Research Methods for Contract Law and Scholarship

ELGAR STUDIES IN LEGAL RESEARCH METHODS

This highly topical series provides a focus on the role of research methods in current legal scholarship. It explores the diverse range of approaches from within the legal discipline as well as the growing role of interdisciplinary methods, and highlights the impact of different research methods on our understanding of the law. The series offers a place both for studies which are defined by their choice of method, and also for discursive work analysing the nuanced insights brought to light by different methodological approaches.

For a full list of Edward Elgar published titles, including the titles in this series, visit our website at www.e-elgar.com.

Research Methods for Contract Law and Scholarship

Edited by

Yuliya Chernykh

Full Professor of Law, University of Inland Norway, Norway

Joshua Karton

Full Professor and Associate Dean, Faculty of Law, Queen's University, Canada

ELGAR STUDIES IN LEGAL RESEARCH METHODS

Edward Elgar PUBLISHING

Cheltenham, UK · Northampton, MA, USA

Published by

Edward Elgar Publishing Limited
The Lypiatts
15 Lansdown Road
Cheltenham
Glos GL50 2JA
UK

Edward Elgar Publishing, Inc.
William Pratt House
9 Dewey Court
Northampton
Massachusetts 01060
USA

Authorised representative in the EU for GPSR queries only: Easy Access System Europe – Mustamäe tee 50, 10621 Tallinn, Estonia, gpsr.requests@easproject.com

A catalogue record for this book is available from the British Library

Library of Congress Control Number: 2025940882

This book is available electronically in the **Elgar**online
Law subject collection
https://doi.org/10.4337/9781035316472

MIX
Paper | Supporting responsible forestry
FSC® C013056

ISBN 978 1 0353 1646 5 (cased)
ISBN 978 1 0353 1647 2 (eBook)
ISBN 978 1 0353 7277 5 (ePub)

Printed and bound in Great Britain by
TJ Books, Padstow, Cornwall

Contents

PART III CHALLENGING THEMES/PERSPECTIVES

List of contributors

Mads Andenas KC is Professor of Law at the Institute of Private Law, Faculty of Law, University of Oslo and Professor II at the University of Inland Norway. He is a Member of the Panel of Arbitrators maintained by the International Centre for Settlement of Investment Disputes (ICSID) since 2016, and was Director of the British Institute of International and Comparative Law, 1999–2005, and Director of the Centre of European Law at King's College, University of London, 1991–1999. He was the United Nations *Président-rapporteur* on Arbitrary Detention 2009–2015, and the General Editor of the *International and Comparative Law Quarterly* (Cambridge University Press), and currently of *European Business Law Review* (Kluwer). He is on the editorial boards of *European Public Law* (Kluwer), *Peking University Law Journal* (Routledge) and *Studies in European Economic Law and Regulation* (Springer).

Victoria Barnes is Reader in Commercial Law at Queen's University Belfast. Her research examines contract, commercial and corporate law from transnational, comparative and interdisciplinary perspectives. She unpicks pivotal historic events, such as landmark cases, and places them in context. Her work traces the way organisations, legal principles and doctrines have developed through time.

Jeff Berryman is a Distinguished University Professor and Professor of Law at the Faculty of Law, University of Windsor, Canada, where he has been for the past 35 years. A specialist in the Law of Remedies, he has also taught, contract law, restitution and trusts. His many published articles have appeared in journals in Canada, Australia, New Zealand, the United States and England. He has advised the New Zealand Ministry of Justice, the Ontario Law Reform Commission and the Federal Court of Canada. His most recent publication is *The Law of Equitable Remedies* 3rd ed. (Irwin Law, 2023).

Yuliya Chernykh is a Full Professor of Law at the University of Inland Norway, ICC International Court of Arbitration member (mandate 2024–2027), Chartered Arbitrator, and CEDR-accredited mediator. Yuliya is a co-rapporteur of the ILA Committee on ADR and Public International Law, and she is also a member of the Steering Committee of the ISDS Academic Forum and the editorial board of the *Journal of World Investment and Trade*. Yuliya researches questions related to contract law and public international law, including interpretation of legal texts and the intersections between national, international and transnational law in international adjudication.

Osny da Silva Filho is Professor of Law at Fundação Getulio Vargas in São Paulo, Brazil (FGV Direito SP), where he teaches courses on private law and legal theory. He holds a PhD from the University of São Paulo School of Law (FD-USP) and was a visiting researcher at Harvard Law School and Max Planck Institute in Hamburg. He practices law in São Paulo.

Liviu Damsa is an Independent Researcher from Brussels, Belgium. Liviu has an LLB obtained in Romania, an LLM from University of Illinois College of Law and a PhD from the University of Warwick and has been working for the past 20 years in private practice (including transactional contract drafting and contract litigation) in Romania and the US, and in the United Kingdom as an EU law post-doctoral fellow.

Alan Hanna is an Associate Professor in the Faculty of Law at the University of Victoria, and a member of the Law Society of British Columbia, Law Society of the Northwest Territories, Indigenous Bar Association, Canadian Bar Association and Canadian Association of Law Teachers. He holds a PhD from the University of Victoria and teaches intersocietal contract law at the intersection of the common law and Indigenous legal orders in the dual JD/JID degree program at the University of Victoria.

Joshua Karton is a Full Professor and the Associate Dean for Graduate Studies and Program Development in the Faculty of Law at Queen's University, Canada. His research encompasses international dispute resolution (especially international commercial and investment arbitration), international and comparative contract law, transnational legal theory, globalization and law, and linguistic issues in law. He is a Book Review Editor of the *American Journal of Comparative Law* and a co-founder and the Managing Editor of the *Canadian Journal of Commercial Arbitration*. He holds a BA in International Relations and Humanities from Yale, a JD from Columbia, and a PhD in International Law from Cambridge. Aside from his scholarly activities, Professor Karton practices as an independent arbitrator and legal consultant in domestic and international commercial disputes.

Mitja Kovač is a full-time Professor of Civil and Commercial Law at the University of Ljubljana, School of Economics and Business, Slovenia, and a visiting lecturer at the Erasmus University Rotterdam, The Netherlands, and at University of Ghent, Belgium. Mitja graduated law with "cum laude" at the University of Ljubljana, Slovenia and gained his LLM and PhD at Utrecht University, Faculty of Law, Economics and Governance, The Netherlands. He publishes in the fields of comparative contract law and economics, new institutional economics, consumer protection, contract theory and competition law and economics.

Monika Leszczyńska is an Associate Professor at the Texas A&M University School of Law. Monika studies how the institutions of contract law interact with individual contractual behavior in an increasingly data-driven economy. In her work, she employs various empirical methods such as behavioral experiments and vignette studies, as well as systematic content analysis and computational methods.

Kateřina Mitkidis is Associate Professor at the Department of Law, Aarhus University, Denmark. Kateřina is interested in the ways law and legal tools are designed and used to steer behaviour in socially and environmentally sound and responsible directions. Her research particularly focuses on the practice of using typically private law tools, such as contracts, to advance public interests. She has published, contributed to, and co-edited books and academic articles on this topic, including *Sustainability Clauses in International Business Contracts* (Eleven International Publishing, 2015) and *Law and Responsible Supply Chain Management: Contract and Tort Interplay and Overlap* (Routledge, 2019).

Sergio Mittlaender is a Professor of Law at FGV Law School in São Paulo and Senior Research Fellow at the Max Planck Institute for Social Law and Social Policy in Munich. He holds a PhD in Law and Economics, as well as Master's and Bachelor's degrees in both law and in economics. His research focuses on contracts, torts and social policies aimed at reducing corruption and discrimination. He frequently employs an empirical approach that utilizes laboratory or online experiments in his studies.

Pietro Ortolani is a Professor of Digital Conflict Resolution at Radboud University in Nijmegen, the Netherlands. He holds a law degree from the University of Pisa and a PhD in arbitration from LUISS Guido Carli University, Rome. Before joining Radboud University, he was a Senior Research Fellow at the Max Planck Institute Luxembourg for Procedural Law and a Law Research

Associate at Queen Mary, University of London. Pietro is admitted to the Bar in Italy and he also works as a practitioner, mainly in the field of arbitration.

Cătălin-Gabriel Stănescu is Associate Professor in Law at the Faculty for Business and Social Sciences, University of Southern Denmark, Denmark. His current research focuses on topics related to consumer financial protection, informal debt collection regulation and digital law. Cătălin has been a visiting scholar at several renowned research institutions such as the Institute for Advanced Legal Studies, London, the Centre for Commercial Law Studies of Queen Mary University, London; Max Planck Institute for Comparative and Private International Law, Hamburg; the European University Institute, Florence; and the Centre for Banking and Finance Law, Singapore.

Johan Vorland Wibye (MA, MJur, MSt, PhD) is Associate Professor at the Department of Law and Governance, BI Norwegian Business School. His research combines analytical rights theory with legal doctrinal methods and applied ethics, with recent publications on legitimacy, correlativity, legal conflict and the distinction between positive and negative European human rights.

Sally Wheeler is Vice-Chancellor of Birkbeck, University of London. She is a socio-legal scholar working in the area of enforceable transactions and corporate governance.

Introduction: everything is interconnected – can we understand contracts from only one perspective?

Yuliya Chernykh and Joshua Karton

1. CHANGING LANDSCAPE

Contracts reflect society. Just as the context in which they operate changes, they themselves also evolve, and the means by which they are regulated evolve along with them. Globalisation, political trends and disruptions, policy overreach by States, synchronisation of consumer protection across jurisdictions, the growing impact of human rights and environmental concerns on business practices, increasingly influential transnational regulation in specific sectors, standardisation and individualisation, AI and other technological changes, and moral dilemmas arising from crosscutting private choices and public interests—these are just some of the many influences that interact to shape the context of contemporary contracting. Contract law and practice, far from being a stagnant area of scholarship, continues to revitalize old debates and raise new questions of fairness, morality, predictability, and efficiency. It is therefore unsurprising that scholarly interest in contract law and practice remains evergreen.

The way that scholars conduct research on contracts and contract law, particularly their methodological choices, must also adapt to changing contract practices and contexts. While traditional doctrinal analysis remains an indispensable part of contract scholarship, it cannot be the only way of 'doing' research on contracts and contract law. The openness of modern legal research to other disciplines has yielded a generation of scholars who are increasingly engaged with history,[1] philosophy,[2] economics,[3] and other fields to explain or question the rationales behind contract terms and contract law rules. Quantitative and qualitative empirical data, including data derived from experiments, increasingly penetrate into and inform the construction of legal arguments and even doctrinal theorizing.[4] Technology offers advanced tools for data mining, natural language processing, computational linguistic analysis, and other types of inquiries.[5] Critical legal research introduces a variety of epistemological standpoints from which to argue about contracts and contract law, based on feminist,[6] decolonised,[7] and other hitherto unconventional approaches. More generally, wider recognition that contract law has developed largely within a Western paradigm has led scholars to embrace other perspectives, such as those deriving from Indigenous epistemologies. Even themes that were previously seen as *objects* of research, such as comparative[8] or transnational[9] contract law, have themselves evolved into analytical lenses.

---

1 Warren Swain, *The Law of Contract 1670–1870* (Cambridge University Press 2015); Anat Rosenberg, *Liberalizing Contracts: Nineteenth Century Promises Through Literature, Law and History* (Routledge 2018).

2 Gregory Klass, George Letsas and Prinse Saprai (eds), *Philosophical Foundations of Contract Law* (Oxford University Press 2015); Martijn W. Hesselink, *Justifying Contract in Europe: Political Philosophies of European Contract Law* (Oxford University Press 2021).

3 Victor P. Goldberg, *Rethinking Contract Law and Contract Design* (Edward Elgar Publishing 2015); Ejan Mackaay, *Law and Economics for Civil Law Systems* (Edward Elgar Publishing 2013) 413–505.

4 Uri Benoliel, 'The Interpretation of Commercial Contracts: An Empirical Study' (2017) 69 (2) *Alabama Law Review* 469.

5 Julian Nyarko, 'We'll See You in...Court! The Lack of Arbitration Clauses in International Contracts' (2019) 58 *International Review of Law and Economics* 6.

6 Hila Keren, 'Feminism and Contract Law' in Robin West and Cynthia G. Bowman (eds), *Research Handbook on Feminist Jurisprudence* (Edward Elgar Publishing 2019) 406–425.

7 Andrew Hutchison, 'Decolonising South African Contract Law: An Argument for Synthesis' in Luca Siliquini-Cinelli and Andrew Hutchison (eds.), *The Constitutional Dimension of Contract Law* (Springer 2017) 151–184.

8 For comparative contract law as a field, see Pier Giuseppe Monateri (ed), *Comparative Contract Law: Research Handbooks in Comparative Law Series* (Edward Elgar Publishing 2018); for a representative example of comparative research methods applied to contract law, see Mindy Chen-Wishart and Stefan Vogenauer (eds), *Contents of Contracts and Unfair Terms* (Oxford University Press 2022) 1–8.

9 For transnational contract law as a field, see Klaas Hendrik Eller, 'Transnational Contract Law' in Peer Zumbansen (ed), *The Oxford Handbook of Transnational Law* (Oxford University Press 2021) 513–530; Joshua Karton,

These methodological developments have also yielded a reappraisal and reaffirmation of the traditional default legal method—doctrinal—opening it up to enrichment from external influences but also reasserting its critical role for understanding both contract law rules and the ways that contracts are generated and operate in the commercial, consumer, employment, and even family spheres.

While methodological evolution can be mesmerising, particularly for academics, the present volume does not primarily focus on evolution as such; rather, it embraces the *variety* of research methods and their possible combinations in contract law scholarship. Concentrating on variety instead of evolution was a deliberate choice by the editors. Our intention is to avoid creating an impression of certain methods' (emerging or growing) superiority, still less to chase what is 'trendy' in legal scholarship. Instead, it is the editors' conviction that all of the research methods featured in this volume, if performed with rigour, can provide unique insights. Accordingly, we have consciously avoided articulating a predetermined view of the meta-methodological significance of any individual research method.

Readers of the book will develop an appreciation for the potential contributions of methods with which they are unfamiliar and deepen their knowledge of familiar methods. Researchers, both experienced and inexperienced, will better understand the range of available options, and more importantly, which methods can provide which kinds of insights for which kinds of research questions. Equally, they can review individual chapters for a primer or a refresher on a given research method.

2. METHODOLOGICAL REINTEGRATION

Ever since contract scholarship splintered into dozens of distinct methodological approaches, scholars have been seeking to reintegrate them, whether by reaffirming doctrinalism's central place in legal scholarship or by engaging in interdisciplinary projects that combine various methods and perspectives. At the same time, social, technological and economic developments have put pressure on the traditional boundaries of contract law, and on more recently established understandings of the roles and methods of contract scholarship.

This book contributes to that process of methodological reintegration in contract law scholarship. It does so in three ways, corresponding to the three parts of the book. Part I focuses on the various *internal* methodologies and

---

'The Rise of Sectorally Fragmented Contract Law' (2017) 111 *AJIL Unbound* 106. On transnational law as an object of legal theory more generally, see William Twining, *Globalisation and Legal Theory* (Northwestern UP 2001).

perspectives that can be brought to bear to understand contract law and practice from the inside of the law. The purely internal perspectives of doctrinal methods are complemented by traditional and doctrine-adjacent philosophical and comparative methods. Part II invites readers to examine contract law and practice from outside the boundaries of law itself, offering *external* approaches premised on historical, empirical, experimental and economic perspectives. Part III focuses on contemporary phenomena—social, economic, technological, and environmental—that pose challenges for contract theory and practice and that can only be understood by employing methodological packages. Each chapter in Part III cuts across the methodologies discussed in the previous parts, guiding researchers toward a more multifaceted understanding of these modern challenges. While Parts I and II present a series of single or relatively homogeneous research methods, Part III addresses methodological choice within contracts scholarship on cross-cutting contemporary topics. No part of the book, nor the book as a whole, purports to present an exhaustive taxonomy of research methods or challenging topics, but rather aims to cover the most salient methodological frameworks and approaches.

While each contributor had the freedom to address what she or he found important to highlight in a particular method or topic area, the editors tasked contributors, to the extent possible, with giving thought to three themes. For the first two parts, contributors were invited to comment on: (1) the capacity of the method or methods to explain and argue about contracts and contract law (what kind of questions, what kind of answers, what is at the core of the argument); (2) the limits of the method or methods (which questions the method or methods are ill-suited to answer, taking into account underlying assumptions of the method); and (3) the current use of the method in researching contract law and potential future uses. For Part III, the contributors were invited to reflect on: (1) the specific research challenges their particular theme poses for contracts and contract law; (2) the implications of the theme for various ways of thinking about contracts and contract law; and (3) the research methods (individually or in combination) most capable of advancing understanding of the contractual aspects of the theme.

Accordingly, although the resulting chapters are not entirely uniform, they still combine harmoniously and collectively provide clarity and insight on research methods and scholarship in the field of contracts and contract law.

Part I opens with the doctrinal research methods—the traditional default tool for contract law research. Barely two generations ago, contract scholarship consisted of only one method: reading laws and cases, and thinking about them. Although of course this is a flippant characterisation, it is only a small exaggeration. Today, while purely doctrinal legal research persists (and not only in practitioner writing), it has become only one method among many that contract researchers employ. Nevertheless, doctrinal research remains the method most characteristic of legal research, and the only one unique to it.

It is the only occasion in the book where a single research method is split between two chapters. Osny da Silva Filho unveils the method from the perspective of the civil law tradition (Chapter 1), and Jeff Berryman uncovers the doctrinal research method as practised in the common law (Chapter 2). While both the common law and civil law legal families contain numerous internal variations, and the borderline between the two is not always sharp or reflective of the entire world, the two-part approach is nevertheless informative. Readers will be able to follow the emergence of legal doctrine and the doctrinal method, its precise content and contemporary role, existing challenges and enduring resilience, and change within each of the two main legal systems, with their distinct dynamics in norm- and rule-production. Each author offers a strategy for keeping doctrinal research methods relevant. Da Silva Filho calls for more interdisciplinarity, creativity and particularity to reclaim the relevance of legal doctrine to legal practice. Berryman, by contrast, stresses the centrality of law for the common law doctrinal method, as any suggestion for improvement of a legal doctrine still needs to be translated into the language of legal rules. Berryman's ultimate observation that there is 'no substitution to a sound knowledge of the law' provides indispensable advice to contract law scholars regardless of their methodological preferences. The doctrinal method as legal scholarship's 'own' research method thus receives thorough coverage, a nuanced literature overview, and insightful discussion of the interrelations between legal doctrinal scholarship and practice.

Having mapped the doctrinal research methodology for civil law and common law jurisdictions—and thus already exposed readers to an implicit comparative exercise—the book proceeds to clarify comparative research methods (Chapter 3). In their chapter, Yuliya Chernykh and Mads Andenas KC bring to light the diversity of comparative contract law scholarship and applied comparative methods and perspectives. Contemporary comparative research in the field of contract law is still largely doctrinal and focused on similarities and differences in the operation of legal rules and doctrines across jurisdictions. Yet, traditional methods are increasingly complemented by empirical, interdisciplinary and critical perspectives. Furthermore, the most debated 'native' comparative law method—the functional method—breaks easily with the borders of specific doctrines and rules to enable researchers to understand the law in a given social, economic and cultural context. With both ongoing loyalty to doctrinal methods and openness toward other considerations, comparative research methods have huge yet underexplored potential for advancing legal theories.

The next chapter, on philosophical methods, addresses legal theories and, more precisely, in Johan Vorland Wibye's words, 'their methodological commitments' (Chapter 4). Clearly and persuasively, Wibye guides readers through the two main strands within the philosophy of contract law—conceptual and normative theories—as well as their mutual interplay. Wibye argues that even if there is no single overarching theory of contract law that provides full coverage of legal doctrines, there is methodological value in approaching the study of contracts from different conceptual and normative angles. Wibye's chapter reveals the fragmented yet overlapping coverage of contract law theories, the philosophical commitments that are necessarily baked into the study of contract law, and the potential of theoretical approaches for highlighting and challenging facets of legal doctrines.

Part II starts with historical perspectives. In their nuanced reflection, Victoria Barnes and Sally Wheeler thoroughly outline two basic historical approaches to contract law research (Chapter 5). The first is centred on 'legal material' in contract law—a doctrine, a legal rule, or a legal issue—and the second on the social role that contracts play in society, or the economic, cultural, and social circumstances that shape how contracts are perceived, drafted, and observed. Relevance for contemporary understanding of law or existing methods of governance appears to be an important legitimising strategy for both historical approaches. Barnes and Wheeler warn against oversimplified engagement with historical material as context only, and demonstrate how an understanding of contemporary contract laws and practices may benefit from a historical perspective.

The following three chapters invite readers to consider socio-legal perspectives, covering empirical, law and economics, and experimental methods. Instrumental and revealing, these non-doctrinal methods require specific expertise, although the precise borderline between each of these methodological instruments is not always sharp. Monika Leszczyńska explains the emergence of empirical contract methods and guides readers through qualitative and quantitative studies of contracts and contract law, including systematic content analysis, surveys, experimental methods, and automated text analysis (Chapter 6). Law and economics research, especially in its more quantitative forms, can seem like a universe in itself; it is associated with specific kinds of empirical research methods, but also embeds a theory of human behaviour with important implications for contracts and contract law. Mitja Kovač offers a brief historical account of the evolution of law and economics methods as applied to contract law, the emergence of behavioural economics insights on non-rational behaviour, an overview of the key concepts and theories, and a discussion of what could be referred to as normative and positive contract law and economics (Chapter 7). Helpfully, Kovač identifies the potential for interdisciplinary and empirical advancement of law and economics methodological toolsets and elucidates a promising direction forcomparative contract law and economics. Experimental methodology may be considered as part of the arsenal used by law and economics and other empirical legal researchers. However, the methodological demands of experimental research are matched only by its capacity to yield deep insights into the actual operation of legal principles. For this reason, it requires separate treatment. Sergio Mittlaender (Chapter 8) explains the roots of the experimental method in psychology, its core principles and rules in economic research, its application to contract law, and the kinds of important causal questions that can only be effectively answered through experiments. The theory-building and policy-guiding potential of experiments are yet to be explored thoroughly in contract law research. Mittlaender concludes by identifying avenues for future experimental studies capable of answering more advanced questions on causality in the presence of several competing legal rules and principles.

Rotating the kaleidoscope to a new position, Part III invites readers to consider the research methods that have been applied to the interface between contracts and a selection of contemporary challenges. Kateřina Mitkidis provides a meticulous overview of the research methods capable of addressing contracts and sustainability, and of grasping the core social, environmental and economic considerations that will continue to shape contract law in an age of environmental crisis (Chapter 9). Sustainability clauses have become a common feature of supply chain contracts. These clauses mesmerise in their ambition to fill regulatory gaps, and to thereby achieve public interest goals with private contractual duties. As traditional doctrinal methods are not sufficient to address all of the challenges that sustainability poses for contract law, contract law scholars are compelled to broaden their methodological toolkits to encompass theoretical and empirical explorations. More diverse methodological packages in turn necessitate clear and express recognition of methodological choices needed to avoid counter-productive accusations of environmental radicalism. In a similar spirit, Pietro Ortolani addresses contracts and digital technology by describing how technological change has forced contract law to reconsider its fundamentals and by explaining the digital methods and tools that are revolutionising research methods in contract law and practice (Chapter 10). Cătălin-Gabriel Stănescu and Liviu Damsa address the challenges that consumer contracts pose in an era of digitalisation and increased use of profiling and automation (Chapter 11). They argue that classical contract theory, developed in the 19th century and still used dominantly in courtrooms or by the legal professions, is inadequate to address these challenges when applied to 21st-century consumer contracts. Without interdisciplinary approaches, contract law scholars appear to be unable to find theoretical and practical solutions capable of rebalancing the parties' otherwise asymmetric positions, which have only been aggravated by technology. The next chapter, on research methods for contracts in Indigenous legal orders, tests our capacity to reconsider the foundations of contract law to its limits (Chapter 12). Alan

Hanna unsettles traditional perceptions premised on colonial understandings of binding legal agreements and constructs an understanding of *relation* as the core of the Indigenous perspective on what the positive law calls contractual relationships. This methodology emphasises the social function of contracts in binding communities beyond just those who exchange mutual promises. From this perspective, contract 'remedies' are means to reconcile rifts in a community, not to 'right wrongs' in a binary system of counterparties. In the concluding chapter, Joshua Karton sheds light on contracts and globalisation, and introduces transnational contract law as a methodological tool or perspective, not just as an object of research (Chapter 13). This chapter shows how the operation of contract law in modern economies transcends the limitations of traditional contract theory. Karton's approach avoids 'the blind spots of an exclusive focus on state-made law', revealing the pluralistic character of law in the transnational space: hard and soft, public and private, and global, regional, and sectoral.

3. CROSSING BRIDGES, OR HOW TO READ THIS BOOK

The chapters of this book can be read separately, as resource texts for researchers working within different methodological paradigms. However, the book is also designed to be read cover-to-cover, including as a textbook for courses on research methods. It is intended as a sort of travelogue, roaming through the distinct-but-neighbouring realms of contract scholarship. As with any travel writing, the book invites readers to retrace the routes of earlier travellers (here seen as the methodological choices made by established scholars) and to chart their own paths. Readers may follow the journey envisaged by the editors (from Part I to Part III), or selectively choose those destinations of greatest interest. Through the chapters of this book, readers will discover new terrains, revisit familiar territories, and find themselves propelled toward both popular destinations and 'hidden treasures'.

Despite their disparate foci and perspectives, all of the chapters in this volume extend bridges to each other. Traversing those bridges can, in itself, be a stimulating exercise. Let us provide a brief travel guide.

To start with, all the chapters, in one way or another, illuminate aspects of the doctrinal method—still seen as simply as 'the legal method', 'the internal method' or 'the default method', or even just as 'legal research'. Our contributors indeed offer two chapters entirely focused on the doctrinal method, which both endorse and challenge traditional perspectives on legal research. But suppose one begins with a different chapter. For instance, let us pick up Barnes and Wheeler's historical chapter (Chapter 5). When addressing different disciplinary agendas, this chapter names *legal doctrinal history* as one of the disciplinary approaches researchers may choose or be caught by. It further clarifies the perspectives that circulate within historical research in contract law and elucidates what the doctrine actually is. Now suppose one chooses Wibye's chapter on philosophical methods as a starting point: one will learn how doctrinal research can be 'rooted' in different philosophical accounts and that conceptual and normative approaches can never be fully separated from doctrinal research, but rather are used to 'support, direct and challenge legal reasoning' (Chapter 4). Interestingly, methods and approaches of contract law and economics inform doctrinal studies on the efficiency of specific rules and approaches (Chapter 7). Mittlaender's study on experimental research (Chapter 8) unveils its capacity to inform doctrinal studies by demonstrating the implications that legal rules have for the perceptions and conduct of individuals subject to these rules. Revealing broadening horizons, Hanna's chapter on Indigenous research methods for studying contracts unpacks a distinct notion of legal doctrine—the one in Indigenous legal orders—and its role in giving structure and reproducing predictable outcomes in Indigenous communities (Chapter 12). Leszczyńska's take on empirical methods shows how crucial insights from contract law doctrines and theories may be for informing and shaping empirical research and vice versa; drawing upon empirical findings is essential to inform the doctrine and theory of contract law (Chapter 6). Addressing sustainability and expressly engaging with the doctrinal method, Mitkidis provides deep insights into doctrine as a reference point for conceptualising sustainability clauses, but also demonstrates its shortcomings. Overall, one can learn more fully about doctrinal research when engaging with each of the chapters and reading across them.

Similar exercises can be made with respect to other methods. The chapter on historical approaches (Chapter 5) complements the chapter on comparative methods (Chapter 4), as does Karton's chapter on transnational contract law, since codified transnational law instruments are typically informed by comparative analysis. The use of comparative methods for apprehending Indigenous legal orders for contract law is traced in Hanna's chapter (Chapter 12) and can also be observed in Mitkidis's chapter on contracts and sustainability (Chapter 9). The list of examples could go on. The point is that reading thematically across chapters enables one to revisit methods and approaches from different standpoints and perspectives.

4. ADVANCING A DIALOGUE

In addition to promoting awareness of methodological options, this display of the range of research methods also helps to overcome other challenges. Progressing in different directions and applying diverse modes of inquiry and argumentative techniques, contract law scholarship has become increasingly fragmented into isolated sub-fields. These sub-fields might speak to different audiences, often in different jargon, such that arguments in one may be intimidating or even incomprehensible to scholars trained in a different methodological paradigm. Attempts to engage with the arguments informed by different methodological premises or to mix several approaches in a single study may invite accusations of dilettantism or methodological illiteracy. Cataloguing the existing approaches will accordingly help boost methodological awareness, foster more meaningful dialogue within contract law scholarship, and facilitate bridging of methodological disagreements (instead of purporting to conclusively resolve them). It will also help younger scholars or those seeking to expand their methodological repertoire to scrupulously implement various research methods.

Reading this book, contract scholars will become conversant in the leading research methodologies. Each chapter, separately and especially when read together, demonstrates the parity of different methodological approaches. There is no one 'correct' way to do contract scholarship, nor even 'better and worse' ways, although of course, each method can be employed sloppily or with rigour. Rather, every methodological approach discussed in Parts I and II has potential but also limitations, unique insights only it can provide but also blind spots, questions that it is well-suited to answer and those to which it can make no significant contribution. Moreover, the contemporary challenges discussed in Part III can only be addressed by resorting to multiple approaches. The modern contract scholar need not themselves work in every possible methodology; indeed, no one researcher could be sufficiently competent in all of them, and attempting to combine them indiscriminately would yield a conceptual muddle. However, every scholar conducting research into contract law and practice must have a basic understanding of each method's strengths and weaknesses. Such an understanding is necessary not only to appreciate the existing literature but also to design research studies capable of tackling modern contract law's most pressing questions.

By focusing on research methods in contracts and contract law, the volume fills an unfortunate gap in the existing methodological literature. The gap has arisen between the flourishing line of generalist publications focused on various methods for legal research[10] and the growing line of methodological

---

10 Dawn Watkins and Mandy Burton (eds), *Research Methods in Law* (Routledge 2018); Mike McConville and Wing Hong Chui (eds), *Research Methods for Law* (2nd edn, Edinburgh University Press 2017); P. Ishwara Bhat, *Idea and Methods of Legal Research* (Oxford University Press 2020); Mátyás Bódig, *Legal Doctrinal Scholarship: Legal Theory and the Inner Workings of a Doctrinal Discipline* (Edward Elgar Publishing 2021); Mark Van Hoecke (ed), *Methodologies of Legal Research: What Kind of Method for What Kind of Discipline?* (Hart Publishing

publications dealing with specific legal sub-fields/disciplines—a line that still does not include a robust publication on the full scope of research methods applicable to contract law.[11] This book is among the first to systematically address a broad range of research methods as they are applied specifically to contract law and practice.

5. CONCLUDING OBSERVATIONS

We conclude this introductory chapter with three observations.

First, a continuously updated understanding of contractual practice is indispensable for any work being done on contract practice and contract law. Contracts are not a phenomenon of nature, although the two share similarities.[12] For this reason, the book does not moralise, does not seek to identify a single best or most prominent approach, and does not attempt to provide methodological recipes. It will be up to individual researchers to translate their curiosity into research questions and to implement their own research designs. Nevertheless, Berryman's message that there is no substitute for a sound knowledge of legal rules must also be kept in mind.

Second, the plurality of research methods that permeates this book suggests a need for caution. Obviously, there are many methods, approaches, and perspectives, and not all of them are addressed in this book. They are all

---

2011); Jaako Husa, *Interdisciplinary Comparative Law: Rubbing Shoulders with the Neighbours or Standing Alone in a Crowd* (Edward Elgar Publishing 2022); Marija Bartl and Jessica C. Lawrence (eds), *The Politics of European Legal Research: Behind the Method* (Edward Elgar Publishing 2022); Ryan Whalen (ed), *Computational Legal Studies: The Promise and Challenge of Data-Driven Research* (Edward Elgar Publishing 2022); Maurice Adams and Mark Van Hoecke (eds), *Comparative Methods in Law, Humanities and Social Sciences* (Edward Elgar Publishing 2021); Jan M. Smits, *The Mind and Method of the Legal Academic* (Edward Elgar Publishing 2012).

[11] Rossana Deplano and Nicholas Tsagourias (eds), *Research Methods in International Law: A Handbook* (Edward Elgar Publishing 2021); Hans-W. Micklitz, Anne-Lise Sibony and Fabrizio Esposito (eds), *Research Methods in Consumer Law: A Handbook* (Edward Elgar Publishing 2018); Andreas Philippopoulos-Mihalopoulos and Victoria Brooks (eds), *Research Methods in Environmental Law: A Handbook* (Edward Elgar Publishing 2017).

[12] In his lecture 'The Relation of Physics to Other Sciences', the theoretical physicist Richard Feynman observed: 'If our small minds, for some convenience, divide this universe into parts—physics, biology, geology, astronomy, psychology, and so on—remember that nature does not know it!' (available at https://www.feynmanlectures.caltech.edu/I_03.html, last accessed 1 June 2024). We draw some analogies from this phrase and apply it to contract law research.

enriching. However, they cannot all be used at once or blindly mixed together. A choice of multi-method approaches and of a mono-method approach can both be justified; what matters is that the choice is made in a deliberate and informed manner.

Third and most importantly, we hope that the book poses at least as many questions as it answers.

ACKNOWLEDGEMENT

Open access publication became possible due to financing by the Open Access Publishing Fund at the University of Inland Norway.

PART I

Internal perspectives

1. Doctrinal methods in contract law in civil law jurisdictions

Osny da Silva Filho[1]

INTRODUCTION

For a long time, making use of doctrinal methods based on identification, interpretation, and systematization of law was understood to be the main, if not the only, task of legal research. This was especially true for contract law in civil law jurisdictions, as connecting black letter law to different types of contracts and stipulating the rules applicable to issues uncovered by civil codes and particular statutes were assumed to represent the entire scope of tasks necessary and sufficient to fill the gaps between legal practice and academic research. Legal doctrine seemed to reign sovereign in the realm of legal scholarship.

This perception, however, has undergone a notable shift. Since the 1990s, transformations such as the rise in full-time professorships at leading law schools and the growing specialization within the legal profession have raised questions about the relevance of legal doctrine. This doubt is amplified by a growing sense of distrust between academic and practical lawyers. While practitioners have increasingly abandoned the search for guidance in doctrinal scholarship, tenured scholars have shifted their research towards philosophy, sociology, and economics, to the detriment of doctrinal methods that once distinguished legal studies.

In light of this, one may question whether doctrinal methods still have a place in legal research—specifically, whether a chapter on 'legal doctrine in civil law jurisdictions' is warranted in a book dedicated to state-of-the-art research methods in contract law. The ensuing discussion affirms that legal doctrine can still be relevant for contract practice. However, for this sort of scholarship

[1] Sergio Lima Dias Junior and Yasmin Bewiahn Saba Relvas provided excellent research assistance. I am also grateful to Yuliya Chernykh, Joshua Karton, Emerson Fabiani, Bruno Salama and Mario Engler Pinto Junior for corrections and comments. Translations are mine unless specified.

to regain its prominence, it must address the criticisms leveled against it, even if these criticisms appear contradictory, misinformed, or unjust.

The remainder of this chapter is divided into three sections and a brief conclusion. Drawing on civil law references, section 1 elaborates on the idea of legal doctrine as a comprehensive and methodologically variegated model of legal scholarship. Section 2 describes the ways in which legal doctrine and legal practice connect in order to present two sets of attacks directed at this connection. Section 3 discusses three strategies for reclaiming the relevance of legal doctrine.

1. THE IDEA OF LEGAL DOCTRINE

In civil law jurisdictions, the label 'legal doctrine' is commonly used to identify ideas conveyed by scholars that employ methods—procedures, modes of reasoning, composition patterns, rhetoric, and communication strategies—that lawyers qualify as *doctrinal*.[2] This intentionally broad concept of legal doctrine is typically contrasted with legislation and case law, so that civil law students learn early on that in order to solve a case or advise a client, a good lawyer should apply not only legislation but also relevant case law *and* the applicable doctrine.[3]

In contrast to legislation, since it has no binding force, and to case law, as it does not rest on the official power inherent to the Judicial Branch to interpret the law (see section 3.2.2 below), legal doctrine consists of a 'magisterial teaching' written by legal scientists 'on recognition by their peers as knowledge worthy of uniform and repeated acceptance'.[4] Doctrinal writings play the central role of identifying, interpreting (including suggestions of gap-filling),

---

2 Aleksander Peczenik, 'A Theory of Legal Doctrine' (2001) 14(1) *Ratio Juris* 75: 'Legal doctrine in Continental European law (*scientia iuris*, *Rechtswissenschaft*, *Rechtsdogmatik*), "doctrine of law" (legal dogmatics) consists of professional legal writings, e.g., handbooks, monographs, etc., whose task is to systematize and interpret valid law'.

3 In this regard, with an emphasis on case law, Cesare Massimo Bianca, *Istituzioni di diritto privato* (Giuffrè 2014) 25: 'An understanding of the legal system, in conclusion, cannot be separated from knowing the case law'. As for legal doctrine, see Ignacio de Cuevillas Matozzi, 'Dottrina degli autori e giurisprudenza: una necessaria complementarietà' (2020) 9 *Annali della Facoltà Giuridica dell'Università di Camerino* – Studi 12: 'the law cannot exist without a jurist who day after day improves it, advances it', based on the words of the Roman jurist Pomponius and noting that legal doctrine plays 'an important steering task'.

4 Otavio Luiz Rodrigues Junior, 'Dogmática e crítica da jurisprudência (ou da vocação da doutrina em nosso tempo)' (2010) 891 *Revista dos Tribunais* 65–68.

and eventually systematizing current law, so that it can be used by judges and practitioners in general.

In order to better understand this idea, it is useful to stipulate the frontiers of legal doctrine. Approaching legal philosophy and socio-legal studies (as well as law and economics) by comparison, one can better visualize what legal doctrine is and which roles it plays (1.1). In this way, we shall be able to identify some different methods of doctrinal scholarship, as well as what they have in common (1.2).

1.1 The Frontiers of Legal Doctrine

For civil lawyers, legal doctrine is a model of legal research, writing, and communication: a model of legal scholarship.[5] It is usually characterized as non-binding, allegedly impartial opinions about how the law is (*de lege lata* doctrine) or should be (*de lege ferenda* doctrine) contained in PhD dissertations, handbooks, commentaries, journal articles, blogs, or any other sort of purposive writing. Since legislation is not self-interpreting, it must be interpreted (or at least discovered, comprehended, paraphrased, applied).[6] Consequently, legal interpretation (in a broad sense) is understood to be the primary task of doctrine in civil law.

So defined as a particular model of legal scholarship, legal doctrine—be it about the law in general or about some particular legal field such as contract law—falls within the same *genus* as legal philosophy (or jurisprudence, as it is usually called by English and North American common lawyers),[7] and socio-legal studies (or empirical legal studies, though of course not all socio-legal scholarship is empirical and not all empirical legal study is sociological in its perspective). Legal doctrine, legal philosophy, and socio-legal studies may be primarily distinguished by their content, methods, and target audiences (or,

[5] Dietrich Maskow, 'Hardship and Force Majeure' (1992) 40(3) *The American Journal of Comparative Law* 657–669; James Gordley, 'Mistake in Contract Formation' (2004) 52(2) *American Journal of Comparative Law* 433–468. On similarities, differences, and 'functional substitutes' between civil law and common law, see Mariana Pargendler, 'O direito contratual comparado em nova perspectiva: revisitando as diferenças entre os sistemas romano-germânico e de common law' (2017) 13(3) *Revista Direito GV* 796–826.

[6] Friedrich Carl von Savigny, *System des heutigen Römischen Rechts I* (Veit 1840), § 33, 213 and § 50, 318–319, famously argued that even clear laws need to be interpreted. This is a highly controversial point in modern hermeneutics.

[7] See fn. 35 below.

for that matter, their 'eavesdroppers', such as practitioners in the case of legal philosophy).[8]

Of course, these different models of scholarship should be understood as *ideal types*. They are *types* because they are species of the same genre, which is legal scholarship; and they are *ideal* because they are, as Weber famously put it, 'formed by the one-sided accentuation of one or more points of view', according to which 'concrete individual phenomena [...] are arranged into a unified analytical construct'.[9] By treating them as ideal types, it is possible to better identify their specific, 'clear and unambiguous'[10] characteristic elements, in order to achieve an adequate understanding of them,[11] and, with it, the indispensable *raison d'être* of each form of legal scholarship. Such a construct allows for the analytical development of each of these models and their respective and indispensable functions. It also plays a didactic role, insofar as accentuating their status as ideal types can at the same time make their nuances more comprehensible.

1.1.1 Legal doctrine and legal philosophy

The distinction between legal doctrine and legal philosophy is as much an analytical finding as a historical fact.[12] While the doctrinal and the philosophical models of legal scholarship are not mutually exclusive and may well supplement each other, legal philosophy as applied to contract law scholarship first appeared as an epistemic challenge to prevailing contract doctrine.

In fact, an autonomous philosophy of contract law only emerged when legal scholars decided to break with their own intellectual tradition, which in this case was partly Aristotelian, partly Christian, and was epitomized by the works of late Scholastics and Natural Lawyers such as Francisco Suárez

---

8 Meir Dan-Cohen, 'Listeners and Eavesdroppers: Substantive Legal Theory and Its Audience' (1992) 63 *University of Colorado Law Review* 569–594.

9 Max Weber, 'Objectivity in Social Science and Social Policy (1904)' in Edward A. Shils and Henry A. Finch (eds), *The Methodology of the Social Sciences* (The Free Press 1949) 90.

10 Tore Lindbekk, 'The Weberian Ideal-type: Development and Continuities' (1992) 35 *Acta Sociologica* 285, 290.

11 Sven Eliaeson, 'Max Weber's Methodology: An Ideal-Type' (2000) 36(3) *Journal of the History of the Behavioral Sciences* 246, citing Louis Schneider's translation of Max Weber's ideal-type procedure, through which there is an 'intensification of features of empirical social reality for purposes of causal understanding'. For this commented translation, see Louis Schneider and Max Weber, 'Marginal Utility Theory and "The Fundamental Law Of Psychophysics"' (1975) 56(1) *Social Science Quarterly* 21, 22.

12 Osny da Silva Filho, *Fundamentos do direito contratual: doutrina, teoria e empiria* (Almedina 2022).

(1548–1617) and Jean Domat (1625–1695).[13] The modern jurists that contributed to the development of legal-philosophical scholarship in contract law abandoned the moral philosophy (of Aristotle and Aquinas) which was embedded in past contract scholarship (that was both doctrinal and philosophical at the same time)[14] in favor of a new set of concepts and reasoning schemes—as well as a new view of politics[15]—based on a far-reaching concept of the will of contracting parties.

The resulting 'will theory' is still debated in civil law, even when it only functions as a straw man for alternative views.[16] Though the will theory is commonly used to clarify different aspects of contract law—such as formation, performance and breach, nullity, modification and termination, and remedies—its main function is still theoretical. As noted by James Gordley, the innovation 'was not simply to use the concept of will, but to use it almost exclusively'.[17] And, I would add, without primary preoccupations with the practice of law—or without due consideration for legal certainty. An excessive emphasis on the will alone, which is an element internal to the subject and difficult, if not impossible, to know, goes against the need for security in the conclusion of contracts, detaching itself from practical needs.

1.1.2 Legal doctrine and socio-legal studies

The emergence of socio-legal studies (both in contract law and other fields)[18] represents a much more recent development in the history of legal thought.

---

13 James R. Gordley, *The Philosophical Origins of Modern Contract Doctrine* (Clarendon 1991).

14 This syncretism, typical of the method of the time, which resulted from different political, cultural, and social circumstances, in no way prevents the current understanding of legal doctrine and legal philosophy as ideal types: today, we can separate them, emphasizing their unambiguous elements and clearly identifying their specific differences. At that historical moment, this understanding procedure was not yet mature enough.

15 Duncan Kennedy, 'Three Globalizations of Law and Legal Thought: 1850–2000' in David M. Trubek and Alvaro Santos (eds), *The New Law and Economic Development* (Cambridge University Press 2006) 26.

16 See different contributions in Gregory Klass, George Letsas and Prince Saprai (eds), *Philosophical Foundations of Contract Law* (Oxford University Press 2016).

17 Gordley (n 13) 161.

18 Carrie Menkel-Meadow, 'Uses and abuses of socio-legal studies' in Naomi Creutzfeldt, Marc Mason and Kirsten McConnachie (eds), *Routledge Handbook of Socio-Legal Theory and Methods* (Routledge 2019) 35–57. See, regarding contract law, Peter Vincent-Jones, 'Contract and Business Transactions: A Socio-Legal Analysis' (1989) 16 *Journal of Law and Society* 166. On family law, Richard

Such studies are generally characterized by a quantitative or qualitative approach to understanding the lived reality of individuals and societies who interact with the legal system and are based on descriptive or causal inference rules first developed in social sciences and statistics.[19] As these methods originally matured outside law schools, the use of interdisciplinary methodologies became essential for legal scholars interested in working with it.[20]

The history of this sort of empirical scholarship intertwines with the development of the law & society movement, which, in the 1960s, began to challenge research models viewed as hegemonic in law schools in the United States,[21] and quickly affected legal thought in civil law countries as well.[22] Its impact on contract law scholarship has been profound. One of its key contributions has been the study of 'relational contracts', a concept introduced by Ian R. Macneil. Macneil famously argued that many contracts are not discrete transactions but rather long-term relationships that evolve over time, with parties adjusting their behavior and expectations in response to changing circumstances and mutual needs.[23] Other scholars have further investigated how

---

Collier and Sally Sheldon, *Fragmenting Fatherhood: A Socio-Legal Study* (Hart 2008).

[19] See generally Lee Epstein and Andrew D. Martin, *An Introduction to Empirical Legal Research* (Oxford University Press 2014); and for the civil law context, Sergio Tuthill Stanicia, 'Doutrina e pesquisa empírica: um diálogo difícil' (2023) 14 *Revista do Curso de Direito da Unifor-MG* 167–181.

[20] Lynn M. LoPucki, 'Disciplining Legal Scholarship' (2015) 90 *Tulane Law Review* 1, 5–6.

[21] Richard A. Posner, 'The Decline of Law as an Autonomous Discipline: 1962-1987' (1987) 100 *Harvard Law Review* 761, 761–790; *Idem*, 'Legal Scholarship Today' (2002) 115(5) *Harvard Law Review* 1314 (explaining why interdisciplinarity has grown so much in US legal doctrine since the 1970s).

[22] See, for example, Jose Reinaldo de Lima Lopes and Roberto Freitas Filho, 'Law and Society in Brazil at the Crossroads: A Review' (2014) 10 *Annual Review of Law and Social Science* 91.

[23] Ian R. MacNeil, 'The Many Futures of Contracts' (1973) 47 *Southern California Law Review* 691, 720 et seq.; Ian R. Macneil, 'Contracts: Adjustment of Long-Term Economic Relations under Classical, Neoclassical, and Relational Contract Law' (1977) 72 *Northwestern University Law Review* 854, 886 et seq. The idea of relational contracts was disseminated in Brazil by Ronaldo Porto Macedo Jr., *Contratos relacionais e defesa do consumidor* (2nd ed. Revista dos Tribunais 2007). According to Antonio Junqueira de Azevedo, a renowned Brazilian jurist in the field of private law, two points related to the origin of the theory of relational contracts would complicate its reception in civil law legal systems, such as the Brazilian one; namely, its source in sociology and in the 'North American intellectual universe'. Antonio Junqueira de Azevedo, 'Natureza jurídica do contrato

social norms actually influence behavior in 'non-contractual' or 'extralegal' relations in commerce and industry.[24]

More recently, socio-legal scholarship on contracts has expanded to include studies on 'hybrid organizations' and 'contractual networks'. Familiar hybrid organizations, such as franchising and industrial subcontracting, often combine elements of markets and hierarchies, presenting unique challenges for contract law.[25] In the same vein, research on contractual networks has focused on how these organizations navigate legal and regulatory frameworks, manage conflicting interests, and achieve their goals through innovative arrangements.[26]

1.1.3 The emergence of law & economics

During a parallel timeframe, law & economics emerged in the US and spread around the civil law world as a conservative or libertarian response to the growing influence of the law & society movement.[27–28] Leading law & economics

---

de consórcio. Classificação dos atos jurídicos quanto ao número de partes e quanto aos efeitos. Os contratos relacionais. A boa-fé nos contratos relacionais. Contratos de duração. Alteração das circunstâncias e onerosidade excessiva. Sinalagma e resolução contratual. Resolução parcial do contrato. Função social do contrato' (2005) 832 *Revista dos Tribunais* 115, 124.

[24] Stewart Macaulay, 'Non-Contractual Relations in Business: A Preliminary Study' (1963) 28 *American Sociological Review* 55, 56 onwards; Lisa Bernstein, 'Opting out of the Legal System: Extralegal Contractual Relations in the Diamond Industry' (1992) 21 *The Journal of Legal Studies* 115, 132 onwards.

[25] Oliver E. Williamson, *The Mechanisms of Governance* (Oxford University Press 1996) 215 onwards. Drawing on Williamson's categories, Osny da Silva Filho, 'Entre mercado e hierarquia: repercussões da desverticalização na disciplina dos contratos empresariais' (2012) 51 *Revista de direito mercantil, industrial, econômico e financeiro* 120–137.

[26] Walter W. Powell, 'Neither Market Nor Hierarchy: Network Forms of Organization' (1990) 12 *Research in Organizational Behaviour* 295, 300 onwards; Marc Amstutz and Gunther Teubner (eds), *Networks: Legal Issues of Multilateral Co-Operation* (Hart 2009); and Fabrizio Cafaggi (ed) *Contractual Networks, Inter-Firm Cooperation and Economic Growth* (Edward Elgar Publishing 2011).

[27] Ronald H. Coase, 'The Problem of Social Cost' (1960) 3 *Journal of Law and Economics* 1–44; Richard A. Posner, *Economic Analysis of Law* (Little, Brown and Company 1973); Lawrence M. Friedman, 'The Law and Society Movement' (1986) 38(3) *Stanford Law Review* 763–780.

[28] Although that was the origin of the movement, the field is no longer necessarily linked to neoclassical economics perspectives, whose premises have already been challenged, for instance, by the authors of behavioral law & economics. Thinking about 'actual human behavior' has helped to question the typical assumptions of the movement. See, for example, Christine Jolls, 'Behavioral Law and Economics' (2007) NBER Working Paper No. 12879 1–45, and Christine

scholars exhibited, until quite recently, a marked reluctance towards embracing experimental methods, having used, on the other hand, empirical and statistical models since at least the 1970s.[29] In any case, in general, they traditionally gravitated towards a philosophical approach when scrutinizing the law.[30]

This preference for philosophy over empiricism is also underscored by the fact that early critiques of economic approaches to legal scholarship were predominantly rooted in philosophical perspectives.[31] In so doing, they left behind the (oftentimes faulted) empirical premises of law & economics.[32] In any case, while socio-legal studies and legal philosophy—as well as law & economics for that matter—consistently emulate methods first developed in non-legal fields, legal doctrine remained the quintessential model of *legal* scholarship.

As for the historical fact, the development of doctrinal commentaries and treatises in the medieval period, distinct from compilations of legal opinions like the Justinian *Digest*, represented a transformative shift in the accessibility of legal knowledge. According to prevailing narratives, this development broke away from the exclusive realm of religious and political elites, rendering legal knowledge more widely available to the general public. This not only enhanced understanding of the law but also yielded positive economic outcomes—something that was only recently recognized by law & economics literature.[33]

Jolls, Cass R. Sunstein and Richard Thaler, 'A Behavioral Approach to Law and Economics' (1997–1998) 50 *Stanford Law Review* 1471–1550.

[29] William M. Landes, 'The Empirical Side of Law & Economics' (2003) 70(1) *The University of Chicago Law Review* 167–180, 169: 'I present data on the frequency of empirical articles in different subject matter areas of law and economics that have been published in the Journal of Legal Studies since its inception in 1972'.

[30] See, as the ultimate example of this, Richard A. Posner, *The Economics of Justice* (Harvard University Press 1981) 48–87, in which the author deals with utilitarianism, economics, and social theory in order to analyze the ethical and political bases of wealth maximization in the following chapter.

[31] Ronald Dworkin, 'The Model of Rules I' in *Taking Rights Seriously* (Harvard University Press 1978) *passim*.

[32] See, for instance, Chris W. Sanchirico, 'Taxes Versus Legal Rules as Instruments for Equity: A More Equitable View' (2009) 29 *Journal of Legal Studies* 29 (2000) 797, 820, concluding that 'the ability to redistribute by income tax does not make it appropriate to ignore redistributive goals in evaluating legal rules'.

[33] Hans-Bernd Schäfer and Alexander J. Wulf, 'Jurists, Clerics, and Merchants: The Rise of Learned Law in Medieval Europe and Its Impact on Economic Growth' (2014) 11 *Journal of Empirical Legal Studies* 266, 298–300.

1.2 The Methods of Legal Doctrine

Doctrinal methods are research methods employed by legal scholars to identify, interpret, and systematize legal rules, concepts, and institutions, as well as to analyze and make sense of the legal system as a whole.[34]

Particular doctrinal methods can be distinguished in historically rooted genres such as legal dogmatics, legal science, and legal theory, but we should not equate these genres with legal doctrine in analytical terms, as they usually involve a melange of methods. For instance, while legal dogmatics is most often primarily doctrinal—*de lege lata* doctrinal, it could be said—legal science and legal theory may not be qualified as that. It is indeed usual that legal theory is considered a subgenre of philosophy of law or jurisprudence, particularized by its concern with the functioning of the law, as opposed to its grounds or foundations.[35]

The doctrinal method *par excellence* is the *problem-solving method*.[36] It is generally characterized by the confrontation of opposing arguments on the same issue, as in the medieval *disputationes*.[37] To be sure, the problem-solving method is actually an array of loosely formalized techniques employed to solve either legal or practical problems. Basic problem-solving techniques aim to (i)

---

[34] Aleksander Peczenik, 'A Theory of Legal Doctrine' (2001) 14(1) *Ratio Juris* 75, mentioning legal doctrine's task of systematization and interpretation of valid law.

[35] On the legal theory/philosophy of law divide, see Robert Alexy and Ralf Dreier, 'The Concept of Jurisprudence' (1990) 3 *Ratio Juris* 1, 2–5. The same hesitation on the doctrinal status occurs in adjacent areas such as legal history: while history is generally qualified as a social science, it is not unreasonable to bring it closer to philosophy of law or even legal doctrine. Historical research was indeed the basis of important doctrinal movements, as we will see later in this chapter.

[36] Mario Engler Pinto Junior, 'Pesquisa Jurídica No Mestrado Profissional' (2018) 14 *Revista Direito GV* 27, 39–41.

[37] Especially common in Oxford and Cambridge, the *disputationes* were not limited to law. Similar exercises were also employed by professors of arts, theology, and medicine. Depending on their nature, the *quaestiones* extracted from the *disputationes* received specific titles. For example, there were the so-called *sabbatinae*, named as such because they were developed from *disputationes* held on Saturday afternoons (although we no longer attend the academy on Saturdays, we still use the term 'sabbatinae' to designate certain tests that students and candidates for important positions in the State and the market undergo). Furthermore, between the 12th and 13th centuries, but this time exclusively in law, we find the so-called *quaestiones legitimae*, a genre characterized by debates concerning direct contradictions between *leges*. See Hermann Kantorowicz, 'The Quaestiones Disputatae of the Glossators' (1939) 16 *Tijdschrift voor Rechtsgeschiedenis* 1.

identify relevant sources of law—be they legal rules, principles, case law, customs, and so on—(ii) make sense of the sources according to different canons of interpretation; and (iii) relate the resulting understandings to hypothetical or actual facts, which may themselves also need to be interpreted. Occasionally, the problem-solving method also involves (iv) confronting local sources of law with foreign materials that provide alternative solutions, as well as (v) exploring historical roots of different laws to assert complementary reasons for some favored interpretation.

Another approach to doctrinal scholarship is the *exploratory enquiry*, which is of particular interest in contract law, as we shall further argue. Exploratory works aim to (i) identify and cast light on sub-formalized legal practices, or those primarily based on autonomous rules; and (ii) identify emerging trends or areas of law. These inquiries may involve conducting 'non-disciplinary' empirical research (by doing interviews or surveys, for instance) with a view to bringing to light or formalizing practices.[38] Such works can be particularly useful for identifying areas of law that require further research, or for providing insight into the broader social, political, and economic forces that shape the development of law.

Case studies, which also appear in the form of *case comments*, can also be a valuable form of doctrinal scholarship.[39] There is an important difference between civil law and common law concerning this point. In common law, legal doctrine departs primarily from cases. In civil law, it departs from codes and statutes. Since the content of these latter sources is highly abstract, its use needs a proper method that devises ways of making it concrete. Case studies are an excellent way of doing this.[40] It is worth mentioning that studies can also perform important didactic roles by enabling students to effectively reason with abstract categories as applied to concrete situations.[41]

2. LEGAL DOCTRINE AND LEGAL PRACTICE

Critics argue that legal doctrine fails to justify its own premises and struggles to address real-world complexities. On the one hand, it is said that doctrinal

---

38 LoPucki (n 20).

39 Alexander L. George and Andrew Bennett, *Case Studies and Theory Development in the Social Sciences* (MIT Press 2005) 85.

40 Bernardo B. Queiroz de Moraes, *Parte Geral – Código Civil. Gênese, difusão e conveniência de uma ideia* (YK 2018) 154–159, emphasizes the abstract nature of the General Part of the Brazilian Civil Code and the importance of Roman case law in helping make its concepts more concrete.

41 Osny da Silva Filho, 'Caso Lake River' (2023) 2(1) *Revista Jurídica Profissional* 88, 93.

propositions, besides being regarded often as 'arcane' or 'tedious',[42] are also based on fragile or outdated grounds,[43] especially when compared to normative philosophy and sociology.[44] On the other hand, since, as already said, civil law doctrine mainly departs from codifications and statutes—and not from case law, as is the case of common law—it is argued that it has not been able to keep pace with the rapid changes legal practice has undergone in the last few decades.

Scholars generally refute these critics as if the burden of proof were on their opponents. For legal doctrine operates precisely to the extent that it refuses to question its starting points; the normative sophistication of its premises would be secondary to the practicality of its propositions. And its generality, i.e., its capacity to answer issues that are not even present when its propositions are developed, would compensate for its recognized lack of up-to-dateness. In fact, those challenges seem to be a consequence of the fact that legal doctrine is a sort of a 'hybrid between legal science and legal practice'.[45] It should, therefore, come as no surprise that it suffers 'from an incurable epistemological

---

[42] Christian Boulanger, 'The Comparative Sociology of Legal Doctrine: Thoughts on a Research Program' (2020) 21 *German Law Journal* 1362–1377, 1362.

[43] Pauline C. Westerman, 'Open or Autonomous? The Debate on Legal Methodology as a Reflection of the Debate on Law', in Mark Van Hoecke (ed), *Methodologies of Legal Research: Which Kind of Method for What Kind of Discipline* (Hart 2011) 87–110, 101–102: 'legal doctrine always comes too late, running behind legal and social developments, dusting [off] concepts that are outdated and no longer in use'. According to the author, this statement was also made in the famous text by Julius von Kirchmann, *Die Wertlosigkeit der Jurisprudenz als Wissenschaft: ein Vortrag, gehalten in der juristischen Gesellschaft zu Berlin* (3rd ed. Springer 1848) 10–13.

[44] Aleksander Peczenik, 'Can Philosophy Help Legal Doctrine?' (2004) 17 (1) *Ratio Juris* 108: 'Jurists themselves accepted, though often superficially, the world picture of analytical philosophy, in essence incompatible with legal doctrine. No wonder that legal sceptics treat theories of juristic doctrine as rhetorical devices, at best making people happy and at worst deceiving them'.

[45] Marietta Auer, 'What is Legal Theory?' (2021) 29 *Rechtsgeschichte – Legal History* 31. The full citation is as follows: 'Legal doctrine, understood as a hybrid between legal science and legal practice, seems to suffer from an incurable epistemological contradiction in terms: What if theory cannot be practice or vice versa'.

contradiction in terms',[46] insofar as its theory may not be practical enough 'or vice versa'.[47]

In order to better understand these challenges, it is useful to distinguish two different connections established between legal doctrine and legal practice.

2.1 Two Opposite Directions of Fit

Legal doctrine and legal practice share a close relationship. From a practical standpoint, doctrinal scholarship assumes the role of a user guide for the law. Just as a user guide assists individuals in comprehending and optimizing the use of a product or system, doctrinal scholarship endeavors to steer legal practice, specifically that of professional lawyers, towards adherence to legality.

This task involves two distinct epistemic courses, akin to what the philosopher John Austin referred to as 'directions of fit'.[48] The first encompasses a *practical commitment* to bringing doctrine into line with actual or future problems, reflecting a 'word-to-world' direction of fit. The second direction involves a *positive attachment* to ensure that doctrine accurately represents the realities of the relevant positive law, illustrating a 'world-to-word' direction of fit.

2.1.1 Practical commitment

Legal doctrine displays its practical commitment by providing epistemic frameworks for the identification, interpretation, and systematization of law in light of practical situations, either past or future, real or hypothesized. It is no accident that the *quality* of the doctrine usually overlaps with its 'word-to-world' fit, i.e., its applicability: doctrinal language is intended to effect change in the real world.

The practical commitment of doctrine also serves as a foundation for legal education and research,[49] be it doctrinal, philosophical, or empirical. Of course,

---

[46] Marietta Auer, 'What is Legal Theory?' (2021) 29 *Rechtsgeschichte – Legal History* 31.

[47] Marietta Auer, 'What is Legal Theory?' (2021) 29 *Rechtsgeschichte – Legal History* 31.

[48] John L. Austin, *'How to Talk' in Philosophical Papers* (3rd ed. Clarendon Press 1990). The idea was further developed by John R. Searle, *Intentionality* (Cambridge University Press 1983); and *Making the Social World: The Structure of Human Civilization* (Oxford University Press 2010).

[49] 'A critical legal education is centrally concerned with legal doctrine', as once argued by Alan Hunt, 'The Case for Critical Legal Education' (2010) 20(1) *The Law Teacher* 10, 18.

legal education does not always reflect the latest doctrinal advancements.[50] But even if their main references are outdated, legal scholarship provides a common language to communicate and discuss legal concepts and rules.

2.1.2 Positive attachment

The 'world-to-word' direction of fit in legal doctrine corresponds to its attachment to positive law (*lex*). Legal doctrine aligns with positive law either by providing frameworks for understanding the existing law (*de lege lata*) or by proposing legal innovations and reforms (*de lege ferenda*).[51] Classifying doctrinal scholarship as either *de lege lata* or *de lege ferenda* can be useful for distinguishing between different levels of applicability. Of course, this distinction can become blurred in the context of contract doctrine because a contract may align to varying degrees with its legal classification; that is, its *type*.[52]

Legal doctrine also reveals its positive attachment when it takes positive law as a starting point for proposing categories that justify exceptions to general rules. These exceptions are sometimes obtained through efforts to justify seemingly *contra legem* case law. In any case, it is not up to legal doctrine to decide whether positive law is legal because it is posited, or it is posited because it is legal. Such an important quest is to be sought by legal philosophy. Equally, legal doctrine makes no claim to reveal the truth of its inputs and outputs. The empirical premises and outcomes of legal doctrine are simply assumed. It is for socio-legal studies to verify them. This, of course, exposes legal doctrine to a wide array of criticism.

---

[50] There can be an unwanted distance between these two spheres, as observed in the Canadian context by David Sandomierski, *Aspiration and Reality in Legal Education* (University of Toronto Press 2020) 178 et seq.

[51] Christian Courtis, 'El juego de los juristas. Ensayo de caracterización de la investigación dogmatica' in Christian Courtis (ed), *Observar la ley. Ensayos sobre metodología de la investigación jurídica* (Trotta 2006) 113–118.

[52] Lorenzo Passerini Glazel, *La forza normativa del tipo: pragmatica dell'atto giuridico e teoria della categorizzazione* (Quodlibet 2005). In this regard, see also Mariana Pargendler, 'Desenho contratual em perspectiva comparada: reflexões sobre a relação entre tipificação legal e inovação contratual' (2016) 61(1) *Revista da Faculdade de Direito UFPR* 224: 'In turn, it is a characteristic feature of civil law codification that it contains […] specific rules applicable to different types of contract […] Each type of contract disciplined reflects, in principle, a different category of economic operation'.

2.2 Two Opposite Orders of Criticism

As mentioned earlier, a first common criticism directed at legal doctrine suggests that it is too focused on practicalities, so it lacks academic rigor.[53]

2.2.1 Legal doctrine is too practical ...

The 'too practical' accusation can be unfolded into at least three further strands: (i) legal doctrine is not up to date with philosophical and social science advances; (ii) legal doctrine cannot have an academic status due to its self-referential nature; and, finally, (iii) legal doctrine has become shallow literature, primarily focused on preparation for legal career exams.

The first strand suggests that legal doctrine has not kept pace with recent advancements in philosophy and social science. In this regard, doctrinal scholarship exhibits a 'relative lag' compared to philosophical and sociological works. Though such criticism is not peculiar to civil law and is often mentioned by common lawyers, it is further complicated by the fact that law is an undergraduate degree in civil law countries, meaning that civil lawyers usually have no prior academic experience with other academic disciplines before graduating. For this very reason, it is argued, interdisciplinary studies should be encouraged to overcome traditional doctrinal methods.[54] Of course, this argument assumes that the stage of development of different fields of knowledge is perfectly commensurable, which is highly debatable.

According to the second strand of criticism, legal doctrine cannot claim academic status, not because of the quality of its instances, but due to its function within the structures of reproduction of legal knowledge in civil law jurisdictions.[55] This argument is not entirely new. Its first and most well-known version was the one presented by the jurist and philosopher Julius von Kirchmann in 1848: 'three rectifying words from the legislator and entire libraries become waste paper'.[56]

---

53 See, for example, William Baude, Adam S. Chilton and Anup Malani, 'Making Doctrinal Work More Rigorous: Lessons from Systematic Reviews' (2017) 84(1) *University of Chicago Law Review* 37–58, 39.

54 See Marcos Nobre, *O que é pesquisa em direito?* (Saraiva 2002). Within a common law context, the same point was made before by George Priest, 'The Growth of Interdisciplinary Research and the Industrial Structure of the Production of Legal Ideas: A Reply to Judge Edwards' (1993) 91 *Michigan Law Review* 1929.

55 Philipp Lassahn and Thomas Steenbreker, 'Gedanken zur Rechtsdogmatik' (2015) 11 *Juristische Rundschau* 558.

56 Julius von Kirchmann, *Die Wertlosigkeit der Jurisprudenz als Wissenschaft* (3rd ed. Springer 1848) 23.

This line of criticism turns the 'world-to-word' fit of legal doctrine—that is, its positive attachment—into a burden: the 'ephemerality' of positive law, argues Marietta Auer, prevents legal doctrine from being considered a 'serious scholarly inquiry', for many recurring problems in private law are actually social issues, better understood through the lens of social structure rather than categories like freedom of contract or contractual justice.[57]

The third strand of criticism argues that legal doctrine has become overly focused on preparing candidates for legal career exams, such as those for judicial positions. As a result, it has devolved into trivial literature, focused on providing Q&A of black letter law without any concern for the actual complexities of real-world issues. This transformation can be attributed to several factors, including changes in legal education, the increasing emphasis on standardized testing, and a corresponding decline in the intellectual rigor of doctrinal scholarship.[58]

This sort of trivialization can also be related to deficiencies in the intellectual grounding of jurists themselves, which may be exacerbated by local peculiarities: estimates suggest, for example, that the number of law schools in Brazil exceeds the total number of law schools in the rest of the world.[59]

2.2.2 … or not practical enough

Another extreme in the critique of legal doctrine questions its practical relevance. The flaw of the doctrine, in this case, would lie in its 'word-to-world'

---

[57] Marietta Auer, 'Der privatrechtliche Diskurs der Moderne revisited' (2020) 53 KJ 47: 'This means that numerous recurring problems of private law thinking present themselves as structural manifestations of the aporias of modern society and can thus be better understood precisely in their insolubility than on the basis of superficially socio-critical categories such as the materialization of contractual freedom or contractual justice'.

[58] Otavio Luiz Rodrigues Junior, 'Dogmática e crítica da jurisprudência (ou da vocação da doutrina em nosso tempo)' (2010) 891 *Revista dos Tribunais* 65, 86–93. See also Judith Martins-Costa, 'Autoridade e utilidade da doutrina: a construção dos modelos doutrinários' in Judith Martins-Costa et al. (eds), *Modelos de Direito Privado* (Marcial Pons 2014) 18–26.

[59] Luiza Tenente, 'Brasil tem mais faculdades de direito que China, EUA e Europa juntos; saiba como se destacar no mercado' (2017), https://g1.globo.com/educacao/guia-de-carreiras/noticia/brasil-tem-mais-faculdades-de-direito-que-china-eua-e-europa-juntos-saiba-como-se-destacar-no-mercado.ghtml. On the other hand, the discrepancy in the number of lawyers per capita is less significant. Brazil (474 lawyers per 100k) is behind Israel (694 lawyers per 100k) and the Dominican Republic (565 lawyers per 100k) and not far ahead of Italy (403 lawyers per 100k), according to https://worldpopulationreview.com/country-rankings/lawyers-per-capita-by-country.

direction of fit, i.e., its practical commitment. The German comparatist Hein Kötz goes as far as to say that '[s]ometimes we come across dogmatic works whose practical relevance cannot be found even with a magnifying glass'.[60]

In addition, critics argue that legal doctrine, often developed in an overly academic and purportedly theoretical manner, may struggle to address the nuances of real-world legal issues. In this regard, Heinrich Stoll once stated in a lecture that 'those in the practice are easily inclined to accuse' legal scholars 'of living in gray theories far removed from reality'.[61] Moreover, it is also said that the legal abstraction of concepts may not reflect the complexities of practical reality, which is reflected in inconsistent or even contradictory case law.[62]

It is also true, however, that legal practice often demands solutions to intricate problems that legal doctrine alone may not sufficiently address. Skeptics argue that an overemphasis on legal doctrine may limit innovative and context-specific approaches to legal problem-solving. They advocate for a more dynamic and pragmatic engagement with legal issues that incorporates practical considerations alongside theoretical analysis.[63]

In any case, addressing these challenges requires a reevaluation of the role and scope of legal doctrine. Embracing interdisciplinary perspectives, engaging with new normative perspectives, incorporating empirical research, and fostering collaboration between scholars and practitioners are essential steps in enhancing the academic rigor and practical applicability of legal doctrine.

3. RECLAIMING LEGAL DOCTRINE

As we have seen, legal doctrine is often criticized for being either too practical or not practical enough. Still focusing on contract law, in what follows I explore three complementary strategies for restoring the relevance of doctrinal scholarship without losing sight of what makes legal doctrine properly 'doctrinal'—namely, its aspiration to inform legal practice (i.e., its *practical*

---

60 Hein Kötz, 'Rechtsvergleichung und Rechtsdogmatik' (1990) 54 *RabelsZ* 211.

61 In the original, Heinrich Stoll, 'Ueber die Beziehungen der Rechtslehre zur Praxis (Pädagogische Aufgaben; Bedeutung der Rechtsgeschichte und Rechtsvergleichung für die Rechtsanwendung). Vortrag, gehalten auf der Tagung des Badischen Richtervereins in Freiburg am 25. April 1926' (1926) 126 *Archiv für die civilistische Praxis* 174.

62 Marcelo Neves, 'Rechtswissenschaft versus Rechtspraxis und sozialer Kontext in Brasilien – vom Autoritarismus zur Demokratisierung' (1998) 8 *Comparativ* 33.

63 Osny da Silva Filho, *Fundamentos do direito contratual: doutrina, teoria e empiria* (Almedina 2022) 202.

commitment) and its conscious dependence on the sources of law (its *positive attachment*). These three strategies are integrating interdisciplinarity (3.1), enabling creative functions (3.2), and zooming in on contract clauses (3.3).

3.1 Integrating Interdisciplinarity

Unlike philosophical and socio-legal scholarship, legal doctrine tends to legitimize itself by rejecting interdisciplinarity.[64] This is not only an epistemic (i.e., field-based descriptive) rejection but also a professional (i.e., role-based moral) one. For, unlike Socio-Legal Studies (which are, of course, undertaken by lawyers but also by social scientists) and Philosophy of Law (developed not only by jurists but also by professional philosophers),[65] the argument goes that doing doctrinal scholarship is a task reserved for trained lawyers.[66]

I shall argue, however, that defending the relevance of legal doctrine by rejecting interdisciplinarity represents a serious error. The importance of doctrine will not be guaranteed by the reproduction of self-referential discourses. On the contrary, interdisciplinarity can contribute to the renewal of doctrine if it reinforces, rather than diminishes, its positive attachment. This can be achieved, for example, through the use of interdisciplinary methods to identify customs that serve as sources of law. Additionally, economic and sociological methods can enhance the efficiency and effectiveness of applying legal rules.[67]

Incorporating interdisciplinarity in this manner would also allow legal doctrine to enhance its practical commitment. By including elements from other disciplines, legal frameworks would be better equipped to address real-world situations. For instance, recognizing that contracts are legal translations of complex economic transactions[68] is essential for understanding their applications. Many contracts, such as insurance policies, can only be fully

---

[64] Examples in Jan M. Smits, *The Mind and Method of the Legal Academic* (Edward Elgar Publishing 2012) 75–86. For an example of criticism of interdisciplinarity, focusing on law & economics, see Karl-Heinz Fezer, 'Nochmals: 'Kritik an der ökonomischen Analyse des Rechts' (1988) 43 *JuristenZeitung* 223–228.

[65] Norberto Bobbio, *Giusnaturalismo e positivismo giuridico* (2nd ed. Edizioni di Communità 1972) 44 (discussing the differences between the Philosophy of Law made by jurists and by philosophers).

[66] It is worth noting that outside the United States, as in the majority of civil law countries, law is an undergraduate course, not a graduate one.

[67] For examples of sociological methods that would be useful for private law, see Andreas Heldrich, 'Die Bedeutung der Rechtssoziologie für das Zivilrecht' (1986) 186 *Archiv für die civilistische Praxis* 88–89.

[68] Enzo Roppo, *Il contratto* (1977), translated by A. Coimbra e M. Januário C. Gomes, *O contrato* (Almedina 2009) 9.

comprehended through an interdisciplinary approach—say, applications of actuarial science—that captures both the essence of the economic transaction and its potential legal challenges.

3.2 Enabling Creative Functions

Doctrinal arguments are often assumed to be limited to determining whether something is permissible within the legal system, such as whether it is legal or illegal, valid or invalid. Similarly, there is a belief that legal doctrine only gains relevance when used to resolve disputes. These assumptions pose significant hurdles to the development of creative functions in legal doctrine. To overcome these challenges, it is essential to understand and address these restrictive views.

3.2.1 By going beyond legality and validity ...

Being primarily trained to engage with legislative sources, civil lawyers may view the focus on legality and validity—which indeed highlights the positive attachment (2.1.2)—as both necessary and sufficient for doctrinal research. However, the practice of law demands more than binary propositions. It requires a nuanced approach encompassing benchmarking, risk assessment, best practices, context analyses, and other strategic arguments. Lawyers must navigate complex legal landscapes, balancing statutory interpretations with practical considerations to craft compelling and effective legal arguments.

Consider, for instance, contracts between freelance software developers and tech companies. These agreements could be qualified as employment contracts, independent contractor agreements, works contracts, or even *sui generis* agreements that incorporate elements from multiple contract types—mixed-type atypical contracts, as civil lawyers call them.[69] Each qualification carries distinct implications. For example, an employment contract might entail certain benefits and protections for the developer, while an independent contractor agreement could offer more flexibility but fewer legal safeguards. Works contracts might focus on the delivery of specific software projects, whereas *sui generis* agreements could blend aspects of both employment and project-based contracts.

Choosing the appropriate contract type involves far more than determining its legality or validity; it requires a strategic assessment of the risks and benefits associated with each option. Legal doctrine can assist in this process. It may consider factors such as the duration of the project, the level of control the company wishes to exert over the developer, the nature of the work being

69 Pedro Pais de Vasconcelos, *Contratos atípicos* (2nd ed. Almedina 2009) 231.

performed, and the legal obligations each party is willing to assume. By doing so, doctrinal scholarship can help tailor and perform agreements to best serve the interests of both the developer and the company, ensuring compliance with legal standards while also addressing practical needs and business objectives.

This multidimensional, strategic approach highlights the importance of legal doctrine as an evolving and adaptable discipline, capable of addressing the complexities of modern legal practice. It underscores the necessity for lawyers to go beyond mere compliance and engage in sophisticated legal reasoning that considers the broader context and implications of their decisions.

3.2.2 … and focusing on advisory practice

The Roman lawyer Gaius, in his book *Institutiones*, noted that Roman law consisted of comitial enactments, plebiscites, and constitutions of the emperors, as well as the advice given by jurists: the *responsa prudentium*.[70] It can be said that these *responsa*, later compiled in the Justinian *Digest*, constitute a prototype of what would come to be known as legal doctrine. Since the post-classical period of Roman jurisprudence (*circa* 230 to 530 AD), the answers provided by the jurists, the *iuris prudentes*, acquired an unequivocal role in defining what counts as legal—a constitutive role, if we may—as it functioned as a source of law.[71]

In modern times, however, the use of doctrine as a source of law has become exceptional, being admitted only in very specific circumstances. In particular, legal doctrine is no longer considered a source of law endowed with a status equivalent to that of legislation. Yes, it may function as a source of law in those cases when legislation and case law run out. But even in these cases, it does not qualify as *mandatory*, but as a *permissive* source: 'a complete legal answer, but not a required legal answer', as John Gardner puts it.[72] This means that judges and arbitrators are not obligated to consider permissive sources, though they have the discretion to do so. Thus, while it may be legally justified for a judge to use doctrinal scholarship as a source of law, it is not legally wrong if they choose not to.

The distinction between mandatory and permissive sources implies that legal doctrine only becomes relevant to the extent it is employed to resolve a

---

[70] Gai. 1, 2. Translation by Francis de Zulueta, *The institutes of Gaius* (Clarendon 1958) 3: 'The laws of the Roman people consist of leges (comitial enactments), plebiscites, senatusconsults, imperial constitutions, edicts of those possessing the right to issue them, and answers of the learned'.

[71] Eva Cantarella, *Diritto romano: istituzioni e storia* (Mondadori 2010) 91.

[72] John Gardner, 'Concerning Permissive Sources and Gaps' (1988) 8 *Oxford Journal of Legal Studies* 458. See also Fábio P. Shecaira, 'Sources and Reasons' in *Legal Scholarship as a Source of Law* (Springer 2013) 23–34.

dispute. However, this perspective significantly undervalues the role of doctrinal scholarship in supporting advisory practices. Doctrinal scholarship is not confined to judicial decision-making and its formal constraints; it can extend its influence into other relevant functions of legal professionals. This broader understanding of the role of legal doctrine enables legal scholars to go beyond what is established by courts and black letter law, enhancing their ability to provide materials for comprehensive legal advice and nuanced legal solutions.

It is worth noting that the use of legal doctrine for supporting advisory practice is not a novelty. A classic Portuguese work written by José Homem Corrêa Telles in the early 19th century provides some excellent examples of this function. Corrêa Telles gives pieces of advice to buyers in hypothetical situations: 'if you are selling a rented farm, you should stipulate the upkeep of the caretaker';[73] 'if you do not want to guarantee the defects of the thing sold, it is allowed to do so, but you must declare it'[74] and, in the case of buying wine, 'it seems more prudent to buy by measure than by eye; never buy without tasting'.[75]

True, advisory scholarship has gradually taken a back seat in legal scholarship, but revisiting it is essential. Doctrinal works can be invaluable in guiding the negotiation, drafting, and performance of contracts. During negotiations, lawyers often rely on doctrinal analyses to understand the implications of various contractual terms and to craft provisions that are both legally sound and tailored to their clients' needs. In the formalization stage, doctrinal scholarship ensures contracts are drafted with precision and clarity, reducing the risk of future disputes. Furthermore, in the performance of contracts, doctrinal insights aid in interpreting and implementing contractual obligations, ensuring that parties adhere to their agreements effectively and efficiently.

3.3 Zooming in from Contracts to Clauses

The organization of contractual regimes around specific types of contracts is a characteristic feature of contract law in civil law systems.[76] Once again, it

---

[73] José Homem Corrêa Telles, *Manual do tabelião ou ensaios de jurisprudência euremática: contendo a coleção de minutas dos contratos e instrumentos mais usuais, e das cautelas mais precisas nos contratos e testamentos* (3rd ed. Imprensa Nacional 1842) 25.

[74] ibid.

[75] ibid 34.

[76] José Reinaldo de Lima Lopes and Osny da Silva Filho, 'Contratos (verbete)' in Andréa Slemian, Bruno Aidar, and José Reinaldo de Lima Lopes (eds), *Dicionário histórico de conceitos jurídico-econômicos (Brasil, séculos XVIII-XIX)* (Alameda 2021) 213–214.

is an ancient tradition, though it was only theorized much later. The Roman jurists of the classical period of the *iurisprudentia* (*circa* 130 BC to 230 AD) did not develop a general concept of contract nor a comprehensive 'contract law', but focused instead on specific rules for obligations derived from a small set of consensual agreements—namely, *emptio venditio*, *locatio conductio*, *societas*, and *mandatum*. In doing so, they asserted a principle of *numerus clausus*, whereby only those specific *obligationes contractae* were recognized as legally binding.[77]

One of the main differences between modern contract law and Roman law of contracts lies in the overcoming of the *numerus clausus* principle through the acknowledgment of freedom of contract and, correspondingly, the general concept of contract.[78] These two major developments, however, posed significant challenges for connecting legal practice and academia. The use of pre-established contract types worked as a safe harbor for jurists. Ultimately, the radicalization of freedom *of* contract would lead to freedom *from* contract, a kind of escape from contract law—a phenomenon well-mapped by the literature on so-called 'relational contracts'.[79] So it begs the question: can we address what appears to be an ever-growing distancing between legal doctrine and the practice of law caused by the desirable expansion of the freedom of contract?

One promising path could be moving focus from types of contracts to specific contract clauses. This approach, which has already been carried out in different civil law countries,[80] brings different practical advantages.

For starters, focusing on individual contract clauses allows for a deeper examination of the specific issues which often go unnoticed in more general

---

77 Fritz Schulz, *Classical Roman Law* (Clarendon 1961) 465.

78 José Reinaldo de Lima Lopes and Osny da Silva Filho, 'Contratos (verbete)' in Andréa Slemian, Bruno Aidar, and José Reinaldo de Lima Lopes (eds), *Dicionário histórico de conceitos jurídico-econômicos (Brasil, séculos XVIII-XIX)* (Alameda 2021) 214–215.

79 References in note 23 *supra*.

80 As for Italy, Massimo Confortini (ed), *Clausole negoziali*: profili teorici e applicativi di clausole tipiche e atipiche (vol. 1, UTET 2017) and Massimo Confortini (ed), *Clausole negoziali: profili teorici e applicativi di clausole tipiche e atipiche* (vol. 2, UTET 2019). In France, William Dross, *Clausier: dictionnaire des clauses ordinaires et extraordinaires des contrats de droit privé interne* (4th ed. Lexis Nexis 2020); and Geneviève Helleringer, *Les clauses du contrat: essai de typologie* (L.G.D.J. 2012). In Brazil, Francisco Paulo De Crescenzo Marino, Marcelo Vieira von Adamek and Osny da Silva Filho (eds), *Cláusulas contratuais* (Almedina 2025).

and abstract studies.[81] This approach facilitates the identification of potential pitfalls, ambiguities, and interpretive challenges that might not be apparent when analyzing contracts at a broader level.

Consider, for instance, the representations and warranties clauses. These clauses serve to allocate risk between the parties by asserting and providing assurances about certain facts or conditions. A detailed analysis can uncover how these assurances impact the negotiation process, the drafting of contracts, and the resolution of disputes. Similarly, entire agreement clauses, which aim to consolidate all terms of the agreement into a single document, can be scrutinized to understand their effectiveness in preventing parties from relying on pre-contractual statements or extrinsic evidence.

In the same vein, indemnity clauses, which are designed to anticipate and provide for compensation for loss or damage, can be dissected to reveal their implications for risk management and liability. By examining these clauses closely, one can better appreciate how they allocate financial responsibility and influence the behavior of contracting parties. Best efforts clauses, which require a party to exert a certain level of effort to fulfill contractual obligations, can be studied to determine how courts interpret and enforce these obligations, particularly in varying jurisdictions. Examples abound.

The second practical advantage of zooming in on contract clauses is that it facilitates comparative analysis by identifying and comparing different applicable legal regimes. Take the case of conditions precedent, a set of clauses first developed in the common law.[82] These clauses specify that certain conditions must be met before certain obligations arise. Civil codes do not provide rules for these specific clauses. However, they do contain rules on typical suspensive and resolutive conditions.[83] This requires legal doctrine to step in and interpret

---

81 As highlighted in an Italian work on the study of contractual clauses, Massimo Confortini (ed), 'Prefazione', in *Clausole negoziali: profili teorici e applicativi di clausole tipiche e atipiche* (vol. 1, UTET 2017) n.p. 1: 'In the aspiration, by this way, to stimulate the student's interest in themes and problems that rarely penetrate the architecture of traditional textbooks or treatises'.

82 Osny da Silva Filho and Sergio Lima Dias Junior, 'Condições precedentes: atipicidade e disciplina jurídica', in Francisco Paulo De Crescenzo Marino, Marcelo Vieira von Adamek and Osny da Silva Filho (eds), *Cláusulas contratuais* (Almedina 2025).

83 Although similar on several points, the concepts of suspensive and resolutive conditions, typical of the civil law system, do not coincide with the concepts of conditions precedent and subsequent, established in the common law tradition. Hence the need for a careful legal translation of conditions precedent under Brazilian law. See, in this regard, Osny da Silva Filho and Sergio Lima Dias Junior, 'Condições precedentes: atipicidade e disciplina jurídica', in Francisco Paulo De Crescenzo Marino, Marcelo Vieira von Adamek and Osny da Silva Filho (eds),

which rules from the Civil Code's regime of typical conditions should govern them. By doing so, scholars can adapt and translate existing legal regimes to fit these specific clauses, ensuring that they are effectively integrated into the legal framework.

CONCLUSION

Doctrinal methods play a crucial role in guiding legal practice by providing frameworks for identifying, interpreting, and systematizing law. They also bridge the gap between legal academia and the practice of law by offering a common legal language. In doing so, legal doctrine distinguishes itself from the philosophy of law, which focuses on the concept and general features of law, and socio-legal studies, which examine the broader social conditions and implications of law.

Despite the acknowledged importance of doctrinal scholarship, it has faced two seemingly opposing criticisms. On one hand, it is perceived as excessively practical, lagging behind recent methodological innovations in philosophy, sociology, and other academic disciplines. On the other hand, legal doctrine is also deemed insufficiently practical, failing to address the complex challenges encountered in contemporary legal practice. These criticisms also take on particular contours in civil law systems, where law is an undergraduate degree, and there is no shortage of either lawyers or inconsistent case law.

In order to overcome these criticisms, this chapter proposes three complementary strategies. These strategies are integrating interdisciplinarity (3.1), enabling creative functions (3.2) by going beyond mere considerations of validity and invalidity (3.2.1) or by focusing on the uses of doctrine in advisory practice (3.2.2), and finally, zooming in from contract types to specific contract clauses (3.3). By incorporating these strategies, legal doctrine can evolve and remain a valuable tool for both legal scholars and practitioners without losing what makes it properly doctrinal, namely, its positive attachment and its practical commitment.

Cláusulas contratuais (Almedina 2025), and, in relation to the European tradition, Ulrike Babusiaux, 'Conditions', in Nils Jansen and Reinhard Zimmermann (eds), *Commentaries on European Contract Laws* (Oxford University Press 2018) 1934, pointing out that 'not all clauses described as "conditions precedent" in contractual practice should be regarded as suspensive conditions'.

2. Doctrinal methods in contract law in common law jurisdictions

Jeff Berryman

INTRODUCTION

Professor Steve Hedley is an astute observer of private law theory, both as curator of the highly-read Private Law Theory Blog[1] and in his own writings. In earlier writing, Hedley lamented the gap between theorists who took a strictly 'internal' point of view without acknowledgment of what an 'external' point of view can offer to explicate and improve the quality and usefulness of legal theory on private law.[2] Recently, Hedley has written that private law theorists of both stripes, internalists and externalists, have come to some rapprochement that allows space for actual dialogue.[3] Hedley poignantly observes, 'Without the internal viewpoint, without at least *some* attention to structure and process, the legal system is not a "system", and arguably isn't legal either'. And later on, 'That the need for *some sort* of structure has never been denied (the dispute has been over the adequacy of the structures on offer, and the need for better ones)'.[4] This is a view I share. A theory of private law is a meta or grand theory designed to unify all of the law of obligations; contract, torts, and restitution, and the place of property within obligations. A grand theory of private law may be useful in identifying an appropriate classificatory structure that accounts for the outputs of private law. In this sense, it may assist in identifying what the law *is*. But the real value of a theory is its predictive value, showing us a way to what the law ought to be.

1 Private Law Theory Blog http://www.private-law-theory.org

2 Steve Hedley, 'Looking Outward or Looking Inward? Obligations Scholarship in the Early 21st Century' in Andrew Robertson and Tang Wu (eds), *The Goals of Private Law* (Hart Publishing 2009) 193.

3 Steve Hedley, 'Private Law Theory: The State of the Art', posted 7 September, 2021 and available at SSRN: https://papers.ssrn.com/sol3/papers.cfm?abstract_id=3917777, last accessed on 16 February 2024.

4 Above note 2 at 195 and 208 respectively.

In earlier writing, Hedley outlines the historical structure of the common law.[5] The common law was structured around its writ system, focusing on the procedures to be followed in obtaining a particular legal remedy. It is in the twentieth century that transformation in structure emerges; at the same time, legal treatises proliferated and the establishment of academic university legal education, as opposed to the apprenticeship model that preceded it, was adopted. In contract law, Hedley notes that we have a 'general law' of contract that is 'duty-based' coupled with a 'rights-based' approach for a number of particular specific types of contracts; a structure which Hedley describes as being quite stable.[6] Hedley attributes this stability to the general attitude of common law lawyers to eschew debates about structure and the disinterest by any government to be concerned with structural issues, certainly with regard to contract law other than some specific piecemeal reforms to discrete substantive areas (e.g. the law of frustration) and particular types of contracts (e.g. insurance contracts). Contract law lies as a constituent element of the law of obligations, and its doctrinal structure is a product of historical antecedents found in reported cases governed by a system of *stare decisis*, and doctrinal writing. Unlike civilian legal systems, there is no foundation code.[7] For common law systems, contract law must be 'found' through doctrinal research.

In sections 1 to 3 I set out a brief history of the development of common law doctrinal contract law and give reasons for its enduring relevance. I then develop an understanding of doctrinal contract law research methodology through three different approaches. These approaches illustrate how common law contract law meets the challenge of remaining relevant while consistent with notions of what it means to act justly and within the boundaries of what it is legitimate for common law judges to do when finding the common law of contract.

1. WHAT IS DOCTRINAL RESEARCH?

As will be argued below, there is a professional obligation on lawyers, and a reasonable expectation of graduates of accredited law faculties to know, or

---

5 Steve Hedley, 'Remedies: The Key to the Common Law System?' in Jeff Berryman and Rick Bigwood (eds), *The Law of Remedies: New Directions in the Common Law* (Irwin Publishing 2010) 305.

6 *Ibid* at 312.

7 For differences between civil and common law systems and methodology, see Sarah Worthington, 'The Unique Charm of the Common Law' (2011) 19(3) *European Review of Private Law* 345.

be able to find, 'the law' before advising a client.[8] 'The law' to be known, found, and used to advise clients in contract law is found in contract doctrine. Contract doctrine, like any legal doctrine, is defined by three attributes. One, a minimal requirement is law studied from an internal point of view. Doctrinal law is usually researched by an insider (lawyer, judge, academic, law student) in a system relying upon sources created by those same actors in the system, largely decided cases and statutes.[9] Two, legal doctrine uses legal arguments and language (i.e. as opposed to economic arguments)[10] to give an understanding of the law. Three, what makes good legal doctrine is what the late Professor Stephen Smith characterized as the incorporation of 'self-understanding'.[11] Smith saw this as incorporating two facets. First, because law is a human practice, it is important that law treats itself as being '*in fact* authoritative'. The legitimacy of law to the populace is that it is regarded as authoritative; it gives good reasons to citizens to act in one way rather than another. Second, that 'law provides its own characteristic method of organizing legal rules and decisions', its own 'self-organization'. That is, the role and importance of legal doctrine is to make the law intelligible and coherent, and doing so requires classification. We are bombarded by millions of sensory experiences which we both consciously and unconsciously compartmentalize in our own classificatory systems to make our lives intelligible and livable. We would simply be paralyzed if required to consciously process every experience without a classificatory system. As with an individual, law's classificatory system is just a more complex and explicit system for ordering our world.

Legal doctrine is not in opposition to legal theory, and in fact, as will be sketched below, much contractual legal doctrine reflects differently held legal

---

8 Law Society of Ontario *Rules of Professional Conduct* 3.1 Competence, https://lso.ca/about-lso/legislation-rules/rules-of-professional-conduct

9 Christopher McCrudden, 'Legal Research and the Social Sciences' (2006) 122 *Law Quarterly Review* 632 at 633, and David John Ibbetson, 'Historical Research in Law' in Mark Tushnet and Peter Cane (eds), *Oxford Handbook of Legal Studies* (Oxford University Press 2003) 864.

10 For example, while there is considerable discourse by law and economics proponents on the economic efficiencies or various aspects of contract law, and these arguments may, although rarely from my review of Canadian case law, buttress contract law doctrine, no legal counsel or judge would commence their pleadings or judgment with an assertion that the only economically efficient resolution to the parties' litigation is *xyz*. In my review of Canadian case law, I have seen reference to 'Pareto optimality' (a critical term in the economic analysis of law) in fewer than 14 cases, and in all situations, it is as a supportive argument or as a reference to some academic writing.

11 Stephen A. Smith, 'Taking Law Seriously' (2000) 50 *The University of Toronto Law Journal* 241, 249.

theories. However, what traditional legal doctrine does hold is that the influence of any particular legal theory becomes authoritative only through the self-organizing structures of the law, and not through morality or any other external legitimating force. These self-organizing principles for common law legal regimes require an understanding of common law methods as well as adoption of a particular theory of adjudication of disputes. Key to common law methodology is the principle of precedent and, more specifically, *stare decisis* (that a lower court is bound by the decision of a higher court). Basing decisions on precedent implies that a court must render a decision, and that a court's judgment is an explicit articulation of the dominant reasons for that decision. Judges and other actors in the legal system internalize these understandings through their discipline and professional training. Academic writing synthesizes court decisions within existing legal doctrine. Academic writing critiques either the coherence of the decision to established doctrine or the intelligibility of the doctrine to explain the judgment and its decision on the facts, and it is here that the particular legal theoretical lens adopted by the writer may influence their critique. While the authority of any decision will be determined by the doctrine of *stare decisis*, the actual precedent value and its persuasiveness will still be influenced by academic writing. In common law systems, one has to wait until the dust has settled – pursuit of any potential appeal, other court decisions and interpretations, and academic writing – before one can determine the impact of any one decision on established doctrine. This comes in contrast with civil law systems, where it may be easier to achieve methodological agreement between theory, doctrine, and praxis because the identification of who has the authority to 'make law' in civil systems is arguably narrower in scope and more explicit. In particular, the more limited role ascribed to judicial decisions as a generator and repository of legal doctrine.[12] The common law is akin to pointillism in art; each case represents a single dot, and only after sufficient cases have been determined does a clearer picture emerge of what the law is.

In a 2019 address, Lord Sales of the United Kingdom Supreme Court gave a defence of common law method and, implicitly, the value of traditional legal scholarship.[13] In his words:

> The common law method informs both the articulation of common law rules in the pure sense of judge-made law and the process of statutory interpretation by the courts. The combination of flexibility and stability capable of being attained within

[12] See Martijn Hesselink, 'A European Legal Method? On European Private Law and Scientific Method' (2009) 15 *The European Law Journal* 20.

[13] Philip Sales, 'The Common Law: Context and Method' (2019) 135 *Law Quarterly Review* 47.

> a common law system has been noted many times. The basic techniques used to achieve this are a system of precedent and locating courts within a strong legal culture which supplies objective criteria for judgment and criticism. Analysis of the concept of precedent indicates that it makes little sense apart from the principles supplied by the legal culture according to which case can be regarded as analogous or distinguishable.

Traditional doctrinal research is often disparaged today in common law developed countries,[14] although there has been some recent resurgence in private law theory.[15] In Canada, a transformation in legal scholarship arose with the report *Law and Learning.*[16] In that report, its author, Harry Arthurs, called for a more academic and intellectual stream to legal scholarship and education, one that would 'cultivate critical distance from doctrine, and the profession'.[17] As Smith noted, no aspiring academic colleague gives a job talk espousing traditional legal doctrine.[18] For law academics, the way ahead is largely through social science research, and universities, motivated by research performance-based indicators, give every encouragement to a transformation in legal scholarship. In the United States, the realist movement and its long tail through

[14] See Andrew Burrows, 'Challenges for Private Law in the 21st Century' in Kit Barker, Karen Fairweather and Ross Grantham (eds), *Private Law in the 21st Century* (Hart Publishing 2017) 29, 32, and Brian Coote, 'Contract: An Underview' in John W. Carter (ed), *Contract as Assumption II: Formation, Performance and Enforcement* (Hart Publishing 2016) 207.

[15] Steve Hedley, 'Is Private Law Meaningless?' (2011) 64 *Current Legal Problems* 89.

[16] Harry Arthurs, *Law and Learning: Report to the Social Sciences and Humanities Research Council of Canada* by the Consultative Group on Research and Education in Law (Ottawa, Information Division, The Council, 1983). For a more recent critique of the influence of the Arthurs report, see Catherine Dauvergne, 'New Crossroads and the Opportunity for a Crisis: The State of Canadian Legal Education' (2023) 101 *The Canadian Bar Review* 708.

[17] See David Sandomierski, reviewing Harry Arthurs' book, 'Law and Living: *Connecting the Dots: The Life of an Academic Lawyer*' (2021) 58 *Osgoode Hall Law Journal* 467, 474.

[18] *Supra* note 11 at 241. Stephen Smith repeated the same sentiment in his review of recent scholarship on tort law, noting that although judges, lawyers, and students still gravitate toward doctrinal legal reasoning, few legal scholars champion the approach. Stephen Smith, 'Taking Tort Seriously' (2021) 71 UTLJ 415, 416.

to critical legal studies,[19] together with the law and economics movement,[20] maligned doctrinal legal research as 'black letter law', law which is unconnected to what really determines cases or simply perpetuates some particular form of unjust hegemony.[21] Legal education that legitimates doctrinal research is viewed as being nothing more than a trade school, and – worse – one that runs counter to the pursuit of social justice; something that is beneath an academic institution that aspires to be integral to the social sciences and humanities.

The most cynical attacks on doctrinal legal research, and indeed, law itself, view law as nothing more than politics written in a different language. For these critical theorists, the very notion of dignity, justice, and objective reasonableness and fairness are all contingent. For other critical theorists, notions of dignity, justice, and objective reasonableness and fairness have transcendent value. They call for better doctrine informed by the perceptions of current legal doctrine drawn from their particular critical lens. For these critics, a knowledge of legal doctrine is necessary to determine the appropriate corrective salve. Drawing from the other dominant camp that critiques traditional legal scholarship, law and economics, even the most ardent advocate Richard Posner calls for more, not less, doctrinal scholarship.[22]

While academic scholarly interest in the exposition of contract doctrine has waned, it still retains importance in the practice of law for lawyers and judges. As observed by Lord Sales above, the culture of the common law and its system of judge-made rules is based upon understanding and reading cases. As

---

19 See Brian Leiter, 'Legal Realism and Legal Doctrine' (2015) 163 *The University of Pennsylvania Law Review* 1975, and Duncan Kennedy and Corinne Blalock, 'Provocation as Strategy: An Interview with Duncan Kennedy' (2022) 121 *The South Atlantic Quarterly* 377, particularly at 388–390.

20 See Jedediah Britton-Purdy, Davide Grewal, Amy Kalczynski, and Sabel Rahman, 'Building a Law-and-Political-Economy Framework: Beyond the Twentieth-Century Synthesis' (2020) 129 *The Yale Law Journal* 1784, particularly at 1794, and calling for a new framework that refocuses legal scholarship and the role of law toward the notion of a political economy that is truly built on equality and democratic ideals.

21 See the chapter by Jan Smits, 'What is Legal Doctrine? On the Aims and Methods of Legal-Dogmatic Research' in Rob van Gestel, Hans-W. Micklitz and Edward Rubin (eds), *Rethinking Legal Scholarship: A Transatlantic Dialogue* (Cambridge University Press 2017) 207, particularly at 209, also noting the decline in doctrinal legal scholarship but providing a defence of its importance.

22 Ironically, Posner noted in 2009 that such doctrinal scholars in the academy would in fact draw higher salaries than their theorist colleagues because the legal profession would compete for their labours. R. Posner, 'The State of Legal Scholarship Today: A Comment on Schlag' (2009) 97 *The Georgetown Law Journal* 845, 854.

will be explored below, the evolution of doctrinal treatises was a distillation of common law cases originally classified under the writs used to bring forward a case, and then to a system of rights and duties created by the parties from their legally recognized promises.

2. TRADITIONAL DOCTRINAL CONTRACT RESEARCH – A BRIEF HISTORY

If one were designing a legal system anew, it is doubtful that a rational actor would seize upon a common law system. Unlike most civil systems that can look to some defining written code of legal principles, the common law is the product of evolution, taking time to build a coherent body of rules into doctrine from court decisions.[23]

Despite the almost primordial nature of contracting, the development of contract doctrine in common law is of relatively recent origin. Feudal systems relied upon status, and it was only once citizens could exercise free will that a climate for contracting behaviour was developed.[24] Even then, the predominant form of contract was the executed contract. Prior to the Industrial Revolution, contracting in law was enforced by resorting to a number of royal writs: covenant, debt (particularly used through reciprocal penal bonds), and later assumpsit (from Latin 'he promised'), detinue, and trespass.[25] In addition, litigants, particularly merchants, had a variety of courts in which to pursue their action: Common Law, Chancery, Ecclesiastical Courts, Courts of Law Merchant, and Courts of Request. Moreover, the dominant interest litigated was the passing of property. Writing in 1760, William Blackstone needed only ten pages to describe the law of contract, which he then placed within 'Rights of Things', a volume devoted to property rights.[26] Blackstone's works formed part of an age in which legal treatises were beginning to be published to make the common law intelligible and coherent. While the structure of some of these treatises modeled civilian approaches, some were simply annotations of cases

23 The common law process was famously likened to building a cathedral by Guido Calabresi and Douglas Melamed in their article 'Property Rules, Liability Rules and Inalienability: One View of the Cathedral' (1972) 85 *Harvard Law Review* 1089.

24 See Henry Maine, *Ancient Law: Its Connection with the Early History of Society, and its Relation to Modern Ideas* (John Murray 1861) 304.

25 A.W.B. Simpson, *History of the Common Law of Contract* (Clarendon Press 1975) 90.

26 William Blackstone, *Commentaries on the Laws of England* (Clarendon Press 1765–69) 442–452.

grouped under a particular concept or maxim, and others consisted of lists of leading cases and abridgements.[27]

The transformation of the common law on both sides of the Atlantic, hewed from the Industrial Revolution, has been the subject of works by Patrick Atiyah,[28] Morton Horwitz,[29] and Lawrence Friedman.[30] During the Industrial Revolution, the popular notion that law could be systematized as a science was an article of faith consistent with the emerging political discourse over liberalism and laissez-faire economics. This became what could be regarded as a golden age for the contract treatise. Pollock[31] and Anson[32] writing on English contract law, and Williston[33] and Corbin[34] writing on American contract law, are regarded as the greatest systematizers of their era, writing treatises on the principles of contract law, and in the case of America, resulting in a form of codification of the law in the Restatement on the Law of Contract.[35]

Some of the treatise titles from the golden era continue today, obviously under new editorship,[36] and there are new contemporary treatise writers,[37] who mostly follow the models and structures adopted in the past. Some

---

27 A.W.B. Simpson, 'The Rise and Fall of the Legal Treatise: Legal Principles and the Forms of Legal Literature' (1981) 48 *The University of Chicago Law Review* 632.

28 Patrick Atiyah, *The Rise and Fall of Freedom of Contract* (Clarendon Press 1979).

29 Morton J. Horwitz, *The Transformation of American Law* (Harvard University Press 1977).

30 Lawrence Friedman, *A History of American Law* (Oxford University Press 2019).

31 Frederick Pollock, *Principles of Contract* (5th edn, Stevens 1889).

32 W.R. Anson, *Principles of the English Law of Contract* (2nd edn, Clarendon Press 1882).

33 Samuel Williston, *The Law of Contracts* (Baker, Voorhis & Co. 1920).

34 Arthur L. Corbin, *Corbin on Contracts: A Comprehensive Treatise on the Working Rules of Contract Law* (West Publishing Co. 1950).

35 *Restatement (first) of the Law on Contracts* (Philadelphia: American Law Institute 1932).

36 For example, *Chitty on Contract* (28th edn, London: Sweet & Maxwell 1999) is now edited by Hugh Beale. *Corbin on Contracts* is now edited by Joseph Perillo. Atiyah's *Introduction to the Law of Contract* (2006) was taken over by Stephen Smith, and *Treitel on the Law of Contract* (2020) is now edited by Edwin Peel.

37 In Canada, see Stephen Waddams' *The Law of Contracts* (7th edn, Toronto: Thomson Reuters 2017); John McCamus, *The Law of Contracts* (3rd edn, Irwin Law 2020); and Angela Swan, Jakub Adams and Annie Na, *Canadian Contract Law* (4th edn, LexisNexis Canada Inc. 2018).

common points emerge from these treatises, which influence the content of the respective treatises. First, audience matters: treatises written for the profession include more cases, are more pragmatic in approach, and are less ideological in theory,[38] while those written for students focus more on key cases, explore underlying theory, and contextualize material.[39] Second, referential authority matters: the fact that the most senior appellate courts in common law countries repeatedly cite a contract treatise legitimates the treatise as an authoritative repository and exposition of doctrinal contract law. Through the publication of multiple editions, a particular treatise and its author contribute to a dialogue with senior appellate courts on the development of the law consistent with common law methodology. Third, universality and language matter: the fact that all the contract treatises address similar topics, rely upon similar cases and statutory material, and address their subject material in the language of the law, is a self-fulfilling argument of doctrinal contract law's potency, legitimacy, and utility to legal practitioners. In a world where the reporting of cases and electronic databases have proliferated, the treatise separates the relevant from background chatter, making the law accessible and influencing what becomes a precedent.

3. WHAT IS THE ENDURING VALUE OF TRADITIONAL CONTRACT DOCTRINE?

Unlike other areas of common law in which there is dispute as to the boundaries of any particular classificatory system (think how the boundaries of the law of unjust enrichment have been much discussed, as have the laws of torts – particularly negligence in the past), the law of contract has rather stable boundaries because it is built upon a particular model, the synallagmatic contract,[40] a

---

38 Although note the more ideological approach by Ian Macneil, *The New Social Contract* (New Haven CT: Yale University Press 1980), who builds a contract theory around a legal framework designed to foster and preserve relationships rather than focusing upon a forensic search as to why a discrete transaction failed. See also the iconoclastic work of Stewart Macaulay, *Contracts: Law in Action* (3rd edn, NJ: LexisNexis 2010), focusing upon empirical research to determine the real boundaries of contract doctrine.

39 James Goudkamp and Donal Nolan, 'Scholars of Contract Law: Individuals and Themes' in James Goudkamp and Donal Nolan (eds), *Scholars of Contract Law* (Hart Publishing 2022) 41.

40 The term is taken from French Law and was used by Lord Diplock in *Hong Kong Fir Shipping Co. Ltd. v. Kawasaki Kisen Kaisha Ltd.* [1962] 1 All ER 474 (CA) at 485. A fuller description of the model was given by Lord Diplock in *Photo Production Ltd. v. Securicor Transport Ltd.* [1980] 1 All ER 556 (HL) at 565.

contract created through the consensual bilateral exchange of executory promises (consideration in common law) between two parties. The foundation of doctrinal contract law is the consensual exchange between two parties of equal bargaining power. Through an exchange of reciprocal promises, the parties 'write law' between themselves and create binding obligations. A distinguishing feature of traditional contract doctrine from areas of behavior prescribed by other common law doctrines is that it is a system of rules made available to parties to use rather than being imposed. Thus, the rules associated with offer and acceptance prescribe the path by which parties access contract doctrine. The rules on representations, interpretation, terms and conditions prescribe how parties order their obligations. The rules on breach, mistake, frustration, and illegality prescribe the rules for dealing with disputes over promised performance. The rules on duress, undue influence, and unconscionability deal with deficiencies in the ability of one party to make a genuine consent, and the rules on failure to perform giving rise to applicable remedies deal with the consequences of breach of contract. Some of these rules are amoral; like rules of the road (i.e. whether one drives on the left-hand side or the right): whatever side one comes down on, what matters is that a decision is made and consistently applied. (An example in common law countries is the postal rule of offer and acceptance, which states that a contract is formed when acceptance is delivered to the post office rather than on receipt by the offeror.)

Traditional contract doctrine works because it largely does what it is meant to do: provide rules to parties to facilitate exchange, commercial activity, and the security of property. Among common law countries, there is no clamour to abandon markets built upon contract doctrine as a means to efficiently move resources through an economy or to satiate individual wants. In other words, traditional contract doctrine meets the interests of those who use it. However, where the underlying premise of 'equality of bargaining power' fails, legislatures have intervened through statutory intervention, often resurrecting a form of contract regime based upon status, i.e. tenant and landlord, consumer and retailer, employee and employer. Nevertheless, these statutory interventions use the language of traditional contract doctrine to prescribe how the power relationship is changed to ameliorate the particular inequality identified in the contractual relationship.

Traditional contract doctrine provides certainty, universality, and predictability over promissory behavior. Because it is based upon a consensual model, the parties are at liberty to define their own contractual relationship subject only to fairly minimal legislative limits that work mostly to protect weaker parties. The rules of contract doctrine provide a shorthand of the background rights that parties would otherwise have had to come to agreement on themselves, but are saved the time, trouble, and effort of negotiation.[41] Rules that address illegitimate exploitative behaviour due to a power imbalance between the parties cannot be avoided. However, where other rules of contract don't work for the parties in individual cases, they are at liberty to draft their own terms with the legitimate expectation that they will be enforced if the product of a free consensual exchange.

We live in a risk-averse world.[42] Risk is either absorbed, mitigated, or insured against. For the business community, a contract is one way to assign risk associated with contractual performance through the inclusion of a specific term, often through the use of exclusions of liability or limitations on damages clauses. The drafting and interpretation of these clauses is made against a backdrop of known judicial decisions based upon contract doctrine applied to the clause under review.[43] Once risk is assigned, it is often covered through insurance. Above all else, insurers require certainty to be able to assess risk and assign a premium value to their coverage. Traditional contract doctrine provides that certainty which allows the secondary insurance market to price risk efficiently.

Other practical considerations exist in support of traditional contract doctrine. Contract doctrine is regarded as a foundational block of the common law of private obligations, next to the law of torts and the law of restitution. As a foundation block, it supports other legal doctrinal areas, including but not limited to commercial law, real estate, shipping, insurance, corporate law, consumer law, and aspects of family law. These areas can only be understood through the lens of contract doctrine, from which they are derived, and in which all have generated their own doctrinal treatises using the language of the law and drawing from an internal point of view.[44] More often, such courses are

---

41 The epitome of this phenomenon is the enactment of the Sale of Goods Act in all Commonwealth jurisdictions. In Ontario, see *Sale of Goods Act*, RSO 1990, c. S.1. The English Act was drafted by Sir Mackenzie Dalzell Edwin Stewart Chalmers as a codification of common law principles relating to the sale of goods.

42 Marc Oliver Rieger, Mei Wang and Torsten Hens, 'Risk Preferences Around the World' (2015) 61(3) *Management Science* 637–648, and Olivier L'Haridon and Ferdinand Vieider, 'All Over the Map: A Worldwide Comparison of Risk Preferences' (2019) 10(1) *Journal of Quantitative Economics* 185, 185–215. While these studies differ in conclusions, both affirm the notion of risk aversion, particularly in wealthier countries.

43 For example, note developments of the *Himalaya clause* taking its name from the case *Adler v. Dickson (The Himalaya)* [1955] 1 QB 158 (CA), dealing with the ability of a third party to take advantage of a limitation of liability in a carriage contract and avoiding the privity of contract rule.

44 For example, consider the prodigious writings of Professor Edward Ivamy, who at one time had 16 book titles simultaneously in print on areas of commercial,

taught in the academy by legal practitioners because they are (mis)perceived as being only practical 'black letter law' rather than engaging theoretical dimensions. Within the academy, traditional contract doctrine holds broad appeal to law students because it often accords with a layperson's understanding of what the law is, posited rules of universal application.[45]

Ultimately, traditional contract doctrine imposes an important constraint on idiosyncratic and arbitrary judicial decision-making. As mentioned above, traditional legal doctrine is legitimated through its internal point of view and self-organization and must be justified within a system of *stare decisis* and explained using the language of the law. Individual court judgments that stray from this legal orthodoxy invite correction on appeal. Apex courts couch their judgments within this orthodox framework in recognition of their constitutional position within common law jurisdictions. The doctrinal language of court judgments has an objectivity and rationality that differs appreciably from the subjectivity and emotionalism of political debate.

Another important constraint on arbitrary or unjust decision-making is the interaction between legislatures, courts, and the law. For example, most common law countries have statutory provisions dealing with consumer transactions. A common feature that underpins these statutory reforms is the empirical fact that there is often a power imbalance between consumers and retailers/manufacturers. Left to traditional contract doctrine, the more powerful party will often exploit this power imbalance to unfairly advance its self-interest and secure more favorable contractual terms. Legislatures redress the power imbalance in a variety of ways.[46] However, all these means of redress utilize the language of contract doctrine and have been enacted on the basis that the particular mode of redress will be applied to the identified deficiency

---

shipping, and insurance law. His obituary in the *Guardian* newspaper poignantly noted: 'Unlike that of many academic writers on law, his work became well established with the legal profession, not only for the comprehensive nature of the treatment and the accuracy of detail, but also because he instinctively knew the needs of the practical lawyer'. Bernard Hargrove, 'Edward Ivamy: Mercantile lawyer whose works retain their practical value', *The Guardian* (London, 27 September 2005).

[45] Most North American law students arrive at their place of study with some knowledge of the film *The Paper Chase* and the actor John Houseman's role as Professor Charles Kingsfield, the brilliant and demanding contract instructor in their first year at Harvard Law School.

[46] In the UK, a broader but more specific legislative provision has been created in the *Misrepresentation Act* 1967, chapter 7. Whereas in Australia a far more encompassing provision relating to misleading and deceptive conduct has been enacted, which includes misrepresentations. See *Competition and Consumer Act 2010, Schedule 2, The Australian Consumer Law.*

in contract doctrine. In other words, a sound knowledge of traditional contract doctrine is a prerequisite to understanding the legislative change. Further, the legislature has enacted the legislation on the assumption that it will be applied by the courts in the manner they have traditionally operated. In fact, it is often through academic scholarship that deficiencies in common law doctrine are demonstrated, and legislative changes, or differences in doctrinal interpretation, are provided through academic writing. In the area of contract doctrine, most legislative law reform has originated through either law reform commissions or legal expert panels.

4. RESEARCH METHODOLOGY – CONTRACT DOCTRINAL RESEARCH

The traditional contract doctrinal scholars that gave rise to the great treatise discussed earlier were essentially formalists and approached their tasks by looking at law from an internal point of view. In this sense, they were not instrumentalists.[47] Modern theorists who take posited law seriously are more likely to come from rights-based[48] and corrective justice theories.[49] For the former, the centrality of contract law is a promise, which is an expression of a person's free will and an exercise of personal autonomy. The reason for enforcing a promise is not because it advances utility (that is, advances a social good) but because it is either intrinsically a good thing to do (i.e. it reifies the liberal ideal of acts of personal autonomy and social relationships) or it is the morally correct thing to do. For the latter, justice is either corrective or distributive. Corrective justice governs the normative relationships between one individual and another. Distributive justice governs the web of interconnected relationships of a society. Corrective justice focuses on maintaining the correlativity between two individuals where wrongdoing is seen as creating a normative imbalance between the victim that only the wrongdoer can correct. Courts applying the common law can only legitimately practice corrective justice. Acts of distributive justice are the prerogative of legislatures. Rights-based and corrective justice theories are as much theories about the limits of the legitimate adjudicative function of courts applying the common law, as they

---

[47] See William Twining, 'Afterword: Understanding Contracts – A Realist Perspective' in James Goudkamp and Donal Nolan (eds), *Scholars of Contract Law* (Hart Publishing 2022) 385.

[48] Stephen Smith, *Contract Theory* (Oxford University Press 2004), and Charles Fried, *Contract as Promise* (Harvard University Press 1981).

[49] Ernest Weinrib, *The Idea of Private Law* (Harvard University Press 1995), and Ernest Weinrib, *Reciprocal Freedom: Private Law and Public Right* (Oxford University Press 2022).

are about justice. For both theories, when can a court alter existing, or create new rights, without undermining either the claim of the immutability of rights or the acquisition of practicing illegitimate distributive justice?

Rights-based and corrective justice theories have been highly persuasive in Canadian courts, but the courts have never slavishly adhered to any particular legal theory. Rather, the Supreme Court of Canada has repeatedly asserted a doctrine of incremental change to the common law and has classified its approach as being principled.[50] Incrementalism is the Supreme Court's response to the need to keep the common law current while at the same time maintaining the virtue of certainty, intelligibility, and coherence. It is a doctrinal response drawn from an internal point of view of law and is ultimately an expression of the authority of law itself.

So far, this chapter has sought to explain the relevance of doctrinal research and provide a justification for the continued importance of traditional contract doctrine. The chapter has been largely silent on research methodology. In an important research project, David Sandomierski has undertaken an empirical study of what Canadian contract law professors aspire to do and what they actually teach in their classrooms.[51] Sandomierski identifies a somewhat conflicted contract law professorship. Although a majority hold a deep affinity with realist ideas ('that law is indeterminate; that rules are mutable and contingent; that one must look to underlying factors or judicial personality, politics, and policy considerations to explain legal doctrine; that social contexts and non-state normativity are relevant to law; and that critical perspectives that evaluate law from external normative positions are essential to a complete understanding of the law'[52]), their approach to legal reasoning is more akin to their more traditionally doctrinal colleagues. According to Sandomierski, 'most describe legal reasoning as a distinct form of discourse, take the content of rules and judicial reasoning seriously, believe legal reasoning primarily consists in drawing lines between what is relevant and irrelevant, and espouse the importance of structure and coherence'.[53] At another point, Sandomierski

---

50 See, for instance per McLachlin J. in *Peel (Regional Municipality) v. Canada* [1992] 3 SCR 762 at 785; Iacobucci J. in *Garland v. Consumers' Gas Co.* [2004] 1 SCR 692 at para 41; Brown J. in *Nevsun Resources Ltd. v. Arya* 2020 SCC 5 at para 226; McLachlin J. in *Watkins v. Olafson* [1989] 2 SCR 750 at 760, paras 13–16; Cromwell J. in *Bhasin v. Hrynew* [2014] SCC 71 at para 34; Iacobucci J. in *R v. Salituro* [1991] 3 SCR 654 at para 37.

51 David Sandomierski, *Aspiration and Reality in Legal Education* (University of Toronto Press 2020).

52 *Ibid* at 179.

53 In an earlier chapter, Sandomierski describes how the dominant contract law casebooks used in Canada are also wedded to the formalist approach to an

notes the prevalence amongst professors of all theoretical stripes, that an understanding of contract doctrine comes before critique.[54] Thus, for Sandomierski, the majority of Canadian contract professors approach the teaching of contract law by valuing an understanding of doctrine, seeing legal reasoning as being a distinctive form of reasoning, requiring their students to learn how to discriminate between relevant and irrelevant facts and spot legal issues, how to legally distinguish and analogize between cases, and evaluating their students on the student's knowledge of substantive rules and ability to apply them to fact hypotheticals.

It is not surprising that, despite varying theoretical approaches taken by teachers of contract law, they should coalesce around the legal reasoning skills identified above. These same skills are at the heart of the common law and distinguish it from civilian approaches to law. It is the methodology recognized by Lord Sales above, and utilized by a succession of treatise writers, as well as forming the basis of most common law legal education.[55] To discuss doctrinal contract law research methodology would largely reproduce well-worn material covered in a legal systems course: how to read a case and identify its *ratio decidendi* (or 'holding'), how to analogize and distinguish facts, and how to understand the impact of precedents through the application of *stare decisis*. Rather than pursue that line, I will use three examples to illustrate how the common law meets the much-vaunted claim that common law doctrine simultaneously provides both stability and flexibility.[56] The examples have been chosen to illustrate three doctrinal methods to keep doctrinal contract law current. The first outlines the process of incremental change to doctrine through common law methodology now explicitly recognized by the Supreme Court of Canada. The second draws upon a distinguishing feature of contractual obligations as being voluntarily assumed through consent, and thus the contracting parties can 'write' their own law. The third illustrates limitations in contract doctrine and where legislation has been enacted to counteract doctrinal abuse.

---

exposition of doctrine and contract rules over other realist approaches to legal reasoning. See *ibid* at 81.

54 *Ibid* at 240, echoing the position of Hedley above note 2.

55 Stephen Waddams, *Introduction to the Study of Law* (8th edn, Carswell 2016), and A.T.H. Smith, *Glanville Williams: Learning the Law* (18th edn, Sweet & Maxwell 2023).

56 Roscoe Pound, *Interpretations of Legal History* (The University Press 1923) 1.

4.1 Incremental Change in Common Law Doctrine – A Contractual Principle of Good Faith and a Duty of Honest Performance

The Supreme Court of Canada's decision in *Bhasin v. Hrynew*[57] addressing 'good faith' provides an object lesson in doctrinal contract law methodology on how the common law is kept relevant to changed circumstances. Contract is a classification within the law of obligations, which together with tort and unjust enrichment make up the constituent elements of private law. The law of obligations describes the rights and duties created or imposed between legal entities. One way of locating the intensity of these rights and duties with respect to a voluntary and consensual relationship is to draw a continuum between self-interested behaviour and selfless behaviour. Even beyond self-interested behaviour lies self-reliance and *caveat emptor* (from Latin 'let the buyer beware'), although even here, there is a minimal requirement not to act fraudulently.[58]

At stake in *Bhasin* was whether a duty of good faith existed between Bhasin, the plaintiff, and the defendant, Can-Am, touching the performance of a contractual obligation concerning contractual renewal. Bhasin had held a highly successful dealership agreement for over twelve years with Can-Am to market education savings plans in Calgary. The dealership agreement would automatically renew unless one party gave six months' notice of intent to terminate. Prior to the date for renewal, Can-Am had been in discussions with another of

---

57 Above note 50.

58 Paul Finn, 'The Fiduciary Principle' in Timothy Youdan (ed), *Equity, Fiduciaries and Trusts* (Carswell 1989) 1, argued that three standards of intensity of relationships can be located within the continuum: 'unconscionability', 'good faith', and 'fiduciary'. 'Unconscionability' accepts that one party is entitled to act self-interestedly in its actions towards the other. Yet in deference to that other's interests, it then proscribes excessively self-interested or exploitative conduct. 'Good faith', while permitting a party to act self-interestedly, nonetheless qualifies this by positively requiring that party, in its decision and action, to have regard to the legitimate interests of the other. The 'fiduciary' standard enjoins one party to act in the interests of the other – to act selflessly and with undivided loyalty. Finn (at page 20), then identified the following factors to assist courts in determining whether to impose a fiduciary relationship: [1] A past course of dealing between the parties in which reliance for advice, etc., has been an accepted feature; [2] The explicit assumption by one party of advisory responsibilities; [3] The relative positions of the parties, particularly in their access to information and in their understanding of the possible demands of the deal; [4] The manner in which the parties were brought together, and the expectation that could create in the relying party; and [5] Whether "trust and confidence" knowingly has been reposed by one party in the other.

its dealers, Hrynew, a competitor to Bhasin, concerning the future marketing of educational savings plans in Alberta, including the area covered by Bhasin. The outcome of those discussions was an agreement to give Hrynew all the rights to market educational savings plans in Alberta, thus effectively eliminating Bhasin's agency. None of these plans were ever shared or discussed with Bhasin, and, in fact, Can-Am continued to discuss renewal with Bhasin as if it would be forthcoming. On a related matter, and at the direction of the Provincial Securities Commission, Can-Am appointed Hrynew as its 'single provincial trading officer', an office that would allow Hrynew to review Bhasin's accounts. Upon Bhasin's refusal to allow Hrynew, its competitor, access to its accounts, Can-Am failed to renew Bhasin's agency agreement. As agreed with Hrynew, Can-Am passed all Bhasin's business to Hrynew, and Bhasin sued.

The single issue before the court was whether there was, or should be, any obligation upon Can-Am to act honestly or in good faith with respect to the performance of the contract with Bhasin. Cromwell J., for the Court, states in an overview the conclusion of his analysis:

> [32] The notion of good faith has deep roots in contract law and permeates many of its rules. Nonetheless, Anglo-Canadian common law has resisted acknowledging any generalized and independent doctrine of good faith performance of contracts. The result is an "unsettled and incoherent body of law" that has developed "piecemeal" and which is "difficult to analyze": Ontario Law Reform Commission ("OLRC"), *Report on Amendment of the Law of Contract* (1987), at p. 169. This approach is out of step with the civil law of Quebec and most jurisdictions in the United States and produces results that are not consistent with the reasonable expectations of commercial parties.
>
> [33] In my view, it is time to take two incremental steps in order to make the common law less unsettled and piecemeal, more coherent and more just. The first step is to acknowledge that good faith contractual performance is a general organizing principle of the common law of contract which underpins and informs the various rules in which the common law, in various situations and types of relationships, recognizes obligations of good faith contractual performance. The second is to recognize, as a further manifestation of this organizing principle of good faith, that there is a common law duty which applies to all contracts to act honestly in the performance of contractual obligations.
>
> [34] In my view, taking these two steps is perfectly consistent with the Court's responsibility to make incremental changes in the common law when appropriate. Doing so will put in place a duty that is just, that accords with the reasonable expectations of commercial parties and that is sufficiently precise that it will enhance rather than detract from commercial certainty.[59]

---

[59] Above note 50.

What are the methodological steps that take Cromwell J. to his conclusion? There are four phases in his analysis. The first is assembling common law artifacts including: a short summary of the history of good faith found in Roman and early English contract law [35]; an outline of earlier Canadian cases that have discussed the concept of a general duty of good faith [38]–[39]; a survey of the current state of the common law with a focus upon academic commentary and treatises [43]–[48]; an analysis of the Supreme Court's own earlier jurisprudence [54]–[56]; and developments in senior United Kingdom and Australian courts [57]–[59]. The second phase is a discussion of the expectation of commercial parties as revealed in academic commentary [59]–[62], followed by the formulation of a general organizing principle of good faith within the context of the Supreme Court's own jurisprudence [63]–[71].

Having recognized good faith as an organizing principle, Cromwell J. turns to its operationalization as an enforceable legal duty, but one that does not undermine certainty in commercial contracts. Important to Cromwell J. is confining good faith to acts of actual contract performance and not to the process of contract negotiation. In the final phase of his analysis, Cromwell J. explains how good faith is to be applied and indirectly why it constitutes an incremental development in common law contractual doctrine. This phase includes meeting criticism of creating a particular duty [79]–[81]; reviewing the experience of Quebec and United States law under the Uniform Commercial Code, which does have such a duty [82]–[87]; drawing an analogy between the duty and other areas of law, particularly promissory estoppel [88]; and discussing the limitations and implications flowing from the recognition of the duty [90]–[92].

Cromwell J. summarizes what the court has done:

> (1) There is a general organizing principle of good faith that underlies many facets of contract law.
> (2) In general, the particular implications of the broad principle for particular cases are determined by resorting to the body of doctrine that has developed which gives effect to aspects of that principle in particular types of situations and relationships.
> (3) It is appropriate to recognize a new common law duty that applies to all contracts as a manifestation of the general organizing principle of good faith: a duty of honest performance, which requires the parties to be honest with each other in relation to the performance of their contractual obligations.[60]

Applied to the case, the Court held that the duty of honest performance was infringed by Can-Am in deliberately misleading Bhasin with respect to Can-Am's intentions for its business going forward and the role that Hrynew was

---

60 *Ibid* at [93].

playing in those plans. Bhasin was entitled to an award of damages measured as the value of his business at the date of the non-renewal. The valuation took into account the difficulties Bhasin may have experienced renewing the contract even if he was made aware of the changes Can-Am wished to put in place and therefore could have terminated the agreement legitimately and without breaching the duty of honest performance.

Bhasin v. Hrynew is an exemplary demonstration of common law doctrinal contract legal reasoning and the notion of incrementalism to keep the law current. As in all common law jurisdictions, the case commences with a detailed factual analysis to support a claim. In this case, the evidence demonstrated how the defendant had acted in a disingenuous and deceptive manner toward the plaintiff, although not amounting to deceit. Did this level of conduct warrant legal condemnation, and if so, where did it fit within the doctrinal structure of contract law? If not within an existing category, how should the law be changed to accommodate the wrong established? The judgment is the product of a deliberative exercise in legal reasoning. It is determinative because of the authority of the court, but it is also defensible because it is comprehensive in the artifacts gathered and the coherent fit to other existing contractual doctrines. The justificatory language of the judgment is the language of the law.

4.2 Contractual Revision of Common Law Doctrine – The Problem of Conditional Contracts and Conveyancing

Traditional contract doctrine looks to a point where offer and acceptance have been exchanged, crystallizing a binding contract (a consensus *ad idem*). From this perspective, an agreement to agree constitutes no contract. A situation that has caused problems arises when an offer includes a condition that states it is subject to contract, subject to inspection, subject to finance, or subject to planning consent. Simply put, when does the contract become binding, and what, if any, obligations are assumed by the parties between the offer being made and the condition being met (or if it is never met)? An immediate ambiguity is whether the term 'condition' is used to describe a future state of affairs that must exist before the contract becomes binding, or whether the contract is immediately binding but subject to a condition that, if not met, results in the contract terminating by mutual consent upon the non-fulfillment of the conditional term. Such contractual terms are called conditions precedent, and the division is whether it is a condition precedent to formation, or whether it is a condition precedent to further performance or obligation. In the former, no binding contract comes into existence; in the latter, there is the possibility of a binding contract, although it may still fail for uncertainty or lack of consideration. A further issue in conditions of the latter type is whether they impose any obligation on the parties to ensure the condition is met, i.e. to attempt to secure finance, planning consent, or a building inspection, and if so, whether that condition can be waived, and by whom.

In Canada, answers to these issues were provided by two decisions of the Supreme Court of Canada in *Turney v. Zhilka*[61] and *Barnett v. Harrison.*[62] In both cases, a contract for the purchase of property was entered into but made subject to planning approval by a third-party municipal planning authority, and in both cases, the purchaser had sought to unilaterally waive the condition, making the contracts unconditional and thus enforceable, without the consent of the municipal planning authority having been obtained. In both cases, the Supreme Court rejected the purchaser's argument. While it held that a binding contract had come into existence, the presence of the subject-to-planning-approval clause described a state of affairs which required fulfillment before the contract became unconditional and fully binding. The interim time was an *inchoate* period during which the parties had to wait for the determination of the third party on whether to give planning consent, and neither party held a right to unilaterally waive compliance. In essence, conditional terms that were dependent on the actions of a third party, i.e. a municipal planning authority, were always to be construed as for the benefit of both parties, and required both to waive if there was a desire to dispense with the necessity of securing planning consent.

The decision in *Barnett v. Harrison*, which had simply applied the earlier decision in *Turney v. Zhilka*, was badly received by the real estate industry. The decision itself was not unanimous, and in fact a strong dissent was written by Chief Justice Laskin, who would have held that the conditional precedent had been included for the purchaser's advantage and could thus be unilaterally waived.

The underlying basis for these doctrinal decisions, and the confusion they caused, can be traced to an over-reliance on English legal authority without taking account of the differences in real estate commercial practices. In England, a real estate contract only becomes binding after an exchange of contracts is made by the conveyancing bar. Up to that point in time, both purchaser and vendor are vulnerable to a change of heart by either party, who is bound to nothing pending the exchange of agreements. In fact, this has led to the phenomenon of 'gazumping'[63] in which the vendor accepts a higher offer or demands a greater payment after initially purporting to verbally accept the original purchaser's offer. In contrast, in Canada and most other common law jurisdictions, real estate agents acting for the purchaser write up the contracts

[61] [1959] SCR 578.

[62] [1976] 2 SCR 531.

[63] See David Capper, 'Good Faith, Gazumping and Lock-Out Agreements: Comments and Notes' (1994) 45 *Northern Ireland Legal Quarterly* 408.

and present them to the vendor, creating conditional contracts. Purchasers and vendors operate on the basis that they have a binding contract and that the purchaser must make genuine efforts to obtain financing, planning consent, or a building inspection, but that they can also make the contract unconditional by unilaterally waiving the term which they have requested be included and which is for their advantage.

The ultimate outcome of these decisions was a revision of the standard form agreement of purchase and sale used by the real estate industry in Canada. In the model form, a conditional term in the contract (finance, planning, building inspection) specifically states it is for the advantage of the purchaser and can be unilaterally waived by the purchaser. During the inchoate period before the condition is satisfied, the vendor may continue offering their property for sale and, if another better offer comes, can require the original purchaser to lift the condition and make the agreement immediately unconditional. The resolution in Canada can be contrasted with that in New Zealand and Australia, where similar contractual doctrine was interpreted to meet the underlying difference in real estate conveyancing practice by creating an obligation on the purchaser to use best efforts to secure compliance with the conditional term in the contract.[64] However, this was a matter of contractual and doctrinal interpretation without the need for a change in the model standard form. In other words, the minority decision of Chief Justice Laskin in Canada was the position originally adopted in those countries and from which Laskin C.J. drew support for his own dissenting opinion.

The fact that within an appellate court, or between jurisdictions (provincial and national), there can be differing opinions when applying essentially similar common law doctrines, is simply an admission of interpretative differences. Under a doctrine of *stare decisis*, the opinion of a majority of judges of the highest appellate court resolves doctrinal differences for that particular jurisdiction and at that particular time. However, implicit within varying interpretative differences are questions of doctrinal coherence and how particular doctrines meet users' expectations.

The treatment accorded conditional contracts and conveyancing illustrates an important principle of traditional contract doctrine, namely, that contract doctrine is made available to parties who wish to use the regime of enforcement provided by the state through the law, but that the parties 'write' their own 'law', in that they have control over the terms of their contractual promises. It also illustrates an important limitation in doctrinal analysis when that

64 For the development of this approach in New Zealand, see Don McMorland, 'A New Approach to Precedent and Subsequent Conditions' (1980) 4 *The Otago Law Review* 469.

analysis is out of step with commercial practice. In contract law, such a disjunction can be corrected by the parties individually or through changes in commercial practices (i.e. the adoption of standardized terms). In New Zealand and Australia, judges accurately reflected user expectations in their doctrinal interpretations and application. In Canada, users have corrected what they perceived as an incorrect doctrinal position.

The wider issue is how judges inform themselves of user expectations; in essence, how is the 'outsider's point of view' reflected by the 'insider' applying doctrine? I offer the following three arguments. First, common law jurisdictions place a great deal of weight on the experiential levels of those appointed to judicial office. By and large, judges are appointed from the profession based upon their legal experience[65] in the matters that will come before them as judges. Second, under common law theories of adjudication, judges are only required to consider the evidence and arguments placed before them. They remain passive on the factual evidence tendered by counsel and have no role in undertaking independent inquiries. On matters of the law, in civil matters they are largely limited to the legal arguments made by counsel before them. Thus, any particular decision is strictly binding only between the parties. Its precedent weight is only decided by others who read the judgment and determine its *ratio decidendi*, and even then, the reading of a judgment will differ over time, and its placement within a system of rules will change.[66] Third, the common law is a 'messy' system and its source material grows with each new case.[67]

Contract doctrine is the work of the 'cartographer' creating a map of the common law.[68] Not everything is included in the map, but one function is to make the common law intelligible by omitting what is irrelevant and locating any particular case within its doctrinal structure. Choices exercised over doctrinal structure infuse the law with underlying moral, philosophical, historical, and economic arguments. Such mapping exercises save the user from having to locate and read every relevant judgment and other secondary sources for themselves. But a map is only useful to the extent that it can be understood by the user; that it uses a common terminology intelligible to the user to advance

---

[65] In Canada, judges are required to be barristers or advocates with a minimum of 10 years standing at the bar. *Judges Act*, RSC 1985, c J-1, s.3.

[66] Robert Samek, 'The Dynamic Model of the Judicial Process and the Ratio Decidendi of a Case' (1964) 42 *The Canadian Bar Review* 433, 446.

[67] Dan Priel, 'Not All Law is an Artifact: Jurisprudence Meets the Common Law' in Luka Burazin (ed), *Law as an Artifact* (Oxford University Press 2018) 249.

[68] Stephen Smith, 'A Map of the Common Law?' (2004) 40 *The Canadian Business Law Journal* 364.

a legal argument.[69] A legal argument is one that conforms to the norms of what is regarded by courts as being within the law's domain and utilizes the language of the law, something over which courts have both competence and constitutional jurisdiction. It is through this process that external values are translated into and facilitate interpretation of what is law.[70]

4.3 Legislative Revision of Common Law Doctrine – Damages for Innocent Misrepresentation

As indicated above, contract doctrine is built upon a model that presupposes that two parties of equal bargaining power bargain to create a consensual agreement. Much of contractual behaviour does not conform to this model because there is an actual or assumed power imbalance, there is no negotiation, and the contracts may be unilateral or executed at the point of formation. Consumer contracts often suffer all three impediments and, as such, most jurisdictions have enacted specific consumer legislation to redress power imbalances and/or create specific rights, or confer broad discretionary powers on courts to ameliorate the power imbalance.

Sales of products or services are often induced by a flow of statements from the seller by way of advertising, puffery, expressions of opinion, statements of facts, and answers to questions. What to make of this information and when should the seller be liable for error? The common law traditionally adopted an approach of self-reliance endorsed in the concept of *caveat emptor*. If a particular attribute or statement is important to the buyer, the buyer always has the option of requesting it as a legal term of the contract, requiring the seller to warrant (promise) the correctness of the statement.[71] The law would

---

69 Doctrinal scholars can differ widely on the contours of the map, but they share a common terminology in their descriptions, which can be compared and evaluated. For example, in contract law, significant contours differ at the margins of what is within contract law and what is now within the domain of restitution, itself once called the law of quasi-contract. Similarly, for example, differences exist over the doctrine of consideration, the place of various forms of estoppel, and even over the appropriateness of specific relief for breach as against an award of damages.

70 As Herbert Lionel Adolphus Hart states in *The Concept of Law* (2nd edn, Clarendon Press 1994) at 269: '… the existence of law can be identified by reference to the social sources of law (e.g. legislation, judicial decisions, social customs) without reference to morality except where the law thus identified has itself incorporated moral criteria for the interpretation of the law'.

71 *Heilbut Symons v. Buckleton* [1913] AC 30 (HL).

not tolerate fraudulent misrepresentations,[72] and gave very limited relief in equity for innocent (including negligent) misrepresentation (a false statement made by the promisor who believed in its truth at the time it was made) where the remedy was confined to rescission of the contract, also subject to further limitations.[73] The lacuna in contract doctrine is that damages are not available at common law for breach of an innocent misrepresentation, and it is into this lacuna that legislation has intervened.

Ontario's statutory provision is contained in the *Consumer Protection Act 2002*.[74] The legislation was introduced as part of an overhaul of consumer protection in a number of discrete areas and to reflect changes in the consumer marketplace brought about by technology that offered new services to consumers and changed existing ways of contracting. The government's Ministry of Government and Consumer Services took the opportunity to update a number of consumer protections regarding unfair practices and remedies for default.[75] The legislation was supported by all political parties in the legislature. The act does not speak of innocent misrepresentation; rather, it creates an 'unfair practice' which is described as a 'false, misleading or deceptive representation' (s.14(1)). The Act captures more than what was included within the common law's notion of rescission for innocent misrepresentation, but the Act applies only to consumer transactions where the possibility of a power imbalance is more likely than in other commercial transactions. The section also provides an inexhaustive list of what can constitute a false, misleading, or deceptive misrepresentation (s.14(2)). The gravamen of the statutory provision is s.18(1) and (2), which allows damages for an 'unfair practice' where rescission is unavailable on two grounds: one, because the return of the goods or service is no longer possible; and two, third-party rights which have been obtained in good

72 *Derry v. Peek* (1889), 14 App Cas 337 (HL), *Bruno Appliances and Furniture Inc. v. Hryniak* 2014 SCC 8.

73 *Dick Bentley Productions Ltd. v. Harold Smith (Motors) Ltd.* [1965] 2 All ER 65 (CA). Rescission would be denied in equity for any of the following reasons: if the innocent party had affirmed the contract after knowledge of the innocent misrepresentation; for delay (laches) in bringing rescission; the intervention of third-party rights; and where the contract had been executed (although this has been undermined somewhat in Canada. See *S-244 Holdings Ltd. v. Seymour Building Systems Ltd.* [1994] 8 WWR 185 (BCCA)).

74 S.O. 2002, c. 30, ss.14 and 18. Now the *Consumer Protection Act 2023* S.O. 2023, c. 23 (yet to be proclaimed in operation).

75 See the Ministry of Government and Consumer Services discussion paper, *Improving Ontario's Consumer Protection Act: Strengthening Consumer Protection in Ontario*, December 2020. https://www.ontariocanada.com/registry/showAttachment.do?postingId=35387&attachmentId=46616

faith and for value have intervened. Damages are permissible without the need for proof that the innocent party 'relied' upon the unfair practice (a requirement that is necessary for rescission for innocent misrepresentation).[76]

The interpretation of the statutory provision must accord with the rules of statutory interpretation. In Canada, the modern principle is that 'words of an Act are to be read in their entire context and in their grammatical and ordinary sense harmoniously with the scheme of the Act, the object of the Act, and the intention of Parliament'[77] and, in Ontario, this is supplemented by s.64(1) of the *Legislation Act 2006* that states, 'An Act shall be interpreted as being remedial and shall be given such fair, large and liberal interpretation as best ensures the attainment of its objects'.[78] One can only understand the 'context' and 'objects' through an understanding of the common law contract doctrine the legislative provision is purporting to remedy. Further, the legislation does this by couching the remedy and its limited application in the same language as that used to explicate the particular contract doctrine on innocent misrepresentations.

This example illustrates the limitations in the current contractual doctrine. As mentioned above, contract doctrine is built on a single model of contractual behaviour that, outside a few exceptions (undue influence, duress, and unconscionability), assumes equality of bargaining power between contracting parties. The legislation imposes a status relationship, that of a 'consumer', and grants additional contractual rights regarding contracts for goods and services entered into between a consumer and a supplier (defined in the Act as one who is in the business of selling, trading, or leasing goods or services to a consumer).[79] However, the Act is written in the language of the law well familiar to lawyers and judges and can only be understood by those who have a knowledge of contract doctrine and thus are able to appreciate the legislative remedy to the perceived deficiency in contract doctrine.

The three examples just described feature three different common law doctrinal approaches to contract law. Example 4.1 is contract doctrinal research at its best and illustrates how the twin demands of Roscoe Pound for a modern legal system – maintaining certainty and sufficient flexibility to adapt to changing demands[80] – can be met incrementally and thus within the confines of what is constitutionally the role of common law courts. The judgment and its changes to the common law are explained on its own terms, using

[76] See *Ramdath v. George Brown College of Applied Arts and Technology* 2015 ONCA 921.

[77] *Bell ExpressVu Ltd. Partnership v. Rex* [2002] 2 SCR 559 at [26].

[78] S.O. 2006, c.21, Sched. F, s.64(1).

[79] *Ibid* ss. 1 and 2.

[80] Above at note 56.

the language of the law. The coherence and integrity of contract law doctrine are maintained while permitting a small degree of flexibility. To suggest that judges are engaged in a process to mask some other instrumental agenda that drives their decisions requires us to believe that judges are engaged in some type of legal charade and have been for a long time. While the changes made may amount to good economics or some other instrumental goal, to suggest that that particular goal drives the judgment is to suggest that the tail wags the dog. Example 4.2 illustrates the particular nature of contractual obligations as opposed to other imposed obligations. Within the constraints of a limited number of objective principles (i.e. the avoidance of unconscionability, undue influence, duress, illegality, and now in Canada, the duty of honest performance), parties are at liberty to write their 'own law', again with the expectation that it will ultimately lead to enforcement according to the principles of contract doctrine. Example 4.3 accords with our notions of democratic and constitutional law. Beyond incremental changes, the legislature may change common law doctrine, but in doing so, it expects courts to interpret that legislation consistent with the understanding of the common law doctrine the legislation purports to reform.

5. CONCLUSION

The common law is the distillate of an ever-increasing number of case reports of conflict and its resolution between litigants. Traditional common law doctrine records (imposes) a classificatory structure to these reports utilizing the language of the law as articulated in the reasons for decision. Common law doctrine is what courts do, and judges and the lawyers who appear and advise their clients bring their claims and defences applying this same doctrine. Whatever may be the state of other common law doctrines, doctrine on contract law has been, as indicated above by Steve Hedley, remarkably stable. Doctrinal change is evolutionary rather than revolutionary, as in example 4.1. The fact that contractual obligations are premised on voluntary consent gives the parties latitude to determine the extent of the particular obligations assumed, as in example 4.2. Legislative intervention adds to or corrects rather than supplants contract doctrine, as in example 4.3. At a functional level, what is necessary to understand is that contract doctrine is the product of a sound education in practical legal reasoning; a view shared by the majority of Canadian contract law scholars according to Sandomierski's study.[81]

Apart from servicing the immediate needs of clients and courts, doctrinal contract research is necessary to meet the other pillar of the common law,

[81] Above at note 51.

namely flexibility to keep doctrine relevant. Incremental change, drawn by analogy and extrapolation from existing doctrine and cases, is one approach, and one, as seen in *Bhasin v. Hrynew*, that can be buttressed by research that draws from an outsider's perspective. When turning to the evaluation of contract doctrine against normative claims of fairness, justice, and economic efficiency, or undertaking the groundwork for law reform through legislation, resort is profitably made to other research methodological approaches, including the lived experiences and empirical evidence of those affected by contract doctrine and what this research may illuminate on doctrinal contract law's impact, as seen in the government reports that supported the legislative change in example 4.3 and the practicing bar's reaction in example 4.2. This research is often pursued to effect better doctrine, a point Sandomierski's study reveals dominates the contract professorship in Canada, or to shape legislation, which itself is often an exercise in translating the observations of the outsider into the language of the insider. In seeking to effect better doctrine, ironically, this work reifies doctrinal analysis. It sort of proves the point that there is no substitution for a sound knowledge of the law. As Andrew Burrows (now Lord Burrows of the UK Supreme Court) recently opined:

> In other words, studying the law first and foremost requires that one truly knows and understands the details of the law; and one acquires that knowledge and understanding by practical legal reasoning.[82]

[82] Andrew Burrows, 'Professor Sir Guenter Trietel (1928–2019)' in James Goudkamp and Donal Nolan (eds), *Scholars of Contract Law* (Hart Publishing 2022) 292.

3. Comparative methods in contract law

Yuliya Chernykh and Mads Andenas

INTRODUCTION

One may think that little in contract law remains *uncompared*. Some would perhaps continue that the tools used for comparison are all fully mapped and well settled. No doubt, comparative law has progressed very far, especially in private law, resulting in an extensive body of scholarship on similarities and differences, as well as numerous harmonised international and transnational instruments and standards that owe their existence and their content to comparative law methods. Contract law has long been at the forefront of comparative law research.[1] Nevertheless, as we will discuss in this chapter, there are still many areas where comparative contract law can and must advance and, what is more important (at least for this chapter), the methodological approaches to comparison are far from settled.

Paradoxically, the comparative methodological discussion has highlighted disagreements and different approaches, leaving the discipline still in search of a common language.[2] It had more of this common language and common aims before the turn of the century/millennium. The deconstruction and erection of methodological requirements have made actual outputs or applications of comparative law more onerous, impracticable, or outright impossible. As a result, the current methodological status of comparative law highlights the potential more for animated disagreements than for actual results in the form

[1] Jaakko Husa, 'Traditional Methods' in Mathias Siems and Po Jen Yap (eds), *The Cambridge Handbook of Comparative Law* (Cambridge University Press 2024) 15; Hein Kötz, 'Comparative Contract Law' in Mathias Reimann and Reinhard Zimmermann (eds), *The Oxford Handbook of Comparative Law* (2nd edn, Oxford University Press 2019) 903–904.

[2] Mads Andenas and Duncan Fairgrieve, 'Courts and Comparative Law: In Search of a Common Language for Open Legal Systems' in Mads Andenas and Duncan Fairgrieve (eds), *Courts and Comparative Law* (Oxford University Press 2015) 3.

of application to concrete comparative exercises. It is unsurprising that a growing literature on the purposes and methods of comparative law demonstrates a wide range of views, even some fundamentally opposed to one another.[3] The idea of comparative law also meets resistance from domestic law,[4] as well as from European law[5] and public international law[6]—all of which would claim autonomy even as they rely on methods that have much in common with comparative law.

This chapter does not attempt to offer yet another, supposedly authoritative or comprehensive, account of comparative methodological approaches in contract law research. It is neither possible nor desirable to recreate a universally accepted methodological system.[7] Instead, we have chosen to address common methodological approaches, identify how they can contribute to comparison in the field of contract law, and reflect on their possible uses and limits.

A selection, or *bricolage*, of different tools and approaches instead of a single coherent system might sound unsophisticated. However, if we consider that researchers come to a comparative exercise with different purposes, standpoints, perspectives, and different expectations, a recognition of a variety of tools can be more productive than another *advocacy* for a single coherent system. We are not advocating for another extreme—a plurality of comparative approaches to be applied *at once*—but rather for a conscious approach built on a combination of different methodological methods appropriate to solve

---

[3] See, for example, the following authors representing some of the divergence in comparative private law scholarship: Pierre Legrand, 'European Systems Are not Converging' (1996) 45 *International Comparative Law Quarterly* 52; Mauro Bussani and Ugo Mattei, 'The Common Core Approach to European Private Law' (1997) 3 *Columbia Journal of Comparative Law* 339; Duncan Fairgrieve and Horatia Muir Watt, *Common law et tradition civiliste. Convergence ou concurrence?* (Presses Universitaires de France 2006).

[4] See Martha Minow, 'The Controversial Status of International and Comparative Law in the United States' in Mads Andenas and Duncan Fairgrieve (eds), *Courts and Comparative Law* (Oxford University Press 2015) 513–535.

[5] Koen Lenaerts and Kathleen Gutman, 'Comparative Law and the Court of Justice of the European Union: Interlocking Legal Orders Revisited' in Mads Andenas and Duncan Fairgrieve (eds), *Courts and Comparative Law* (Oxford University Press 2015) 141–176.

[6] Eirik Bjorge, 'The International Court of Justice's Methodology of Law Ascertainment and Comparative Law' in Mads Andenas and Duncan Fairgrieve (eds), *Courts and Comparative Law* (Oxford University Press 2015) 213–231.

[7] For different views and attempts to systematise, see for instance, Esin Örücü, 'Methodologies for Comparative Law' in Jan M. Smits, Jaakko Husa, Catherine Valcke and Madalena Narciso (eds), *Elgar Encyclopedia of Comparative Law* (Edward Elgar Publishing 2023) 46–43.

a comparative question or task that a contract law researcher might have. In doing so, we encourage researchers to step beyond the endless methodological debates in comparative law to make practical use of comparative research to solve conceptual and practical problems in contract law.

In this chapter, we first identify what makes contracts a fruitful object of comparative law research and provide a brief account of comparative law efforts in the field of contract law (section 1). We then proceed to a *panorama* of different methodological approaches, with examples of their application and accompanying reflections as to research design and the kinds of research questions each approach is fit to address (section 2). We then identify future avenues of comparative methods in research focused on contracts and contract laws (section 3) and conclude the chapter (section 4).

We have structured the selection of methodological approaches in section 1 into four major groups: (1) classical, (2) empirical, (3) interdisciplinary, and (4) critical. The division between these groups is not mutually exclusive, and various approaches can be combined, although the underlying methodological core of each category is distinct. Classical, or traditional, methods relate to the actual comparison of legal rules against legal rules in different jurisdictions and encompass a spectrum of different approaches, with the functional method among the core methods. The empirical methods join empirical legal studies with a comparative exercise to enable researchers to make causal links in real-life situations across different jurisdictions or other constitutive units of comparison. Interdisciplinary methods rely, as the name suggests, on the meeting of different disciplines, such as law and economics, law and language, or law and literature, and numerous other 'law ands …', to produce a synergistic effect and unpack dimensions beyond the doctrinal perspective on law. Finally, critical approaches invite comparatists to actively reflect on their own positionality and unveil hidden presumptions and power imbalances embedded in and perpetuated by contract law rules and contracting practices.

1. IDEAL OBJECTS IN COMPARATIVE LEGAL RESEARCH?

Contracts not only penetrate all fields of life; they absorb, reflect, and react to the economy, finance, and trade, as well as to political, social, historical, and cultural peculiarities and trends in society. Contracts reach far in creating private governance in specific areas or otherwise shaping existing regulatory frameworks. At the same time, contracts do not operate in a legal vacuum. Applicable laws define the scope of party autonomy, provide default background regulation, and impose mandatory rules that are not subject to variations. National, regional, religious, or industry cultures also shape contracting practices and even the applications of contract law rules to the extent that they shape what is considered 'reasonable' or 'good faith' conduct or interpretations. The legal field created is extremely rich for comparison and responsive to explanations offered by various theoretical strands and methodological approaches in comparative law.

Historically, doctrinal perspectives dominated comparative contract law research, by which different regulations and contractual solutions were compared. Such research tended—and still tends—to contrast civil and common law systems and the different solutions they produce.[8] With time and the rise of harmonisation projects, more efforts were devoted to identifying a common core of contract law principles.[9] This work required tools that would transcend the formal and enable researchers to integrate the operation of the rules and their functions. The functional method and its factual component became central to some important comparative efforts in the field (starting from Schlesinger's factual approach[10] to the comparative exercise that, since the Cornell project on contract formation, produced a lasting methodological impact on the field of comparative law[11]). With time, a broader understanding of law has opened up for interdisciplinary and critical inquiry. This

---

8 Kötz (n 1) 907–908.

9 Without attempting to write a complete history of comparative contract law, it is possible and helpful to name some highlights. The selection of these highlights may itself be an object of critical investigation as the view and perspectives might change depending on the standpoint of a comparatist and her own jurisdiction and intellectual home. The European projection on this question would inevitably highlight codification efforts and the impressive influence of contract law rules originating from German, France, Switzerland, and England on national codes across the globe. It would also reiterate all 'grand' harmonisation projects, starting with the success story of the Convention on International Sales of Goods (CISG) in 1980 and moving through the Principles of European Contract Law (PECL) and the Draft Common Frame of Reference (DCFR) towards the UNIDROIT Principles of International Commercial Contracts and ongoing—yet fragmented—harmonisation of European contract law. And while some of these grand harmonisation efforts resulted in practical solutions and others did not, the point is that they were the product of comparative efforts, comparative compromises, and provoked a strand of literature that continues to explore the results and its similarity or differences from national solutions.

10 Rudolf Berthold Schlesinger, 'Formation of Contracts – A Study of the Common Core of Legal Systems: Introduction' (1969) 2 *Cornell International Law Journal* 1, 36–41.

11 Paola Monaco, 'Making Comparative Law Projects: A Matter of Methodology' in Jacques Hartmann, Benjamyn I. Scott, Steven Truxal, Andrea Bertolini and Anna Masutti (eds), *Civil Regulation of Autonomous Unmanned Aircraft Systems In Europe* (Edward Elgar Publishing 2024) 8–9.

development is not necessarily linear or evolutionary. Comparison focused on legal rules and doctrines is still of value, and so are cultural and critical perspectives. What these methodological developments do demonstrate, though, is that contracts, contracting, and contract laws seem to represent a very attractive—ideal—object for comparative law.

Thinking about an ideal object or objects of comparative law, one may say that it must demonstrate similarities and differences or be *comparable*. These similarities and differences must be open to explanations of various theoretical strands of comparative law and comparative methods and approaches. The object itself must be capable of being split into numerous smaller elements equally significant for comparison, also easily combined or rearranged into bigger parts, creating a vast and rich comparative terrain. The meaningful material for comparison must be *available* and *accessible*. The results of comparison must *matter*, either for practical or theoretical concerns or, best of all, for both. Finally, there must be an overarching societal significance that justifies knowing more about the object of study beyond a single jurisdiction. Contracts, contracting, and contract laws easily satisfy these criteria for an ideal object of comparative law, whereas the concrete objects of comparison may vary among contractual provisions, contract law rules, reasoning of arbitral tribunals and courts on questions pertaining to contract law, as well as comparison of education in the contract law field, borders between contract law and other fields, interrelation between contract law and human rights, cross-border aspects of politics in contract law, the role of the state, and different roles of regulatory instruments.

This description by no means attempts to create a theoretical construction of an *ideal object* within comparative law. It attempts only to give shape to the reasons why some specific areas of comparative law, like comparative contract law, remain an evergreen and attractive field of research. Different reasons that may explain this include considerations of practicality playing a central role. Results of comparison matter for the field where sparse mandatory regulation is combined with a broad unregulated scope for parties' agreements, and where ideas of similarities/differences, origin, legal transplants, harmonisation, and analogies still carry weight for practical purposes. Historically, an interest in comparative contract law can be explained by practical reasons in international trade, when parties in choosing the law applicable to their contracts were inevitably engaged in a comparative exercise: whether the solutions will be the same or similar in the jurisdictions under scrutiny? Whether contractual provisions will be enforceable under different applicable rules? These are only some of the questions the parties may be interested in asking. Furthermore, awareness of differences and similarities has prompted harmonisation efforts of various kinds (see also the chapter 'Research methods for transnational contract law' in this book). International or transnational commercial law has been an active field for unification at an international level for the last hundred years or more. These efforts were either aiming at—and successfully achieving—the creation of binding instruments in the form of conventions[12] or the creation of various types of soft law instruments.[13] Some efforts, though, failed because of fundamental disagreements and splits among national contract laws.[14] In view of the

---

12 One of the most significant is the United Nations Convention on Contracts for the International Sale of Goods, CISG (Vienna, 1980). Other conventions include, for instance, the International Convention for the Unification of Certain Rules of Law Relating to Bills of Lading for the Carriage of Goods by Sea (Hague Rules) (1924); the United Nations Convention on the Limitation Period in the International Sale of Goods (1974); the UNIDROIT Convention on International Interests in Mobile Equipment (Cape Town Convention) (2001); the Hague Convention on the Law Applicable to Certain Rights in Respect of Securities Held with an Intermediary (2006); the United Nations Convention on Independent Guarantees and Stand-by Letters of Credit (New York, 1995); the United Nations Convention on the Assignment of Receivables in International Trade (New York, 2001); the United Nations Convention on the Use of Electronic Communications in International Contracts (New York, 2005); the United Nations Convention on Contracts for the International Carriage of Goods Wholly or Partly by Sea (New York, 2008) (the "Rotterdam Rules"); the United Nations Convention on International Effects of Judicial Sales of Ships (the Beijing Convention on the Judicial Sales of Ships); the United Nations Convention on the Carriage of Goods by Sea (Hamburg, 1978) (the "Hamburg Rules"); the UNIDROIT Convention on International Financial Leasing (1988); the UNIDROIT Convention on International Factoring (1988); the United Nations Convention on International Bills of Exchange and International Promissory Notes (New York, 1988); the UNIDROIT Convention on Stolen or Illegally Exported Cultural Objects (1995); and the UNIDROIT Convention on Substantive Rules for Intermediated Securities (2009).

13 Non-binding international instruments include, for instance, UNIDROIT Principles of International Commercial Contracts (1994, 2004, 2010, 2014, 2016); UNCITRAL Model Law on International Credit Transfers (1992); UNCITRAL Model Law on Electronic Commerce (1996); UNCITRAL Model Law on Electronic Signatures with Guide to Enactment (2001); UNIDROIT Guide to International Master Franchise Arrangements (2007); UNIDROIT Model Law on Leasing (2008); UNIDROIT Legal Guide on Contract Farming (2015); Hague Principles on Choice of Law in International Commercial Contracts (2015); UNCITRAL Model Law on Secured Transactions (2016); UNCITRAL Model Law on Electronic Transferable Records (2017); Tripartite Legal Guide to Uniform Legal Instruments in the Area of International Commercial Contracts (with a focus on sales) prepared by UNCITRAL, HCCH and UNIDROIT.

14 For instance, an attempt to create a legal instrument that would uniformly address what in civil law jurisdictions are called 'penalty clauses' and in common

above, it is not surprising that comparative law has contributed immensely to progress in the field of contract law. But as contracting, contracts, and contract laws are not frozen in time,[15] they continue to mesmerise scholars.

2. COMPARATIVE METHODS AND APPROACHES

2.1 Classical

Comparatists frequently associate classical or traditional approaches to comparison with the so-called *functional method*. While the functional method is sometimes referred to as 'the method' of comparative law,[16] little remains settled about it.[17] Debates continue as to the precise aspiration behind the method, its operation, limitations, and contribution.

The core of the method, as the name suggests, emphasises *the function* of a given legal rule or set of rules subject to comparison. This focus enables researchers to transcend the expression or words of a particular rule or doctrine and look at their operation, purpose, and consequences in different legal systems subject to comparison. The method has an *antiformalist* aspiration that steps beyond the traditional doctrinal perspective to produce valuable observations that different rules and doctrines might actually lead to the same

---

law jurisdictions 'liquidated damages' failed—see UNCITRAL Uniform Rules on Contract Clauses for an Agreed Sum Due Upon Failure of Performance (1983).

15 English contract law presents one of the best illustrations of continuous development, including on the most sensitive—and largely misunderstood and misrepresented—topic of good faith. See George Leggatt, 'The Emerging Concept of a Relational Contract in English Law' in Maren Heidemann (ed), *The Transformation of Private Law Principles of Contract and Tort as European and International Law: A Liber Amicorum for Mads Andenas* (Springer 2024) 455–480.

16 Konrad Zweigert and Hein Kötz, *An Introduction to Comparative Law* (transl Tony Weir, 3rd edn, Oxford University Press 1998) 32–47.

17 On various views on the functional method, see, for instance, Ralf Michaels, 'The Functionalist Method of Comparative Law' in Mathias Reimann and Reinhard Zimmermann (eds), *The Oxford Handbook of Comparative Law* (Oxford University Press 2019) 345–389; Jan Smits, 'Taking Functionalism Seriously: On the Bright Future of a Contested Method' (2011) 18 *Maastricht Journal of European and Comparative Law* 554; Catherine Valcke and Mathew Grellette, 'Three Functions of Function in Comparative Legal Studies' in Maurice Adams and Dirk Heirbaut (eds), *The Method and Culture of Comparative Law: Essays in Honour of Mark Van Hoecke* (Hart Publishing 2014) 99–112; Giovanni Marini, 'Critical Comparative Contract Law' in Pier Giuseppe Monateri (ed), *Comparative Contract Law* (Edward Elgar Publishing 2018) 95–110.

or similar results and, vice versa, similar rules or doctrines might operate differently and lead to different results. Above all, the method makes it possible to identify the purpose behind the rules or doctrines and (intended and unintended) consequences. This aids not only in the direct comparison of rules but also in the identification of common principles for legal harmonisation or transplantation purposes.

While the method seems to be comprehensive, it is far from simple or straightforward. The basic premise that rules and doctrines do have some functions and that these functions are comparable can trigger a legitimate question about whether the method is capable of embracing the cultural aspects of laws and translating them into functional equivalents. In response to this, it may be given that there is no single understanding of 'the function' of law or even of any given legal rule (since law is a normative discipline), and what the function is may be located somewhere on the spectrum between *legally defined* and *socially loaded* concepts. Engagement with the functional method, however functions are understood, accordingly varies from research devoted fully to functionalism to studies that rely only partly on the functional method as an initial research inquiry, and a wide range of research in between these poles (so-called moderate functionalism). The supra-national dimension of rule production, such as in the EU, may also demand recalibration of the method from horizontal (between different legal systems) to vertical (within one system).[18] Increasingly and unsurprisingly, comparisons are made between national and international or transnational legal rules, or across industry sectors regardless of jurisdictional boundaries. New axes of comparison will continue to arise as the commercial and social context of contracting evolves.

All this indecisiveness or plurality of views about the method's framing opens up opportunities, but also endless criticism and, paradoxically enough, aresulting absence of an agreed standard in the application of what is still framed as the traditional method for comparative research.

Regardless of the differences in views over what the method is, or actually because of these differences, the functional method continues to contribute to comparative contract law. And while it may appear to be a single stringent method, there are different framings and variations that permit the functional method, or methods, to adjust to the concrete needs of a comparatist engaging in a specific research project. James Gordley helpfully summarises that comparatists rely on the functional method not because it is 'clear or compelling',

---

18 On the need to adapt the functional method to the EU-dimension (with the example of property law), see Bram Akkermans, 'The Use of the Functional Method in European Union Property Law', (2013) 2(1) *European Property Law Journal* 9.

but simply because 'it helps them to make sense of some of the similarities and differences among different legal systems'.[19]

The framing of the functional method in comparative contract law can vary. The method can be used in broader collective endeavours or in individual research. It can also inform the entirety of a comparative exercise or serve as an entry point into comparison. Finally, the method can be applied in a strictly doctrinal manner, comparing only legal perspectives or functions, or it can be more socially and culturally informed. Regardless of the framing, the common denominator is the pursuit of the function behind contractual clauses, regulations, or doctrines as opposed to their wording or theoretical characterisation.

Apart from defining the overall research design, the functional method can also help to avoid initial misunderstandings in terminology and concepts and serve as an *entry point* into a foreign legal system. This may be particularly helpful for an individual researcher who does not have an expert team to support the research and who is interested in not missing the entire picture of how a legal system operates in specific areas. Catherine Valcke offers helpful methodological reflections on how and why to use the functional method as a starting point.[20] According to this approach, a researcher enters the system on the basis of certain *approximations* of the functions of specific rules or doctrines but does not remain caught by this initial point of investigation and dives deeper, trying to understand the internal operation of the systems under comparison 'on their own terms'[21] before comparing across jurisdictions. Rather than entertaining relatively easily observable differences and similarities, Valcke's series of publications comparing English and French contract laws[22] enable us to investigate nuances without losing sight of the entirety of each system.

[19] James Gordley, 'The Functional Method' in Pier Giuseppe Monateri (ed), *Methods of Comparative Law* (Edward Elgar Publishing 2012) 107.

[20] Catherine Valcke, 'Reflections on Comparative Law Methodology – Getting inside Contract Law' in Maurice Adams and Jacco Bomhoff (eds), *Practice and Theory in Comparative Law* (Cambridge University Press 2012) 29–34.

[21] Ibid 48.

[22] Catherine Valcke, 'Comparative History and the Internal View of French, German, and English Private Law' (2006) 19 *Canadian Journal of Law & Jurisprudence* 133; Catherine Valcke, 'The Different Rhetorics of the French and English Law of Contractual Interpretation' in Jason W. Neyers, Richard Bronaugh, Stephen G.A. Pitel (eds), *Exploring Contract Law* (Hart Publishing 2008) 77–114; Catherine Valcke, 'Convergence and Divergence among English, French, and German Conceptions of Contract', (2008) 16 *European Review of Private Law* 29; Catherine Valcke, 'On Comparing French and English Contract Law: Insights from Social Contract Theory', (2009) 4 *Journal of Comparative Law* 69.

The functional method does not only help to identify but also to *evaluate*. Using the work of Arthur Taylor von Mehren on offer and acceptance as an illustration, James Gordley observes that the method implicitly invites evaluation of whether and how the functions, or aims, of legal rules and doctrines are pursued and achieved.[23] In this sense, Gordley suggests that, of itself, the functional method is not specific to comparative law and can be used domestically without any cross-jurisdictional observations. Yet, that does not diminish its central role in comparative studies to produce lasting insights in everything from grand harmonisation projects to specific micro comparative investigations.

The functional method is often exercised in collaborative studies. Questionnaires and multi-jurisdictional research teams help mitigate the risks of dilettantism in comparative law, associated with insufficient expertise in foreign law and knowledge of foreign languages. By way of example, no fewer than 30 submissions from national rapporteurs on the role of good faith in given factual scenarios facilitated editors' comparative observations in *Good Faith in European Contract Law*,[24] wherein contributors focused on the operation, or function, of good faith. Similarly, the series *Studies in the Contract Laws of Asia* benefited from the expertise of numerous national rapporteurs from Asia who were asked to focus on remedies, formation and third-party beneficiaries, contents of contracts and unfair terms, invalidity, etc.[25] The same structure, relying on national rapporteurs informing general rapporteurs, is used by the International Academy of Comparative Law for its congresses.[26]

However, questionnaires do not automatically ensure the application of the functional method, as much depends on the wording of the questions and subsequent analysis. Much also depends on the quality of factual scenarios that

---

23 Gordley (n 19) 107.

24 Reinhard Zimmermann and Simon Whittaker (eds), *Good Faith in European Contract Law* (Cambridge University Press 2000).

25 Mindy Chen-Wishart, Alexander Loke and Burton Ong (eds), *Remedies for Breach of Contract* (Cambridge University Press 2016); Mindy Chen-Wishart, Alexander Loke and Stefan Vogenauer (eds), *Formation and Third Party Beneficiaries* (Cambridge University Press 2018); Mindy Chen-Wishart and Stefan Vogenauer (eds), *Contents of Contracts and Unfair Terms* (Cambridge University Press 2020); Mindy Chen-Wishart, Hiroo Sono and Stefan Vogenauer (eds), *Invalidity* (Cambridge University Press 2022).

26 On the International Academy of Comparative Law and its method, see Katharina Boele-Woelki and Diego Fernández Arroyo, 'International Academy of Comparative Law' in Jan M. Smits, Jaakko Husa, Catherine Valcke and Madalena Narciso (eds), *Elgar Encyclopedia of Comparative Law* (Edward Elgar Publishing 2023) 248–252.

editors invite their contributors to answer. Proper 'training' of the participants is also indispensable. One such volume in *Studies in the Contract Laws of Asia* provides helpful reflections on how to strike a proper balance between ensuring that contributors address the same issues, but also are capable of exploring those that are '*of particular attention or controversy in their jurisdictions*'.[27] In this way, editors may choose to give detailed terms of reference, set reading lists for all contributors to align their minimum understanding of the comparative exercise, organise colloquia to discuss the ideas and, inevitably, employ extensive editorial efforts to harmonise national reports and synthesise them in a comparative analysis. Above all, clear framing of the project and observance of deadlines are indispensable to avoid risks of potentially outdated information associated with grand projects with numerous contributors.[28]

Collaboration no doubt contributes to the quality of functional comparative research. Still, there are successful examples of studies where individual scholars also use the functional method. In *International Commercial Contracts: Contract Terms, Applicable Law and Arbitration*, Giuditta Cordero-Moss observes that clauses that are repeatedly included in contracts with the hope of achieving predictable results may operate differently depending on governing law and some other factors.[29] Relying on a variety of factual scenarios, Cordero-Moss verifies the effect, or function, of different contractual provisions, such as entire agreement clauses, no waiver, no oral amendments, subject to contract, termination, representations and warranties clauses, liquidated damages clauses, *force majeure* clauses, and hardship clauses.

---

[27] Mindy Chen-Wishart and Stefan Vogenauer, 'Introduction' in Mindy Chen-Wishart and Stefan Vogenauer (eds), *Contents of Contracts and Unfair Terms* (Cambridge University Press 2020) 4.

[28] Ewoud Hondius in his book review of *Good Faith in European Contract Law* observes: '*A disadvantage of teamwork such as this is that it often takes years before the work is completed. National reporters who respected the deadline may be punished in finding that their reports are no longer fully up to date. An example is the Dutch national report by J.H.M. van Erp. The report is well done and can be wholly supported in its findings. But in the footnotes, references to the most recent case law and to new writings such as Hesselink's doctoral thesis are, naturally, absent. The two main authors have made this up to some extent by referring to the most recent national cases and writings in their General Introduction*'— Ewoud Hondius, 'Good Faith in European Contract Law – A First Publication of the Trento Common Core Project' (2002) 10(3) *European Review of Private Law*, 471, 474.

[29] Giuditta Cordero-Moss, *International Commercial Contracts: Contract Terms, Applicable Law and Arbitration* (2nd edn, Cambridge University Press 2024) 441–443.

While the functional method may be used to explore law in context more fully, well beyond doctrinal rules, it still largely remains in the hands of doctrinalists for contract law research. As the examples above demonstrate, doctrinalists investigate good faith, interpretation, and other specific contractual doctrines, as well as the role of specific contractual terms. Nevertheless, doctrinally driven comparative research has moved the methodological frontiers towards seeing the operation of law in society. In this respect, Jaakko Husa suggests that 'functionalism in comparative law meant a methodological step forward for doctrinally trained legal scholars'.[30] That is, the functional method offers a spectrum that a researcher may fully explore, from a focus on legal rules and doctrines isolated from their context to legal rules and doctrines as embedded in social, historical, cultural, and economic contexts. The functional method, properly exercised, enables the advancement of either end of the spectrum and much in between. The traditional or classical approach thus does not preclude researchers from investigating law in context.

Indeed, contemporary comparative contract law must not, in our view, reject the achievements and contributions that the doctrinal end of the spectrum offers, but must also be capable of embracing the other end of the spectrum when needed. The overarching task is not to disconnect and under-evaluate both pure doctrinal and pure sociology of law; to the contrary, the goal should be to connect them and further advance the understanding of the modern development of contract law, taking into account empirical, critical, and interdisciplinary perspectives (as further advanced in this chapter). Classical comparative law methods help strike a necessary balance between looking at law through its functions and understanding it from within.

The knowledge thus produced can be used in different contexts, or in the words of Jürgen Basedow, by many 'clients' of comparative law.[31] The purposes also vary, and include *mere knowledge* of similarities and differences as a foundation for evaluation and (possible) transformation of legal solutions under national laws, more active *borrowing, cross-fertilisation*, and *inspiration* leading to changes in national laws and prevailing legal reasoning, etc. Indeed, much of comparative law that takes place in the context of the legislative process and in adjudication[32] can benefit directly from legal scholarship. Comparative law users need clear and up-to-date insights on similarities and

30 Husa (n 1) 25.

31 Jürgen Basedow names legal practitioners, courts, legislators, unification agencies, and various public and private institutions as 'clients' of comparative law, see (2014) 62(4) *American Journal of Comparative Law* 821, 821.

32 See Mads Andenas and Duncan Fairgrieve, 'Intent on Making Mischief: Seven Ways of Using Comparative Law' in Pier Giuseppe Monateri (ed), *Methods of Comparative Law* (Edward Elgar Publishing 2012) 25.

differences in rules, doctrines, legal reasoning, and overarching solutions. In practice, however, comparative law thus exercised often takes place without substantial assistance from scholarship.[33] Not only with respect to outcomes, but also with methodological enquiries, scholarship must aim at assisting these forms of comparative-law-in-action. In this endeavour, scholarship can produce informative insights and (most importantly) assist in calibrating the classical methods that legislators, judges, and arbitrators might need for their practical purposes. The way forward must not be overcomplicated; it should be based on a few simple steps that the classical comparative law method endorses, and that, in one way or another, include *identifying* a basis for comparison, *describing* the objects of comparison, *comparing*, and *critically assessing* the results.[34]

2.2 Empirical

While it is still difficult to talk of an empirical *turn* in comparative legal studies, its bright future, particularly in the field of contract law, seems to be predetermined. Indeed, the promise of empirical methods can be observed in various fields of legal studies. Empirical legal scholars unite in associations and launch journals specifically dedicated to empirical legal research. Empirically informed papers have become increasingly observable (even in jurisdictions previously indifferent to empirical legal studies) and increasingly influential in challenging legal doctrines, informing specific regulations/policies, and otherwise changing prevailing legal perspectives. Contracts offer endless opportunities for investigating the reality of contracting and the effect of legal rules and doctrines. And it appears to be just one step from looking at empirical material in the context of a single jurisdiction to implementing empirical perspectives in comparative law studies across jurisdictions focused on contracts, contracting, and contract laws.

Crucially, comparative law is intrinsically empirical; it places law in context rather than focusing exclusively on black-letter provisions and doctrines. The core point for empirical comparative research is to look at the real-life expressions of law and legal systems—in their quantitative and qualitative dimensions—and add a *comparative lens* to it. For example, comparatists may

---

[33] Of course, some examples can be found. For instance, Lord Hoffman, of the UK's House of Lords, relied on the article of Catherine Valcke, 'On Comparing French and English Contract Law: Insights from Social Contract Theory', calling it 'illuminating'—see *Chartbrook Ltd v. Persimmon Homes Ltd* [2009] UKHL 38, 39.

[34] Mathias Siems, *Comparative Law* (3rd edn, Cambridge University Press 2022) 15.

ask why certain contract laws dominate the parties' choice? What contractual choices prevail for certain industries? What outcome does a particular rule bring for contract practice in different jurisdictions? Whether a particular doctrine, pertinent in one legal system and absent in another, delivers what it promises? These and many other questions need an anchoring in social reality, either through large-scale empirical investigations or other forms of empirical studies, such as experiments. With a long tradition of going beyond what legal rules or doctrines say, comparative law seems to be well-tuned to embracing contractual reality and getting a sense of it across jurisdictions. In this sense, comparative contract law is destined to interact with empirical methods—at various levels of comfort for comparatists.

While empirical studies may be used for answering causal questions, empirical methods broadly perceived do not exclusively relate to explanatory investigations and may contribute to descriptive and exploratory studies. When an empirical component in a comparative exercise becomes more explicit, comparativists may, for instance, be interested in addressing what is happening with the use of a specific type of contractual provision in certain industries across jurisdictions (description) or investigate what legal issues the use of technology brings for contract drafting across jurisdictions (exploration).

The way comparatists approach empirically loaded questions reflects the methodological plurality known to empirical legal studies. These methods can be loosely divided into two groups, quantitative and qualitative. While quantitative methods *measure*, qualitative methods *grasp* the depth of the phenomenon under study. Both provide unique empirical data for a comparative exercise.

The works of Gilles Cuniberti on choice of law illustrate the use of quantitative methods. Cuniberti evaluated the most attractive contract laws by looking at choice of law clauses in arbitration agreements from different parts of the world. While one may question whether such contracts—all of which came from actual disputes submitted to arbitral tribunals—are representative of the whole universe of commercial contracts, the point remains clear. Disputes do *illustrate* the most frequently chosen contract laws and—arguably—the most preferred laws for commercial disputes. In the first of three articles,[35] Cuniberti studied 4,400 international contracts concluded by approximately 12,000 parties who participated in arbitrations under the ICC Arbitration Rules. The study demonstrated that English and Swiss laws were chosen three times more often than their closest competitors. The article further enquired

---

[35] Gilles Cuniberti, 'The International Market for Contracts – The Most Attractive Contract Laws' (2014) 34 *Northwestern Journal of International Law & Business* 455.

into the features of English and Swiss law as well as rationales behind parties' choices. In the second article,[36] Cuniberti assessed choices of law in Asia on the basis of unpublished data from the four arbitral institutes active in Asia for the years 2011 and 2012. Three laws appeared to be most preferred: English law, US law, and, to a lesser extent, Singapore law. Not only did the article demonstrate that contractual choices in Asia are somewhat different than in Europe, but it also identified different circumstances under which English law and US law were chosen, as well as the reasons for English law as an attractive option even for parties and transactions with no connection to England. In the third article,[37] Cuniberti and Manuel José Segovia González conducted an empirical analysis of data from arbitral institutions active in Latin America, focusing on the years 2011 and 2012. They observed that parties rarely choose the law from a jurisdiction that was the home jurisdiction of neither party, and that most often parties chose the law of the seat of arbitration to also govern the substance of their dispute. Across all three articles, the focus was on whether there is an international market for contract laws and, if so, how and why it differs across the three regions considered.

These examples put empirical investigation first in the research design and then let the comparative exercise (to a varying degree) explain or otherwise get a sense of 'the reality'. Another approach might be to have a comparative inquiry from the very beginning and to rely on empirical methods as a companion or supportive tool to the overarching comparative question. By way of example, Christoph Engel and Andre Schmelzer conducted an experiment to test the doctrinal divide between civil and common law jurisdictions on the issue of consideration.[38] More precisely, the researchers designed an experiment to investigate whether *conditional* promises are better performed than *unconditional* ones. Their hypothesis was that conditional promises (comparable with consideration) are more capable of inducing performance than unconditional, meaning that the doctrine of consideration has clear practical anchors. 180 participants were selected from a pool of about 6,000 in the Bonn EconLab. All were students; however, law students were excluded in order not to contaminate the findings with views influenced by legal education. The

---

[36] Gilles Cuniberti, 'The Laws of Asian International Business Transactions' (2016) 25 *Washington International Law Journal* 35.

[37] Gilles Cuniberti and Manuel José Segovia González, 'Choice of Law in Latin American Arbitration: Some Empirical Evidence and Reflections on the Latin American Market for Contracts' (2020) 77 *THĒMIS-Revista de Derecho* 35.

[38] Christoph Engel and André Schmelzer, 'Committing the English and the Continental Way: An Experiment' Preprints of the Max Planck Institute for Research on Collective Goods, No. 2017/16, Max Planck Institute for Research on Collective Goods.

experiment demonstrated what the authors called 'a surprising finding', namely that conditional promises were not more obeyed than unconditional ones.[39]

And while it is possible that further experiments may show different results, the findings on the historical contingency of doctrines, as opposed to moral or practical bases,[40] remains illustrative for the *refreshing* contribution that qualitative empirical studies may bring in affirming or challenging the dominant views in comparative contract law. There is a serious synergistic effect between comparative and empirical studies capable of shedding new light on well-accepted doctrines or otherwise contributing to a comparative exercise regardless of the ultimate aim. The stimulating insights that empirical comparative contract law offers are underexplored, and there is huge potential to advance based on available (non-comparative) empirical insights that are progressing nowadays (see also the chapter 'Empirical methods in contract law' in this book).

In principle, and as seen from the above examples, contracts, contracting, and contract laws open up endless areas for empirical curiosity. Empirical methods in comparative contract law not only nourish law and legal scholarship with data and trends; they also, on a more profound and nuanced level, may affirm or challenge prevailing doctrinal perspectives. A comparative lens magnifies the reach of observations and arguably the persuasiveness of empirical conclusions. While quantitative studies can provide a necessary correction and reality check, qualitative work can give a nuanced perspective that unsettles dominant doctrinal views across different fields. Empirical studies may also contribute to non-doctrinal comparative law perspectives by identifying aspects of the socio-legal context for contract law with greater precision than would otherwise be possible. Empirical studies can also assist in revisiting classificatory approaches (legal traditions, families, cultures) by either corroborating or challenging these macro-perspectives on contract law.

While undoubtedly helpful, empirical methods also bear some risks and challenges for researchers. Some of these are of general character pertinent to empirical studies as such; others are more closely connected to the specificity of law, including comparative law. General risks are primarily associated with

---

39 The authors were clear about not making a normative claim, and their contribution to challenging the rationale behind the doctrine can be further explored and tested.

40 Ibid, 15.

data quality[41] and research replicability.[42] Risks specific to legal research are those connected to the nature of law as a normative and intrinsically endogenous discipline that is created by what it seeks to regulate. Still further, risks specific to comparative empirical legal research are those related to the units of comparison, primarily countries that are not homogenous.[43] Countries differ not only in their legal systems and socio-economic context but also in the accessibility of data. It can be difficult to assemble multijurisdictional data sets that are not only large enough to be statistically robust and of relatively equal size but which also represent high-quality *comparative* law data.[44]

While data quality is a complex issue to tackle, more transparency and access to data can potentially enhance it along with the changing culture expected from empirical legal studies, including within comparative law, to be more open and encouraging attempts to replicate the findings. Challenges that arise from the nature of law being the object of comparison are more difficult to address. The social sciences are somewhat heuristic in their methods, not aiming at the same conceptual precision that the law and legal scholarship aim for. The combination of quantitative and qualitative empirical methods can be particularly helpful in facing the inherent endogeneity of law and validating conclusions.[45] Overall, applying rigorous methods, being transparent and open about the limits of one's data, and being cautious about what conclusions are supported by the data—these are absolutely essential for empirical legal studies to progress in comparative law.

---

41 See, for instance, Alec Stone Sweet, Wayne Sandholtz and Mads Andenas, 'Dissenting Opinions and Rights Protection in the European Court: A Reply to Laurence Helfer and Erik Voeten' (2021) 32 *European Journal of International Law* 897 (criticizing Helfer's and Voeten's study for misclassification and overclaiming). In the subsequent publication, Stone Sweet, Sandholtz and Andenas how how a group of erroneous quantitative studies could engender fundamental stakes: Alec Stone Sweet, Wayne Sandholtz and Mads Andenas, 'The Failure to troy the Authority of the European Court of Human Rights' (2022) 21 *The Law ractice of International Courts and Tribunals* 244. While being in the field of n rights and international adjudication, the examples show debates that can voked around the quality of empirical findings.

son Chin and Kathryn Zeiler observe that: '*Although progress* [with repli- —our comment] *is underway, the picture is bleak relative to other social* –Jason Chin and Kathryn Zeiler, 'Replicability in Empirical Legal (2021) 17 *Annual Review of Law and Social Science* 239, 242.

(n 34) 271, 282.

Spamann, 'Empirical Comparative Law' (2015) 11 *Annual Review of ial Science* 131, 148.

34) 268–282.

2.3 Interdisciplinary

The call for interdisciplinary research, which for the purposes of this chapter means research that combines doctrinal comparison with insights from other non-legal fields, has also gained increasing support and become more visible in comparative law.[46] As discussed earlier, comparative law itself transcends doctrinal borders. Just as it is predisposed to empirical studies, it is also open to interdisciplinary scrutiny. Yet, the discussion at present seems to be largely limited to the conceptual level, namely on the desirability of *having more* interdisciplinary research within comparative law, rather than actually doing it. As a result, and save some limited exceptions,[47] interdisciplinary perspectives within comparative contract law have not yet resulted in a solid line of research being *actually conducted.*

The most likely explanation for this is the simple difficulty of drawing on two or more disciplines. Practising interdisciplinarity is not easy. It requires familiarity with the 'other' field and skilled methodological 'translation'. It also requires time and (often) collaboration, in circumstances where productive working relationships among teams with varied methodological backgrounds can be difficult to manage. As a result, it is much easier to address the usefulness of interdisciplinarity in conceptual terms than actually to demonstrate it in practice.

Effort to overcome these hurdles is worth expending, since interdisciplinary methodological tools can produce helpful insights, both for doctrinal and non-doctrinal understanding of contract law across jurisdictions. Interdisciplinarity for comparative contract law is about adding a comparative level to interdisciplinary research as otherwise practiced. Similar to empirical comparative research, a comparative lens can magnify the reach of interdisciplinarity. Among many possible interdisciplinary directions, one of the most pronounced is comparative contract law and economics (also addressed in this book in the chapter 'Research methods and techniques in contract law and economics'). This approach enables researchers to rely upon economic perspectives in the exercise of comparison, for instance by using efficiency and wealth maximisation (as 'the economically-inspired objective evaluation method'[48])

---

[46] Jaakko Husa, *Interdisciplinary Comparative Law: Rubbing Shoulders with the Neighbours or Standing Alone in a Crowd* (Edward Elgar Publishing 2022) 227–231.

[47] For instance, on law-and-literature comparison see Daniela Carpi, 'Contracts in Literature: From Doctor Faustus to Vampires' in Pier Giuseppe Monateri (ed), *Comparative Contract Law* (Edward Elgar Publishing 2018) 322–360.

[48] Mitja Kovač, *Comparative Contract Law and Economics: New Horizons in Law and Economics series* (Edward Elgar Publishing 2011) 378.

in assessing the results of comparison. Further examples may include adding a comparative perspective to law and literature views on contracts and contract laws in order to uncover 'supremely sensitive' insights.[49] Or one can add a comparative perspective to law and psychology studies, for instance, to uncover the role of emotion in contracting across borders.[50] A comparative perspective can also be added to law and language[51] views on contract law, including for instance the area of mandatory plain language requirements across jurisdictions.

At the same time, engagement with interdisciplinarity may be obstructed or complicated because of the particular development of contract laws in different jurisdictions. Klaas Hendrik Eller gives an illuminating analysis of how the 'disciplinary framing' of US and English contract laws is more open to interdisciplinary (primarily sociological) investigations than German contract law.[52] Differences in the reception of legal realism—more influential in the US and UK and less visible in Germany—seem to be one cause of divergent attitudes. This results in what Eller calls 'societally contextualized conceptions of contract', which are more visible in the US and England and less so in Germany. Similarly, Mariana Pargendler reflects on the US-centric bias of the law and economics literature as one of the reasons for insufficient comparative investigation of the economic effects of contracts law.[53]

Despite the difficulties involved, interdisciplinary comparative contract law can progress in the years to come and will advance a better understanding of the operation of contract law across borders. Similar to empirical comparative research, interdisciplinarity can produce insights that are relevant for challenging and further advancing doctrinal understanding of contract law. As always, it is important to reflect on what questions cannot be solved doctrinally, what questions are open to genuine interdisciplinary inquiry within comparative contract law, and, most importantly, what questions can advance understanding of contract law when addressed from interdisciplinary perspectives.

---

49 Luke Wilson, 'Contract' in Lorna Hutson (ed), *The Oxford Handbook of English Law and Literature, 1500–1700* (Oxford University Press 2017) 393.

50 Emma Jones, 'You Don't Pay 100,000 to a Lawyer Unless You Care about Something: The Role of Emotion in Contract Law' in Susan A. Bandes, Jody L. Madeira, Kathryn D. Temple and Emily Kidd White (eds), *Research Handbook on Law and Emotion* (Edward Elgar Publishing 2021) 248.

51 Husa (n 46) 48–54.

52 Klaas Hendrik Eller, 'Comparative Genealogies of "Contract and Society"' (2020) 21 *German Law Journal* 1393, 1396, 1409.

53 Mariana Pargendler, 'Comparative Contract Law and Development: The Missing Link?' (2018) 85 *The George Washington Law Review* 1717, 1730–1733.

Emerging 'non-traditional units of comparison'[54] that go beyond jurisdictions and state law and are more firmly anchored in history, sociology, literature, and other fields can further open comparative contract law towards more interdisciplinarity.

2.4 Critical

Critical approaches can further advance comparative contract law research. Not only do these approaches bring necessary *self-reflection* upon the underlying—and frequently disguised—premises of comparison; they can also serve as tools for *uncovering hidden or otherwise unarticulated premises*, essentially debunking neutrality in the comparative work done by others. One may look to the extent to which Western approaches to contract law define and dictate the selection of themes and jurisdictions for comparison,[55] to what extent the notion of legal tradition may advance or suppress various comparative projects,[56] or to what extent gender considerations are or are not fully embraced in dealing with specific types of contracts, such as marriage contracts[57] or surrogacy agreements, for example.[58]

In comparative law, the advancement of critical perspectives/ideas is largely associated with the works of Günter Frankenberg. In a 1985 article,

---

54 Mathias Siems, 'The Power of Comparative Law: What Types of Units Can Comparative Law Compare?' (2019) 67(4) *The American Journal of Comparative Law* 861, 881 (naming as 'possible new units' such as 'new and old law of different countries', 'old laws of different countries', 'new and old law of same country', 'law and nonlaw of different countries', 'law and nonlaw of same country', 'existing law and fictional law', 'fictional laws', 'foreign country implicit', 'local laws', 'private lawmaking', 'different areas of law', 'domestic and international law', 'different int'l law, same topic', 'different int'l law, different topic').

55 Dominance of Western perspectives in comparative law is increasingly criticised, see Ugo Mattei, 'Comparative Law and Critical Legal Studies' in Mathias Reimann and Reinhard Zimmermann (eds), *The Oxford Handbook of Comparative Law* (2nd edn, Oxford University Press 2019) 820; Lena Salaymeh and Ralf Michaels, 'Decolonial Comparative Law: A Conceptual Beginning' (2022) 86 *Rabels Zeitschrift für ausländisches und internationales Privatrecht / The Rabel Journal of Comparative and International Private Law* 166, 166–188.

56 Marini (n 17) 98.

57 Peter Goodrich, 'Gender and Contracts,' in Anne Bottomley (ed), *Feminist Perspectives on the Foundational Subjects of Law* (Cavendish Press 1996) 17, 19–22.

58 Mirela Župan and Martina Drventić, 'Gender Issues in Private International Law' in Gabriele Carapezza Figlia, Ljubinka Kovačević and Eleonor Kristoffersson (eds), *Gender Perspectives in Private Law* (Springer 2023) 17.

Frankenberg specified that his 'methodological suggestions' were 'such as a deviant reading of comparative works, the identification of those mechanisms with which perspective is denied, the analysis of what is left out, marginalized or taken for granted by the official discourse'.[59] Later on, Frankenberg further elaborated on methodological advancements of critical perspectives, including an acknowledgement that comparative law is not neutral or objective, and a need to enrich it 'with context information—rather than thin taxonomies, meagre functional analyses, or bony factual positivism'.[60] Almost 40 years later, co-authoring with Fernanda G. Nicola, Frankenberg brought into focus advancements that the critical approach can bring to comparative *contract* law.[61] This is an important work, that apart from discussions on potential (rather illusory) contributions, engages instead with concrete examples and suggestions. More precisely, according to Nicola and Frankenberg, critical perspectives can challenge the dominant civil/common law distinction and connected overemphasis on similarities in comparative exercise in contract law. Critical researchers incorporate important insights from anthropology, sociology, economy, critique of market individualism, ideology ('negative world-making'), feminism, and critical race theory to reveal hidden biases and unpronounced assumptions in comparative contract law research.[62] These observations resonate well with other scholars who have advanced the critical perspective either in terms of principles, both theoretically and as applied to concrete comparative projects.[63]

Overall, rather than being an independent method of legal research, critical comparative law is primarily about *perspective*. Still, because the critical approach assists in organising *how* to think about legal problems, the critical perspective brings to bear a methodological character.[64] A researcher either self-reflects on their own approaches or focuses on failures to acknowledge power imbalances or hidden biases in the research of others. In this sense,

---

[59] Günter Frankenberg, 'Critical Comparisons: Re-thinking Comparative Law' (1985) 26 (2) *Harvard International Law Journal* 411, 455.

[60] Günter Frankenberg, 'Critical Histories of Comparative Law' in Markus D. Dubber and Christopher Tomlins (eds), *The Oxford Handbook of Legal History* (Oxford University Press 2018) 61.

[61] Fernanda G. Nicola and Günter Frankenberg, *Comparative Law: Introduction to a Critical Practice* (Edward Elgar Publishing 2024) 70–97.

[62] Ibid, 84–93.

[63] Marini (n 17) 95–110; Mattei (n 55) 805–825.

[64] For a similar idea on the methodological core behind the critical approaches, see Katharine T. Bartlett, 'Feminist Legal Methods' (1989) 103 *Harvard Law Review* 829–888.

Thomas Coendet's helpful observations capture the methodological core of the critical approach:

> Critical comparative law should stand for an ethos, an attitude that requires the comparative lawyer to position and reposition her- and himself time and again towards the received methodological tools and the themes currently in vogue. That positional work will result in specific methodological proposals and advances – as in this chapter – but not in grand, overarching methods or projects for comparing law.[65]

Interestingly, a similar approach can be found in critical rhetoric, a direction that came to life in the same period as Frankenberg's pioneering article on critical comparative law. Its founder, Raymie E. McKerrow, defined critical rhetoric 'as a performance of a rhetor advocating a critique as a sensible reading of the discourse of power'.[66] Such performance or practice required both engagement with power misbalance, hierarchy, and dominance, on one side, and self-reflection as to the exercised critique, on the other side. In this sense, the outward and inward reflections are characteristic of the critical approach in comparative law and rhetoric. Given that law can be conceptualised as rhetoric,[67] such parallels in the development of critical perspectives are unsurprising.

While the 'critical' no doubt brings an evaluative and analytical component, it by no means refers to a single or even harmonious approach. Many ideas may form the foundation for critical exercises, bringing pluralism and eclecticism to the forefront. They may synchronise with critical legal studies (CLS) or go beyond the established directions that unpack the intertwinement of law and inherent social biases. Furthermore, critical approaches are not exercised exclusively within the space of comparative law and frequently step further to advance points beyond similarities and differences. For instance, their ultimate aim might lie in revealing and confronting the underlying injustices in existing contract law rules.[68] In this sense, the critical approach helps to boost the theory-building capacity of comparative contract law.

---

65 Thomas Coendet, 'Critical Methods' in Mathias Siems and Po Jen Yap (eds), *The Cambridge Handbook of Comparative Law* (Cambridge University Press 2024) 70.

66 Raymie E. McKerrow, 'Critical Rhetoric: Theory and Praxis' (1989) 56(2) *Communication Monographs* 91, 108.

67 James Boyd White, 'Law as Rhetoric, Rhetoric as Law: The Arts of Cultural and Communal Life' (1985) 52(3) *The University of Chicago Law Review* 684.

68 Martijn W. Hesselink, 'EU Private Law Injustices' (2022) 41 *Yearbook of European Law* 83, 115; Thomas Wilhelmsson, *Critical Studies in Private Law* (Kluwer Academic Publishers 1992) 1–16.

Like zooming in and out from different positions, critical approaches enable the comparatist to choose a perspective, or an attitude. Whether a foundation for criticism is accentuated and pronounced or merely adds to more vigilance does not make a big difference in terms of methodological advancement, as long as a comparatist is aware of their own biases and possible pitfalls. Such 'mental training' will become even more important when academics use generative AI as their 'academic partners' in comparative exercises and a resource for possible exploration.[69]

3. FUTURE USES OF COMPARATIVE METHODS IN CONTRACT LAW RESEARCH

Contract law is a paradox.

From one perspective, it is one of the most progressive areas of legal practice and rule-making, with contract practice and contract rules rapidly reacting to societal changes and contemporary challenges. An example is the clauses allocating risks in relation to international sanctions that popped up in many contracts immediately after the phenomenon became widespread. Another is the recent recognition of emojis as an expression of consent, or the use of AI technology to review, negotiate, and enforce contract terms.

From another perspective, however, contract law is one of the most traditional and often conservative areas of practice. Contract statutes in many jurisdictions have remained largely unamended for over a century.[70] Deep-rooted doctrines anchored in historical and cultural antecedents that may no longer apply, such as the common law doctrines of consideration and the parol evidence rule, continue to persist. Across legal families, we still view contracting through the idealised doctrinal model of equal parties negotiating every single clause of their contracts.

Unsurprisingly, change and resistance surrounding contracts and contracting can be best understood through *comparative lenses*. These lenses, though, need some adjustments:

---

[69] As of the date of writing, there seems to be already a growing scholarship on the use of AI in comparative law studies. For instance, Lutz-Christian Wolff, 'Artificial Intelligence Ante Portas: The End of Comparative Law?' (2019) 7(3) *The Chinese Journal of Comparative Law* 484; Han-Wei Ho, Patrick Chung-Chia Huang and Yun-chien Chang, 'Machine-Learning Methods' in Mathias Siems and Po Jen Yap (eds), *The Cambridge Handbook of Comparative Law* (Cambridge University Press 2024) 176–207.

[70] For instance, the Contract Law Act remains largely unamended in Norway from 1918 (save for very few changes).

- Use of diverse comparative tools chosen depending on the tasks and standpoints that a comparatist has.
- Careful reconsideration of the object of comparison. While legal doctrines and rules are no doubt central to the comparative *law* exercise, comparison can be directed towards other less conventional objects of comparison, such as contract negotiation practices, contractual choices/contractual design, and the effects of contract governance. Going beyond rules and doctrines to elements embedded in the society will be most productive for understanding contract law in its context, and thus more illuminating for understanding rules and doctrines. Comparison can assist in revisiting the role of contract law and its governance potential.[71]
- Careful reconsideration of the basis of comparison. Clearly, a focus on western laws and the civil/common law divide unnecessarily limits the potential of comparative law research in contract law and does not fully embrace the dynamic and evolving character of contract law around the world. However, our claim goes further than this (by now) conventional critique of comparative law. We believe that comparison across fields and sectors, between national and transnational, between national and international, between past and present, between contentious and non-contentious, etc. can offer valuable perspectives.
- Use of comparative methods that go beyond doctrinal perspectives, but also beyond the private dimension of contract law to embrace studies of contract governance and the public law dimensions of contracting and contract laws.[72]
- Finally, we believe that the future stands both with comparative research as the sole methodological highlight for the work and as an integral part of the more complex methodological package that combines different methods and approaches.

4. CONCLUSION

With comparison, a contract law researcher can sing in their highest octave range. Comparison can be exercised *inside* contract law at the level of legal rules and doctrines, as well as *outside* it, transcending the borders of law

71 For instance, by verifying if observations of Catherine Mitchell on the fading role of contract law resonate with developments in other jurisdictions—Catherine Mitchell, *Vanishing Contract Law Common Law in the Age of Contracts* (Cambridge University Press 2022).

72 See, for instance, Luca Siliquini-Cinelli and Andrew Hutchison (eds), *The Constitutional Dimension of Contract Law: A Comparative Perspective* (Springer 2017).

and engaging with larger historical, social, economic, and cultural contexts. Comparison can be performed in pursuit of practical and pragmatic goals such as law reform, and for the sake of theory building. Comparison can be used as an end destination or as an interim step in an overarching research design. It is also the reason why the intensity of engagement with comparison varies dramatically. Even individual comparative observations, insufficient to centre an entire work as comparative, enable lawyers to become aware of their own biases and blind spots when they assess their 'home' legal systems or otherwise advance knowledge. And while thoroughly performed deep and multi-layered comparative research is still very welcome in contract law, our chapter does not call for comparative *puritanism*. Any genuine comparative effort at a macro or micro level still might be worth exploring so far as it helps to answer a research question or achieve a theoretical or policy goal.

As much as being about research methods, comparison is also and primarily about research approaches and designs. Its *vaporous* structure enables other (non-comparative) methods and approaches to be used along with comparison. Unsurprisingly, empirical and interdisciplinary highlights are very welcome in modern/contemporary comparative contract law studies, as are critical approaches.

While not offering a single system of methodological approaches, we have still proposed some structure in how to address comparative methods and approaches. We have first structured the methods around different methodological cores of *classical*, *empirical*, *interdisciplinary*, and *critical* perspectives, and then placed them within the *radiating spectrum* of doctrinal research. The idea is not simply to mark certain approaches as being 'doctrinal', while others as being 'less' doctrinal or 'non-doctrinal' altogether. Nor are these categorisations absolute, as the same approaches may show fluidity in contributing to doctrinal research fully or partially, or escaping it altogether and approaching contract law from external perspectives. Rather, the idea is to offer a reflection on how different comparative tools, approaches, and methods can relate to what can be defined as a *default* research method and what they can offer to a researcher interested in studying contract law in a broader societal context. Even what is predominantly perceived as the core of comparative doctrinal research—the functional method—is fully capable of embracing all relevant context, enabling a researcher to see well beyond the borders of legal rules and doctrines.

Regardless of whether comparison is perceived as a method, an approach, or a research design, it could fail. Not fully committing to comparison risks engaging in a superficial imitation of comparison without actually exercising it to elicit real insights. Comparison is capable of delivering on many fronts, but only if a researcher is committed to it. While the challenges to conducting deep comparison—such as lack of relevant language skills or training in foreign laws—are well known, they are manageable, and commitment ensures that proper efforts are being put in place to if not overcome, then at least minimise them.

To conclude, comparative law research in the field of contracts and contract law looks very much like the House in Susanna Clarke's popular novel *Piranesi*: its beauty is also *immeasurable* and its kindness *infinite*.[73] It is up to the comparatist to explore its potential in order to unfold the vibrant world of contracts, contracting, and contract law.

---

73 Susanna Clarke, *Piranesi* (Bloomsbury 2020) 245.

4. Philosophical methods in contract law

Johan Vorland Wibye

1. INTRODUCTION

Contract law shapes behaviour throughout society, and the enforcement of contracts requires coercion. The discipline of contract theory aims to explain, and potentially justify, these features of contract as a legal practice. While doctrinal legal scholars seek insight by immersing themselves in a body of legal sources and discourse,[1] contract theorists seek to examine and confront our notions about the nature and content of law. The aim of this chapter is to outline how scholars can take on both roles, rooting doctrinal research in a philosophical account. By opting to view law through the lens of contract theory, we are better placed to account for the normative and conceptual roots of legal doctrines, to align these doctrines with core principles, and to make a more convincing case for necessary adjustments.

Contract theory is legal theory applied to contract law. Just as there are two general domains in the field of legal theory, there are, broadly speaking, two methodological branches within contract theory. The first and most recognisable branch is that of normative reasoning.[2] Normative theories of contract seek to identify the organising moral principle that makes contract law distinctive. These theories are founded on the notion of a fundamental unity in contract law—a basic value or moral commitment which binds all contract law together and can be used to explain the formation and enforcement of

[1] Jan Smits, 'What is Legal Doctrine? On the Aims and Methods of Legal-Dogmatic Research' in Rob van Gestel, Hans Micklitz and Edward L. Rubin (eds), *Rethinking Legal Scholarship: A Transatlantic Dialogue* (Cambridge University Press 2017) 211.

[2] The broader distinction drawn in legal theory is between normative and analytical jurisprudence; see, for example, Brian Bix, 'Conceptual Questions and Jurisprudence' (1995) 1 *Legal Theory* 465; H.L.A. Hart, *Essays in Jurisprudence and Philosophy* (Clarendon 1983) 271.

particular legal doctrines.[3] The methodological upshot is an ability to examine doctrine by way of a single, coherent account of contract law as a legal and moral institution.

The second branch of contract theory can be termed conceptual explanation.[4] Whereas normative reasoning seeks to explain contract law from the perspective of the whole, conceptual reasoning seeks to explain contract law by breaking it down into its constituent parts. The main tools of such analysis are: tracking linguistic usage, ascribing meaning to legal terms and concepts, positing categories, and drawing conceptual boundaries.[5] Conceptual tools are value-neutral and context-independent, and their value is measured in clarity and explanatory power.

It should be noted that neither of these tracks is intended to supplant legal doctrinal analysis. Their purpose, rather, is to support, direct, and challenge legal thinking.[6] Most normative contract theories have revisionary implications.[7] Normative reasoning and conceptual explanation are also mutually supportive. This is in some ways obvious, as all contract theory must rest on conceptual foundations. Sharpened conceptual tools help to reveal hidden factors and assumptions shaping our understanding of contracts, their distinctiveness, and their function.

This chapter surveys the most prominent contract theories in modern scholarship and their methodological implications. Section 2 examines conceptual approaches, focusing in particular on tools for analysing the language of contractual rights and obligations. Section 3, which takes up the lion's share of the chapter, examines intrinsic moral accounts of contract law. According to such theories, there is a moral core within contract law, and its enforcement protects something that is inherently worthy of respect. Section 4 is devoted to instrumental accounts of contract law. These theories anchor the institution

---

3 "Legal doctrine" is used narrowly here as a means of referring to descriptive statements about the content of legal norms.

4 Jody S. Kraus, 'Legal Theory and Contract Law: Groundwork for the Reconciliation of Autonomy and Efficiency' in Enrique Villanueva (ed), *Legal and Political Philosophy* (Brill 2002) 385.

5 Robert Alexy, *Theorie der Grundrechte* (Suhrkamp 1986) 34.

6 Thilo Kuntz and Paul B. Miller, 'Introduction to Methodology' in Thilo Kuntz and Paul B. Miller (eds), *Methodology in Private Law Theory: Between New Private Law and Rechtsdogmatik* (Oxford University Press 2023).

7 For a discussion of the potential limitations of moral contract theories and the need to distinguish "private" and "public" morality, see Randy E. Barnett, 'Contract Is Not Promise; Contract Is Consent' in Gregory Klass, George Letsas and Prince Saprai (eds), *Philosophical Foundations of Contract Law* (Oxford University Press 2014) 55–56.

and enforcement of contract law in its beneficial effects. Section 5 examines pluralistic accounts, which jettison the requirement of a unitary organising principle for contract law in favour of a composite account. Section 6 concludes by drawing out some of the overarching themes for legal research. Two stand out. The first is that there may be more to gain by treating the various contract theories as complementary perspectives rather than as mutually exclusive accounts. The second, related point is that when we judge the merits of a contract theory, we should do so not only on the basis of coverage—the degree to which a theory can accommodate any and all contract doctrines—but also on the theory's ability to pinpoint facets of contract law that may otherwise be overlooked. Some initial caveats are also in order. It is necessary to be selective both in the choice of contract theories and literature.[8] Furthermore, some detail is sacrificed to emphasise major fault-lines, methodological implications, and utility—that is, how contract theory sheds light on contract as a tangible, legal practice.

2. CONCEPTUAL CONTRACT THEORY

At the moment a contract is entered into, the normative landscape changes. Previous rights and obligations are altered or superseded, and new rights and obligations come into being. To make these legal effects intelligible, we need a vocabulary and framework. The ideal framework should provide clarity while tracking legal doctrine and practice as closely as possible.

A starting observation is that legal practitioners tend to couch their arguments in the language of logical consistency. Legal research may thus fall within the conceptual domain simply by virtue of testing the coherence of such arguments, potentially exposing contradictions and hidden implications. Take, for example, scholarship on the relationship between contractual obligations and remedial liabilities. Jody Kraus charts a default mode of thinking on this topic, which holds that a breach of promise is what inherently gives rise to liability. Since breach and liability are logically linked, so the thinking goes, they share a legal basis and moral justification.[9] This mode of reasoning seems straightforward, but it is conceptually fraught. Performance obligations and liabilities in case of breach have distinct prerequisites and legal effects, as is

[8] The chapter relies heavily on Gregory Klass, George Letsas and Prince Saprai, *Philosophical Foundations of Contract Law* (Oxford University Press 2014). The anthology pursues the same overall objective as this chapter, summarising and contrasting different philosophical perspectives, albeit with a greater focus on theoretical rather than practical implications.

[9] Jody S. Kraus, 'The Correspondence of Contract and Promise' (2009) 109(7) *Columbia Law Review* 1603, 1628.

evident from the broad menu of remedial mechanisms that contracting parties can choose from. Thus, as Kraus notes, the content of moral or legal remedial claims following a breach "cannot be determined by pure logic or brute intuition alone".[10] Equating the two leads to a loss of nuance. Furthermore, every argument that liability follows from breach can be met with a demand to show independent, substantive grounds for liability.

The terminology in this starting example indicates a further need for conceptual explanation. Upon being presented with terms such as "obligation" and "liability", we may ask what, exactly, these terms refer to. In attempting to ascribe precise meaning, we may then discover that the content of an "obligation" or a "liability" can vary according to context. Tools are needed in order to further differentiate the possible components of these terms and to describe how components can be combined into different types of obligation and liability. We need, in short, a language of rights.

When it comes to rights, according to Hillel Steiner, "[t]he beginning of wisdom [...] is widely agreed to be the classification of juridical positions developed by Wesley Newcomb Hohfeld".[11] The Hohfeldian framework for sorting and classifying rights has become the standard tool of legal theorists and is woven into the fabric of general legal reasoning that contract theory relies on.[12] Hohfeld's key observation was that scholars and practitioners use the same term—"right"—to denote various legal relations that are analytically distinct. Such indiscriminate usage obscures differences and invites confusion. His solution is to replace the one aggregate term with four sub-types of rights, distinguished according to their legal effects: claims, liberties, powers, and immunities. Although the Hohfeldian framework is seldom mentioned explicitly in contract theory, these four categories and their associated meanings should be fairly recognisable to legal scholars.

Contractual *claims* require the duty bearer to do or refrain from doing some act. In a simple delivery contract, for instance, one party possesses a claim to the delivery of a good and the other a claim to payment. *Liberties*, meanwhile, allow the right holder to act or refrain from acting without breaching a duty. A delivery contract that only stipulates a fulfilment window gives the promisor the liberty to choose the exact time of performance. Although both claims

---

10 Ibid. See also Dori Kimel, *From Promise to Contract: Towards a Liberal Theory of Contract* (Bloomsbury Publishing 2003) 95.

11 Hillel Steiner, *An Essay on Rights* (Blackwell 1994) 50.

12 For an overview of the framework's current range of applications, see Kit Barker, 'Private Law, Analytical Philosophy and the Modern Value of Wesley Newcomb Hohfeld: A Centennial Appraisal' (2018) 38 *Oxford Journal of Legal Studies* 585; Heidi M. Hurd and Michael S. Moore, 'The Hohfeldian Analysis of Rights' (2018) 63 *The American Journal of Jurisprudence* 295.

and liberties can be referred to as "having a right", one regulates the actions of the duty bearer and the other the actions of the right holder. In the words of Leonard Sumner, we cannot have claims to do, only claims that others do. Conversely, we cannot have liberties that others do, only liberties to do.[13]

Claims and liberties are both static. We need two further sub-types—powers and immunities—to describe the conditions under which contractual relations may change.[14] *Powers* grant the right holder the ability to effect changes to their own rights or the rights of others. A prime example is the power of waiver, the exercise of which cancels contractual commitments. *Immunities*, meanwhile, render attempts to change the distribution of rights and obligations ineffectual. If, for instance, stipulated conditions for pricing adjustment are not met, then the promisee enjoys an immunity to the promisor's attempted price adjustment.

The Hohfeldian approach to describing rights is devoid of any normative commitments. The system does not arrange rights in a hierarchy or prefer some kinds of rights to others; it is only a tool for distinguishing and labelling their content.[15] The system does, however, come with some important conceptual commitments, two of which are particularly significant for contract scholars. The first is correlativity. There are four rights but eight possible positions to occupy in a contractual relationship, because any contractual right must be tied to a corresponding contractual burden. For every holder of a contractual claim to delivery, there is someone who bears the corresponding performance duty. Similarly, there is a liability for every power, a no-right for every liberty, and a disability for every immunity.[16]

---

13 Leonard W. Sumner, *The Moral Foundation of Rights* (Clarendon Press 1987) 25.

14 Wesley N. Hohfeld, *Fundamental Legal Conceptions as Applied in Judicial Reasoning* (Lawbook Exchange 1964) 39. The distinction between static rights (claims and liberties) and dynamic rights (powers and immunities) coincides with Hart's distinction between primary and secondary rules, respectively; see H.L.A. Hart, *The Concept of Law* (Oxford University Press 2012) 81; Lon L. Fuller, *The Morality of Law* (Yale University Press 1969) 134 n. 50.

15 Pierre Schlag, 'How to Do Things with Hohfeld' (2015) 78 *Law & Contemporary Problems* 185, 189; Barker (n 12) 586.

16 Two separate terms are in play here: "obligation" and "duty". This is due to varying preferences in the literature. Rights theorists tend to use "duty", while contract theorists alternate between "duty" and "obligation". For the present purposes, we may treat the two terms as synonymous, with the caveat that some authors sort them into conceptually distinct categories. Theorists may, for instance, follow Hart in using "duty" as the broader term and reserving "obligation" for duties that are self-imposed; see Hart, *Essays in Jurisprudence and Philosophy* 101; Kraus, 'The Correspondence of Contract and Promise' (n 9) 1614.

The correlativity of contractual rights and obligations is not merely a contingent feature; it is a matter of conceptual necessity. A claim is *defined* as the correlate of a duty, in the sense that the two terms denote placements in the same legal relation between promisor and promisee.[17] The promisee's claim is equivalent to the promisor's performance duty because both the claim and the duty are part of the same legal relationship. Furthermore, correlativity is the only necessary link between legal positions.[18] This has far-reaching implications. Whenever a legal argument is framed in terms of necessity, we may always ask whether this necessity stems from correlativity or requires a substantive basis in contract interpretation and statute. We have already seen an example of this above. Kraus argues that contractual liabilities cannot be logically derived from contractual duties because the two rights are conceptually distinct.[19] The same conclusion follows from Hohfeldian analysis, since the relationship between a contractual obligation and liability is not one of correlativity.

The second and perhaps more impactful insight from Hohfeldian analysis is that most of the time we refer to a "right", we are, in fact, referring to a composite structure of rights. The "right to waiver", for instance, is a composite of a power (because its exercise cancels claims and their correlative duties) and of a liberty (because the right holder may choose whether to exercise the right of waiver or not). If we take a given contract and subject it to conceptual analysis, what emerges after disassembly is a composite and potentially shifting bundle of rights and obligations. Its various components can be slotted in or out according to the preferences of the parties, legislative choices, and interpretation.

What we do with this tool will vary. For a doctrinal lawyer, conceptual analysis makes for a robust and widely recognised method of disassembly. After such disassembly, there would be no need, however, to identify any one of the constituent parts of a contract as its "core". Things are different for normative contract theorists. In their hunt for an organising moral principle

17 To explain this relationship, Kramer asks us to imagine a right holder (promisee) and a duty bearer (promisor) standing at the top and bottom of a hill. The hill represents their contractual relation. For the promisee, the hill appears as a descent, and for the promisor, it appears as an ascent, but they are both looking at the same contractual relation. See Matthew Kramer, 'Rights Without Trimmings' in Matthew Kramer, Nigel Simmonds and Hillel Steiner (eds), *A Debate Over Rights* (Clarendon Press 1998) 26.

18 Matthias Brinkmann and Johan Vorland Wibye, 'Towards Non-essentialism–Tracking Rival Views of Legitimacy as a Right to Rule' (2023) 43 *Oxford Journal of Legal Studies* 497, 505.

19 Kraus, 'The Correspondence of Contract and Promise' (n 9) 1628.

of contract law, theorists tend to home in on a single aspect. Thus, competing theories anchor contract law in the duty to keep one's word,[20] or the power to take on duties,[21] or the duty to avoid harm,[22] or the power to waive contractual rights,[23] or the power to take on liability,[24] and so on.[25] In each case, positing a unitary organising principle makes the candidate theories mutually exclusive. And in each case, a conceptual framework allows us to distinguish normative theories according to which rights or obligations they focus on.

It is often up to the reader to determine the conceptual assumptions at work in scholarship on contracts. There are frequent examples, however, of authors highlighting specific assumptions as a springboard for doctrinal or normative analysis. Liam Murphy, for instance, distinguishes the possible functions of contracts in conceptual terms in order to arrive at an account that is ultimately rooted in the beneficial effects of a contract regime.[26] Then there are contract theories where conceptual explanation takes centre stage. David Owens takes as his point of departure the orthodox notion that promises somehow "transfer" a right from the promisor to the promisee. This transfer, so the argument goes, converts what was previously a liberty into a performance duty (correlated with a claim at the hands of the promisee). According to Owens, the notion of a transfer is not conducive to clear thinking about contracts. He instead portrays contracts as granting the promisee a power of choice: to insist on performance or to exercise a power of waiver.[27] From its point of divergence to its conclusion, this is a theory where the interplay between conceptual and normative reasoning is on full display.

---

20 See, e.g., Charles Fried, *Contract as Promise: A Theory of Contractual Obligation* (Oxford University Press 1981).

21 Joseph Raz, 'Is There a Reason to Keep a Promise?' in Gregory Klass, George Letsas and Prince Saprai (eds), *Philosophical Foundations of Contract Law* (Oxford University Press 2014).

22 Thomas M. Scanlon, *What We Owe to Each Other* (Harvard University Press 1998).

23 David Owens, 'Does a Promise Transfer a Right?' in Gregory Klass, George Letsas and Prince Saprai (eds), *Philosophical Foundations of Contract Law* (Oxford University Press 2014).

24 Barnett (n 7) 48.

25 These debates resemble efforts to identify a single legal norm at the heart of tort and property theory; see James E. Penner, 'The Bundle of Rights Picture of Property' (1996) 43 *The UCLA Law Review* 711, 721.

26 Liam Murphy, 'The Practice of Promise and Contract' in Gregory Klass, George Letsas and Prince Saprai (eds), *Philosophical Foundations of Contract Law* (Oxford University Press 2014).

27 Owens (n 23) 79. See also Hanoch Dagan and Michael Heller, *The Choice Theory of Contracts* (Cambridge University Press 2017) 33.

The methodological value of conceptual tools is best demonstrated through application, and the remaining sections of this chapter provide ample opportunity. Throughout the survey, candidate theories of contract will be contrasted according to which Hohfeldian right or obligation they place at the core of contracts. As will become clear, there is a major fault-line between contract theories that treat the core function of contract law as power-conferring and those that treat the core function as duty-imposing.[28]

3. NORMATIVE CONTRACT THEORY—INTRINSIC ACCOUNTS

The focus now turns from the conceptual to the normative. Normative contract theories seek an organising principle within contract law. In the words of Gregory Klass, "[j]ust as a language has a grammar, contract law might have basic rules or commitments that structure the practice as a whole".[29] That structure, once determined, can help us frame research questions, explain particular contract doctrines, and formulate revisionist critiques. We begin with accounts that justify contract law on the basis of its intrinsic moral features, while the next section examines accounts based on the instrumental value of contract law. Four intrinsic theories are selected for analysis. These are, in order of appearance, that contract law serves to uphold promises, that it enforces a duty to avoid harm, that it enhances autonomy, and lastly relational accounts of the contract.

Contract as Promise

The most prominent account in modern theory holds that contract law is made distinctive by its commitment to the enforcement of promises. Such a view seems to line up with doctrinal terminology. We speak of contracts between "promisors" and "promisees", and some treatises expressly define contracts in terms of promises.[30] Stipulated definitions and linguistic usage can only

---

28 See Gregory Klass, 'Three Pictures of Contract: Duty, Power, and Compound Rule' (2007) 83 *New York University Law Review* 1726.

29 Gregory Klass, 'Introduction to Philosophical Foundations of Contract Law' in Gregory Klass, George Letsas and Prince Saprai (eds), *Philosophical Foundations of Contract Law* (Oxford University Press 2014) 2.

30 See, e.g., art. 1.6(2) UNIDROIT Principles of International Commercial Contracts 2016 (UNIDROIT) art. 5.2.1; Principles of European Contract Law – PECL (https://www.trans-lex.org/400200) art. 6:110. In the Restatement (Second) of the Law of Contracts (1981) § 1, a contract is defined as a "promise or set of

take us so far, however. In order for an account of contract as promise to do explanatory work, legal scholars must understand what it means to promise. They must also track the (dis-)similarities between promises of the everyday sort and promises as expressed in legally binding contracts. Only then can they begin to apply a conception and justification of promissory morality to the study of legal doctrine.

The leading proponent of promise theory is Charles Fried. In his seminal work, *Contract as Promise*, Fried grounds contract law in the principle of promise; "that principle by which persons may impose on themselves obligations where none existed before".[31] A promise is understood here as an act of communication signalling an intention to take on an obligation to perform or refrain from performing a specified act, and where the parties understand the commitment as being taken on by the act of communication.[32] By viewing legal contracts as promises, contract law is conceived of as an intrinsically moral institution. Fried acknowledges that the practice of self-imposing duties and holding others to theirs promotes welfare but rejects the notion that such downstream benefits play a justificatory role. Instead, the morality of promissory compliance is grounded in the deeper morality of autonomy, respect for persons, and trust.[33] Contract law, then, is justified to the extent that it upholds and reflects corresponding moral duties to keep one's word.[34] To quote Fried, "since a contract is first of all a promise, the contract must be kept because a promise must be kept".[35]

The methodological upshot of adopting promise theory is that lawmaking and adjudication can only be properly understood by viewing legislative,

---

promises for the breach of which the law gives a remedy, or the performance of which the law in some ways recognizes as duty".

[31] Fried, *Contract as Promise* (n 20) 1.

[32] John Finnis, *Natural Law and Natural Rights* (Clarendon 1980) 298. The United Nations Convention on Contracts for the International Sale of Goods, 1489 UNTS 3 ("CISG") art. 14(i) states that a contractual offer is made when a party "indicates the intention of the offeror to be bound". The Restatement of Contract art. § 2(1) defines a promise as "the manifestation of intention to act or refrain from acting in a specified way, so as to justify a promisee in understanding that a commitment has been made".

[33] Fried, *Contract as Promise* (n 20) 16. Charles Fried, 'The Ambitions of Contract as Promise' in Gregory Klass, George Letsas and Prince Saprai (eds), *Philosophical Foundations of Contract Law* (Oxford University Press 2014) 20. See also Seana Valentine Shiffrin, 'The Divergence of Contract and Promise' (2012) 120(3) *Harvard Law Review* 708, 721.

[34] Stephen A. Smith, 'Performance, Punishment and the Nature of Contractual Obligation' (1997) 60 *Modern Law Review* 360, 367.

[35] Fried, *Contract as Promise* (n 20) 132.

adjudicative, and practitioners' choices in light of the moral duty to keep promises. Promise theorists can support this argument with various doctrinal observations. For one, legal contracts and moral promising are similar. Both actions give rise to content-independent and voluntarily acquired obligations owed to a designated person or set of persons.[36] Both come into being when promisees perceive in the promisor an intention to take on obligations through an act of communication. A further similarity is that the breach of both moral and legal promises can trigger liability in the absence of fault. For example, promisors may be held liable even when contractual performance is unexpectedly burdensome or hindered by third parties.[37]

Promise theorists also see evidence of promissory morality in the gulf between contract law and tort law. Remedial contract law is organised around expectation damages,[38] according to which the promisor must pay damages approximating contractual performance. The sought-after result is that the promisee is put in a position equivalent to what they would have enjoyed after contractual performance. For example, if the promisor fails to deliver promised widgets, the damages cover the cost of sourcing widgets from a third party. Tort law, on the other hand, is organised around reliance damages. These are damages designed to return parties to their prior state, as if no tort had been committed (or, in the context of contract, as if no promise had ever been made). According to promise theorists, the legal safeguarding of a promised outcome demonstrates that contract as a body of law is devoted to enforcing promises.[39]

Two points are worth noting here. The first is that the same differentiation of contract and tort features in classical will theories of contract, where being forced to honour contracts is justified by virtue of the fact that contractual duties are self-imposed.[40] In fact, Fried presents his account as a defence of the classical view of contract proposed by will theorists.[41] The second point is that the evidentiary role of expectation damages is still up for debate. To critics, expectation damages do not go far enough. If the law was truly committed to

36 Klass, 'Introduction to Philosophical Foundations of Contract Law' (n 29) 2.

37 Cf. Robert A. Hillman, 'The Future of Fault in Contract Law' (2014) 52 *Duquesne Law Review* 275.

38 For example, art. 1231-2 of the French Civil Code states that "[d]amages due to a creditor are, as a rule, for the loss that he has suffered and the profit of which he has been deprived". See also Restatement of Contract § 344 (a).

39 Fried, *Contract as Promise* (n 20) 17.

40 Fried, 'The Ambitions of Contract as Promise' (n 33) 2. For further discussion, see Barnett (n 7) 44.

41 Fried, *Contract as Promise* (n 20) 6.

promissory morality, the criticism goes, enforcement should be geared towards specific performance and not just equivalent outcomes.[42]

Critics of promise theory may also cite its lack of coverage, in the sense that certain legal doctrines are difficult to reconcile with promissory morality. Three of the most important criticisms concern standards of interpretation, contractual gaps, and mitigation doctrines. Starting with interpretation, promise theory justifies the enforcement of contractual duties on the basis that they are self-imposed. This would suggest that enforcement is only appropriate when the promisor assented to the contractual obligations being enforced. The problem is that assent is a subjective state of mind, and it is impossible for courts and other observers, or indeed the promisee, to verify the promisor's true intentions. Absent subjective verifiability, legal systems have instead turned to objective standards of interpretation based on default rules, general principles, and so on. The upshot for promisors is that they risk being held to terms they did not intend to impose on themselves (that is, obligations they did not consent to). Fried accommodates this criticism and responds by placing such standards of interpretation outside the scope of promise theory. Objective standards of interpretation are thus incompatible with his stated account, imposing "an external standard on the parties" that cannot be justified within a promise-based justification of contract law.[43]

Fried makes a similar concession when it comes to contractual gaps. Take the case of parties to a delivery contract that have failed to anticipate fluctuations in the market for raw materials. Arbitrators and courts cannot settle such disputes on the basis of promissory morality because the gap lies, by its very nature, outside of what the parties have agreed on.[44] We must once again resort to objective criteria.

Promise theory also struggles to explain certain mitigation doctrines. Promisees may be required to act reasonably in order to reduce losses. For example, a buyer may be required to obtain the promised goods from another party; the remedial damages cover the difference in price. If the law of contract were wholly concerned with promissory morality, then the promisee should not be required to accept a substitute. We should expect, instead, that remedies would require promisors to keep their promises rather than making demands on the victim of non-performance.[45]

---

[42] See, e.g., Kimel (n 10) 95. T.M. Scanlon, 'Promises and Contracts' in Peter Benson (ed), *The Theory of Contract Law: New Essays* (Cambridge University Press 2001) 92.

[43] Barnett (n 7) 45.

[44] Fried, *Contract as Promise* (n 20) 61.

[45] Ibid; Shiffrin (n 33) 724.

To some, such doctrinal incompatibilities are enough to rule out a promise theory of contract law. It is possible that these and other challenges may be overcome, but that likely requires a more developed theory of the background assumptions held by contracting parties when they make promises.[46] Another, more pragmatic path is to admit that promise theory has certain limitations while still holding onto its explanatory power. This leads us neatly to an underlying question: what are the methodological implications of viewing contract law through the lens of promissory morality?[47]

Perhaps the most important implication of promise theory is that it puts the interests of the promisee in the limelight. This will make the theory appealing to scholars who attach particular normative significance to the promisee side of contractual relationships.[48] A common example in the literature is the debate on efficient breach. Economic analysis supports a justification of expectation damages on the basis that promisors should be able to escape onerous performance duties. The efficient breach hypothesis in contract theory goes one step further, arguing that the wide availability of expectation damages in legal systems actually encourages breach.[49] For the promise theorist, this instrumentally grounded analysis of liability dilutes the idea of complying with a moral commitment for its own sake.[50] Supporting expectation damages because of the advantage of contractual breach serves, on this view, to erode the foundational principles of contract law as a whole. Additionally, promise theorists may argue that the value gained from efficient breach doctrines accrues to the wrong party; a contract law anchored in promissory morality should be more oriented towards the claims of the promisee than systemic efficiency.[51]

In conceptual terms, promise theory is oriented towards the duty-imposing aspects of contract, making it generally suited to highlighting promissory duties in legislative choices and interpretation practices. It should be noted,

---

46 See, e.g., Kraus, 'The Correspondence of Contract and Promise' (n 9) 1607.

47 One immediate implication is definitional. "Contract law" may be understood broadly as the body of law governing voluntary economic exchanges. For Fried, however, "contract law" is *defined* as the domain of legal rules that are derived from promissory morality. Doctrines that clash with promise theory are treated as falling outside the domain of contract law, properly conceived; see Fried, *Contract as Promise* (n 20) 61; Kraus, 'The Correspondence of Contract and Promise' (n 9) 1607 fn 10.

48 Klass, 'Introduction to Philosophical Foundations of Contract Law' (n 29) 2.

49 Kraus, 'The Correspondence of Contract and Promise' (n 9) 1606.

50 Shiffrin (n 33) 740.

51 Richard Craswell, 'Contract Remedies, Renegotiation, and the Theory of Efficient Breach' (1988) 61 *The Southern California Law Review* 629, 640.

however, that the orientation towards duty is a feature of Fried's particular brand of promise theory. It is possible to take the account in other directions, as Joseph Raz does when reconstructing promise theory around autonomy and the power-conferring functions of contract law. Raz stresses the ability of promises—and by extension, contracts—to enhance our moral lives.[52] This perspective brings out how promises are a particularly valuable tool for pursuing personal ends. They allow us to shape our own responsibilities and pursue goods that would otherwise be inaccessible. Raz uses this feature of promising as the basis for a broader account of the power-conferring function of contract law as a vehicle for autonomy and self-realisation.

Raz's take on promissory morality allows us to explain further patterns in legal systems. It is common for there to be limits on what kind of rights the promisor can give up, as in the absence of power to enter into immoral contracts or sell oneself into servitude. In a contract theory based on enhancing moral lives, such limitations are necessary to avoid detrimental effects for the promisor. This account also supports morally grounded limits on the power to stipulate remedies for non-performance.[53] For instance, supercompensatory remedies such as punitive damages may be judged too harmful to moral lives to be accepted and enforced.[54]

Harm-Avoidance

The development of promise theory has been driven, in part, by the desire to separate contract law and tort law.[55] There are alternative theories that do away with this imperative by leaning into the similarities of contract and tort. Contract breach, like tortious behaviour, typically has tangible costs—hence the "contract as tort" theories that were prominent before promise theories became mainstream.[56] If we conceive of reliance costs caused by contract

---

52 Raz (n 21) 64.

53 According to Dori Kimel, the power to self-impose duties is not only a manifestation of autonomy but also a threat to it, depending on how the promisee opts to exercise the power of waiver. See Dori Kimel, 'Personal Autonomy and Change of Mind in Promise and in Contract' in Gregory Klass, George Letsas and Prince Saprai (eds), *Philosophical Foundations of Contract Law* (Oxford University Press 2014) 99.

54 Alan Schwartz and Robert E. Scott, 'Contract Theory and the Limits of Contract Law' (2003) 113 *Yale Law Journal* 541, 584.

55 Fried, 'The Ambitions of Contract as Promise' (n 33) 19.

56 See, e.g., Grant Gilmore, *The Death of Contract* (The Ohio State University Press 1974).

breach as harms, then the function of contract law can be tied to the promisor's duty not to harm the promisee.

One of the leading exponents of harm-avoidance theory is T.M. Scanlon. His *Principle of Fidelity* states, in simplified terms, that if a promisor voluntarily and intentionally provides the assurances that a promisee seeks, and if both parties are mutually aware of, and rely on, their respective intentions to take on obligations, then the promisor has an obligation of fulfilment unless the promisee waives contractual claims.[57] Note that this approach does not ignore the moral significance of promising.[58] Promises still feature, but they no longer serve as the organising principle of contract law. That role belongs to the avoidance of detrimental reliance caused by making promises and then breaching the expectations that those promises create.

Harm-avoidance theory, like promise theory, resonates with moral intuitions. It seems plausible that, in the words of Patrick Atiyah, contract law should be concerned with the correction of harms caused by unfulfilled promises and unjust enrichment.[59] Doctrines such as mitigation or the common law promissory estoppel—upholding promises that contractual parties have relied on to their detriment—mesh well with a portrayal of the law as a tool for harm-reduction and avoidance.

What are the methodological implications of grounding contract law in harm-avoidance? In conceptual terms, the theory is once again oriented towards the duty-imposing rather than power-conferring aspects of contracts. It anchors contract law in what agents should do, rather than what is in their power to do. Its implications are particularly clear for remedial mechanisms. If the organising principle of contracts is to avoid harm, we have a supporting argument for treating reliance damages as the default over expectation damages. According to Scanlon, expectation damages are only warranted when the contracting parties manifestly commit to this form of remedy.[60] Therein also lies a challenge, for reliance damages are, in fact, seldom the default.

Basing an account on harm-avoidance leads Scanlon to introduce several caveats pertaining to the knowledge and status of contracting parties that are not clearly reflected in legal doctrine. For the promisor, he posits that enforcement of expectations should only happen if the burden of fulfilment is not

---

[57] Scanlon (n 22) 304.

[58] Charlie Webb, 'Contract as Fact and as Reason' in Gregory Klass, George Letsas and Prince Saprai (eds), *Philosophical Foundations of Contract Law* (Oxford University Press 2014) 142.

[59] Patrick S. Atiyah, 'Contracts, Promises and the Law of Obligations' (1990) 94 *Law Quarterly Review* 193.

[60] Scanlon (n 22) 99.

"excessive" and if the promisor had "adequate opportunity" to avoid the harm.[61] Legal doctrine, meanwhile, typically only allows exemptions from liability in unforeseeable and unavoidable circumstances such as *force majeure*.[62] For the promisee, Scanlon holds that only "reasonable" expectations trigger the moral justification of harm-avoidance. Jurisdictions often lack obvious legal equivalents, especially in contract regimes without mechanisms for liability exception upon providing advance warning of a possible breach. The harm-based view is also hard-pressed to account for liability in the absence of reliance costs or insistence on liability even when the promisee had prior grounds for doubting the ability of the promisor to meet their obligations.

Clearly, the thresholds introduced by Scanlon require some fleshing out. This ties in with an underlying challenge: harm-avoidance theory does not provide much in the way of legislative, judicial, or practical guidance.[63] The view is compatible with a wide range of enforcement mechanisms; harm can, after all, be avoided in different ways. This need not be a flaw. For the practically minded contract theorist, harm-avoidance theory offers a foundational account of contract law with intuitive support and relatively few conceptual and normative commitments.

Autonomy-Preservation

As noted, Fried's promise theory is anchored in the deeper morality of autonomy, respect for persons, and trust. Other theorists have singled out the first of these—autonomy—as the true focal point of contract law. Randy Barnett argues in this vein that what sets contract law apart is not promise but rather consent, meaning the manifested intention to be legally bound.[64] The philosophical move is perhaps best expressed using our language of rights: promising is about taking on *duties*, while consent is about taking on *liability*. On Barnett's account, then, the core of a contract is the consent that opens the way for ramifications in case of non-performance.[65] The law, in turn, gives expression to and protects the autonomy of contracting parties by facilitating their exercise of self-binding power.

---

[61] Ibid.

[62] See CISG art. 79.

[63] According to Craswell, intrinsic theories suffer from this problem generally; see Richard Craswell, 'Contract Law, Default Rules, and the Philosophy of Promising' (1989) 88 *Michigan Law Review* 489, 495.

[64] Barnett (n 7) 48. For a recent overview and discussion of autonomy-based theory, see Dagan and Heller (n 27).

[65] Barnett (n 7) 48.

The implication of taking autonomy as our starting point is a contract law structured around the need to help parties exercise the power to consent regardless of their previous relational status, to explore the full breadth of contractual relationships, and to ensure that enforcement mechanisms respect the boundaries of their consent. Commercial entities with no previous dealings should be able to rely on a legible and standardised framework of interpretation and enforcement to facilitate their joint consent. This stance can be taken further to include, for instance, a normative demand on legislators to take a proactive role in adapting contract law to new contract types and commercial settings.[66]

Autonomy-based theories of contract, and especially those with libertarian roots, are closely tied to both classical will theories and contract as promise. All highlight the role of contract law in conferring self-binding power.[67] They nonetheless result in diverging views on enforcement. According to Barnett's theory of contract as consent, state enforcement of contracts is only justified to the extent that the parties clearly intended to be bound.[68] Since, as noted above, the true subjective intentions of a promisor are unverifiable, emphasising autonomy suggests we should place greater weight on factors that are accessible to the contracting parties. Consent theory is therefore well equipped to explain the prevalence of objective standards of interpretation. An autonomy-based view also meshes well with consideration doctrines requiring evidence of mutual advantage through promises and performances that are bargained for.[69]

Scholars may also find autonomy theory to be a useful staging point for doctrinal research.[70] As with the other theories surveyed, however, there are challenges related to coverage. Contract law does not always look like a system designed with autonomy-preservation in mind.[71] An example is the practice of setting aside supercompensatory provisions as overly punitive or exclusion of liability clauses as unconscionable. If sophisticated contracting parties have chosen specific remedies—a choice that is presumably reflected in their pricing agreement—then the choice to strike those remedies down is hard to

66 Dagan and Heller (n 27) 4.

67 Barnett (n 7) 49; Duncan Kennedy, 'From the Will Theory to the Principle of Private Autonomy: Lon Fuller's "Consideration and Form"' (2000) 100(1) *Columbia Law Review* 94, 1728.

68 Barnett (n 7) 57.

69 Randy E. Barnett, 'Some Problems with Contract as Promise' (1992) 77 *Cornell Law Review* 1022, 1029.

70 Craswell argues against this stance, suggesting that autonomy theory offers little guidance for the content of default legal rules. See Craswell, 'Contract Law, Default Rules, and the Philosophy of Promising' (n 63) 395.

71 Schwartz and Scott (n 54) 584.

reconcile with autonomy.[72] Similarly, consent theory cannot straightforwardly explain legal boundaries on contractual freedom. The inability to consent to servitude, for example, is better explained with a theory that contracts serve to enhance our moral lives.[73] A further challenge to autonomy theory is the occurrence of promises that are made on the condition that promisees do not seek legal enforcement. In such cases, attempting to trigger liability would have the effect of cancelling the underlying obligation.[74] If contract is consent, and consent is understood in terms of self-imposed liability, then such arrangements seem to fall outside the contractual domain.

Relational Accounts

Contracting parties are not strangers to one another. A further group of contract theories stresses the relational nature of contracts. James Penner, for example, organises his theory around the notion that contracts should be conceived of as agreements rather than promises.[75] The distinction hinges on promises being unilateral obligations, and agreements being bilateral or multilateral obligations. In conceptual terms, the relational account is more aligned with the principle of correlativity than theories focused on either the promisor- or promisee-side of a contractual relationship. Viewed from the perspective of correlativity, a contract is not a property of contracting parties but rather the thread that ties contracting parties together. This is a conceptual departure from previously surveyed contract theories that alternate between the perspectives of the promisor and the promisee. Penner's argument is that the contracting parties together create something new—a joint venture or undertaking. Parties who enter into an agreement take on the interests of their counterpart, creating exclusionary reasons to facilitate performance and not to take actions which undermine their shared purposes and goals.[76]

---

72 Fried, 'The Ambitions of Contract as Promise' (n 33) 27.

73 Raz (n 21) 64.

74 Restatement (second) of Contract § 230.

75 James Penner, 'Promises, Agreements, and Contracts' in Gregory Klass, George Letsas and Prince Saprai (eds), *Philosophical Foundations of Contract Law* (Oxford University Press 2014) 117.

76 Ibid. According to Penner, the joint venture is "morally prior" and promises parasitic, meaning that the morality of agreements is what motivates the actions of contracting parties; promises are typically appropriate in instances of breach. For the seminal account of exclusionary reasons, see Joseph Raz, *Practical Reason and Norms* (Oxford University Press 1999).

Relational accounts are arguably more familiar to civil law jurisdictions that embrace a cooperative view of contracts.[77] The relational account of contract law is not incompatible with evidence from common law jurisdictions, however.[78] A relational theory may be formulated that places the doctrine of good faith at the core of contracts, thus emphasising the duty of promisors and promisees to recognise each other's independence and special normative status.[79] Whether the focus is on civil law or common law systems, relational accounts seem well-placed to explain some of the realities of contractual relationships. The scholarly notion of a contract is of a legal relationship that is either extant or not. In practice, however, parties often agree to partial terms and then simply start performing.[80] In such cases, contracting becomes an incremental process based on trust and organic solidarity rather than a single act of promise or consent.

A relational perspective can also be used to put forward a moral function that is unique to contract law. Daniel Markovits, for instance, argues that contracts create a distinctive moral relationship of solidarity and good faith.[81] While this approach is reminiscent of the trust-based arguments in Fried's account, Markovits makes the implications of good faith more explicit. The relational duty of good faith includes a duty to show flexibility in the face of changed circumstances, facilitating the "success of the contractual collaboration's shared plan".[82] One implication is a shift in the moral division of labour. In a dispute concerning a contractual gap, we may think that the work of completing the incomplete is done by adjudicators. Within the distinctive moral relationship of solidarity and good faith, however, the contracting parties themselves hold the responsibility for filling contractual gaps with altruistic solutions as

---

77 See, e.g., the Draft Common Frame of Reference (DCFR) of 2009, art. III. 1:104, which sets out an explicit duty of cooperation.

78 For a discussion of civil and common law perspectives on cooperation, see Robert Hardy, 'The Feasibility Study's Rules on Contract Interpretation' (2011) 19(6) *European Review of Private Law* 825.

79 See, e.g., Uniform Commercial Code (UCC) § 1–304; Restatement (second) of Contract § 205.

80 Stewart Macaulay, 'Relational Contracts Floating on a Sea of Custom? Thoughts about the Ideas of Ian Macneil and Lisa Bernstein' (2000) 94(3) *Northwestern University Law Review* 778; Melvin A. Eisenberg, *Foundational Principles of Contract Law* (Oxford Academic 2018) 733.

81 Daniel Markovits, 'Good Faith as Contract's Core Value' in Gregory Klass, George Letsas and Prince Saprai (eds), *Philosophical Foundations of Contract Law* (Oxford University Press 2014) 282.

82 Ibid.

befitting a shared enterprise; others can only rely on the principle of good faith as interpretational guidance.

4. NORMATIVE CONTRACT THEORY—INSTRUMENTAL ACCOUNTS

We now move away from accounts of contract law based on an intrinsic moral justification to accounts that justify contract law using empirical data about its capacity to generate value. A calculus evaluating contract law according to its effects can be designed in different ways. The leading account, and main contender to promise theory, is the instrumental analysis of wealth maximisation championed by Richard Posner in *The Economic Analysis of Law*.[83] The theory is so prominent that a distinction is commonly made between "philosophical" and "economic" theories of law, where the former refers mainly to promise theory and the latter mainly to empirical study of wealth maximization. While it is true that proponents of intrinsic theories tend to be philosophers and proponents of economic analysis tend to be doctrinalists,[84] it should also be acknowledged that economic analyses can be carried out with differing philosophical ambitions and on different normative levels.[85] On one end of the scale are normatively agnostic studies, such as plotting out the economic impact of a suggested policy on punitive damages without taking a moral standpoint. On the other end of the scale are theories of the kind evaluated here, which make the normative claim that welfare maximization is the organising principle at the core of contract law. This is why the present chapter makes a distinction between intrinsic and instrumental theories rather than "philosophical" and "economic" theories.

Contract theories rooted in economic analysis can be traced back to David Hume and his observation that human affairs can be conducted to greater mutual advantage by relying on established procedures and institutions.[86] One of these advantages relates to incentives. As emphasised in the literature on effective breach, contracting parties may find themselves in situations where contractual breach is more advantageous than performance. If they were to always pursue this short-term gain, however, trust and the prevalence of

---

[83] Richard A. Posner, *Economic Analysis of Law* (Aspen Publishing 1973); Fried, 'The Ambitions of Contract as Promise' (n 33) 400.

[84] Jody S. Kraus, 'Philosophy of Contract Law' in Jules L. Coleman, Kenneth Einar Himma and Scott J. Shapiro (eds), *The Oxford Handbook of Jurisprudence and Philosophy of Law* (Oxford University Press 2004) 697.

[85] Richard A. Posner, 'Utilitarianism, Economics, and Legal Theory' (1979) 8 *The Journal of Legal Studies* 103, 109.

[86] David Hume, *A Treatise of Human Nature* (Clarendon Press 1896) pt. II.

contracts would suffer. Contract law serves to align the immediate interests of promisors with the long-term societal benefits of a robust contract regime.[87] A *justificatory* economic theory thus holds that contracts should be enforced to the extent that such enforcement maximises welfare and efficiency.[88]

Perhaps the most formidable methodological advantage of economic analysis is its transparency. The justificatory argument rests on claims that are both accessible and testable, making the theory appealing to legal scholars engaged with the bottom-up work of explaining particular legislation and precedent. Hence Murphy's argument that economic analysis offers "the only sustained attempt at explaining how legal rules affect behavior" and should feature in any contract theory.[89] Economic analysis as a discipline is especially apt in the context of contracts entered into by artificial and commercial entities.[90] The analysis also lends itself to revisionary critiques. If it can be demonstrated that reliance damages generate greater welfare and efficiency than expectation damages, for instance, then doctrine should be revised accordingly.

Are these advantages enough to embrace wealth maximisation as the organising principle of contract law? Such a position is suggested by Schwartz and Scott when they argue that "the law should pursue the first-order goal of maximising contractual surplus when it chooses rules to regulate merchant-to-merchant contracts".[91] Note, however, the justificatory leeway allowed in their phrasing. Assessing any and all legal doctrines solely on the basis of efficiency is bound to challenge our intuitions. To the extent that the moral foundation of an intrinsic theory of contract is plausible, that foundation acts as an immediate counterpoint to wholesale instrumental analysis.

Law-and-economics scholars who never engage with intrinsic theories may attempt to defuse possible criticisms by pointing out that their analysis is agnostic with regards to the moral foundation of contract law. On this view, economic analysis and intrinsic contract theories simply have different objectives. The former aims only to identify efficiency considerations that explain past outcomes and predict future judgments,[92] whereas only the latter is

87 Craswell, 'Contract Law, Default Rules, and the Philosophy of Promising' (n 63) 496.

88 Schwartz and Scott (n 54) 541; Kraus, 'The Philosophy of Contract Law' (n 84) 694.

89 Murphy (n 26) 163.

90 Avery W. Katz, 'Economic Foundations of Contract Law' in Gregory Klass, George Letsas and Prince Saprai (eds), *Philosophical Foundations of Contract Law* (Oxford University Press 2014) 176.

91 Alan Schwartz and Robert E. Scott, 'Contract Interpretation Redux' (2010) 119 *The Yale Law Journal* 926, 928.

92 Kraus, 'The Philosophy of Contract Law' (n 84) 689.

concerned with the normative principles that explain and unify contract law. Yet this response only sidesteps the challenge. A scholar who tries to explain something in terms of reasons for it cannot be unconcerned with the justification of that thing.[93] The justification, then, is not absent but merely concealed. Moreover, assessing contract law solely on the basis of welfare maximisation suggests a degree of consequentialist thinking about welfare as the good.[94]

Further challenges relate to scope. Should a welfare and efficiency calculus include psychological and reputational costs? What of the long-term economic value of fostering a trust-based society? And will the absence of contracting strictures not favour those who are already economically privileged, thus perpetuating inequality? John Rawls argues in this vein that a free and efficient market may allow those who are already in a position of strength to capture more of the contractual advantage; the invisible hand ends up "maintaining unjustified inequalities and restrictions on fair opportunity".[95] The same concern leads Atiyah to question the traditional liberal values of free choice in contract law. Since some individuals are better equipped to exercise free choice than others, greater freedom ends up perpetuating or worsening economic inequality.[96]

Such criticisms may be disarmed by combining the instrumental justification with a broader instrumental calculus. If contract law is conceived of as part of the basic structure of society, for instance, then it can be made subject to Rawlsian principles of justice and fairness.[97] Economic analysis that tackles justice and fairness falls within the ambit of what may be termed "contract law egalitarianism".[98] This method can operate on the level of institutional design as well as particular legal outcomes. Aditi Bagchi attempts to specify how legislative choices and enforcement practices can be made more sensitive

---

93 John Gardner, 'What is Tort Law for? Part 1. The Place of Corrective Justice' (2010) 30 *Law and Philosophy* 1, 2. This kind of objection cuts both ways, however. A counterargument is that something cannot be justified until it is explained, and that economic analysis offers the only means to such pre-theoretical explanation.

94 For a discussion and critique of this perspective, see Richard Posner, 'Utilitarianism, Economics, and Legal Theory' (1979) 8 *Journal of Legal Studies* 1, 104–107.

95 John Rawls, *A Theory of Justice* (Harvard University Press 2009) 266.

96 Patrick Selim Atiyah, *The Rise and Fall of Freedom of Contract* (Clarendon Press 1979) 6.

97 Josse Klijnsma, 'Contract Law as Fairness' (2015) 28 *Ratio Juris* 68.

98 It can be argued, for instance, that mitigation is not grounded in a promissory morality but should rather be conceived of as a special application of the principle of fairness. See George Letsas and Prince Saprai, 'Mitigation, Fairness, and Contract Law' in Gregory Klass, George Letsas and Prince Saprai (eds), *Philosophical Foundations of Contract Law* (Oxford University Press 2014) 327.

to distributive effects by interpreting ambiguous terms in a way that promotes the interests of the economically disadvantaged.[99] Similarly, Todd Rakoff argues that interpretational discretion can be used to fill contractual gaps in ways that favour the weaker, less sophisticated contractual party.[100] A further option is to submit contract interpretation and enforcement to a doctrine of unconscionability, meant to protect consumers, employees, and other weak contracting parties from asymmetrical bargaining power. This approach, in effect, grants courts the power to enforce a set of negative duties not to take advantage of others in the absence of rules guaranteeing distributive justice.[101]

Yet by responding to worries about fairness, the instrumental justification of contract opens itself to new criticisms. The first is that asking courts to incorporate justice and fairness in their legal reasoning runs counter to the division of labour between judges and political institutions. Courts, critics may argue, should not be in the business of ensuring distributive aims, even if that means upholding unconscionable and unfair contracts. The second observation is that the expansion of the instrumental calculus worsens the problem of feasibility. It is hardly realistic to ask judges to chart all the possible economic consequences of their decisions. Note that this problem is not limited to contract law egalitarianism. Any instrumental justification of contract law runs into challenges of institutional competence. The third possible criticism is that by expanding its scope, the supposedly instrumental analysis seems to have taken a step closer to the idea of intrinsic moral values in contract law. This also paves the way for normative disagreement. An autonomy theorist, for instance, may argue that the doctrine of unconscionability is paternalistic and inconsistent with the power and liberty of contracting parties to make such promises as they deem necessary.[102] On a liberal account, regulating and overruling contractual clauses to serve aggregate societal needs may unfairly burden individual parties.[103] Alternatively, one may object that enforcing distributive aims is to treat contracting parties as means and not as ends in themselves.[104]

99 Aditi Bagchi, 'Distributive Justice and Contract' in Gregory Klass, George Letsas and Prince Saprai (eds), *Philosophical Foundations of Contract Law* (Oxford University Press 2014) 199.

100 Todd D. Rakoff, 'The Five Justices of Contract Law' (2016) *Wisconsin Law Review* 733, 779.

101 Bagchi (n 99) 207.

102 Fried, 'The Ambitions of Contract as Promise' (n 33) 35.

103 Thomas Nagel, *Equality and Partiality* (Oxford University Press 1995) 86.

104 Klijnsma (n 97) 78.

5. PLURALIST ACCOUNTS

A general pattern is beginning to emerge. While the proposed contract theories offer plausible accounts of particular doctrines, none of them offer complete coverage. As proponents seize on a feature of contract and hold it up as the organising principle, detractors stand ready with counterexamples. There are few signs that this back-and-forth in the literature will ever culminate in a single dominant and comprehensive account. The alternative is to ask whether there is something wrong with our starting point: the insistence that contract theories are mutually exclusive. The reality may be that competing justifications are rooted in distinct and jointly significant aspects of contract law.[105]

The paradigm pluralist account combines intrinsic and instrumental perspectives. For law-and-economics scholars, pluralism could take the form of a methodological caveat: the analysis, so the argument would go, only provides a set of empirical results to be held up against a yet-to-be-determined normative standard. Such pluralism would seem to address some of the more notable vulnerabilities of a purely instrumental analysis. It may also boost explanatory power. One example is the modest but growing literature examining how contracting parties are motivated by reputational and psychological costs as well as internalised norms.[106]

Aside from this methodological caveat, scholars may also take the more active approach of combining different justificatory perspectives. Because both intrinsic and instrumental theories are concerned with the project of making rules from the *ex ante* perspective of parties, such pluralist accounts have the potential to demonstrate considerable overlap.[107] Different contract theories may, once their implications are fully unpacked, converge on similar doctrinal conclusions.[108] The efficient breach hypothesis, for instance, may be reconceived in order to be rendered compatible with promissory morality.[109] In the words of Gregory Klass, "one need not be a promise theorist to think that a clear understanding of the morality of promising is likely to cast new light on the law of contract".[110] Or we could adopt a convergence thesis stating that contract law simultaneously promotes both autonomy and social welfare.[111]

---

105 The scholarly bent towards mutual exclusivity is common within legal theory; see, e.g., Leif Wenar, 'Rights and What We Owe to Each Other' (2013) 10 *Journal of Moral Philosophy* 375, 378.

106 Kraus, 'The correspondence of contract and promise' (n 9) 1637.

107 Fried, 'The Ambitions of Contract as Promise' (n 33) 41.

108 Ibid; Kraus, 'The Philosophy of Contract Law' (n 84) 688.

109 Kraus, 'The correspondence of contract and promise' (n 9) 1638.

110 Klass, 'Introduction to Philosophical Foundations of Contract Law' (n 29) 8.

111 Kraus, 'The Philosophy of Contract Law' (n 84) 688.

Such joint accounts are vulnerable, however, to the same challenge faced by pluralist normative theories generally: they must still explain how their explanations are defensible in the absence of a (singular) principle for ranking the different values invoked.[112] Without any such unified ranking principle, there seems to be no way of making final determinations when values and commitments collide.

6. METHODOLOGICAL FINDINGS

The chapter has charted intrinsic and instrumental theories, their conceptual roots, and their ability to explain, justify, and challenge legal doctrines. Fried's promise-based and Scanlon's harm-avoidance theories both support a view that the function of contract law is duty-imposing. Barnett's consent-based account is oriented towards the power-conferring function of contract law, as is, arguably, Raz's account of promises as tools for enhancing moral lives. Penner's relational account stresses the interests contained within the joint venture that contracting parties enter into. All these candidate theories mesh with certain contract doctrines while struggling to accommodate others.

For the practically minded scholar, there is a recurring question here: what is the relationship supposed to be between contract theory and doctrinal analysis? This question drives much of the tension between intrinsic and instrumental theories. Intrinsic theorists adopt a top-down approach, examining contract doctrines through the lens of an overarching normative theory, while economic analysts are more concerned with explaining patterns in legal outcomes. Continuing disagreement may be as much a function of different objectives as of different conceptions of contract. If our goal is to explain particular judicial and legislative outcomes, economic analysis may be more informative. If our goal is to explain the desired endpoint and overall evolution of legal doctrine, however, economic analysis needs to be combined with some form of normative account (even if that account is welfare maximization).

A default methodological stance for a contract scholar is to use conflicts between theory and practice either as a basis for revisionist critique of the law or as proof that the theory is flawed. On the latter approach, the merits and demerits of a contract theory are judged according to its extensional fit––how much of contract doctrine it is able to accommodate and explain. There are good reasons, however, to adopt a more open methodological stance. The body of contract law has evolved—and continues to evolve—through a complex interaction between courts, legislators, parties, and practitioners. We must acknowledge not only that these participants can have diverging priorities and

112 Ibid.

reasoning processes, but also that decisions made at different points in time are subject to shifts in priorities and reasoning. There are also limits on how far we can go in demanding that legislators and judges operate on the basis of a deliberate and coherent account of contract law.[113] In light of all these factors, the divergence of theory and doctrine seems unavoidable.

How, then, do we reconcile the absence of an all-encompassing theory of contract with the claim that theorising remains worthwhile? For one, the lack of perfect correspondence does not necessarily have to be taken as a lasting indictment. A theorist faced with counterexamples could argue that doctrine is still informed by underlying moral principles, even if practical considerations sometimes require other solutions. Or, perhaps less convincingly, they could argue that the arc of development still bends towards their account of contractual morality. The more open methodological response is that the lack of a one-size-fits-all theory of contract does not take away the value of being able to adopt different normative perspectives. Promise theory may struggle to account for objective standards of interpretation and contractual gaps, but it is exceedingly well placed to highlight the interests of the promisee. Positing harm-avoidance as the function of contract law may offer little concrete guidance but remains a helpful lens through which to evaluate remedial liabilities. Economic analysis turns out, upon closer examination, to benefit from an interplay with intrinsic accounts of contractual morality.

Throughout, competing theories can be categorised and contrasted using conceptual tools. Scholars oriented towards the interests of the promisee can look to duty-imposing justifications of contract doctrines. Those who wish to make observations from the vantage point of personal autonomy and liberalism may look to the various theories focused on the power-conferring aspects of contract law. Together, conceptual and normative toolsets offer so many options, and are so tightly woven into the fabric of contract theory that they can never be fully severed from doctrinal research.

113 Grant Huscroft, Bradley W. Miller and Gregoire Webber, *Proportionality and the Rule of Law: Rights, Justification, Reasoning* (Cambridge University Press 2014) 138.

PART II

External perspectives

5. Historical approaches to contract law

Victoria Barnes and Sally Wheeler

INTRODUCTION

This chapter examines the way history is and can be deployed in the study of contract law. One approach is to use history to explain or illuminate in some way the presence of a doctrine, rule or legal issue in current law. Scholars might look to a key piece of legislation or code provision, such as the Sales of Goods Act 1893 for implied terms, or to landmark cases which developed the law in some way, for example, *Carlill v Carbolic Smoke Ball Company*[1] on offer and acceptance; or by creating new law, causing a new interpretation of existing case law or code provisions,[2] or prompting law reform. Another approach is to look not at the development of law itself but rather at the way contemporary 'users' of law such as businesses, financiers, bankers and private individuals acted in relation to particular legal phenomena; did it satisfy their needs or was there a culture of avoidance, for example? These inquiries might take the form of literary inquiry or quantitative social science studies of contracts and their contents. Studies in this genre would find their material by tracking developments in economic, cultural or social history. The chapter does not suggest that one approach is preferable to another. It suggests that each approach has its own inherent strengths and weaknesses and should be used with an appreciation of those biases in a way that is appropriate and suited to the research question. This chapter adds further thoughts on historical sources, where they might be found, where they are available and how they

---

1 [1892] EWCA Civ 1.

2 Stefan Vogenauer, 'The Avant-project de réforme: An Overview' in John Cartwright, Stefan Vogenauer and Simon Whittaker (eds), *Reforming the French Law of Obligations, Comparative Reflections on the Avant-project de Réforme du Droit des Obligations de la Prescription* (Hart Publishing 2009) 3.

might be used to facilitate these enquiries. It introduces what is often referred to as the manuscript tradition and favoured use of archival sources.[3]

1. DISCIPLINARY AGENDAS

Historical approaches to research in contract law are numerous, but all must be positioned somewhere within the scope of the two disciplines. Neither law nor history, as disciplines or fields of study, is fixed; both enjoy a broad range of methods, approaches, and aims that have changed and evolved over time. This leads to the development of disciplinary agendas and divisions within disciplines. These divisions are endless and somewhat meaningless; they are as much about the audience as about methods, style, and aim. It is both interesting and informative to identify an author's intellectual hinterland, where his, her, or their training has taken place and what are their aims.[4] Yet, these discussions are often used as mechanisms to discount scholarship, to silo it and brand it as 'other' and lesser. Statements about the relative strength of one approach over another often say very little about the strengths (and weaknesses) of individual approaches. They say more about historic power structures (closed or otherwise insular), networking, egocentric and unnecessary battlegrounds, and the general whims of solitary and unsociable intellectuals. This is reflected in the types of studies that have been undertaken in relation to contract law. Labels have emerged to differentiate these studies. They act as guides to their genealogical roots, their suggested audiences, and their purposes. These labels are important within the Academy as they indicate the field to which a scholar and their research belongs.[5] As we all know, 'field' determines so much; *inter alia* academic employment opportunities, career progression, and grant funding possibilities.

1.1 Legal History

The rhetoric in legal history has been to question whether legal history is law, history, or something separate from both. British legal historians A.D.E. Lewis and Michael Lobban have sought to segment this scholarship by audience. This

3 See David J. Seipp, 'The Law's Many Bodies, and the Manuscript Tradition in English Legal History' (2004) 25 *The Journal of Legal History* 74.

4 See Edward Hallett Carr, *What Is History?* (2nd edn, Pelican Books 1964).

5 Some thirty years or so ago, the late A.W.B. Simpson, one of the finest legal historians of the post-war era, commented that it was important to 'place clear labels on your work, so that everyone knows what is going on, and the appropriate brownie points can be accumulated', see A.W.B. Simpson 'Legal Iconoclasts and Legal Ideals' (1990) 58 *University of Cincinnati Law Review* 819, 822 n11.

is a useful and sensible mode of division which avoids prolonged entanglement with the definitional debates of either law or history. They consider those who write for legal scholars as 'internal' and those who write for historians and other groups as 'external'.[6] Warren Swain, specifically writing on the history of contract law, redraws this definition by moving the internal and external definitions away from audience and towards the perspective brought to bear on source material. For Swain, 'internal legal history' involves reading from the perspective of those connected to the legal process – lawyers, judges, contemporary textbook writers, and commentators. The 'external' legal perspective arises for him when what is offered is an account from 'outside the legal system', created by drawing on sources based in social and economic history.[7] In his chapter in *The Oxford Handbook of Legal History*, Joshua Getzler has described what Lobban and Lewis refer to as 'internal' legal history as 'doctrinal' legal history.[8] Doctrinal legal history can be split further into two categories. In the first, doctrine is seen as a product of the contemporary social and economic forces that surround it. Patrick Atiyah's magnum opus, *The Rise and Fall of Freedom of Contract*,[9] falls into this category. 'Social' in this context frequently embraces the intellectual mood of the time, and so what results is a legal history that is as concerned with the influence of Adam Smith[10] as it is with business practice and custom. The second category is narrower in scope. It eschews perspectives broader than judicial practice. This is predicated on the idea that judges, in a classic conservative common law sense, do not make doctrine through innovation but instead discover it and then develop it.[11] As Hamburger explains, the legal historian in this instance requires knowledge of the 'external forces', i.e. social and economic developments surrounding

[6] For more on the methodological difficulties in internal legal history, see Andrew Lewis and Michael Lobban (eds), *Law and History* (Oxford University Press 2004) 1–32.

[7] Warren Swain, *The Law of Contract 1670–1870* (Cambridge University Press 2015).

[8] Joshua Getzler, 'Legal History as Doctrinal History' in Markus D. Dubber and Christopher Tomlins (eds), *The Oxford Handbook of Legal History* (Oxford University Press 2018).

[9] Patrick Selim Atiyah, *The Rise and Fall of Contract* (Oxford University Press 1979).

[10] Adam Smith, *The Wealth of Nations* (Printed for W. Strahan and T. Cadell, 1776).

[11] A.W.B. Simpson, 'Innovation in Nineteenth Century Contract Law' (1975) 91 LQR 247.

legal doctrine, but explains its development by reference to an 'internal' debate only.[12]

In the UK, the last 30 years or so have seen socio-legal studies rise to become the dominant paradigm for legal research,[13] including legal history. Before this, despite some excellent studies,[14] there was a risk that the work of the legal historian would be seen not as scholarship in its own right but as providing a contextual background for doctrinal study. A strength of historical inquiry situated within socio-legal studies is that it is possible from a methodological standpoint to combine current qualitative sources with historical sources to produce an account. Mitu Gulati and Robert Scott, in their search to understand the function of *pari passu* clauses in cross-border sovereign debt contracts, combine extensive historical analysis of the origin and use of these contracts between 1823 and 2011 with interviews with lawyers drafting those contracts in the moment.[15] Bernstein uses historical accounts of mercantile behaviour to examine whether the first drafters of the Uniform Commercial Code (UCC), principally Karl Llewellyn in the 1940s, really did capture accurately the way in which businessmen and business institutions conducted business and construed contracts and trade usages. Alongside a contemporary empirical study of business practices, she concluded that the very contextualised adjudicative architecture of the UCC was never how contracting parties saw themselves behaving and, in a contemporary sense, did not reflect what a business community wanted if it resorted to courtroom litigation.[16]

Legal history has long been fertile ground for scholars who see themselves as part of the Critical Legal Studies movement, particularly in the area of contract law,[17] as it allows the construction of a narrative about how and why

---

12 Philip A. Hamburger, 'The Development of the Nineteenth-Century Consensus Theory of Contract' (1989) 7 *Law and History Review* 241, 244.

13 Hilary Sommerlad, 'Developments in Socio-legal Studies: Subjects and Methodologies – the Anglo-Saxon Model' (2015) 36 *Recht der Werkelijkheid* 55, 60.

14 Ferguson's study of the adoption into English law of a number of commercial law codes in the area of business partnerships, the sale of goods, bills of exchange and marine insurance is one such example. Robert B. Ferguson, 'Legal Ideology and Commercial Interests: The Social Origins of the Commercial Law Codes' (1977) 4 *British Journal of Law and Society* 18.

15 Mitu Gulati and Robert E. Scott, *The Three and a Half Minute Transaction: Boilerplate and the Limits of Contract Design* (University of Chicago Press 2013).

16 Lisa Bernstein, 'Merchant Law in a Modern Economy' in Gregory Klass, George Letsas and Prince Saprai (eds), *Philosophical Foundations of Contract Law* (Oxford University Press 2014) 238.

17 The most accessible account of Critical Legal Studies and its project remains Alan Hunt's 'The Theory of Critical Legal Studies' (1986) 6 OJLS 1.

the individualist market-based order emerged and the co-option of law to its service. Horwitz's work provides an excellent example of this. His thesis was, in very simple terms, that judges, as the United States had begun to establish its own legal system, had worked in tort and property law as well as in contract law to establish the supremacy of business interests (in the form of entrepreneurs) over the interests of consumers, workers, and farmers. Once this supremacy was established, it worked to prevent any claims of redistribution.[18] Feminist theory has much in common with critical legal studies. Both dispute, for example, the reification of the market, the accuracy of the public-private divide and the suppression of 'voice' and 'story' for some groups. For feminist theory, debunking the idea of the masculine public realm in the form of the market and the feminine domain of the private sphere in the form of the home is very important. Amy Dru Stanley's work demonstrates the artificiality of these boundaries through her study of contract in the context of marriage, maintaining a home, and waged labour. She explores the connections and tensions between these, using extensively the archives of the Freedman's Bureau, and posits that although waged labour, as opposed to slavery, allowed a male breadwinner to keep a dependent wife who, in turn, in the post-Abolition US, was able to freely enter into a marriage contract, both marriage and waged labour could be seen as undermining the metaphor of contract as freedom. Women had moved from slavery into marriage where their husbands could contract for them, claim their wages, and take their property as their own.[19]

1.2 Law and History

Elsewhere, especially in the United States, where research in law is also produced by those sitting outside the organisational structure of the law school (unlike the UK, the EU, and Australia),[20] the more traditional style of scholarship in legal history explained above is dismissed as 'law school

[18] Morton J. Horwitz, *The Transformation of American Law 1780–1860* (Harvard University Press 1977). Interestingly, Horwitz draw these conclusions about the social and economic consequences of judicial activity from research based only on treatises and decided cases.

[19] Amy Dru Stanley, *From Bondage to Contract: Wage Labor, Marriage, and the Market in the Age of Slave Emancipation* (Cambridge University Press 1998).

[20] The Nuffield Inquiry on Empirical Legal Research offers a series of insights as to why legal scholarship in the UK, unlike the US, is (with a few singular exceptions) conducted from within the Law School. See Hazel Genn, Martin Partington and Sally Wheeler, 'Law in the Real World: Improving Our Understanding of How Law Works. Final Report and Recommendations' (The Nuffield Foundation 2006) 31, 33.

historiography' and 'law office history'.[21] The flagship American legal history journal is called *Law and History Review*. The title indicates a positive shift towards history. There is a general consensus among the American academic community not to regard legal history as a *sui generis* field. Academics based in history faculties and those who see history as opposed to law as their parent discipline would generally be reluctant to label themselves as 'legal historians' for fear of their work being seen as exclusive, narrow, or internally focused. The use of the 'and' in the label 'law and history' suggests that we are not looking at the history of a particular legal phenomenon from the perspective of legal development or even at an interdisciplinary inquiry, but rather at a historically based analysis of what legal structures can tell us about larger social and economic relations. The disciplines of law and history are standing at a respectful distance from each other.[22]

An exemplar account in this vein can be found in the work of Casey Marina Lurtz on the adoption of Mexico's Civil Codes into the lifeworld of small farmers, small merchants, and tradesmen.[23] Lurtz's research draws on registers of contractual debts from 1870 to 1910 found in the archive of a small town in southern Mexico. It is not clear who maintained these registers or why they existed. There is no reference to any Code provision or any judicial activity or intervention. The entries are, as Lurtz explains, traces of everyday activity. It is unlikely that they would be an appropriate starting point for a legal historian as there is insufficient material to describe or analyse evolving legal developments. For Lurtz, however, as a historian of Latin America, they are evidence of a credit market supported by evolving business norms and operating outside elite structures, which drew for its legitimacy on knowledge of recently enacted Civil Codes designed to liberalise fiscal policy.

1.3 Comparative Law, History and Society

With its emphasis on the appropriateness and usefulness of legal transplants,[24] comparative scholarship in legal history addresses empirical questions about legal rules and their suitability for different societies. If we ask where English

---

21 Howard Schweber, 'Lochner v. New York and the Challenge of Legal Historiography' (2014) 39 *Law & Social Inquiry* 242, 246–247.

22 Sally Wheeler, 'Socio-Legal Studies in 2020' (2020) 47 *Journal of Law and Society* S209, 216.

23 Casey Lurtz, 'Codifying Credit: Everyday Contracting and the Spread of the Civil Code in Nineteenth-Century Mexico' (2021) 39 *Law and History Review* 97.

24 The relevant debates are summarised in Mindy Chen-Wishart, 'Legal Transplant and Undue Influence: Lost in Translation or a Working Misunderstanding' (2013) 62 *International & Comparative Law Quarterly* 1, 2.

and US contract law come from, given its relative absence as a distinct body of law in Blackstone's Commentaries, the answer is to be found in translations and citations of the work of Pothier, resulting in the transplant of numerous ideas from civil law into common law[25] and the impact of German theoretical work on US contract law.[26] As Zimmermann explains—through many examples—a rule in a European country code is frequently derived from interaction with Roman law, and a common law rule often comes down one derivation further from a jurist commenting on that Code.[27] The significance of comparative legal history for the academy in an era where there is cross-pollination of cultures, political structures, and markets can be seen in the establishment in 2013 of a journal, *Comparative Legal History*. Scholars working in this area have moved beyond the purely functional idea of comparing solutions to common problems across different traditions[28] to focus on searching for a common core, potentially as a modern replacement for Roman law, ideas of harmonisation, and uniform law-making.[29]

These approaches to comparative legal history draw heavily on contract law as the subject of their inquiry. There have been at least two studies of significance in searching for a common core of contract: the work of Schlesinger on formation, and the more recent Trento project. Both harmonisation and unification have real-world commercial significance as well as being intellectual projects. Obvious examples, one from a widely ratified treaty of the UN and the other from soft law, are the Convention on the International Sale of Goods (UN) and the UNIDROIT Principles of International Commercial Contracts. It is not hard to see why contract is a popular site for exploring these ideas. In Roman law, contracts were the pre-eminent form of private law, which was

---

[25] Joseph Perillo, 'Robert J Pothier's Influence on the Common Law of Contract' (2005) 11 *Texas Wesleyan Law Review* 267.

[26] Stefan Riesenfeld, 'The Impact of German Legal Ideas and Institutions on Legal Thought and Institutions in the United States' in Mathias Reimann (ed.), *The Reception of Continental Ideas in the Common Law World 1820–1920* (Dunker and Humbolt 1993) 89.

[27] Reinhard Zimmermann, *The Law of Obligations: Roman Foundations of the Civilian Tradition* (Oxford University Press 1996).

[28] Dmitry Poldnikov, 'The Functional Method to Study the General Part of Contract Law in Historical Perspective: Pro Et Contra' (2018) 9 *European Journal of Legal History* 92.

[29] Jürgen Basedow, in a similar way to Loban and Lewis (see n. 6), segments the audience for Comparative Law into 'clients'. He identifies, inter alia, professional legal audiences, unification agencies, legal education and legislatures as potential clients. This applies equally well to contract law research in a comparative historical perspective. See Jürgen Basedow, 'Comparative Law and its Clients' (2014) 62 *American Journal of Comparative Law* 821, 837f.

itself the most important discrete legal area. This pre-eminence has transferred to both civil law and common law. Despite key differences between the two traditions, for example, the focus on agreement in common law versus the focus on promise in civil law, there are also common questions around areas such as formation and enforcement. Added to this is the economic significance of contract law in both domestic and international legal contexts.[30]

Contract law has also attracted historical comparative attention from scholars working on legal systems that are not those of the United Kingdom, the United States, or Continental Europe. The 'Asian Contract Law' movement has gathered momentum in the last 15 years or so and can be showcased through two large projects. One is the harmonisation initiative of the Principles of Asian Contract Law[31] and the other is the Studies in the Contract Laws of Asia.[32] In the case of the latter, historical exploration of the origins and descent of particular concepts and rules looms large. Contract law in the jurisdictions that form the project is the embodiment of colonial imposition, with source countries spread across those of the civil law codes: France, Germany, and the Netherlands, as well as the English common law. Some jurisdictions are overtly mixed systems drawing on both civil law and common law. Onto this inheritance national legal cultures have also been grafted transplants from powerful political traditions such as those found in Japan and China. Examining how contract law has developed in these jurisdictions tells us much about how societies create a legal system that reflects their values from an essentially foreign beginning. We can see similar questions about the construction of societies and the choices that are made about the form of laws, legal processes, and concepts being asked by the Global History movement.[33]

---

30 E. Allan Farnsworth, 'Comparative Contract Law' in Mathias Reimann and Reinhard Zimmermann (eds), *The Oxford Handbook of Comparative Law* (Oxford University Press 2006) 899.

31 Aleksander Grebieniow, 'Principles of Asian Contract Law at the Crossroads of Standardization and Legal Pluralism' (2021) 10 *Asian Journal of Law and Society* 1.

32 This is a proposed 6-volume set of books published by Oxford University Press. As of 5 December 2023, four volumes have been published: Mindy Chen-Wishart, Alexander Loke and Burton Ong (eds), *Remedies for Breach of Contract* (Oxford University Press 2016); Mindy Chen-Wishart, Alexander Loke and Stefan Vogenauer (eds), *Formation and Third Party Beneficiaries* (Oxford University Press 2018); Mindy Chen-Wishart and Stefan Vogenauer (eds), *Contents of Contracts and Unfair Terms* (Oxford University Press 2020); Mindy Chen-Wishart, Hiroo Sono and Stefan Vogenauer (eds), *Invalidity* (Oxford University Press 2022).

33 Thomas Duve, 'Global Legal History: A Methodological Approach' *Oxford Handbook Topics in Law* (online edn, Oxford Academic, 2 May 2016), <https://

2. APPROACHES

2.1 Tracing the History of Law

One approach is to write a history of contract law to explain or shed light on a doctrine, rule, or legal issue in the present. This involves unpicking legal change as it occurred. The unit of analysis is law, and the focus is on explaining the law itself by showing how it changed or who changed it. The point that is implicit in this scholarship is that the historical context informed the actions of those in the past, but this information is now lost to those in the present. It has either been forgotten or is not recorded in legal sources, which focus only on the technical aspects of law-making. For example, words such as 'misrepresentation' have a particular meaning in legal discourse today, but that meaning was not always the same in the past. Scholars might look to landmark cases which developed the law in some way, like *Carlill v Carbolic Smoke Ball Company* on offer and acceptance,[34] or by creating new law or by prompting law reform. Others look to show how historical actors, for example Powell, the author of the first treatise on contract law, or Anson, the author of one of the first widely used textbooks, developed legal principles and legal theory.[35] Another approach is to look at how, in colonial contexts, judges and academics combined to 'create' law that reflected both the law of the occupying power and indigenous law. Swain's work on India provides a good example of this, where the result of these endeavours was legislation that codified common law and incorporated some civil law thinking drawn inevitably from Pothier and some very limited pre-colonisation jurisprudence.[36]

In these efforts to study leading legal authorities or explain legal change, the method is sometimes described as being placed 'in context'. Catharine MacMillan's paper on *Grand Trunk Railway Company of Canada v Robinson* (1915) is a good example.[37] 'Context', she says, 'is important in the development of the common law. Each case is a precedent, but each case is best

---

doi.org/10.1093/oxfordhb/9780199935352.013.25>, accessed 22 July 2023; Shaunnagh Dorsett, *Juridical Encounters: Maori and the Colonial Courts, 1840–1852* (Auckland University Press 2017).

[34] A. W. B. Simpson, 'Quackery and Contract Law: The Case of the Carbolic Smoke Ball' (1985) 14 *The Journal of Legal Studies* 345.

[35] James Goudkamp and Donal Nolan (eds), *Scholars of Contract Law* (Hart Publishing 2022).

[36] Warren Swain, 'Contract Codification and the English: Some Observations from the Indian Contract Act 1872' in James Devenney and Mel Kenny (eds), *The Transformation of European Private Law* (Cambridge University Press 2013) 172.

[37] [1915] UKPC 21.

understood in the context in which it arose'.[38] Context is also important for civil law. The underpinning philosophy is one of adapting to change, so context might be social or economic change which has created the case for introducing a particular rule or abandoning another. Zimmerman traces the history of 'fitness for purpose' as a concept in sales of goods cases under the German Civil Code (BGB s.434) from Roman law where it was used to deal specifically with sales of cattle and slaves through the *ius commune* to the BGB where it became a general remedy for those goods that can be said to have a defined or delineated purpose, in part because we no longer sell people.[39] Studies like these deepen our understanding of the law by encouraging us to think about whether the historical context for a rule is still relevant or not. If it is not, then we might advocate for it to be reshaped.

Cases and developments in legal rules can be the vehicle for different contexts and potentially competing contexts. The 'postal rule' is taught as a doctrinal rule in English Law (although it is less well accepted in the US and Australia, so can hardly be described as a common law rule) and dictates that when an offer is accepted by post, that acceptance becomes valid upon posting, unlike the revocation of an offer which is valid only upon receipt. Peter Goodrich considers *Adams v Lindsell* to be a case that comes directly from the ecclesiastical rules governing spousal contracts and promises to marry.[40] Mutuality was required in this instance by the Ecclesiastical Courts much earlier than the common law required it in executory contracts. Regard was extended for the reliance interest of the usually female offeree because of the weight of cultural expectations upon her.[41] Simon Gardiner sees *Adams v Lindsell* as the first, albeit rather limited, expression of the communication rule we now know as the 'postal rule'. He identifies the gradual exposition of this rule in a line of cases running from *Adams* as being grafted into the establishment of the modern Post Office and paid-for postage stamps.[42] Any idea

38 Catharine MacMillan, 'The Mystery of Privity: Grand Trunk Railway Company of Canada v Robinson (1915)' (2015) 65 *University of Toronto Law Journal* 1.

39 Zimmerman (n 27) 327.

40 *Adams and Others v Lindsell and Others* (1818) 1 Barn & Ald 681.

41 Peter Goodrich, 'The Posthumous Life of the Postal Rule: Requiem and Revival of *Adams* v *Lindsell*' in Linda Mulcahy and Sally Wheeler (eds), *Feminist Perspectives on Contract Law* (Glasshouse Press 2005) 75.

42 Simon Gardner, 'Trashing with Trollope: A Deconstruction of the Postal Rules in Contract' (1992) 12 OJLS 170, 178–184.

that this rule on acceptance and communication is anachronistic in the 21st century is negated by the current debates around smart contract formation.[43]

Some studies that do not use contextualisation as a tool prefer periodisation. There are, of course, different ways of using periodisation. If we compare the work of Warren Swain, for example, with that of Morton Horwitz,[44] we can see that they both offer a history of a similar period in the development of contract law, but that is where any commonality ends. Horwitz offers a grand sweeping narrative in which the factors he chooses as relevant are placed together to offer a master plan of development. For Swain, who in contrast offers a more doctrinally based theory of development – a history of legal ideas, if you like – the Horwitz approach does not deal adequately with the idea that contract law emerged at the end of the 19th century in a form that we, as lawyers, recognise even now as a 'product of numerous factors' which often 'pull[ed] in different directions'.[45] Periodisation as history is subject to the criticism that, in whatever form it is used, it is an essentialist approach that seeks to order and consolidate different voices and experiences into 'a critical utopia',[46] which also means ignoring some voices. There are links here to the political positions of feminist legal history and critical legal history, although, as we can see from Horwitz's work, it is often impossible to avoid periodisation as a measure that defines scope. Moving away from periodisation, Sandberg advocates using a counterfactual model; asking what would have happened had a particular legal development not occurred or had occurred differently.[47] He ties this to his idea of 'subversive' legal history, which encourages us to present neat and linear stories for the purpose of then exposing them as mythical.

There are a small number of studies that trace the roots of modern-day legislation. Sean Thomas's study of the United Kingdom's Sale of Goods Act 1893 provides an excellent history of implied terms and contractual remedies.[48]

---

43 Sally Wheeler, 'The Possibilities of IF-THEN-WHEN' in Mark Findlay, Jolyon Ford, Josephine Seah and Dilan Thampapillai (eds), *Regulatory Insights in Artificial Intelligence* (Edward Elgar 2022) 162.

44 Morton Horwitz, 'The Historical Foundations of Modern Contract Law' (1973–1974) 87 *Harvard Law Review* 917.

45 Warren Swain, *The Law of Contract 1670–1870* (Cambridge University Press 2015) 8.

46 Jeanne Boydston, 'Gender as a Question of Historical Analysis' (2008) 20 *Gender and History* 558.

47 Russell Sandberg, *Subversive Legal History* (Routledge 2021) 136f.

48 Sean Thomas, 'The Development of the Implied Terms on Quantity in the Law of Sale of Goods' (2014) 35 *The Journal of Legal History* 281. See also Ingeborg Paulus, *The Search for Pure Food: A Sociology of Legislation in Britain* (Martin Robertson 1974).

The 1893 Act is no longer in force in the United Kingdom because it has been updated by the Sale of Goods Act 1979, and in part replaced by the Consumer Rights Act 2015. Yet, the structure of the 1893 legislation remains relevant in the United Kingdom today, even if the substance of the law has changed. The Sale of Goods Act 1893 is a prominent example of a serious piece of legislative drafting, but it is far from a complete code in the European sense.[49] Through the auspices of the British Empire, the Sale of Goods Act 1893 became part of the law of other colonial jurisdictions. For many of the jurisdictions in the former British Empire, the 1893 Act is still part of the fibre of contract law as the relevant legislation has not been significantly updated.[50] In all of the Canadian provinces, for example, *pace* Quebec, the current sales of goods legislation is the 1893 Act with only minor modifications aside from the impact of consumer protection laws. It is one of many legal authorities which are essential for any student of contract or commercial law in the United Kingdom and for many common law jurisdictions.

2.2 Contract Law in Historical Societies

A rather different way to write a legal history of contracts is not to trace the development of doctrine or the body of law we call contract, but to explain instead how societies, such as in inter alia citizens, enterprises, traders, other commercial actors, and the state (local and national), interpreted or otherwise used the law at a particular point in time or in a particular period of history. The relevance of work like this is that it gives us a set of tools with which to understand and critique debates or propositions in contemporary society. Much is made within current political agendas in the global north of the benefits of a market society in which 'contract' is used as the leitmotif to explain the relationship between citizens and employment; waged labour is a guarantee of freedom bestowing choices that are not available to the unemployed (and historically those enslaved), thus it is a status to be embraced. Hartog's work on pre-Civil War slavery in the northern states of the US demonstrates that the links between waged labour, the market and slavery are far from the clear status categories we are presented with.[51] These observations are useful in critiquing current political discourse.

---

49 Christine Riefa, 'Codification: The Future of English Consumer Law?' (2015) 4 *Journal of European Consumer and Market Law* 12, 14.

50 Fidelma White, 'Sale of Goods Law Reform: An Irish Perspective' (2013) 42 *Common Law World Review* 172, 173–175.

51 Hendrick Hartog, *The Trouble with Minna: A Case of Slavery and Emancipation in the Antebellum North* (University of North Carolina Press 2018).

Scholarship has always had a political dimension because people who write it also have political opinions. In academic scholarship, personal political opinions are often hidden behind seemingly neutral explanations and identifications of ideology. The past is influenced by the present, for the author is situated in the present and his, her or their experience bears some relevance to their study. It is a truism that history is determined by *the questions that we ask* and *the reasons why we ask them*. Goodrich offers us a study of contracts of love adjudicated upon by institutions such as the High Court of Love, the Court of the Reformer General of Abuses of Love, the Court of the Countess of Champagne and the High Court of Flowers. There is no discussion of periodisation here. The events that Goodrich describes took place between 1150 and 1650 in the Royal Palaces of the French Kingdoms and eventually France itself, regarded in this period as the most civilised and culturally sophisticated of the monarchical regimes. We are not offered a description of how these courts worked as institutions in terms of developing the law but are rather invited to think about how emotions such as love and desire might fit into contemporary contract thought and interpretation.[52] We might see this as an expression of anti-market sentiment. Another example is the work of Anat Rosenberg on Victorian novels and their representation of the marriage contract.[53] She uses her historical analysis to suggest that there is an alternative to the market society of the 21st century which revolves around a 'relational liberalism'.

For much of the 18th and 19th centuries, contract law was the province of merchants – a self-regulating group who sought to be legally autonomous. They frequently found their own separate mechanisms for establishing the contents of trading terms and dispute resolution.[54] Exploring the behaviour of these merchants offers insight into the way society operated and the role that contracts played in regulating relationships. Many of the mechanisms they adopted then found their way into established principles of contract law. Ross Cranston's examination of the London and Liverpool commodity markets in the 19th and early 20th centuries explains how practices around market governance, settlement, and arbitration evolved in the shadow of contract law mechanisms. Cranston departs from previous studies in seeing courts as being

52 Peter Goodrich, *The Laws of Love: A Brief Historical and Practical Manual* (Palgrave Macmillan 2007) 65–81.

53 Anat Rosenberg, *Liberalizing Contracts: Nineteenth Century Promises through Literature, Law and History* (Routledge 2017).

54 Derek Roebuck, Francis Calvert Boorman and Rhiannon Markless, *English Arbitration and Mediation in the Long Eighteenth Century* (Holo Books The Arbitration Press 2019).

neither overt supporters[55] nor inflexible hinderers of commercial and contract practice development.[56] The courts, in his view, were open to endorsing and adopting trading community practices in areas such as set-off and novation. In other areas, such as agency and brokerage, where the courts threatened to upset established market trading methods,[57] the relevant trade associations developed standard form contracts to avoid triggering the newly established rules. In this way, the courts operated as the steerers of commercial practice rather than overt regulators.[58] The approach of the courts is similar today. In two recent decisions concerning arbitrator appointments, the judgments reflected support for the rules of industry arbitration bodies and a general pro-arbitration stance.[59] In a different geographical space, Bruce Kercher offers us a rich study of the first colonial settlement of New South Wales and the creation of a system of contract law that was, at one and the same time, both paternalistic in that it favoured supporting a standard of fairness in relation to contracts for the sale and delivery of goods and commercially aware in that it was pro-trade. There was a severe shortage of sterling and a large fluctuation in commodity prices. The NSW Court of Civil Jurisdiction developed a system fordealing with promissory notes that reflected community norms rather than the prevailing rules of equity. The response to commodity shortages and consequent price fluctuations was the recognition of the appropriateness of expectation damages, rather than specific performance, some years before this was a remedy available to parties litigating in London. Kercher notes that at the time of his writing in 1991, New South Wales had no less than five pieces of legislation, the remit of which was to deal with harsh, unfair, or unconscionable contracts, reflecting the inheritance of such practices from its first colonial judges.[60]

---

55 Roy Goode, 'The Concept and Implications of a Market in Commercial Law' (1990) 24 *Israel Law Review* 185.

56 Hugh Collins, *Regulating Contracts* (Oxford University Press 1999).

57 *Robinson v Mollett* (1875) LR 7, HL 802. John Mollett was a prominent London tallow broker. He was used to being involved in legal process, if not as defendant or plaintiff, acting as he did as petitioning creditor and/or official assignee in numerous bankruptcies of fellow tallow brokers during the middle decades of the 19th century, e.g. *ex parte Gull*, Evening Mail, Wednesday, July 14, 1852.

58 Ross Cranston, *Making Commercial Law through Practice 1830–1970* (Cambridge University Press 2021).

59 See the judgments of the English High Court and the UK Supreme Court respectively in *Aldcroft v The International Cotton Association Limited* [2017] EWHC 642 (Comm) and *Halliburton v Chubb* [2020] UKSC 48.

60 Bruce Kercher, 'Commerce and the Development of Contract Law in Early New South Wales' (1991) 9 *Law and History Review* 269, 286. See also Bruce

3. SOURCES

There is a wide diversity of sources used in legal history and law and history. This section examines the range of historical sources, their relative value, and where to find them. The obvious primary legal sources are used, such as law reports, legislation, national, and local government records. As the pieces drawn on in this chapter indicate, material can be found in literary works, newspapers, trade journals, the records of trade associations, and the personal papers of prominent individuals. The novelty of some studies lies in their use of unique or never-before-used historical sources. This is all well and good as a justification for the value of a study. All historical study is an interpretation of the past. That is to say, it is usually thought to have very little in the way of scientific merit and, much like law, to be a branch of the arts and the humanities. As dissenting judgments and differing legal opinions are so frequently given in common law jurisdictions, even the most traditional legal historian must accept that the same source, document, or jurisprudence can be read in several different ways. The same body of jurisprudence can be understood to give different rules.[61] It is even more important, perhaps, to remember this in areas like Roman law where it is unlikely that further sources will be discovered and added to the existing canon.[62] This point about multiple interpretations is prompted by postmodernism in history rather than judicial disagreement, and it has not been accepted so well. Some traditionalists consider that there is only one way to interpret a source.[63] Those seeking to 'read against the grain', to note the omission and the absence of evidence, will quite understandably have a different perspective than those undertaking a literal interpretation of the source. Indeed, it is these studies of overlooked or marginalised groups, by focusing on gender, race, class and social status, that seek to take on a quite deliberately different and non-traditional perspective. Lauren Macivor Thompson's work on the freedom of contract in medical law

---

Kercher, 'Colonial Contracts and Expectation Damages: Girard v Biddulph, New South Wales Supreme Court, 1834 Case Comment' (2001) 1 *Macquarie Law Journal* 129.

[61] See, for instance Watson's reinterpretation of Roman contract law that he stressed was 'consistent with surviving textual data and plausible with regard to human behaviour'. Alan Watson, 'The Evolution of Law: The Roman System of Contracts' (1984) 2 *Law and History Review* 1, 1.

[62] See the comments made about the lack of new or available sources preventing further study of Roman contract law. Andreas Wacke, 'Freedom of Contract and Restraint of Trade Clauses in Roman and Modern Law' (1993) 11 *Law and History Review* 1, 1.

[63] Geoffrey Rudolph Elton, *The Practice of History* (Fontana Press 1967).

takes the perspective of the 'reasonable woman'.[64] This is an important departure from the traditional scholarship on freedom of contract, which generally tracks the switch from subjective to objective reasoning. These different views of the same sources should not be seen as competition, where one is incorrect or correct or as better or worse, but rather as complementary, where one draws out ideas and themes that the other(s) does not.

Legal history has long since followed the manuscript tradition, where handwritten sources are found, transcribed and utilised in research. One must have strong palaeography skills to decipher these sources, and the research itself can be time-consuming.[65] With small or no details given on an archival catalogue,[66] visits to the archive can be fruitful or a loss. Working on archival material can be time-consuming and both rewarding and deeply frustrating. Other handwritten notes of cases were also made in the 18th and 19th centuries. The process for creating a law report was that a barrister,[67] who attended court, would take his own notes of the case. These would include details of the facts of the case, the counsel's arguments and the judge's words in the same way that a law report would be written today.[68] Isaac Espinasse, for example, was a prolific reporter. His law reports were well-known for their

---

64 Lauren Macivor Thompson, '"The Reasonable (Wo)Man": Physicians, Freedom of Contract, and Women's Rights, 1870–1930' (2018) 36 *Law and History Review* 771.

65 Sugarman points out (when discussing legal life writing) that a consequence of the time-consuming nature of accessing archives is that work of this nature is ill-suited to any regime of research assessment that adopts a quantification metric. David Sugarman, 'From Legal Biography to Legal Life Writing: Broadening Conceptions of Legal History and Socio-Legal Scholarship' (2015) 42 *Journal of Law and Society* 7, 16.

66 This is, of course, assuming that there is an archival catalogue. Often, there is not.

67 The only qualification needed for a case to be used as precedent was that a barrister wrote the report. This ended with the passage of the Courts and Legal Services Act 1990. Afterward, reports authored by solicitors would have the same value as those written by barristers. William Thomas Shave Daniel, *The History and Origin of the Law Reports together with a Compilation of Various Documents Showing the Progress and Result of Proceedings Taken for their Establishment and the Condition of the Reports on the 31st December, 1883* (Wildy 1969).

68 It is easy to forget that even 30 years ago reports of all cases were not routinely available through online databases such as BAILII and Austlii. Law reporting was a selective exercise and obtaining unreported decisions was not easy; see Michael Bryan, 'The Modern History of Law Reporting' (2012) 11 *University of Melbourne Collections* 32, 35.

brevity and inconsistency with other law reports of the same case.[69] In the context of contract law, *Stilk v Myrick* (1809) is a case on consideration and the modification of contractual promises during performance where conflicting law reports about its facts and the judgment given offer the opportunity for different interpretations of its importance.[70] The law reports published by lawyers were distinctly different from the formal records created by the process of litigation or the judge's own personal set of notes. The latter group of sources did not have the same function or value in the courtroom. Judicial notebooks (or benchbooks) give insight into the judge's views. James Oldham's work with Lord Mansfield's judicial notebooks sheds much light on the development of contract and commercial law in the 18th and 19th centuries.[71] Much like diaries or other private correspondence, these sources are a prized resource in legal and historical research. As they were authored as an *aide-mémoire* or in case the case was appealed, they are a private record. As such, they represent the author's private thoughts on the case. They are uncensored as they are not written to suit a particular audience or supplement a wider aim.[72] These resources are sometimes left in the Inns in London of respective judges or a local archive.

With such disparate methods of law reporting and commenting on judgments, learning about judge-made law can be seen as disputed and unclear. Yet, to those lawyers who were well-connected and 'in the know', the common law rules were far from undecided. Lawyers and legal writers evidently understood far more about the common law rules than the information available to those who looked through the printed law reports alone.[73] Those writing treatises or digests often had better access to legal information than those who had

---

69 Lord Denman, in *Small v Nairne*, explained that Espinasse's description of cases 'were never quoted without doubt and hesitation; and a special reason was often given as apology for citing that particular case'. *Small v Nairne* (1849) 116 Eng. Rep 1484, 1486; 13 QB 840, 844.

70 Peter Luther, 'Campbell, Espinasse and the Sailors: Text and Context in the Common Law' (1999) 19 *Legal Studies* 526. *Compare*, e.g. *Stilk v Myrick* (1809) 170 Eng. Rep 1168; 2 Camp. 317 (providing the case as reported by Campbell), *with Stilk v Meyrick* (1809) 170 Eng. Rep 851; 6 Esp. 129 (providing the case as reported by Espinasse).

71 James Oldham, *The Mansfield Manuscripts and the Growth of English Law in the Eighteenth Century, Vol. I* (University of North Carolina Press 1992).

72 Ludmilla Jordanova, *History in Practice* (2nd edn, Bloomsbury Publishing 2016).

73 As Oldham explains, these manuscript notes might, inter alia, reveal otherwise unreported sections of judicial opinion. James Oldham, 'Eighteenth-Century Judges' Notes: How They Explain, Correct and Enhance the Reports' (1987) 31 *American Journal of Legal History* 9, 16–21.

only a copy of the printed report itself. Before the advent of modern law reporting, these sources contained information about unreported cases. Digests were what we might term a casebook today and often contained swathes of undigested cases.[74] Treatises might act to bring these cases together in an analytical form to theorise about the connections between them. These treatises, which became textbooks, were a source for legal change so developments in doctrine can be evidenced through them. They are both artefacts of legal history themselves and useful tools for explaining how and when changes in thinking about doctrine occurred. For example, Anat Rosenberg brings together the classic common law case on unilateral offers, *Carlill v Carbolic Smoke Ball Company* (1893), and William Reynell Anson's contract textbook.[75] Her analysis of *Carlill* asserts that it was the case that began the doctrine of puffery in common law, which allows sellers to make *grossly* outlandish claims for their products without attracting liability for them.[76] She uses changes in the 7th edition of Anson's textbook to support her argument by noting that after *Carlill*, it included 'puffery' for the first time.[77] Anson added an explanation of what puffery was and a selection of cases as his examples. Anson's *Principles of the English Law of Contract and of Agency in Its Relation to Contract* is not the only example of changes in textbook editions documenting legal developments.[78] Some authors adopted a path dependency approach, but others were much more radical in restructuring their analysis and ordering of the material they were presenting according to what they saw as doctrinal developments in case law. This scholarship on academic writing and legal theorists, which connects legal scholarship to legal change, is more common in the civil law tradition.[79] In the common law world, the focus has traditionally been on judicial activity. As Sugarman explains, this is changing through

74 For more on the birth of case books in contract law, see Bruce A. Kimball, 'Langdell on Contracts and Legal Reasoning: Correcting the Holmesian Caricature' (2007) 25 *Law and History Review* 345.

75 Swain describes it as the 'first true contract textbook produced for students'. Warren Swain, 'Rescuing Contract Law Pedagogy from the Nineteenth Century' in Warren Swain and David Campbell (eds), *Reimagining Contract Law Pedagogy: A New Agenda for Teaching* (Routledge 2019) 2.

76 Anat Rosenberg, 'Legal Ridicule in the Age of Advertisement: Puffery, Quackery, and the Mass Market' (2021) 61 *American Journal of Legal History* 281, 285.

77 Supra at 285.

78 Goudkamp and Nolan (n 35) 129.

79 Serge Dauchy and others, *The Formation and Transmission of Western Legal Culture: 150 Books that Made the Law in the Age of Printing* (Springer 2016) 319f.

increased interest in legal life biography, which takes as its subjects, in his words, 'women, minorities, displaced persons and outsiders'.[80] The telling of history in this way encourages us to think differently about current challenges.

For those seeking greater detail on the litigants or the facts of cases, original court records are useful sources. These are not always retained, and for some courts, testimony was not always reduced to writing and stored. Newspapers fill a gap here, as do business and local archives. If we take Cranston's work, referred to earlier, as an example of archival research, it uses a wide array of sources, such as the Guildhall Library of the City of London, the Merseyside Maritime Museum, and the Liverpool Record Office, for example.[81] There are plenty of resources that help to understand how legislative drafting and the parliamentary interactions that supported it occurred. The legislation itself is not always online, but specialist legal history libraries have copies. The exception here is private member bills, which can be found in the Parliamentary Archives. Some historical sources are still compiled today but have evolved in their event-recording methodology; Hansard is a rather different historical source from the contemporary verbatim record of the Westminster Parliament. Previously, it was compiled from newspaper accounts of the debates.[82] The newspapers were, as they are today, biased towards political parties. As such, they would carry more detail on one party's speakers and misuse arguments of another party's speakers. Notetaking was also a skill; incomplete notes or misread shorthand could create a strange or misinformed report of the debates. This was also apparent in law reporting.

4. CONCLUSION

This chapter has sought to address historical research on and in contract law from a perspective of reflection. Through this reflection, it makes three contributions that will benefit those who wish to undertake this kind of research. It explains the significance of disciplinary agendas and labels on research and implicitly warns against being captured by them. It focuses, with examples, on two major historical approaches to contract law: the history of contract law per se and the use of contract and associated laws and ideas at a particular historical moment in a particular society. One approach is not inherently superior to the other. And it offers an overview of historical sources and problematises

80 Sugarman (n 65) 7.

81 Cranston (n 58).

82 H. Donaldson Jordan, 'The Reports of Parliamentary Debates, 1803-1908' [1931] *Economica* 437; Olive Anderson, 'Hansard's Hazards: An Illustration from Recent Interpretations of Married Women's Property Law and the 1857 Divorce Act' (1997) 112 *The English Historical Review* 1202.

their interpretation. In some instances, what is special is the use and interpretation of unique, difficult-to-read or access, and never-before-used sources to challenge or revise long-held views about the past.

Historical studies of current law are inherently useful and informative. Indeed, histories must have some relevance to the present, otherwise they would not be accessed and read by contemporary lawyers, which they clearly are.[83] For those researching society, the link to today's law is less obvious. Some thought is needed to make historical study appealing to lawyers as well as historians. It may be, for instance, that those judging, litigating or legislating can learn from past methods of regulation.[84] That claim is key to ensuring this research is not just 'othered' and considered history for history's sake. Writing to improve our knowledge of a society in a particular period is perfectly intellectually respectable for those whose disciplinary designation is history, but rather less so, and indeed somewhat fanciful, for those in law faculties in today's heightened research assessment and ranking culture. Brian Simpson, in the 1990s, wrote so that his work on historical cases 'may show that we can obtain greater enjoyment'.[85] It is worth noting that he was at this point at the height of his career.[86] He could afford to write fairly luxurious pieces about legal history that were openly fun, fanciful and amusing. Such a blasé approach is plainly likeable, intellectually honest, and commendable, but probably no longer tenable. It is unlikely that many early or mid-career scholars today would experience much in the way of approval from their peers or success in probation or promotion applications if they explained the value of their work was to add humour and enjoyment to legal studies. The academy is probably worse off for this.

---

83 Sugarman (n 65).

84 One might look to the arguments on how and where couples in the UK can marry in Rebecca Probert, 'Getting Married: The Origins of the Current Law and Its Problems' (2021) 23 *Ecclesiastical Law Journal* 255.

85 A. W. B. Simpson, *Leading Cases in the Common Law* (Clarendon Press 1996) vii.

86 For more on Simpson's path, see David Sugarman, 'Brian Simpson's Approach to Legal Scholarship and the Significance of Reflections on "The Concept of Law"' (2012) 3 *Transnational Legal Theory* 112.

6. Empirical methods in contract law

Monika Leszczyńska

INTRODUCTION

The purpose of this chapter is threefold: firstly, to explore how empirical methods can effectively address research questions related to contracts and contract law; secondly, to clarify the merits and limitations inherent in various empirical methodologies; and thirdly, to demonstrate the interplay between empirical methods and doctrinal and theoretical research on contract law. In this discussion, I will identify the methods best suited for addressing specific questions, while bearing in mind that no empirical approach is without its imperfections; each method possesses its unique strengths and weaknesses. Nevertheless, researchers can mitigate these shortcomings by adhering to two fundamental principles: selecting a method that aligns with the nature of the research question and, where feasible, employing multiple methods to ensure the robustness of findings, irrespective of the chosen approach.

To accomplish these objectives, I present carefully chosen examples of empirical projects that address questions within contracts and contract law, showcasing various data collection methods. Unlike research design, which involves the overall approach in a project—whether observational, experimental, or a case study—the data collection method refers to how a researcher gathers observations.

I begin with qualitative interviews, a method that offers valuable insights into the dynamics of specific environments. These interviews involve engaging individuals who are either participants in the given environment or experts possessing in-depth knowledge about a particular sector of the world. For instance, we can use qualitative interviews to understand whether and why people rely on contracts or how they conceptualize contracts. Subsequently, I transition to quantitative interviews, which serve multiple purposes, such as uncovering contract content when full texts are not readily available, gauging individuals' perceptions of contracts, and studying behavioral patterns within hypothetical scenarios.

Following this, I explore both experimental and non-experimental data collection methods, which allow for the direct observation of individuals' behavior in contractual contexts. Finally, I present examples of research using traditional as well as modern text analysis techniques that yield valuable insights into contract content and legal cases related to contract disputes.

When discussing these data collection methods and providing examples of studies relying on them, I will demonstrate how these studies were either inspired by longstanding doctrinal or theoretical questions in contract law or were later employed to address relevant issues in the doctrine or theory of contracts. Additionally, I will touch upon potential future directions and methodological developments that may help address some of the shortcomings of the methods used today.

1. QUALITATIVE INTERVIEWS—EXPLORING PEOPLE'S BEHAVIOR AND VIEWS ON CONTRACTS

Stewart Macaulay conducted one of the earliest and seminal empirical studies on the role of contract law in contractual relationships, laying the foundation for what later evolved into relational contract theory.[1] The primary objective of his study was to understand how businesses utilized contracts. To achieve this, Macaulay engaged in interviews with 68 businessmen and lawyers from 43 companies and six law firms. These interviews were largely unstructured, ranging from brief 30-minute sessions to extensive, profound discussions exceeding six hours.

Analyzing the responses from businessmen and lawyers, Macaulay concluded that, with exceptions, the majority of transactions were not thoroughly planned, at least not from the perspective of contractual provisions. Formal legal enforcement was seldom utilized when disputes arose in business relationships. Businessmen, as a principle, leaned towards informal mechanisms to motivate their business partners to fulfill promises, fearing that formal enforcement could strain those relationships.

The significance of Macaulay's findings and approach cannot be emphasized enough. He demonstrated the necessity of looking beyond contract law to comprehend how and whether it fulfills its intended function. This understanding could only be achieved through empirical methods, as traditional legal tools, such as doctrinal methods, lack the ability to shed light on people's behavior and social interactions. Macaulay's work sparked an entire scholarly

1 Stewart Macaulay, 'Non-Contractual Relations in Business: A Preliminary Study' (1963) 28 *American Sociological Review* 55.

pursuit examining relational contracts and attempting to decipher the interplay between formal and informal contractual mechanisms.[2]

An illustrative instance of qualitative interviews used to comprehend the interplay between contracts and the conduct of parties involved can be found in Sadie Blanchard's research.[3] Blanchard conducted semi-structured interviews with market participants and their legal representatives in the sovereign debt arena. Her aim was to explore the motivations of market participants in opting for legal avenues, specifically courts, to resolve sovereign debt disputes. The prevalent use of court processes in these disputes has been perplexing, given the absence of mechanisms for enforcing court orders. Hence, Blanchard sought to discern why market participants persisted in engaging in these resource-intensive court procedures. Such inquiries are aptly addressed through qualitative interviews. While quantitative data might offer insights into the prevalence of resorting to courts in those disputes, it falls short in revealing the motivations of the involved parties in relying on the judicial system for resolution.

In contrast to Macaulay, Blanchard employed a semi-structured approach rather than open-ended interviews. In semi-structured interviews, researchers have a predetermined set of questions for each participant, but subsequent questions depend on the participants' responses and may vary. Blanchard interviewed 20 professionals using a snowballing method, starting with initial contacts and relying on referrals to reach other interviewees. The outcomes of these interviews affirmed the reputational theory regarding the use of formal enforcement in sovereign debt disputes. Blanchard demonstrated that market participants in the sovereign debt realm turn to courts as informational intermediaries. Bringing a case to court initially enables creditors to confirm that the sovereign breached the contract. Subsequently, during court proceedings, creditors gain insights into the sovereign's behavior that led to the default. Lastly, court proceedings shed light on corrupt practices by sovereigns, emphasizing an ethical dimension of these disputes. This information can subsequently be leveraged to bolster the creditor's position during settlement negotiations.

The empirical findings on relational contracts have had a significant impact on doctrinal and theoretical scholarship in contract law. For instance, Robert

---

2 See, e.g., Jean Braucher, John Kidwell and William C. Whitford, *Revisiting the Contracts Scholarship of Stewart Macaulay: On the Empirical and the Lyrical* (Bloomsbury Publishing 2013).

3 Sadie Blanchard, 'Courts as Information Intermediaries: A Case Study of Sovereign Debt Disputes' (2018) *Brigham Young University Law Review* 497.

E. Scott proposed a relational theory of default rules.[4] Scott's theory helps us understand why contractual default rules often adopt a clear, categorical, winner-takes-all approach. According to Scott, this characteristic of contractual defaults allows them to function in parallel with social norms that are relied upon to enforce mutual cooperation. The objective of legal rules is not merely to reflect these social norms but rather to establish norms that work effectively when social norms fail. It appears that clear legal rules with binary risk allocation work best for contractual parties when they need to resort to legal enforcement. Building on this foundation, Scott collaborated with Ronald J. Gilson and Charles F. Sabel to explore the interplay between formal and informal enforcement.[5] They utilized this perspective to evaluate the existing legal doctrines concerning preliminary agreements and the duty to negotiate.[6]

Empirical research helps us understand not only how people behave in contractual relationships but also their comprehension and viewpoints regarding contracts. It allows for the exploration of various types of contracts and diverse populations, such as businesses (as observed in Macaulay's study) and consumers (as demonstrated in Dennis Stolle's study described below).

Dennis Stolle employed focus group interviews to explore consumers' contractual schemas—their understanding and perception of contracts.[7] Instead of opting for one-on-one interviews, Stolle chose to conduct focus groups, involving small groups (typically 4–8 people) engaging in a moderated discussion guided by an interviewer. This approach proved particularly effective for studying contract schemas, which are complex knowledge structures. Stolle aimed to uncover features of these knowledge structures that had not been previously revealed. A focus group environment encourages brainstorming, exposing participants to varied perspectives, facilitating idea generation, and thus identifying features that might not be as apparent in one-on-one interviews. In total, the author conducted three focus groups with 19 participants, compensating them for their involvement in hour-long interviews.

Although the specific questions varied among the groups, all participants were probed about their perceptions and thoughts regarding entering into a contract, as well as the factors they deemed essential for establishing a legally

4 Robert E. Scott, 'A Relational Theory of Default Rules for Commercial Contracts' (1990) 19 *The Journal of Legal Studies* 597.

5 Ronald J. Gilson, Charles F. Sabel and Robert E. Scott, 'Braiding: The Interaction of Formal and Informal Contracting in Theory, Practice, and Doctrine' (2010) 110 *Columbia Law Review* 1377.

6 ibid.

7 Dennis Paul Stolle, 'A Social Scientific Look at the Effects and Effectiveness of Plain Language Contract Drafting' (PhD, The University of Nebraska–Lincoln 1998).

binding contract. The results indicated that participants perceive contracts as lengthy, complex documents filled with legal jargon and potentially tricky elements. Interestingly, the act of signing, symbolized by a signature, was consistently emphasized as crucial for establishing a legally binding contract. What is worth noting is that Stolle leveraged the insights from this qualitative study to conduct a quantitative analysis. This subsequent study aimed to ascertain whether the factors identified by the focus groups indeed influenced participants' perceptions and comprehension of a contract.

Other examples of qualitative interviews used in contract law scholarship include the work by Mitu Gulati and Robert Scott, who interviewed lawyers assisting with transactions involving sovereign debts to explore the reasons for including specific provisions in those contracts, including those that turned out problematic for their clients.[8] Jacobien Rutgers interviewed Dutch lawyers to understand the reasons behind the content of the choice-of-law clauses in commercial contracts.[9] Researchers have also interviewed non-legal market participants, such as borrowers and lenders[10] as well as sales associates[11] and real estate brokers.[12] Ronald Mann explored the motivations of both borrowers and lenders in engaging in secured and unsecured credit transactions.[13] Zev Eigen researched sales agents' perception of form contracts (as either binding or non-binding) and how this perception relates to agents' perception of the contractual relationship (either as transactional or relational).[14] Finally, Doron Teichman wanted to find out why real estate contracts in the Israeli market rely on prices expressed in US dollars, rather than the local currency.[15]

Most of those projects are fundamentally exploratory and descriptive in nature. The authors do not hold specific predictions or expectations regarding

---

8 Mitu Gulati and Robert E. Scott, *The Three and a Half Minute Transaction: Boilerplate and the Limits of Contract Design* (University of Chicago Press 2012) 73–108.

9 Jacobien Rutgers, 'Choice of Law in b2b Contracts: The Law of the Jungle' (2018) 14 *Exploratory Interviews with Dutch Lawyers* 241.

10 Ronald J. Mann, 'Explaining the Pattern of Secured Credit' (1997) 110 *Harvard Law Review* 625.

11 Zev J. Eigen, 'The Devil in the Details: The Interrelationship among Citizenship, Rule of Law and Form-Adhesive Contracts' (2008) 41 *Connecticut Law Review* 381.

12 Doron Teichman, 'Old Habits Are Hard to Change: A Case Study of Israeli Real Estate Contracts' (2010) 44 *Law & Society Review* 299.

13 Mann, 'Explaining the Pattern of Secured Credit' (n 10).

14 Eigen, 'The Devil in the Details: The Interrelationship among Citizenship, Rule of Law and Form-Adhesive Contracts' (n 11).

15 Teichman, 'Old Habits Are Hard to Change: A Case Study of Israeli Real Estate Contracts' (n 12).

what they would observe or the relationships between various aspects of the world. Although they often speculate about the underlying reasons for their findings, they did not subject them to direct testing. In cases where a researcher lacks firm hypotheses or predictions about what to expect in the world, or is not primarily focused on explaining or discovering relationships between different aspects of the world, interviews serve as an apt data collection method. They permit researchers to explore a topic through the perspectives of the individuals involved, enabling the formulation of in-depth inquiries and learning from key stakeholders about the functioning of the world, which might otherwise remain unobservable. Moreover, it allows for uncovering potential mechanisms that stakeholders themselves identify as influential in the observed phenomena. Finally, qualitative interviews are a great tool to explore people's perceptions, views, and motivations, which we cannot learn about simply by observing their behavior.

Nonetheless, qualitative interviews have certain limitations to consider when interpreting their findings.[16] Typically, interviews are conducted with a relatively small group of individuals who have consented to participate. This can lead to a non-representative sample of the entire stakeholder population, either due to the group's limited size or because those who agreed to be interviewed represent specific perspectives on the issues discussed during the interview.

Second, although interviews do allow researchers to identify potential factors driving the observed behavior, one still needs to remember that these are the factors identified by stakeholders themselves. Their views on what is going on might be affected by various elements, such as being involved in the behavior of interest, being exposed to only a fraction of behaviors and not having a complete picture, or being interested in promoting a specific agenda or particular views about the world. Qualitative interviews also do not allow us to test a causal relationship between these factors and the outcomes we are interested in studying.

Finally, the reliability of findings obtained through interviews might be questioned since interviewees' responses may well depend on who conducts the interview. The demand effect may also be particularly pronounced in the interviews—interviewees may respond in a socially desirable way.

16 See also, Royce A. Singleton and Bruce C. Straits, 'Approaches to Social Research' (6th edn, Oxford University Press 2018), 296–298.

2. QUANTITATIVE SURVEYS—STUDYING PEOPLE'S PERCEPTIONS ABOUT AND ATTITUDES TOWARDS CONTRACTS

Some of the shortcomings of qualitative interviews might be addressed by relying on quantitative surveys. Instead of engaging with participants in person, over the phone, or online and asking them open-ended questions, researchers construct questionnaires that are answered using scales or other categorical variables, allowing for quantitative analysis.

Quantitative surveys offer significant advantages. Firstly, they facilitate the collection of a larger number of observations, which would be exceedingly time- and effort-consuming in the case of qualitative interviews. For instance, Evan Starr, J.J. Prescott, and Norman Bishara conducted a large-scale online survey with 11,505 respondents provided by an online panel company.[17] Such companies specialize in recruiting and verifying individuals who regularly participate in consumer or academic research, compensating them with monetary rewards. The study aimed to determine the prevalence of noncompete clauses—clauses that limit an employee's future job prospects—and identify the types of employees most likely to encounter them in their employment contracts. The researchers also sought to explore the relationship between noncompete clauses and various labor-related outcomes, such as training, wages, and job satisfaction.

The results revealed that almost 40% of the US workforce have worked under a noncompete clause at least once in their lives. Additionally, noncompete clauses tend to be lengthy, with the majority lasting for over two years, and they typically apply nationwide rather than to specific regions. Interestingly, these clauses are equally prevalent in states that enforce them as they are in those that do not. Finally, while noncompete clauses are more common in high-wage jobs involving trade secrets, they also occur in low-wage positions with no access to trade secrets.

The authors discuss the implications of the study for the economic theory of non-competes, according to which non-competes serve as an 'efficient contracting device'.[18] While some evidence, such as the frequent use of non-competes in technical positions and the coupling of non-competes with higher wages, supports the economic view of non-competes, other results, such as the existence of non-competes even in states where they are unenforceable and a

---

[17] Evan P. Starr, J.J. Prescott and Norman D. Bishara, 'Noncompete Agreements in the US Labor Force' (2021) 64 *The Journal of Law and Economics* 53.

[18] ibid 80.

high frequency of non-compete clauses in low-wage jobs, speak against that theory.

The study by Starr, Prescott, and Bishara illustrates how quantitative surveys can provide insights into the use of specific contractual provisions where we lack direct access to the contracts themselves. While similar insights can be obtained through qualitative interviews, it is not feasible to conduct them with a large sample, thus offering only a glimpse into the behavior of a small group of people. This limitation was addressed by accessing a large sample of employees with various demographic features. By asking participants to report other features related to their employment, such as the industry they work in or the level of their salaries, the researchers were able to study the relationship between the existence of noncompete clauses and other job-related outcomes. However, this research design of a quantitative survey does not allow for the study of causal relationships between these factors. This is possible using experimental vignette studies, which are also quantitative surveys but include scenarios that differ in only one particular feature that the researcher is interested in studying.

An illustration of such an experimental vignette is a study I conducted with Stefanie Jung and Peter Krebs on people's perceptions of lying in pre-contractual negotiations.[19] We were interested in finding out which lies people find immoral and which they think should give the deceived party a right to rescind the contract. Such lies are treated very strictly in some legal systems, such as Germany,[20] yet in other countries, contract law formulates a high threshold for a contract to be invalidated because of a lie in the pre-contractual stage (e.g., in the US, the deceived party must show that a lie was material and that they justifiably relied on it when entering into a contract).[21] To provide empirical insights into people's perceptions of those lies, we presented our participants with various scenarios describing different lies in pre-contractual negotiations. After reading a scenario, participants were asked to assess whether they find a lie immoral and whether they think it should give the deceived party a right to rescind a contract. We found that participants, in general, are more likely to find lies immoral than to think they should give a right to cancel the contract. This difference also depends on the type of lie. Whereas the probability of assessing a lie about a subject matter of a contract or about the reservation price as immoral and providing a right to rescind a contract did not differ, we observed a large share of participants who found it immoral when a seller lies

19 Stefanie Jung, Peter Krebs and Monika Leszczyńska, 'Does It Matter what People Lie About?' https://papers.ssrn.com/sol3/papers.cfm?abstract_id=3916340 accessed 8 December 2023.

20 German Civil Code (*Bürgerliches Gesetzbuch*) (BGB), s 123(1).

21 E. Allan Farnsworth, *Contracts* (4th edn, Aspen Publishers 2004), 237.

about having an alternative offer or about product availability but did not think that this lie should give a right to invalidate the contract.

The study was initially conducted as a paper-pencil study with students at the University of Siegen in Germany. To determine if the results generalize to a more diverse population and to people from other countries, we also ran a study online on Prolific[22]—a platform that recruits participants interested in taking part in academic research in exchange for small monetary rewards. On Prolific, we were able to reach a more diverse pool of participants with respect to age, education level, and job status from three countries: Germany, Italy, and the US. This way, we were able to show that our results hold regardless of the sample.

Our study was inspired by a long-standing theoretical debate about the normative underpinning of contract law. According to some legal scholars, contract law should reflect, or at least be compatible with, people's morality.[23] Our results contribute to this debate by showing that people may distinguish between behavior that they find wrong and behavior that should trigger legal consequences.[24] Therefore, moral norms may not necessarily be an adequate benchmark for the content of contract law, as people may consider different values than morality when assessing how the law should react to immoral behavior.

Experimental vignette studies, such as the one described above, are increasingly popular among scholars studying contract law questions. They are particularly useful for investigating how specific features of contracts or contract law impact people's views and perceptions. For instance, a whole series of experimental vignette studies was conducted to understand people's views about the breach of contract and contractual remedies.[25] For instance, Tess Wilkinson-Ryan and David Hoffman discovered that people's negative reactions to a breach of contract are influenced by factors such as intentionality, feelings of betrayal, and the resulting inequality.[26] In contrast, Mittlaender

---

22 Prolific Academic Ltd, https://www.prolific.com/ accessed 4 January 2024.

23 Charles Fried, *Contract as Promise: A Theory of Contractual Obligation* (Oxford University Press, 2015); Seana V. Shiffrin, 'The Divergence of Contract and Promise' (2007) 120 *Harvard Law Review* 708.

24 See also Roseanna Sommers, 'Contract Schemas' (2021) 17 *Annual Review of Law and Social Science* 293, 303.

25 See, e.g., Tess Wilkinson-Ryan and David A. Hoffman, 'Breach is for Suckers' (2010) 63 *Vanderbilt Law Review* 1001; Sergio Mittlaender, 'Morality, Compensation, and the Contractual Obligation' (2019) 16 *Journal of Empirical Legal Studies* 119; Matthew A. Seligman, 'Moral Diversity and Efficient Breach' (2019) 117 *Michigan Law Review* 885.

26 Wilkinson-Ryan and Hoffman, 'Breach is for Suckers' (n 25).

demonstrated that if a breach of contract is accompanied by compensation that addresses the unfairness resulting from the breach, the breach itself is not perceived as immoral.[27] Finally, Seligman showed that adding an exit clause to a contract, which provides the right to cancel the contract in exchange for a fee, helps individuals overcome their reluctance to cancel, even when it is efficient for them to do so.[28]

Though experimental vignette studies are indeed valuable for studying people's views, they can only provide us with basic insights into people's behavior. Some experimental vignette studies present participants with scenarios and ask them to report how they would behave in this hypothetical situation. An illustrative study in this context is the one conducted by Tess Wilkinson-Ryan and David Hoffman.[29] The authors aimed to address two fundamental questions: 1) at what stage in the process of forming a contract do individuals perceive that a contract has already been established; and 2) how does this conviction regarding an existing contract influence people's willingness to either fulfill or breach the contract? In this study, the authors presented participants with different scenarios depicting an individual interested in purchasing a used car. Depending on the treatment, some participants were exposed to a scenario in which a person found a car listing and sent an email expressing interest in the offer. Others were exposed to scenarios where the person either emailed the dealership offering a specific amount of money for the car, received an acceptance of the offer via email, or had already signed a contract with the dealer to pick up the car the next day. The participants were then asked whether they would be willing to cancel the contract. The results revealed that even when the contract had not yet been formed (i.e., when a purchaser had only sent an email expressing their interest in the offer or made an offer), only half of the participants declared that they would cancel the deal. Simultaneously, participants showed decreasing willingness to back out of the contract as they progressed further in the process of contract formation. Overall, the findings demonstrate that while the legal binding point of the contract plays a significant role in decreasing the willingness to breach, a considerable number of individuals are hesitant to withdraw from the deal even before it has reached a legally binding status.

Wilkinson-Ryan's and Hoffman's study is an example of research that draws upon current doctrine to formulate empirical research questions. The authors' starting point was the observation that there are doctrines in contract law that

---

27 Mittlaender, 'Morality, Compensation, and the Contractual Obligation' (n 25).

28 Seligman, 'Moral Diversity and Efficient Breach' (n 25).

29 Tess Wilkinson-Ryan and David A. Hoffman, 'The Common Sense of Contract Formation' (2015) 67 *Stanford Law Review* 1269.

look into people's subjective views about contract formation, such as promissory estoppel. This is why the authors wanted to find out whether lay intuitions of contract formation correspond to the legal approach. Although the authors do not use these results to question existing doctrines but rather rely on existing doctrines as an inspiration for their research, often the divergence between people's intuitions and the doctrine is used to criticize the latter.[30]

Hypothetical studies, like the one conducted by Tess Wilkinson-Ryan and David Hoffman, offer essential initial insights into how people's contractual behavior is influenced by their perception of contract formation. However, as the authors acknowledge in the paper,[31] we face uncertainty because we cannot directly observe participants' declared behavior. We cannot be entirely certain if what participants declare they would do in a given situation accurately reflects their actual behavior. Factors such as the potential impact of participants' choices on their welfare or their desire to present themselves as reciprocal and socially oriented individuals could influence their responses. Moreover, even when focusing solely on understanding people's perceptions of specific situations rather than their behavior, it remains unclear if participants would perceive these situations the same way if they were to experience them firsthand. Hypothetical scenarios can still be valuable, particularly when exposing participants to certain situations may be ethically or practically undesirable. Furthermore, there are instances where observing actual behavior through experiments is not feasible due to practical constraints, either due to high costs or the impossibility of reconstructing a real-life situation of interest in a controlled laboratory setting (e.g., when studying people's consumption choices).

3. BEHAVIORAL EXPERIMENTS AND OBSERVATIONAL STUDIES—TESTING PEOPLE'S CONTRACTUAL BEHAVIOR

Some of the downsides of running quantitative questionnaires can be addressed by setting up behavioral labs or online experiments, or directly observing people's behavior in the real world (either in an experimental or non-experimental setting).

Behavioral experiments can effectively investigate complex human behaviors even within abstract contexts. This abstract setting provides researchers with a controlled environment, ensuring that no external variables influence

---

30 See, for instance, Tess Wilkinson-Ryan, 'Intuitive Formalism in Contract' (2015) 163 *University of Pennsylvania Law Review* 2109, 2112.

31 Wilkinson-Ryan and Hoffman, 'The Common Sense of Contract Formation' (n 29), 1296.

the results. Consequently, they can confidently attribute any observed differences between treatments to the experimental manipulation, enhancing the validity of their findings.

An example of this approach is demonstrated in a study conducted by Florian Ederer and Alexander Stremitzer, which investigated the motivations behind individuals' commitment to keeping promises.[32] This exploration is particularly relevant in the ongoing philosophical discourse regarding the interplay between the moral aspects of promise-keeping and the principles of contract law.[33] Behavioral experiments provide valuable insights into the underlying motivations driving promise-keeping behaviors. This empirical knowledge enables us to scrutinize whether these motivations align with the philosophical foundations of contract law. Essentially, the question at hand is whether individuals are genuinely motivated by moral considerations when fulfilling promises, and if so, what specific moral values and principles guide their actions.

The primary aim of the authors was to discern whether the act of keeping a promise is influenced by the expectations of the promisees. Specifically, they investigated whether the promisor's belief about the promisee's anticipation of promise fulfillment had a substantial impact on actual promise-keeping behavior. To investigate these motivations, Stremitzer and Ederer designed a trust game scenario. In this experimental setup, one participant was endowed with a sum of money and had the option to share a portion of it with another participant. Crucially, the trustors in this game had the opportunity to make explicit promises regarding the amount they intended to share. Subsequently, recipients had the option to decide whether they wanted to continue the game, and trustors had to make a decision about keeping their promise.

To test the influence of promisees' expectations, the authors introduced two distinct treatments. In one treatment, both trustors and trustees were informed that there was a high probability that the trustor would indeed have a chance to fulfill their promise. In contrast, participants in the alternative treatment were informed that there was a low probability of the trustor having a choice to keep their promise. In this second scenario, promisees should not have high expectations of promise fulfillment, and promisors should believe that promisees' expectations regarding their performance were relatively low.

The hypothesis underlying this experiment was that the beliefs held by promisees about the expectations of promise fulfillment would significantly

---

32 Florian Ederer and Alexander Stremitzer, 'Promises and Expectations' (2017) 106 *Games and Economic Behavior* 161.

33 See, for instance, P.S. Atiyah, *Promises, Morals and Law* (Oxford Academic Books 1983); Fried, *Contract as Promise: A Theory of Contractual Obligation* (n 23); Shiffrin, 'The Divergence of Contract and Promise' (n 23).

impact promisors' behavior. In other words, if individuals' perceptions of promisees' expectations indeed drive their actions, then we should observe a lower frequency of promise-keeping behavior when the promisor believes that the promisee expects the promisor not to fulfill their promise.

Although the abstract environment created in lab or online experiments allows the experimenter to have full control over all variables that may potentially influence people's behavior, it also raises issues of external and ecological validity—will people behave in the same way in the real world? One way of addressing this problem is to directly observe people's behavior in a real environment, either in an experimental or non-experimental setting. A non-experimental design does not allow us to study causal relationships between some features of contracts and contract law and people's behavior, but it does provide us with valuable insight into how people behave in a contractual setting.

The paper by Yannis Bakos, Florencia Marotta-Wurgler and David Trossen on non-readership of standard form contracts is an example of such a study.[34] For years, consumer and contract law scholars have been discussing the fact that many people do not read contracts. This can be understandable given how complex those contracts are and how many of them one would need to read everyday. Some scholars argue that this should change the way we perceive standard form contracts from a doctrinal perspective;[35] others have raised that the lack of reading may lead to businesses implementing terms unfavorable for consumers and, therefore, requiring legal intervention.[36] The law and economics scholars, however, opposed the legal intervention, claiming that a small number of consumers who read contracts will be sufficient to discipline the businesses and prevent terms that are disadvantageous to consumers.[37]

By directly observing consumers' behavior when it comes to software licenses, Bakos, Marotta-Wurgler, and Trossen showed that the number of consumers is so small that it is not enough to provide incentives for companies

---

[34] Yannis Bakos, Florencia Marotta-Wurgler and David R. Trossen, 'Does Anyone Read the Fine Print? Consumer Attention to Standard-Form Contracts' (2014) 43 *The Journal of Legal Studies* 1.

[35] See, for instance, Mark A. Lemley, 'Terms of Use' (2006) 91 *Minnesota Law Review* 459, 480–482.

[36] See, for instance, Oren Bar-Gill, *Seduction by Contract: Law, Economics, and Psychology in Consumer Markets* (Oxford University Press 2012) 21, 32.

[37] Alan Schwartz and Louis L. Wilde, 'Intervening in Markets on the Basis of Imperfect Information: A Legal and Economic Analysis' (1979) 127 *University of Pennsylvania Law Review* 630; Clayton P. Gillette, 'Pre-Approved Contracts for Internet Commerce Transactions, Information and Emerging Law: Pre-Approved Contracts for Internet Commerce' (2005) 42 *Houston Law Review* 975.

to avoid terms that might impose costs and risks on consumers.[38] The data for this study was received from a large online research company. This company recruited over 90,000 households who agreed to have a program installed on their computers that would track all URL visits. The researchers focused on the software market to study consumers' contract readership behavior. They identified websites where software is sold or made available for download for free and the websites containing end-user license agreements for this software. This way, they were able to observe the readership behavior of over 48k visitors to the websites of 90 software companies for over a month. By measuring the clicks, access to these websites, and time spent on them, the researchers concluded that only one or two out of 1,000 shoppers access these agreements for at least a second. Although the study provides us with only a peek into consumers' behavior, it does show that at least software license agreements are not read by a number of consumers that is sufficient to protect both the reading and non-reading consumers from unfavorable terms.

Finally, a comprehensive approach involves integrating both experimental manipulations and real-world behavioral observations using field experiments. This approach is exemplified by a study conducted by Yair Listokin.[39] The study was inspired by a widespread theory of contractual default rules, according to which gap-filling contractual provisions should reflect the preferences of the majority—i.e., 'what most parties would have contracted for had they written a complete contract'.[40] Yet, as the author concludes, legislators are not equipped to predict those preferences. Therefore, in his study, the author provided empirical evidence on people's preferences for warranty rules to identify the one preferred by the majority. Specifically, the author aimed to investigate whether the default warranty rule of the Uniform Commercial Code (UCC), reflecting a warranty of merchantability, is indeed perceived as the buyer's default rule.

To address this question, Listokin conducted a field experiment on eBay, presenting iPods with four different warranty provisions: 1) 'satisfaction guaranteed', 2) the explicit UCC rule, 3) silent (no explicit warranty provision), and 4) 'as is'. If buyers assumed a default warranty rule different from the actual default rule expressed in the UCC, they might be willing to purchase the iPods at a higher or lower price if there is no explicit warranty provision than if the offer includes an explicit reference to the UCC warranty rule. However, the

---

38 Bakos, Marotta-Wurgler and Trossen, 'Does Anyone Read the Fine Print?' (n 34).

39 Yair Listokin, 'The Meaning of Contractual Silence: A Field Experiment' (2010) 2 *Journal of Legal Analysis* 397.

40 Ian Ayres and Robert Gertner, 'Majoritarian vs. Minoritarian Defaults' (1999) *Stanford Law Review* 1591, 1591.

results revealed that this was not the case. When there was no explicit warranty provision, buyers were willing to purchase iPods at a similar price to those with an explicit UCC warranty provision. On average, they paid $3 more for iPods with 'satisfaction guaranteed' and $12 less for iPods sold 'as is'.

Field experiments allow researchers to study people's real behavior by randomly assigning them to different treatments, thus establishing causal relationships between variables and the behavior of interest. However, they also introduce challenges, leaving certain aspects beyond researchers' control. In the illustrative example, the author was unable to account for fluctuating prices due to the aging model of iPods being sold or seasonal variations related to holidays. Additionally, the reputation of the eBay account used to sell iPods was subject to change, which may have also affected prices and the perception of the warranty provisions. Organizing a field experiment often requires collaboration with companies, which may not always be willing to cooperate with researchers or may only be interested in studying specific questions likely to yield results that are important and beneficial for their business. Implementing field experiments also raises ethical issues, particularly concerning participants being involved in research without their knowledge or incurring some, even if minimal, costs and risks. Lastly, field experiments can be exceedingly costly and time-consuming to implement, and a researcher may not have complete control over how the treatments are implemented and the data is collected. This is why researchers often turn to lab or online experiments as the second-best solution for studying causal relationships.

4. SYSTEMATIC CONTENT ANALYSIS—STUDYING THE CONTENT OF CONTRACTS AND COURT OPINIONS

While the data collection methods described earlier primarily focus on studying people's perceptions or behavior, researchers investigating contracts and contract law often aim to examine the textual aspects of contracts or court opinions in contract cases. However, accessing these contracts is often challenging. In such cases, researchers may opt for a quantitative survey approach, where they ask individuals about the provisions included in their contracts, as in the study by Starr, Prescott, and Bishara on noncompete clauses described above. It's important to note that this method has its limitations, as it relies on self-reporting, and individuals may not always be aware of the specific provisions in their contracts. Furthermore, this approach provides insights into only specific contractual terms, such as noncompete clauses, rather than the entirety of the contract terms.

Recently, due to the digitalization of many documents, researchers are increasingly able to access to the full text of contracts or court decisions. The text of these documents can be analyzed in two primary ways: manually or automatically. An example of a manual systematic content analysis of contracts is illustrated in Meirav Furth-Matzkin's study, which aimed to determine whether residential rental contracts include unenforceable clauses.[41] David Hoffman and Anton Strezhnev also analyzed unenforceable clauses in residential rental contracts, but they did so in an automated manner.[42]

In manual systematic content analysis of contracts, Meirav Furth-Matzkin encountered several challenges. The first challenge was gaining access to the rental contracts. The author employed a snowballing method, reaching out to tenants, landlords, and real estate agents and requesting them to share their rental contracts while also asking them to refer her request within their networks. This approach granted the author access to a total of 70 leases.

The subsequent step involved systematically analyzing the provisions within these contracts. Initially, the author identified mandatory provisions in Massachusetts Landlord and Tenant Law, applicable to the region where the contracts were collected. These provisions were then assigned to 14 distinct categories. During the analysis of the rental contracts, the author assessed each category to determine whether the provisions within the contracts complied with the law, violated the law, were misleading, or if there were no provisions addressing specific issues. The results of the study revealed that more than 70% of the analyzed contracts included at least one unenforceable clause, while over 90% included at least one misleading clause.

A systematic content analysis enables the quantitative examination of contract texts and the exploration of the relationship between the likelihood of specific provisions being present in a contract and other features, such as the type of landlord (private or residential company). However, this approach does come with its set of limitations. For instance, the coding of provisions may vary based on the individual conducting it. One way to address this issue is by employing multiple independent coders to analyze the contract, checking for intercoder reliability, and refining the coding to achieve the highest possible reliability. However, even this solution does not facilitate the analysis of a large number of contracts efficiently due to the substantial time and effort it demands.

An alternative approach to handle this challenge is automated text analysis. Automated text analysis may involve the relatively straightforward use of search patterns to identify clauses of interest, as demonstrated in a paper by

---

41 Meirav Furth-Matzkin, 'On the Unexpected Use of Unenforceable Contract Terms: Evidence from the Residential Rental Market' (2017) 9 *Journal of Legal Analysis* 1.

42 David A. Hoffman and Anton Strezhnev, 'Leases as Forms' (2022) 19 *Journal of Empirical Legal Studies* 90.

David Hoffman and Anton Strezhnev.[43] Similar to Meirav Furth-Matzkin, the authors analyzed residential leases for unenforceable clauses. However, in contrast, Hoffman and Strezhnev studied a vast dataset of over 170,000 lease contracts obtained from a nonprofit organization offering legal advice to low-income individuals.

This organization scraped court dockets in search of landlord-tenant cases. Subsequently, it extracted leases from the documents attached to the complaints and this dataset was shared with the authors. After cleaning and identifying essential data from these leases, such as the names of the tenant and landlord, the rent amount, and the location of the rental apartment, the authors constructed search terms using key phrases.[44] These search terms allowed them to identify four unenforceable and oppressive terms. This strategy was validated using 800 hand-coded contracts.

The results revealed a prevalent and increasing use of unenforceable and oppressive terms. Moreover, these terms were found to be more common in higher rent leases and in wealthier areas of the city. The study illustrates that automated text analysis not only allows for the examination of larger contract samples but also facilitates the investigation of broader patterns, such as temporal trends and the relationship between location features and the presence of unenforceable or oppressive clauses.

Automated text analysis has gained popularity among empirical legal researchers, who are now utilizing advanced text analysis techniques. For example, researchers construct a dataset in which they manually code certain contracts with respect to specific provisions. They then use this dataset to develop an algorithm that can automatically identify these provisions in the rest of the dataset. An example of such an approach is the paper by Julian Nyarko on 'Stickiness and Incomplete Contracts'.[45]

Finally, scholars may seek to analyze not only contractual provisions but also court cases involving questions of contract law. An illustrative analysis

---

43 ibid.

44 A similar approach was employed by Uri Benoliel in his research on parties' preferences for a textualist or contextualist approach to contract interpretation. Uri Benoliel searched through over 1500 commercial contracts using various key phrases to determine whether they included merger clauses, which would indicate parties' preferences for a textualist interpretation: Uri Benoliel, 'The Interpretation of Commercial Contracts: An Empirical Study' (2017) 69 *Alabama Law Review* 469.

45 Julian Nyarko, 'Stickiness and Incomplete Contracts' (2021) 88 *The University of Chicago Law Review* 1.

is presented in a paper by Hannes Westermann and his co-authors.[46] In this study, the researchers aimed to determine the factors that predict outcomes in landlord-tenant disputes over rent reductions. They initially identified a set of factors that courts typically consider in such cases and enlisted annotators to code these factors in 149 cases from a Quebec court. Employing machine learning tools, the researchers developed an algorithm capable of predicting case outcomes based on the factors proven during the trial.

As evidenced by these examples, both manual and automated text analyses play crucial roles in extracting valuable insights from contracts and contract-related court decisions. The advent of digitalization in legal systems and the proliferation of databases containing digitized contracts have exponentially expanded researchers' access to a vast array of contracts. However, to comprehensively analyze this massive corpus, researchers increasingly depend on automated techniques rather than manual coding and analysis. Despite notable advancements in these automated methods, they still face limitations in fully addressing all research inquiries concerning contract content.[47]

5. INTERPLAY BETWEEN EMPIRICAL AND OTHER METHODS IN CONTRACT LAW AND THE WAY FORWARD

As illustrated by the examples above, the interplay between different legal methods in contract law operates in a two-way direction. Discussions in the doctrine and theory of contract law can inspire empirical research, such as those exploring the moral perception of lying in pre-contractual negotiations or examining perceptions of contract formation and contractual breach. Simultaneously, empirical research, like studies on relational contracts, can inspire and trigger doctrinal and theoretical discussions about the interaction

46 Hannes Westermann and others, 'Using Factors to Predict and Analyze Landlord-Tenant Decisions to Increase Access to Justice' (Proceedings of the Seventeenth International Conference on Artificial Intelligence and Law).

47 On the potential of computational methods in law, see Jens Frankenreiter and Michael A. Livermore, 'Computational Methods in Legal Analysis' (2020) 16 *Annual Review of Law and Social Science* 39. On the potential and limits of text mining, see Jo Guldi, *The Dangerous Art of Text Mining: A Methodology for Digital History* (Cambridge University Press 2023).

between legal and social norms in contracts, such as about the function of default rules[48] or the doctrines of preliminary agreements.[49]

Despite this fruitful interaction between various methods in contract law, it could be further enhanced by considering two particularities. These considerations are crucial when informing empirical research with insights from the doctrine and theory of contracts and vice versa—drawing upon empirical findings to inform the doctrine and theory of contract law.

Firstly, researchers conducting empirical studies on contractual behavior or the content of contracts may measure various features of this behavior or content. Identifying and defining these features—operationalizing the variables, in other words—based on the doctrine and theory of contract law can enhance the relevance of these studies for contractual scholarship. This can be exemplified through research on people's views on contract formation. One could investigate the impact of various features on how individuals perceive contracts and contractual consent; however, some of these features will be more relevant to the doctrine and theory of contracts than others.

Regarding consent, psychologists might explore whether participants feel they have genuinely consented to the contract, examining contextual and personal factors that may influence this feeling.[50] On the other hand, legal researchers might be more interested in studying people's perception of consent by manipulating factors that are legally relevant. For instance, they may examine whether individuals consider a contract binding, even if induced by a seller's false representation contradicted by contractual terms, which were later signed without being read by a consumer.[51] Similarly, in contrast to moral psychologists interested in people's evaluation of the moral wrongfulness of a given act, empirical legal researchers might focus on studying people's normative views about the legal consequences of a given behavior.[52]

Secondly, strengthening doctrinal and theoretical legal scholarship in contract law through the use of empirical evidence requires a better understanding of the nature of empirical research. Unlike doctrinal scholarship, empirical research is never definitive; rather, it provides evidence that either supports or

---

48 Scott, 'A Relational Theory of Default Rules for Commercial Contracts' (n 4).

49 Gilson, Sabel and Scott, 'Braiding: The Interaction of Formal and Informal Contracting in Theory, Practice, and Doctrine' (n 5).

50 Vanessa K. Bohns, 'Toward a Psychology of Consent' (2022) 17 *Perspectives on Psychological Science* 1093, 1098.

51 Meirav Furth-Matzkin and Roseanna Sommers, 'Consumer Psychology and the Problem of Fine-Print Fraud' (2020) 72(3) *Stanford Law Review* 503.

52 Jung, Krebs and Leszczyńska, 'Does it Matter what People Lie About?' (n 19).

contradicts a given hypothesis. Gathering more evidence increases our confidence that things operate in the real world as predicted by our hypothesis.

Therefore, it is crucial to review all relevant empirical studies, avoiding cherry-picking those that align with our doctrinal or theoretical arguments. Alternatively, relying on a meta-analysis, which systematically analyzes multiple previous studies, offers insights into the size of the effect of interest. Another approach to enhancing certainty and understanding a phenomenon better is to explore studies that investigate it using various methods (so-called triangulation), such as qualitative and quantitative interviews.

Moreover, legal scholars employing empirical methods in their doctrinal or theoretical research should be aware of the strengths and weaknesses of these methods to properly assess the conclusions drawn from a study. Finally, it is essential not only to examine empirical results but also to consider the underlying theory that informed the hypothesis tested or was developed based on previous empirical research. This theoretical framework helps us understand the assumptions, relationships, and operationalization of variables measured in the study, enabling us to grasp the constraints and make informed generalizations from the research within its exact boundaries.[53]

There are several factors that may play a role in how empirical research in contract law could potentially evolve in the future. First, as has likely been evident throughout previous sections, empirical research in contract law, as well as empirical research in social science in general, is heavily influenced by technological developments. These developments affect empirical research in various ways. For instance, the development of video conferencing and other online communication techniques, with increased accessibility and quality, has had a significant impact on conducting of qualitative interviews. Often, it is logistically challenging and costly to contact interviewees or, in the case of focus groups, to gather them in one place at the same time. Communication technologies remove those boundaries, yet they are not without shortcomings. Issues such as protecting privacy or overcoming the distance created by using online media to connect will need to be addressed to implement these technologies in a responsible and enriching way.[54]

---

53 Kathryn Zeiler, 'Cautions on the Use of Economics Experiments in Law' (2010) 166 *Journal of Institutional and Theoretical Economics (JITE) / Zeitschrift für die gesamte Staatswissenschaft* 178.

54 Sara Thunberg and Linda Arnell, 'Pioneering the Use of Technologies in Qualitative Research – A Research Review of the Use of Digital Interviews' (2022) 25 *International Journal of Social Research Methodology* 757, 762–764.

Technological developments have also assisted with quantitative surveys and experimental research. Platforms such as Prolific, MTurk[55] or similar platforms now allow access to a large pool of participants ready to take part in a study.[56] This enables researchers to gather their data within minutes compared to days spent in a research lab before. Experimental software, such as Otree[57] or Empirica,[58] helps program interactive online experiments.

Software used for qualitative analysis, as well as for annotations, is changing how researchers analyze text data.[59] The incredibly fast developments within Natural Language Processing, including ChatGPT, are opening new possibilities in text analysis. Also, general developments in machine learning data analysis are aiding quantitative research. These developments are not only increasing the efficiency of research but also opening up new research opportunities that were not available before.[60]

The second important development in empirical research in contract law to be expected is linked to an increased importance of empirical legal methods, including the interest of funding institutions in granting research funds to legal research involving empirical methods, as well as the emphasis now placed on teaching empirical methods to law students. These changes will not only increase the volume and quality of empirical research in contracts but also bring new questions that have not been asked before. It is hard to underscore the importance of having legal scholars involved in empirical research—they know what questions can be relevant from the perspective of law and how to operationalize variables measured in empirical research in a legally relevant way. Therefore, it is not sufficient for legal scholars to be only consumers of empirical research done by researchers specializing in other disciplines, such as social sciences or computational science. It is important that they actively

---

55 Amazon Mechanical Turk, https://www.mturk.com/ accessed 4 January 2024.

56 Benjamin D. Douglas, Patrick J. Ewell and Markus Brauer, 'Data Quality in Online Human-subjects Research: Comparisons between MTurk, Prolific, CloudResearch, Qualtrics, and SONA' (2023) 18 *PLOS ONE* e0279720.

57 Daniel L. Chen, Martin Schonger and Chris Wickens, 'oTree—An Open-source Platform for Laboratory, Online, and Field Experiments' (2016) 9 *Journal of Behavioral and Experimental Finance* 88.

58 Empirica, https://empirica.ly/ accessed 4 January 2024.

59 Though there is still room for development, see, for instance, a project aiming at developing an annotation tool designed specifically for legal data: Gijs van Dijck, Carlos Aguilera, Chris van der Lans, Shashank Chakravarthy and Sander van Essel, https://www.lawnotation.org/ accessed 4 January 2024.

60 Frankenreiter and Livermore, 'Computational Methods in Legal Analysis' (n 47).

get involved in this research to ask legally relevant questions. Education and funding can only help with this.

6. CONCLUSIONS

The examples provided above demonstrate the valuable application of empirical methods in tackling a wide range of questions highly pertinent to contract law theory and doctrine. For instance, researchers have the capacity to investigate how the formal enforcement of contracts intersects with informal mechanisms of promise enforcement. Similarly, the analysis of contract content can shed light on the presence of provisions that may be in violation of legal norms. Such datasets can also facilitate the exploration of which types of contracts are more prone to containing unenforceable clauses. This is particularly relevant for legislators contemplating intervention in such scenarios.

Furthermore, empirical methods offer an avenue for delving into individuals' perceptions of contracts and contract law, including their moral convictions regarding contractual relationships. Finally, these methods enable the examination of how people behave in response to contract law institutions.

Addressing these multifaceted issues involves the utilization of diverse data collection methods and research designs. This chapter highlights that each data collection method carries its own set of advantages and disadvantages. Thus, the researcher's role is to discern these pros and cons and select a method that minimizes drawbacks while aligning with the specific research question at hand.

7. Law and economics methods and techniques in contract law

Mitja Kovač

1. INTRODUCTION

Ever since Adam Smith, economists and lawyers have known that commerce and manufacturing rarely flourish without the predictable and effective enforcement of contracts. The importance of contract law for economic growth and development can thus hardly be overstated.[1]

Contract law has long been one of the core subjects of law and economics analysis,[2] and among the most popular. This is not surprising. As Farnsworth notes, contract law is among the practically most salient areas of law, both in terms of social and economic importance and in terms of the realities of

[1] See Douglass North and Barry Weingast, 'Constitutions and Commitment: The Evolution of Institutions Governing Public Choice in Seventeenth-Century England' (1989) 49(4) *The Journal of Economic History* 803, 803–832; Steven Knack and Philip Keefer, 'Institutions and Economic Performance: Cross-country Tests Using Alternative Institutional Measures' (1995) 7(3) *Economics and Politics* 207, 207–228; Daron Acemoglu, Simon Johnson and James Robinson, 'Institutions as a Fundamental Cause of Long-Run Growth' in Philippe Aghion and Steven Durlauf (eds), *Handbook of Economic Growth* (North Holland Elsevier 2005) 385–472.

[2] For a synthesis, see Richard Craswell and Alan Schwartz, *Foundations of Contract Law* (Foundation Press 1994) 16–21; Victor Goldberg, *Readings in the Economics of Contract Law* (Cambridge University Press 1989) 21–14; Steven Shavell, *Foundations of Economic Analysis of Law* (Harvard University Press 2004) 289–387; Hans-Bernd Schäfer and Claus Ott, *The Economic Analysis of Civil Law* (Edward Elgar Publishing 2004) 273–293; Gerrit De Geest, *Contract Law and Economics: Encyclopedia of Law and Economics* (2nd edn, Edward Elgar 2011) 1–9; and Alain Marciano and Giovanni Battista Ramello, *Encyclopedia of Law and Economics* (Springer 2020) 362–370.

international negotiation and litigation.[3] Almost all trade and economic relations nowadays depend on private contracts. Moreover, it may be argued that contracts are an essential part of the modern economy, where practical daily considerations call for further understanding of similarities and differences among the various national legal systems or legal families. Hence, legal practitioners, international business, the bench and the bar, and legislators have an increasing interest in understanding contract law in a transnational context.

In many respects, the impact of contract law and economics has exceeded its early ambitions, in that it has irreversibly transformed classical legal methodology. However, despite notable antecedents tracing back to Adam Smith's discussions on the economic effects of legislation and Bentham's theory of legislation and utilitarianism, it was not until the mid-20th century that the links between law and economics became an object of serious academic pursuit. Even today, despite the powerful analytical reach of economics and recognition of the positive nature of the economic analysis of contract law, misunderstandings and controversies about the uses and impact of law and economics persist.[4]

Classical contract law and economics research assesses how "good" a given rule of contract law is by reference to its "efficiency", by which is meant the maximization of the net increase in social welfare conferred by the rule. In this way, contract law and economics fit broadly within the utilitarian normative tradition. Contract law and economics research focuses on the incentives, risks, and transaction cost effects created by legal rules.[5]

In this context, the "goodness" of a legal rule can refer not only to the content of a law but also to its technical formulation. Most contract law and economics literature is focused on content; it seeks to determine which legal rules have the most desirable effects, irrespective of how these legal rules are formulated. At the same time, contract law and economics may also offer useful advice on how to improve the technical formulation of a given rule. An underlying assumption of much law and economics literature is that lawmakers (legislators and judges) in fact balance the efficiency advantages and disadvantages of

---

3 Allan Farnsworth, 'Comparative Contract Law' in Mathias Reimann and Reinhardt Zimmermann (eds), *The Oxford Handbook of Comparative Law* (2nd edn, Oxford University Press 2008) 899.

4 Richard Posner and Francesco Parisi, 'The Economic Foundations of Private Law: An Introduction' in Richard Posner and Francesco Parisi (eds), *Economic Foundations of Private Law* (Edward Elgar Publishing 2002) 4.

5 For a synthesis of law and economics scholarship, see De Geest (n 2) 5. Also see Richard Posner, *Economic Analysis of Law* (8th edn, Wolters Kluwer Law Publishers 2011) 115; and Victor Goldberg, *Rethinking Contract Law and Contract Design* (Edward Elgar Publishing 2015) 2.

alternative solutions, although this balancing is often hidden (perhaps even to those lawmakers) behind a veil of "fairness" rhetoric. Contract law and economics tries to reduce these advantages and disadvantages to a single measure of efficiency as a way of more accurately assessing them by modelling their consequences. As a result, it may address what lawmakers do—as opposed to what they say they do—and hence, more accurately address the law.

In other words, contract law and economics is not only a theory of how law evolves and what makes laws good, but also a method that can be applied in combination with other legal research methods in order to facilitate discussions about contract law as a whole and the value or effectiveness of individual contract law rules. This chapter offers a synthesis of the normative and positive law and economics methodology as applied to contract law. It seeks to examine (1) the capacity of the contract law and economics method (and its different schools of thought) to explain and argue about contracts and contract law (what kind of questions, what kind of answers, what is at the core of the law and economics perspective); (2) the limits of the method or methods (which questions the method or methods are ill-suited to answer, taking into account underlying assumptions of the method); and finally (3) the current use of law and economics methods in researching contract law and the potential for their use in future research.

Several caveats are warranted. First, the chapter does not aim to offer the final word on the matter but, via an exploratory analysis, seeks to consider different methodological currents within law and economics and to explore potential limitations of the contract law and economics paradigm. Second, due to the vast amount of literature, the chapter selectively emphasizes the most important methodological avenues and currents.

The structure of this chapter is as follows. Section 2 presents key methodological concepts and explains the historical development and analytical currents within contract law and economics. Section 3 describes the methodological tools and concepts employed in classical economic analysis of contracts (i.e. contract theory) and in behavioural contract law and economics. Section 4 discusses some limitations of contract law and economics research and the potential for future use of the contract law and economics approach. Section 5 concludes.

2. HISTORIC DEVELOPMENT, KEY METHODOLOGICAL CONCEPTS AND ANALYTICAL CURRENTS

Law and economics is one of the most ambitious and probably the most influential theories in the US that seeks to explain decision-making by legal actors (legislatures, judges, and private parties), and to place it on an objective basis.

Although a comprehensive examination of the field is beyond the scope of this chapter,[6] the basic methodological concepts will be briefly outlined at the beginning of this section. The central assumption of economics is that all people (except children and the mentally disabled) are rational maximizers of their own welfare (however they define it) in all of their activities. The rational choice approach is the basic methodological principle in classical contract law and economics scholarship, although most economic models are no longer based on an assumption of perfect rationality but now account for the ways in which rationality is limited (bounded) by context and inherent human nature. The notion of welfare-maximizing behaviour comprises the principle of wealth maximization, which can be modeled for predictive purposes as contracting parties' degree of willingness to pay.[7] That is to say, parties that value certain outcomes more will be willing to pay more for them, so if goods are left in the hands of the persons who were willing and able to pay the highest amount, wealth is maximized in the contract as a whole.[8] Much of the first generation of law and economics literature (classical law and economics) combined the analytical tools of adjoining and complementary social sciences in order to develop a critical approach to contract law, conveying a distinctive perspective on the contract law theory, practice, and understanding of the law of contracts of different legal systems.

2.1 Historic Development and Methodological Perspectives

Contract law is one of the core fields of law and was also among the first to be exposed to law and economics treatment. Modern law and economics is broadly acknowledged to have begun in the 1960s with the pioneering work of Coase, Calabresi, Birmingham, and Barton.[9] However, a difference in

---

[6] For such a comprehensive examination, see Mitchell Polinsky and Steven Shavell, *Handbook of Law and Economics* (North-Holland 2007); Robert Cooter and Thomas Ulen, *Law and Economics* (6th edn, Addison-Wesley 2016).

[7] Heico Kerkmeester, 'Methodology: General' in Boudewijn Bouckaert and Gerrit De Geest (eds), *Encyclopedia of Law and Economics* (Edward Elgar Publishing 1999) 34.

[8] See for example Posner (n 5) 20.

[9] Ronald Coase, 'The Problem of Social Cost' (1960) 2 *Journal of Law and Economics* 1, 1–44; Robert Birmingham, 'Damage Measures and Economic Rationality: The Geometry of Contract Law' (1969) 18(2) *Duke Law Journal* 49; John Barton, 'The Economic Basis of Damages for Breach of Contract' (1972) 1(2) *Journal of Legal Studies* 277; and Guido Calabresi and Douglas Melamed, 'Property Rules, Liability Rules, and Inalienability: One View of the Cathedral' (1972) 85(6) *Harvard Law Review* 1089. Moreover, the first monographs on law

methodological approach is discernible between the contract law and economics contributions of the early 1960s and those that followed a decade later.[10] Namely, while earlier studies investigated the effects of contract law rules on the normal functioning of the economic system of exchanges,[11] the subsequent generation of studies utilized economic analysis to achieve a better understanding of the legal system.[12] Moreover, as Posner and Parisi emphasize, methodological differences played an important part in the "uneasy marriage between law and economics".[13] Namely, the Popperian methodology of positive science (positive economics where testable hypotheses or models are derived by means of logical deduction and then tested empirically) was in many respects at odds with the existing paradigms of legal analysis, according to which lawyers use individual judgments, provisions from statutes, or doctrinal writings to construct a general premise of law. The early years of contract law and economics were also marked by the uneasiness of some classical legal scholars with the notion of wealth maximization as a paradigm of justice.[14] Classical law and economics relies on the standard economic assumption that individuals are rational maximizers of their own utility and studies the role of law as a means for changing the relative prices attached to alternative individual actions.

Economic analysis of contract law got a boost in the 1980s, when institutional economics gained popularity and mainstream economists started to

---

and economics already devoted separate chapters to contract law. See e.g. Gordon Tullock, *The Logic of Law* (Basic Books 1971) 37–137; and Richard Posner, *Economic Analysis of Law* (1st edn, Little, Brown 1973) 115–183.

[10] Francesco Parisi (ed.), *The Economic Structure of the Law – The Collected Economic Essays of Richard A. Posner* (Vol. 1, Edward Elgar Publishing 2000) 14. See also Avery Katz, *Foundations of the Economic Approach to Law* (Oxford University Press 1998) 11–18; and Cooter and Ulen (n 6) 45–70.

[11] See e.g. Coase (n 9); Harold Demsetz, 'Toward a Theory of Property Rights' (1967) 57(2) *American Economic Review* 347–359; and James Buchanan, 'Good Economics – Bad Law' (1974) 60(1) *Virginia Law Review* 483–492.

[12] See e.g. James Barton, 'The Economic Basis of Damages for Breach of Contract' (1972) 1(2) *Journal of Legal Studies* 277–304; Anthony Kronman, 'Mistake, Disclosure, Information and the Law of Contracts' (1978) 7(1) *Journal of Legal Studies* 1–34; Alan Schwartz, 'The Case for Specific Performance' (1979) 89(1) *Yale Law Journal* 271–306; Charles Goetz and Robert Scott, 'Enforcing Promises: An Examination of the Basis of Contract' (1980) 89(7) *Yale Law Journal* 1261–1288; and Steven Shavell, 'Damage Measures for Breach of Contract' (1980) 11(2) *Bell Journal of Economics* 466–490.

[13] Posner and Parisi (n 4) and Charles Rowley, 'The Common Law in Public Choice Perspective: A Theoretical and Institutional Critique' (1989) 12(1) *Hamline Law Review* 355.

[14] Posner and Parisi (n 4) 13.

study contracts.[15] Economists conceptualized various types of organizations as solutions to principal-agent problems in the behaviour of business firms, and in contracts as the archetypical form of organization within markets.[16] This stream of literature is now known as industrial organization or sometimes as *contract theory*.[17]

More recently, much of the normative discussion relating to contract law has revolved around the issue of freedom of contract. Today, the economic approach to contract law is based on a limited number of assumptions regarding human behaviour that themselves may be amended if an alternative set of assumptions (e.g. bounded rationality and cognitive limitations) would better fit the particular object of study.[18] Moreover, as De Geest points out, from an analytical perspective, contracts present a bilateral incentive problem, meaning that each party's behaviour creates incentives and disincentives for the other party, with extensive opportunities for information exchange and strategic interaction.[19] This analytical complexity arguably explains why economic literature on contract law is not so well developed and why there is probably less consensus on optimal contract law than, for example, on optimal tort law, which does not involve parties continually reacting to each other's behaviour according to the incentives each creates for the other.[20]

2.2 Classical Methodological Concepts: Wealth Maximization, Risks and Transaction Costs

The concept of wealth maximization is one of the main analytical principles in classical contract law and economics scholarship. Wealth maximization is commonly misunderstood as equating business income to social value. In fact, wealth maximization refers to a sum of all tangible goods and services, weighted by offer prices and asking prices, according to the value each party

15 Gerrit De Geest, 'Introduction' in Gerrit De Geest (ed), *Contract Law and Economics: Encyclopedia of Law and Economics* (2nd edn, Edward Elgar Publishing 2011) 4.

16 ibid 1.

17 Patrick Bolton and Mathias Dewatripont, *Contract Theory* (MIT Press 2005) 72.

18 Gerrit De Geest, *Economische Analyse van het Contracten – en Quasi-Contractenrecht: Een Onderzoek naar de Wetenschappelijke Waarde van de Rechtseconomie* (Maklu 1994) 568.

19 De Geest (n 18) 2. These strategic interactions are the focus of the field of economic analysis usually referred to as game theory.

20 ibid.

subjectively assigns to them.[21] In this context, wealth should be understood as the summation of all valued objects, both tangible and intangible, weighted by the prices they would command if they were to be traded in markets.[22] From a Pareto efficiency perspective, a transaction is wealth maximizing, where, provided that it has no third-party effects and is a product of free, unanimous choice, the transaction has made two people better off and no one worse off.[23]

It should also be noted that those decisions, in order to be rational, need not be well thought out at the conscious level; in fact, they need not be conscious at all since, as Posner states, "rational" denotes only the suiting of means to ends, and much of our knowledge is tacit and our decision-making reflexive.[24] Moreover, it is evident that non-monetary as well as monetary satisfactions enter into each individual's calculus of maximizing their own welfare. It should also be stressed that, despite the valuable insights of new behavioural approaches addressed in more detail in section 3 below, the main reason why many economists continue to work within the rational-choice framework is that it can sharpen conclusions without downplaying the importance of behavioural considerations that make humans "irrational" in predictable ways.

The next methodological principle comprising the foundation of any comprehensive contract law and economics investigation is transaction costs. This is the label given in economic theory to the costs incurred in order to complete a transaction. While the voluntary transaction is beneficial to both parties, transaction costs reduce its value for both contracting parties, who will therefore want to minimize them. In this way, transaction costs slow the movement of scarce resources toward their most valuable uses and should be minimized in order to increase allocative efficiency. This phenomenon was first discussed by Ronald Coase[25] and later developed by other eminent authors.[26] As Coase

---

21 The notion of wealth maximization is that the value of wealth in society should be maximized. See e.g. Parisi (n 10) 88; John Coleman, *Markets, Morals and the Law* (Cambridge University Press 1988) 147; Shavel (n 2) 293; and Richard Posner, 'Utilitarianism, Economics, and Legal Theory' (1979) 8(1) *The Journal of Legal Studies* 103.

22 Posner (n 5) 116.

23 Emanuel Towfigh and Niels Petersen, *Economic Methods for Lawyers* (Edward Elgar Publishing 2015) 29.

24 Richard Posner, *The Problems of Jurisprudence* (Harvard University Press 1993) 354.

25 Ronald Coase, 'The Nature of the Firm' (1937) 4 *Econometrica* 394; Coase (n 9) 22; and Douglass North, *Structure and Change in Economic History* (W. W. Norton & Co. 1981) 18.

26 For a synthesis, see Oliver Williamson and Sidney Winter (eds), *The Nature of The Firm: Origins, Evolution, and Development* (Oxford University Press 1993) 68.

showed, in a world of zero transaction costs, parties would always produce economically efficient results without the need for legal intervention. However, since in reality transaction costs are pervasive in every transaction, intervention becomes necessary. Contract law rules can help to reduce transaction costs imposed upon an exchange, or at least allocate them by default to the party best able to pay them. In so doing, contract law can improve allocative efficiency and help to maximize social welfare. Hence, any sound examination of contract law rules should devote substantial effort to their effects on transaction costs.

Finally, issues of uncertainty and risk form the last pillar of the classical contract law and economics analytical framework. Economists have established that one of the basic characteristics of economic actors is their attitude towards risk. Empirical studies demonstrate most people are risk-averse most of the time—that is, they seek to avoid risks more than they seek to attain equally valuable gains—although a number of institutional responses (such as insurance contracts) may make people act as if they are risk-neutral in many situations.[27] Almost any contract term shifts risk, since contracts by their nature commit the parties to a future course of action, where the future is uncertain. Economic theory suggests that whenever one contracting party can bear a given risk at a lower cost than another, efficiency requires assigning the risk to such a "superior risk bearer" or "least cost avoider".[28] Such a bearer is the party to an exchange who is best able to minimize losses either by taking steps to avoid realization of the risk (such as by taking care to avoid losses due to negligence) or to insure against it. A robust contract law analysis should strive to identify the superior bearer of any given risk in a transaction and allocate the risk to that party.

2.3 Positive and Normative Analysis

One of the central questions of economics is the question of choice under conditions of scarcity and the related attempts of individuals to maximize their desired ends by doing the best they can with the limited resources at their disposal (formation of preferences). In analyzing the question of choice, contract law and economics differentiates between positive and normative analysis.

---

27 See generally Posner (n 5) 10.

28 See e.g. Guido Calabresi and Douglas Melamed, 'Property Rules, Liability Rules, and Inalienability: One View of the Cathedral' (1972) 85(6) *Harvard Law Review* 1089; Kenneth Arrow, 'Uncertainty and the Welfare Economics of Medical Care' (1963) 53(5) *The American Economic Review* 941; Richard Posner and Andrew Rosenfield, 'Impossibility and Related Doctrines in Contract Law: An Economic Analysis' (1977) 6(1) *The Journal of Legal Studies* 83.

This distinction goes back to the 19th-century writings of John Stuart Mill.[29] In economics, the issue became entangled with a different, although related, distinction among philosophical positivists between "is" and "ought", between facts and values, between supposedly objective, declarative statements about the world and prescriptive evaluations of states of the world. Positive analysis investigates what the effects and consequences of certain contractual provisions or contract law rules are, whereas normative analysis revolves around the issue of how contract law should be structured in order to achieve desirable social consequences.[30] For example, positive analysis of the pre-contractual duty of good faith shows the effects of such duty on the behavior of the contracting party, whereas normative analysis investigates the content of social preferences and whether enacting a rule relating to pre-contractual good faith would or would not serve those preferences.

2.4 Comparative Contract Law and Economics

Another fruitful methodological approach to the study of contract law is comparative contract law and economics.[31] This approach serves as a bridge between facts and normative conclusions, between economic theory and policy proposals for an improved legal system.[32] It seeks to complement other legal disciplines by uncovering the underlying economic logic and social effects of assessed legal institutions revealed by comparing those legal institutions against each other within and across jurisdictions.[33] In looking for transparency in the law, the comparative contract law and economics approach connects to what "the best classical legal scholarship aims to do: clarifying the

---

[29] John Stuart Mill, *Principles of Political Economy* (D. Appleton and Company 1885).

[30] See e.g. Benjamin Hermalin, Avery Katz and Richard Craswell, 'Contract Law' in Mitchell Polinsky and Steven Shavell (eds), *Handbook of Law and Economics* (Vol. 1, North Holland 2007) 3–28.

[31] Roger van den Bergh, *The Roundabouts of European Law and Economics* (Eleven International Publishing 2018) 21–28.

[32] ibid. See also Ugo Mattei, *Comparative Law and Economics* (The University of Michigan Press 1997) 80.

[33] Comparative law and economics complement classic legal disciplines by bringing to light the implicit logic decision-makers follow but that they may not acknowledge in their reasons for judgment. It also seeks to make this logic transparent to outside observers. See Anthony Ogus, *Costs and Cautionary Tales: Economic Insights for the Law* (Hart Publishing 2006) 11–16. See also Guido Calabresi, *The Future of Law & Economics* (Yale University Press 2016) 137; and Richard Posner, *Divergent Paths: The Academy and the Judiciary* (Harvard University Press 2016) 211.

underlying order of law as it is; offering tools for fashioning law to cope with novel situations".[34]

The functional method of comparative law generally looks for the way a given social, political, and/or economic problem is solved by different legal systems or different legal institutions. However, the standard functional comparative method itself lacks tools for determining which of the compared laws is better, since the specific function itself cannot serve as a benchmark, and since, as comparatists point out, once the similarity has been established, the same function cannot determine superiority, making a comprehensive evaluation almost impossibly complex.[35] Yet the evaluation criterion is defined as a "practical judgment" or "policy decision" under the conditions of partial uncertainty.[36] In other words, as De Geest and Van den Bergh point out, when comparatists are to decide which of two different rules is the best one, they still make a choice on the basis of pure intuitive thinking.[37]

Comparative contract law and economics,[38] on the other hand, treats legal and institutional backgrounds as dynamic variables and attempts to build models which reflect the ever-changing layered complexity of the real world of law. This method might thus broaden the horizon of the underlying legal discourse and confer an economically informed degree of realism upon the theoretical analysis.[39] For example, I employ this methodology to explore the disclosure duties in the contract law of ancient Rome,[40] while Parisi, on the other hand,

---

34 Ejan Mackaay, *Law and Economics for Civil Law Systems* (Edward Elgar Publishing 2013) 6.

35 Ralph Michaels, 'The Functional Method of Comparative Law' in Mathias Reiman and Reinhard Zimmermann (eds), *The Oxford Handbook of Comparative Law* (Oxford University Press 2006) 374.

36 ibid.

37 Commentators report, for example, that when the Lando commission had to decide which of two doctrines (leading to the same result) was to be chosen for the European contract code proposal, the choice was based on mere intuition (or even majority voting); De Geest (n 2) 11.

38 For a synthesis, see Mattei (n 32) 74. However, for diverse viewpoints, see Florian Faust, 'Comparative Law and Economic Analysis of Law' in Mathias Reiman and Reinhard Zimmermann (eds), *The Oxford Handbook of Comparative Law* (Oxford University Press 2006) 837.

39 Ugo Mattei and Alberto Monti, 'Comparative Law and Economics: Borrowing and Resistance' (2001) 2(1) *Global Jurist Frontiers* 1.

40 They, for example, show that Cicero's more than two-thousand-year-old case, while brilliantly addressing the ever-present issues of morality and ethical behaviour, could be, from the law and economics perspective, regarded as the first recorded example in human history of an asymmetric information problem. Moreover, they show that: (a) the praetorian and, in particular Cicero's decision

argues that its value added is the theoretical rigour of its models and the possibility to engage in a scientific dialogue not hampered by jurisdiction-specific features.[41]

3. THE BEHAVIOURAL REVOLUTION IN CONTRACT LAW AND ECONOMICS

As discussed, classical contract law and economics are founded on the assumption that people make rational choices to maximize their own welfare, as they see it, in a world in which resources are limited. Accordingly, classical contract law and economics assume that contracting parties rationally maximize their returns from contracts in a self-interested manner. This concept of contracting parties as rational, wealth-maximizing, self-interested actors also implies that parties respond to incentives in generally predictable ways. For example, if higher quality goods are valuable to a buyer in a transaction, they will be willing to pay a higher purchase price than would a buyer who is less sensitive to quality. However, this classical rational-choice concept has been challenged on several grounds, aside from the superficial criticism that contractual parties typically do not describe or conceive of their own decisions in such terms. The observed behavioural inconsistencies with the conventional approach have induced scholars to investigate the underlying motivations behind the behaviour of contracting parties, in order to improve existing theories and make more accurate predictions. This new analytical approach is called behavioural contract law and economics. This section explains the importance and methodological concepts of classical contract law and economics and then also

---

in the Rhodes famine case efficiently addresses the problems created by the asymmetric information problem; (b) that lawmaking in ancient Rome produced remarkable legal solutions to omnipresent legal problems; and (c) that the decision in the Rhodes famine case stands the test of time and corresponds with the law and economics suggestions on how to address the asymmetric information problem in circumstances under which an individual has valuable information unknown to the person with whom he transacts. See Mitja Kovač and Margot Callewaert, 'Does Cicero's Decision Stand the Test of Time? Famine at Rhodes and a Comparative Law and Economics Approach" (2023) 12(2) *Comparative Law Review*, 85–113, 112.

41 Parisi also suggests that possible synergies of comparative law and economics with comparative legal research abound, but the organization of academic structures has so far prevented their full exploitation; Francesco Parisi, 'The Multifaceted Method of Comparative Law and Economics' (2023) 12(2) *Comparative Law Review* 25–34, 30.

offers a brief description of the behavioural approach to the study of contract law and how it both challenges and enriches the classical approach.

3.1 Classical Contract Law and Economics

In the economics literature, contract theory explores how economic actors behave in contractual arrangements, and the implications of such behaviour in terms of efficiency.[42] Contract economics pursues two related normative goals: the design of contract terms that create incentives for the contracting parties to act in a welfare-maximizing manner and the development of contract law principles that mitigate welfare losses and maximize welfare at the systemic level. Thus, contract theory provides an analytical apparatus to identify the welfare implications of various bargaining scenarios and contractual arrangements.[43] Commentators agree that the economics of contracts has been successful in identifying sources of market failures where the parties fail to conclude optimally welfare-maximizing contract terms, as well as in explaining how and why contract terms fall short of optimal welfare maximization in practice.[44] The most important source of such market failures is the asymmetric information problem and associated incentive mismatches. Economic analysis can thus be employed as a mitigating mechanism to minimize welfare losses in contract design.

From a methodological perspective, modern contract theory is dominated by three schools of thought: incentive theory, transaction cost theory, and incomplete contract theory. The development of the theory of incentives has been a major advance in economics in the last thirty years. Today, for many law and economics scholars, economics is to a large extent a matter of incentives: incentives to work hard, to produce good quality products, to study, to invest, to save, etc. The economics of incentives can be described as the design of rules and institutions for inducing economic agents to exert appropriate levels of effort, to refrain from opportunism, and to disclose truthfully all socially relevant information they might have. Hence, how to design institutions that provide good incentives for economic agents has become a central question

---

42 Klaus Schmolke, 'Contract Theory and the Economics of Contract Law' in Emanuel Towfigh and Niels Petersen (eds), *Economic Methods for Lawyers* (Edward Elgar Publishing 2015) 96 et seq. See also Oliver Williamson, *The Economic Institutions of Capitalism: Firms, Markets, Relational Contracting* (The Free Press 1985) 183.

43 Schmolke (n 42) 119. See also Steven Shavell, 'Contracts' in Peter Newman (ed), *The New Palgrave Dictionary of Economics and the Law* (Palgrave Macmillan 1998) 436–445.

44 Schmolke (n 42) 119.

of economics. Incentive theory then provides contractual tools for addressing and mitigating inefficiencies generated by, for example, the notorious asymmetric information problem or to design incentives for optimal contractual performance.[45]

Transaction cost theory in turn considers the transaction (contract) as the most basic unit of measure and focuses on how much effort, resources, or cost are necessary for two parties to complete a contractual exchange. The theory pursues an investigation of how parties address the problem of suboptimal mutual trust caused by the impossibility of perfectly foreseeing (and contracting for) all potential events and human behaviour that would prevent optimal *ex post* contractual allocation of scarce resources.[46] Transaction cost theory has enormous significance for contract law and for the analysis of contracts. The theory informs us that institutional frameworks set the limits for contractual arrangements that may be effectively enforced and implemented in practice by contracting parties, and that the study of institutional frameworks should not be limited to their formal rules but should also include informal institutions.[47]

---

45 The theory offers various remuneration models to address the principal-agent problem. It provides a menu of contracts to tackle adverse selection and moral hazard issues. See e.g. Eric Malin and David Martimort, 'Transaction Costs and Incentive Theory' in Eric Brousseau and Jean-Michel Glachant (eds), *The Economics of Contracts: Theories and Applications* (Cambridge University Press 2002) 159.

46 The transaction cost literature offers a set of contractual instruments that deter opportunism and moral hazard and simultaneously induce cooperative behaviour and contractual commitment (e.g. employment of hostages, irreversible investments, length of commitment) and focuses on private conflict resolution mechanisms. See e.g. Oliver Williamson, 'The New Institutional Economics: Taking Stock, Looking Ahead' (2000) 38(1) *Journal of Economic Literature* 595; Oliver Williamson, *The Mechanisms of Governance* (Oxford University Press 1996) 69; Oliver Williamson, *The Economic Institutions of Capitalism: Firms, Markets, Relational Contracting* (Free Press 1985) 200; Oliver Williamson, 'Transaction-Cost Economics: The Governance of Contractual Relations' (1979) 22(2) *Journal of Law and Economics* 233; and Herbert Simon, 'A Formal Theory of the Employment Relationship' (1951) 19(1) *Econometrica* 293.

47 For example, social rules, usages, norms, and traditions imposed by relational networks (e.g. professional, social, and ethnic groups). See e.g. Eric Brousseau and Jean-Michel Glachant, 'The Economics of Contracts and the Renewal of Economics' in Eric Brousseau and Jean-Michel Glachant (eds), *The Economics of Contracts: Theories and Applications* (Cambridge University Press 2002) 27; Douglass North, *Institutions, Institutional Change and Economic Performance* (Cambridge University Press 1990) 167; and Lisa Bernstein, 'Opting out of the

The most recent branch of contract theory is incomplete contract theory, which examines the impacts of the institutional framework on contract design and establishes a direct link between the ability of judicial institutions to observe or evaluate the nature of contractual arrangements that may be effectively enforced and implemented in practice by contracting parties and their efficiency.[48] In a world of imperfect information and positive transaction costs, contracts are inevitably incomplete; that is, the parties cannot possibly predict and account for every possible contingency that could arise. Such an effort would be doomed to failure, and even the attempt to negotiate a complete contract would be wastefully expensive. Thus, the optimal (efficient) design of default rules becomes a crucial component if one attempts to induce efficient behaviour of contracting parties.[49]

Contract theory has been influential in a range of bargaining settings, such as the sale of goods, insurance, employment, and corporate governance. It triggered a fundamental reassessment in all areas of economic analysis, from the study of microeconomic interactions to the various domains of applied economics, finance, international trade, and industrial organization.[50] This analytical approach enables a more economically informed examination of the exact nature of various coordination failures that reduce the level of social cooperation or that can undermine or prevent cooperation among contracting parties. It also helps identify the exact nature of the various contractual provisions that induce or improve coordination,[51] of how agents and principals conceptualize and form the rules and decision-making structures that govern their behaviour and finally to explore the evolution of contractual mechanisms.[52]

Legal System: Extralegal Contractual Relations in the Diamond Industry' (1992) 21(1) *The Journal of Legal Studies* 115.

48 Brousseau and Glachant (n 47) 12.

49 See e.g. Oliver Hart, *Firms, Contracts and Financial Structure* (Oxford University Press 1995) 104; Oliver Hart and John Moore, 'Incomplete Contracts and Renegotiation' (1988) 56(4) *Econometrica* 755; Philippe Aghion, Mathias Dewatripont and Patrick Rey, 'Renegotiation Design with Unverifiable Information' (1994) 62(2) *Econometrica* 257; Jean Tirole, 'Incomplete Contracts: Where Do We Stand?' (1999) 67(4) *Econometrica* 741.

50 Brousseau and Glachant contribute the success of contract theory to the analytical power of the notion of contract, since the concept of contract focuses on elementary social structures that regulate any human coordination at bilateral and multilateral levels; Brousseau and Glachant (n 47) 5.

51 For example, routines, inducement and coercion mechanisms, conflict resolution, and different informal and formal routines.

52 Such investigation supports our understanding of social and contractual changes in the structures that frame economic activity. Brousseau and Glachant (n 47) 5. See also Schmolke (n 42).

For example, its insights have been employed in classic legal analysis to understand the role of various mechanisms that induce better performance of contracts and improve contract drafting.[53]

For all its contributions, classic contract theory also suffers from clear methodological limitations. First, this approach has limited value for the study of economic activity where organizations and institutions are not reducible to simple contractual arrangements, such as a simple contract for the sale of standardized goods in a supermarket.[54] Second, the properties of organizations' collective contractual arrangements may not derive from the bilateral contractual relationship but also from the communal articulation of the interaction among numerous stakeholders (interaction networks) where an exchange is not merely a two-party relation but involves the entire network of human interactions.[55] Third, some of the economic models, due to their high level of abstraction, employ unrealistic assumptions. This can limit the value of these models for classic legal scholarship, practical contracting, and lawmaking. Fourth, theoretical developments in the economic analysis of law are sometimes due to economists' lack of deeper understanding of legal institutions detached from empirical legal reality and should be thus enriched with closer and more sincere collaborations between legal professionals (operational lawyers) and doctrinal contract law scholars who are experts in the related contract law fields and possess a profound understanding of judicial decision-making, case law details, and jurisprudence. Namely, economists often tend to simplify legal reality by focusing merely on certain general provisions of civil codes or simply employ as their explanatory variable "common law" or "civil law". Such generalization lacks a proper understanding of the real law in action, disregards the issues of contract law enforcement and interpretation and the small but super-important factual differences among apparently (to non-lawyers) similar cases, and is thus prone to over-simplification or over-generalization.

The exact description of sound and reliable empirical law and economics analysis exceeds the available space of this chapter and can be found elsewhere.[56] However, it should be emphasized that the concept of empirical law

---

[53] For example, by suggesting incentive mechanisms that may mitigate moral hazard and opportunism, it helps to draft more effective insurance contracts.

[54] Namely, as Brousseau and Glachant emphasize, institutions and organizations have a collective character whereby an individual will join them without negotiating each rule governing the relations between members; Brousseau and Glachant (n 47) 5.

[55] ibid.

[56] See e.g. Lee Epstein and Andrew Martin, *An Introduction to Empirical Legal Research* (Oxford University Press 2014), and Herbert Kritzer, *Advanced Introduction to Empirical Legal Research* (Edward Elgar Publishing 2021).

and economics concerns methodology broadly defined as referring to the process of assembling and analyzing factual information or data. The goal of this research may be simply to empirically describe some legal phenomenon; it may seek to assess how some law-related program is functioning; or it may have the goal to provide a causal explanation of some legal phenomenon.[57] While conducting empirical research, law and economics scholars now employ tools of applied econometrics such as linear regression analysis, panel data econometrics, and difference-in-difference analysis. For example, a linear regression analysis comprises the most fundamental and the most widely accepted tool in applied econometrics, and it is concerned with whether a change in one variable can cause a change in another variable.[58] Regression techniques are essential in such analysis for answering some of the most puzzling questions and dilemmas posed by law and economics scholars, as these techniques enable both the estimation and validation of the model rather than descriptive analysis, which fails to control for the causal relationship between the investigated variables.

The mechanics of econometric analysis are generally based on cross-sectional analysis where researchers perform a regression analysis based on a given sample at a certain point in time.[59] Despite its usefulness and widespread application, cross-sectional analysis ignores the temporal dimension of the outcome of interest since it disallows the observation of the dependent variable both across groups and over time. Such an empirical strategy is possible by constructing a panel that exhibits observations on both dependent and independent variables across multiple years.[60] However, the neglect of the joint temporal and cross-sectional dimensions leads to a lack of control for unobserved effects across both space and time. Such an estimation strategy without control for unobserved effects inevitably leads to (i) omitted variable bias; and (ii) inconsistently estimated effects of independent variables on the dependent variable. Thus, a reliable econometric analysis should address these two issues.[61] Unobserved effects across space are commonly known as fixed-effects, unobserved heterogeneity, or simply heterogeneity bias since unobserved effects necessarily imply a degree of heterogeneity between groups

---

57 Kritzer (n 56) 3.

58 Epstein and Marvin (n 56) 171.

59 Joshua Angrist and Jorn-Steffen Pischke, 'The Credibility Revolution in Empirical Economics: How Better Research Design is Taking the Con Out of Econometrics' (2010) 24(2) *Journal of Economic Perspectives* 3–30.

60 See e.g. Joshua Angrist and Jorn-Steffen Pischke, *Mostly Harmless Econometrics: An Empiricist's Companion* (Princeton University Press 2009).

61 Epstein and Martin (n 56) 173.

with respect to the outcome of interest.[62] Similarly, unobserved effects across time are known as time-fixed effects, which allow the investigator to control for unobserved shocks to the outcome of interest and therefore tackle intertemporal omitted variable bias.[63] Finally, quantitative empirical analysis of exploiting policy changes is commonly known in applied econometrics as a difference-in-difference estimation strategy.[64] In this setup, the investigator is interested in whether an exogenous policy change affects the outcome of interest.[65] Such an effect necessarily depends on which groups, such as firms or individuals, are affected by the policy change and which of them remain unaffected. The group affected by a given policy change is referred to as the treatment group, whereas the unaffected group is known as the control group since it remains uninfluenced by the exogenous policy change.[66]

While employing empirical legal analysis, one has also to address its potential methodological limitations and should thus not overstate obtained results. Namely, Helland and Klick suggest that the fundamental problem in modern empirical economics is one of statistical identification.[67] Namely, estimated relationships may merely be the result of an omitted variable bias[68] and then it is very problematic to draw policy conclusions about the kind of legal institution a certain policy-maker should adopt based on the econometric evidence.[69] Credible empirical law and economics approaches should, in addition also address the problems of endogeneity, reverse causality, sample selection, and simultaneity.[70] Finally, reliable empirical analysis may also employ

---

62 See, e.g., Rok Spruk, 'Reliable Research Methods in Applied Econometrics for Competition Law' in Mitja Kovač and Ann-Sophie Vandenberghe (eds), *Economic Evidence in EU Competition Law* (Intersentia 2016).

63 ibid.

64 Angrist and Pischke (n 59) 185.

65 ibid.

66 Guido Imbens and Jeffrey Wooldridge, 'Recent Developments in the Econometrics of Program Evaluation' (2009) 47(1) *Journal of Economic Literature* 5–86.

67 That is, how can one isolate the causal effect of x on y? Eric Helland and Jonathan Klick, 'Legal Origins and Empirical Credibility' in Michael Faure and Jan Smits (eds), *Does Law Matter? On Law and Economic Growth* (Intersentia 2011) 108.

68 It is almost impossible for a researcher to know all of the important variables affecting the outcome of interest if that outcome is even moderately complex.

69 Sometimes it is also very difficult to obtain relevant data in order to quantify important variables properly. Although proxies sometimes exist, one has to note that they are never perfect.

70 As an example of such a credible empirical law and economics analysis, see e.g. Mitja Kovač, Salvini Datta and Rok Spruk, 'Pharmaceutical Product

natural experiments or quasi-randomizations where the previously mentioned difference-in-difference measure represents the treatment effect of certain legal intervention and the instrumental variables technique wherein a particular instrument affects the regressor of interest but does not directly affect the outcome studied.[71] In addition, to pursue a very robust empirical analysis, one may also employ the so-called regression discontinuity design,[72] extreme bounds analysis,[73] and structured modelling.[74]

Thus, a more rigorous empirical analysis of real contract law in action, where scholars would not resort to oversimplifications or overgeneralizations but would instead, in order to avoid the omitted variable bias problem, carefully investigate even the slightest variations in the facts of the cases and related judicial decision-making and judicial interpretation of abstract, general contract law rules.

3.2 Behavioural Contract Law and Economics

In the last two decades, social scientists and law and economics scholars have learned a great deal about how people actually make decisions. The field of behavioural economics, which was inspired by an observed difference between the predicted and actual behaviour of supposedly rational, self-interested, risk-averse persons, borrows from psychology and sociology to explain decisions inconsistent with classical economic assumptions about rational choice.

Liability, Litigation Regimes, and the Propensity to Patent: An Empirical Firm-level Investigation' (2021) 22(2) *SAGE Open* 18; and Mitja Kovač and Rok Spruk, 'Does the Ban on Trans-fats Improve Public Health?: In Search of the Optimal Policy Response' (2019) 55(3) *Journal of Regulatory Economics* 258–281.

71 Helland and Klick (n 67) 109.

72 Which focuses on observations just above or below some decision threshold that determines the treatment status—such subjects just above or below that threshold are likely to be very comparable. Helland and Klick (n 67) 109.

73 In econometrics, extreme bounds analysis is a type of sensitivity analysis that attempts to determine the most extreme possible estimates for a fixed subset of allowed coefficients and a variable set of linear homogeneous restrictions.

74 Structural modeling uses theory to adjust parameter estimates for any source of bias due to missing data. For example, if we are concerned that self-selection problems bias the estimated treatment effect of certain legal interventions, a structural approach would use microeconomics to model the decision-making related to such a rule and use that information in the estimation process to account for the unobserved heterogeneity that leads to the bias; Helland and Klick (n 67) 110.

Behavioural economics has revolutionized the way economists and (to a lesser extent) lawyers view the world.[75]

The observed behavioural inconsistencies and apparent shortcomings of the classical economic approach have induced some scholars to investigate the underlying motivations behind human behaviour in order to make more accurate models, in turn enabling more accurate predictions about how people act in the context of different legal rules. Simon's pioneering work, in particular his introduction of the concept of 'bounded-rationality',[76] was followed by several significant contributions[77] and, by the late 1970s, the field of behavioural economics was established. In 1979, Kahneman and Tversky published their ground-breaking article on prospect theory in which they introduced fundamental concepts in relation to reference points, loss aversion, utility measurement, and subjective probability judgements.[78] This seminal work has been followed by Thaler's contribution on a positive theory of consumer choice, which introduced the concept of mental accounting.[79]

In short, behavioural economics seeks to improve on classical models by incorporating information about the ways humans are not purely rational in their decision-making.[80] This resurgence of psychology in economics has also inspired some legal scholars to employ additional scholarship from both cognitive psychology and behavioural economics, which suggests that human behaviour often deviates from rational choice in systematic and predictable ways, to explain legal phenomena and to argue for legal reforms.[81] More

---

75 Peter Diamond and Hannu Vartiainen, *Behavioral Economics and its Applications* (Princeton University Press 2007) 4.

76 Herbert Simon, 'A Behavioral Model of Rational Choice' (1955) 69(1) *Quarterly Journal of Economics* 99.

77 See e.g. Harry Markowitz, 'The Utility of Wealth' (1952) 60 *Journal of Political Economy* 2; Maurice Allais, 'Fondements d'une Theorie Positive des Choix Comportant un Risque et Critique des Postulats et Axiomes de l'École Américaine' (1953) 21(4) *Econometrica* 503; Thomas Schelling, *Strategy of Conflict* (Harvard University Press 1960); and Daniel Ellsberg, 'Risk, Ambiguity and the Savage Axiom' (1961) 75(4) *Quarterly Journal of Economics* 643.

78 Daniel Kahneman and Amos Tversky, 'Prospect Theory: An Analysis of Decisions under Risk' (1979) 47 *Econometrica* 263.

79 Richard Thaler, 'Toward a Positive Theory of Consumer Choice' (1980) 1 *Journal of Economic Behavior and Organization* 39.

80 Cass Sunstein, *Behavioral Law and Economics* (Cambridge University Press 2000) 1–13.

81 Douglas Langevoort, 'Behavioral Theories of Judgment and Decision Making in Legal Scholarship: A Literature Review' (1998) 51(6) *Vanderbilt Law Review* 1499, 1450.

recently, behavioural law and economics has devoted considerable attention to the study of contract law.[82]

Behavioural contract law and economics argue that persons display bounded rationality, meaning that their decision-making is affected by a range of inherent and systemic cognitive biases, such as (a) over-optimism and self-serving conceptions of fairness; (b) reliance on heuristics and cognitive biases that lead to mistakes, such as the availability heuristic; and (c) incomplete self-control that induces persons to make decisions in conflict with their long-term self-interest.[83] Moreover, people might have bounded willpower and might be tempted and myopic.[84] Furthermore, people might be concerned with the well-being of others, and this concern and their self-conception can lead them in the direction of altruism (or at least cooperation) at the expense of their own material self-interest.[85] Jolls, Sunstein, and Thaler also suggest that behavioural insights should be employed in order to better explain both the effects and the content of contract law.[86]

Indeed, behavioural insights should be employed to help lawmakers achieve specified ends, such as deterring socially undesirable behaviour. Yet, one might also argue that all of the discussed behavioural insights and observed inconsistencies could be neatly explained from the classical contract law and economics perspective. Observed patterns, including behavioural biases, might actually result from completely rational *ex ante* decision-making in the context of positive transaction costs and asymmetric information. While classic contract law and economics assumes that people exhibit rational behaviour: that people are risk-averse, self-interested utility maximizers with stable preferences and the capacity to optimally accumulate and assess information, a large body of social science literature still demonstrates that these assumptions are not always accurate and that deviations from rational behaviour are both inevitable and predictable.[87] In other words, the employed methodological

---

82 For a synthesis of behaviouralbehavioral approaches to contract law, see Ann-Sophie Vandenberghe, 'Behavioral Approaches to Contract Law' in Gerrit De Geest (ed), *Contract Law and Economics: Encyclopedia of Law and Economics* (Edward Elgar Publishing 2011) 401.

83 Christine Jolls, Cass Sunstein and Richard Thaler, 'A Behavioral Approach to Law and Economics' in Cass Sunstein (ed), *Behavioral Law and Economics* (Cambridge University Press 2000) 13–58.

84 ibid.

85 ibid.

86 ibid.

87 Mitja Kovač, 'Competition Law and Behavioral Evidence in a Courtroom?' in Mitja Kovač and Ann-Sophie Vandenberghe (eds), *Economic Evidence in EU Competition Law* (Intersentia 2016) 104. See also Jolls et al. (n 83) 21.

framework, assumptions, and definitions inevitably affect lawyers' normative and positive analysis, conclusions, and suggestions.

Behavioural contract law and economics methodologically emphasize the role of factors such as promise-keeping and trust and examines how these are affected by the mode of contracting.[88] Numerous studies show that once methodological assumptions of perfect rationality are relaxed, some key conclusions of the economic analysis of contract law are not as robust as previously envisaged.[89] However, one has to note that behavioural contract theory has mainly focused on contracting issues rather than on contract law rules and has highlighted behavioural findings that may be employed in optimal contract design.[90] Namely, experimental studies mainly focus on investigating how commercial parties behave and act when they transact with each other in controlled environments, whereas they generally do not study the impact that different contract law rules might have on the behaviour of contracting parties. Finally, behavioural contract law and economics methodology has also been employed in the extensive study of consumer contracts and to identify effective legal approaches to consumer protection.[91]

---

[88] Eyal Zamir and Doron Teichman, *Behavioral Law and Economics* (Oxford University Press 2018) 238.

[89] For a synthesis, see Melvin Eisenberg, 'Behavioral Economics and Contract Law' in Eyal Zamir and Doron Teichman (eds), *The Oxford Handbook of Behavioral Economics and the Law* (Oxford University Press 2014) 109.

[90] This methodological approach focuses on the issues of desirable levels of contract enforcement, control of performance, compensation schemes, and the optimal design of auctions; Zamir and Teichman (n 88) 239. See also Iris Bohnet, Bruno Frey and Steffen Huck, 'More Order with Less Law: On Contract Enforcement, Trust, and Crowding' (2001) 95(1) *American Political Science Review* 131; Emel Filiz-Ozbay and Erkut Ozbay, 'Auctions with Anticipated Regret: Theory and Experiment' (2007) 97(4) *American Economic Review* 1407; and Armin Falk and Michael Kosfeld, 'The Hidden Costs of Control' (2006) 96(5) *American Economic Review* 1611.

[91] For example, it has been behaviourally demonstrated that practically no one reads standard-form contracts, and that neither professional training nor experience eliminates various cognitive biases; Yannis Bakos, Florencia Marotta-Wurgler and David Trossen, 'Does Anyone Read the Fine Print? Consumer Attention to Standard Form Contracts' (2014) 43(1) *Journal of Legal Studies* 1. These findings confirm previous classic contract law and economics findings on the signing-without-reading and signing-without-understanding problems. See Gerrit De Geest, 'The Signing-Without-Reading Problem: An Analysis of the European Directive on Unfair Contract Terms' in Hans-Bernd Schäfer and Hans Lwowski (eds), *Konsequenzen Wirtschaftsrechtlicher Normen: Ökonomische Analyse des Rechts* (Deutscher Universitätsverlag 2002) 76.

To sum up, behavioural contract law and economics enriches classical law and economics methodology by illuminating the ways that people, while making decisions, (a) display bounded rationality; (b) suffer from certain biases, such as over-optimism and self-serving conceptions of fairness; (c) follow heuristics, such as availability, which leads to mistakes; and (d) behave in accordance with prospect theory rather than expected utility theory.[92]

4. CAPACITY, LIMITATIONS AND THE POTENTIAL OF THE FUTURE USE OF CONTRACT LAW AND ECONOMICS

Previous parts of this chapter have outlined the impact of law and economics research on our understanding of contract law and practice, and the issues that this approach can illuminate. This part provides a brief summary of the capacity of law and economics, its limits (which questions the method, or methods are ill-suited to answer, taking into account underlying assumptions of the method), and its potential for future use in contract law research.

The novelty of the contract law and economics research programs lies in its search for what is good law by analyzing incentives, and the risk and transaction cost effects of legal rules. It attempts to determine which rules have the strongest welfare-enhancing effects and also offers useful advice on how to improve the technical formulation of contract law rules and contract terms. Namely, contract law and economics can be employed as a useful additional methodological tool that may support other doctrinal contract law studies by informing them which contract law rules have the most desirable effects, irrespective of how these contract rules are formulated. Thus, jurisprudence may employ contract law and economics methodology as an additional tool to evaluate contract law rules and norms according to a criterion of wealth maximization that determines whether or not analyzed rules heed or hinder the efficient use of resources. At the same time, contract law and economics may also offer useful advice to other doctrinal studies on how to, from an economic perspective, improve the technical formulation of a given rule. An underlying assumption of much law and economics literature is that lawmakers (legislators and judges) in fact balance the efficiency advantages and disadvantages of alternative solutions, although this balancing is often hidden (perhaps even to

---

[92] Jolls et al. also suggest that people have bounded willpower, are boundedly self-interested, and can be tempted and even myopic. In addition, they argue that people are on average concerned about the wellbeing of others, even strangers in some circumstances, and that a self-conception as a "moral" person might lead them in the direction of cooperation at the expense of their material, narrowly defined, rational self-interest; Jolls et al. (n 83) 23.

those lawmakers) behind a veil of "fairness" rhetoric. Contract law and economics may thus support other doctrinal studies by seeking to reduce these advantages and disadvantages to a single measure of efficiency as a way of more accurately assessing them by modelling their consequences. As a result, it may address what lawmakers or courts do—as opposed to what they say they do—and hence, more accurately address the law.

However, contract law and economics methodology, like any other, have their limits and shortcomings.

First, a more complete account of social welfare could be offered and might also consider competing normative values such as fairness, equity, rent-extraction[93] etc. to the extent that they affect social wealth. Contract law and economics focus on the goal of maximizing the contractual surplus while presuming that contracting parties' preferences are compatible with the tenets of rational choice theory.[94] Posner argues that this normative and positive combination has brought contract law and economics scholars to adopt a laissez-faire attitude toward contract law.[95] This analysis also takes for granted that contract law should avoid placing restrictions on the freedom of the contracting parties to design contractual provisions that best serve their needs. Intervention is justified only to correct for market failures, such as behavioural monopolies induced by one of the contracting parties, non-disclosure of information, and negative externalities.[96] Yet, in the daily operation of law, contract law doctrines reflect competing values, and even some law and economics scholars have expressed doubts about the ability of economic analysis to explain existing law or to come up with workable suggestions about the optimal design of contract law doctrine.[97]

A second shortcoming relates to the need for specifying an initial set of individual entitlements or contract rights, as a necessary prerequisite for operationalizing the methodological maxim of wealth maximization. Namely, in order to be able to achieve wealth maximization, one would have to know the exact values of all resources and then also establish the exact *ex ante* set of all rights and entitlements on those resources. Such *ex ante* specification of all

---

[93] Rent-seeking behaviour (or rent-seeking) is an economic concept that occurs when an entity seeks to gain added wealth without any reciprocal contribution of productivity. In other words, rents are profits that would not have been earned in a perfectly competitive and transparent economy.

[94] Eric Posner, 'Economic Analysis of Contract Law after Three Decades: Success or Failure?' (2003) 112(1) *Yale Law Journal* 832, 843.

[95] ibid 842.

[96] Alan Schwartz and Robert Scott, 'Contract Theory and the Limits of Contract Law' (2003) 113(2) *Yale Law Journal* 609, 633; and Shavell (n 2) 320–322.

[97] Posner (n 5).

individual entitlements or contract rights might be, due to the positive transaction costs and asymmetric information problems, prohibitive or at least very costly.

Third, as Zhou suggests, the assumptions of perfect rationality and perfect information are the main shortcomings of the contract law and economics approach.[98] Information in the real world is almost always imperfect, making any such analysis largely unreliable. More generally, if the assumptions about human behaviour that inform an economic model are inaccurate, any conclusions and predictions from that model will be unreliable and perhaps outright misleading. In addition, the recent breakthroughs in behavioural law and economics cannot completely cure this shortcoming, since the external validity of behavioural laboratory experiments may be questioned. Namely, the behavioural analysis is inductive where the effects of certain rules are analyzed in laboratory settings (and field experiments), but such experiments face a serious problem of external validity. There is actually no guarantee that people will make the same choices outside the laboratory, behavioural findings may point in opposite directions, it is hard to estimate the size of the behavioural effect, there may be selection biases, and it may not be clear which of the identified biases will take the overhand in individual real-world decision-making. All these issues represent important limitations from a legal point of view, which requires that legal rules are objective and generally applicable.[99]

Moreover, there are different reasons why lawyers, officials, and judges may be hesitant to adopt a full-fledged economic approach to contract or tort law. Van den Bergh offers two main reasons: (a) they may be subject to the cognitive bias that an economic approach boils down to an adoption of libertarian capitalist views, which are seen as biased in favor of corporate interests; and (b) they may have difficulties accepting the results of economic analysis that are counter-intuitive and contradict common expectations and ideas.[100]

In addition, economists who study contract law should also recognize that legal scholars often employ different methodologies than they do, and hence should not disregard their findings as irrelevant or insignificant.[101] Namely, economic literature dealing with contracts may not be sufficiently informed and lawyers relying on it should be aware of such potential limitations. As Katz suggests, non-lawyers should not misinterpret the mixed nature of legal

98 Qi Zhou, 'What can Contract Lawyers Learn from Law and Economics' (2011) 30(1) *The University of Tasmania Law Review* 157, 159.

99 Van den Bergh (n 31) 34.

100 ibid 43.

101 For example, they do not make such a sharp distinction between positive and normative analysis or between *de lege lata* and *de lege ferenda*; Hermalin et al. (n 30) 13.

discourse in order to avoid incorrect or misleading interpretations of legal phenomena.[102]

The future vitality of contract law and economics methodology is contingent on progress in the following areas: (a) the measurement and collection of data; (b) departures from the narrow assumption of rationality and effective modeling of bounded rationality; (c) uses of laboratory experiments to uncover the real incentive effects of different contract law rules and doctrines; (d) collaboration with professionals and scholars in other disciplines; (e) understanding of inductive legal reasoning and corresponding methodology; and (f) clear implementation and communication of the methodological approach to avoid unnecessary misunderstanding and confusion.

In other words, methodological developments remain highly dependent on an improved understanding and grasp of empirical reality.[103] Accordingly, contract law and economics scholarship should benefit from more intensive collaboration with professionals and scholars from other disciplines. Research in psychology, history, management, political science, administrative science, sociology, and behavioural economics should methodologically stimulate contract law and economics by offering both methodological concepts and tools, concepts and hypotheses, or empirical evidence and issues that ought to be addressed. Moreover, a more complete account of social welfare could be offered and might also consider competing normative values to the extent that they affect social wealth.

5. CONCLUSIONS

The contract law and economics approach dominates the intellectual discussion of nearly every doctrinal area of law in the United States, and it is again gaining relevance in other regions. After several decades of ground-breaking work, and despite continuing controversy, law and economics now occupies a secure position within the legal (and economic) academy. It has proved to be an effective methodological tool to structure policy debates and to analyze the potential effectiveness and/or efficiency of policy choices at both the systemic and individual contract levels.

As shown, by adopting an *ex ante* approach, contract law and economics provides information about the real-life effects of legislation, regulatory intervention, and case-law that remain hidden in an *ex post* perspective. Contract law and economics also provide an analytical framework to structure the policy

---

[102] Avery Katz, 'Positivism and the Separation of Law and Economics' (1996) 94(7) *Michigan Law Review* 2229.

[103] Brousseau and Glachant (n 47) 29.

discussion and enable a substantive understanding of the core of the regulatory problem that lawmakers are facing while designing an optimal policy response and boost recognition of false arguments.

Moreover, despite the approach's admitted limitations, contract lawyers can benefit from the economic analysis of contract law in at least three ways. First, economic analysis can be a method to evaluate the effectiveness of contract law rules. Second, it can help us in identifying the winners and losers created by the law. Third, it can broaden our understanding of business behaviour so that we can make contract law meet legitimate commercial and social expectations. Recent breakthroughs in behavioural, comparative, and empirical contract law and economics show that the discipline is intellectually vital and will certainly be improved further, as it engages with a wider and wider range of empirical data and analytical approaches. Finally, one must acknowledge that substantial blind spots remain for law and economics, which continues to struggle to provide satisfying descriptive and normative accounts of complex and voluminous legal acts, and of social functions of the law that cannot be conceived in terms of welfare maximization.

ACKNOWLEDGEMENTS

The author acknowledges financial support from the Slovenian Research Agency (research core funding No. P5-0128).

8. The experimental methods in contract law

Sergio Mittlaender

1. INTRODUCTION

Experimental research is empirical research. It often seeks to provide causal evidence of how people act and react, think and perceive, or judge and evaluate. While other empirical methods, such as observational studies, might also support causal inferences under certain conditions, the degree of control that experiments provide is stronger and permits more precise claims on what causes people to behave or think in a certain manner. In the study of contract law, experiments provide evidence on the factors driving decisions such as breaching a contract, renegotiating a deal, or investing in reliance that the promisor will keep the deal. This knowledge is valuable not only for academics developing theory, but also for lawyers drafting contracts or for judges and politicians implementing or changing policies. Therefore, experimental research is not an exclusively academic inquiry; it has normative implications relevant for practice and policy.

Experiments are, in general, particularly useful in the study of individual behavior, cognition, and perception. This is because they require human participants, who will be randomly allocated to act, decide, judge, or think either in the absence or in the presence of a factor that the researcher is interested in. The strength of an experimental investigation lies in the identification and measurement of the causal effect of this single factor. Questions related to the effect that a certain norm of contract law will have on individual behavior or cognition can hence be studied systematically with experiments. This applies to the behavior of the parties to a contract and to the decisions and judgments of judges and jurors. In addition, the way in which different factors affect how individuals interpret contractual or legal norms can also be studied with experiments, as it is up to a person to interpret the norm. In contrast, questions that are typical of doctrinal and jurisprudential studies, such as the classic 'What is law?' cannot be directly studied with experiments, as they do not immediately depend on how people behave or think.[1] They are also not useful for efforts to systematize the law, to understand the intent or reason for a legal norm, or to determine the validity of a legal norm. Experiments can, however, inform dogmatic studies by asserting, for instance, how a certain interpretation of a legal norm will impact the behavior, cognition, or perception of the individuals subject to that norm.

Much of the experimental literature in law has therefore focused on studying individual decision-making or cognitive processes by actors in different legal environments. By way of example, the initial experiments of Hoffmann and Spitzer investigated how pairs of subjects would bargain under different conditions, thereby testing the predictions from the Coase theorem, namely that individuals will bargain, in the absence of transaction costs, to achieve an efficient outcome independent of the initial allocation of rights.[2] Other experiments have focused on pretrial bargaining and the decision to litigate or settle.[3] But experiments have also studied how judges decide cases; for example, Guthrie, Rachlinski, and Wistrich have systematically examined how cognitive biases affect decision-making processes of judges and arbitrators.[4]

---

1 See Gareth Davies, 'The Relationship between Empirical Legal Studies and Doctrinal Legal Research' (2020) 13 *Erasmus Law Review* 3.

2 Elizabeth Hoffman and Matthew L. Spitzer, 'The Coase Theorem: Some Experimental Tests' (1982) 25 *The Journal of Law and Economics* 73. See also Elizabeth Hoffman and Matthew L. Spitzer, 'Entitlements, Rights, and Fairness: An Experimental Examination of Subjects' Concepts of Distributive Justice' (1985) 14 *The Journal of Legal Studies* 259; Elizabeth Hoffman and Matthew L. Spitzer, 'Experimental Tests of the Coase Theorem with Large Bargaining Groups' (1986) 15 *The Journal of Legal Studies* 149; Don L. Coursey, Elizabeth Hoffman and Matthew L. Spitzer, 'Fear and Loathing in the Coase Theorem: Experimental Tests Involving Physical Discomfort' (1987) 16 *The Journal of Legal Studies* 217.

3 Don L. Coursey and Linda R. Stanley, 'Pretrial Bargaining Behavior Within the Shadow of the Law: Theory and Experimental Evidence' (1988) 8 *International Review of Law and Economics* 161. See also Linda R. Stanley and Don L. Coursey, 'Empirical Evidence on the Selection Hypothesis and the Decision to Litigate or Settle' (1990) 19 *The Journal of Legal Studies* 145; George Loewenstein, Samuel Issacharoff, Colin Camerer and Linda Babcock, 'Self-Serving Assessments of Fairness and Pretrial Bargaining' (1993) 22 *The Journal of Legal Studies* 135; Linda Babcock, George Loewenstein, Samuel Issacharoff and Colin Camerer, 'Biased Judgments of Fairness in Bargaining' (1995) 85 *The American Economic Review* 1337.

4 See Chris Guthrie, Jeffrey J. Rachlinski and Andrew J. Wistrich, 'Blinking on the Bench: How Judges Decide Cases' (2007) 93 *Cornell Law Review* 1. See also Jeffrey J. Rachlinski, Sheri Lynn Johnson, Andrew J. Wistrich and Chris Guthrie, 'Does Unconscious Racial Bias Affect Trial Judges?' (2009) 84 *Notre Dame*

Scholars have further studied the factors that impact how jurors decide cases, ranging from the effect of caps on damages[5] to how jurors' votes are aggregated.[6] Individual decisions taken alone (such as those of judges), in pairs (such as those of parties negotiating or contracting), or even in groups (such as those of jurors) are the fundamental object of study of experiments.

The experimental method holds significant promise for advancing research in contract law, offering a rigorous framework for testing theoretical propositions and evaluating the effectiveness of legal interventions. Through carefully designed experiments, researchers can simulate real-world contractual scenarios, isolating variables to assess their impact on outcomes such as contract formation, interpretation, and enforcement. Experimental studies can provide valuable insights into the causal mechanisms underlying contractual behavior and legal decision-making, holding the potential to deepen our understanding of legal principles and to inform policy debates and shape the development of more equitable and efficient contractual regimes.

First, the foundations of the experimental method are described in section 2. Section 3 further discusses how experiments are and can be designed to study relevant legal questions. In section 4, important findings of experimental research in contract law are presented. The aim of this section is not to provide an exhaustive list of experiments in the area but rather to illustrate how the method, explained in the previous sections, is applied in the area, highlighting its limitations and implications. The chapter concludes by presenting avenues for future research.

2. THE EXPERIMENTAL METHOD

It is perhaps no exaggeration to say that the experimental method is the gold standard for determining cause and effect in empirical research. As a scientific procedure, an experiment is designed and implemented, most often, to test a hypothesis derived from a theory, aiming to provide evidence for a causal

---

Law Review 1195; Jeffrey J. Rachlinski, Chris Guthrie and Andrew J. Wistrich, 'Probable Cause, Probability, and Hindsight' (2011) 8 *Journal of Empirical Legal Studies* 72; Rebecca K. Helm, Andrew J. Wistrich and Jeffrey J. Rachlinski, 'Are Arbitrators Human?' (2016) 13 *Journal of Empirical Legal Studies* 666.

5 See Edith Greene, David Coon and Brian Bornstein, 'The Effects of Limiting Punitive Damage Awards' (2001) 25 *Law and Human Behavior* 217.

6 Serena Guarnaschelli, Richard D. McKelvey and Thomas R. Palfrey, 'An Experimental Study of Jury Decision Rules' (2000) 94 *American Political Science Review* 407. See also Marco Battaglini, Rebecca B. Morton and Thomas R. Palfrey, 'The Swing Voter's Curse in the Laboratory' (2010) 77 *The Review of Economic Studies* 61.

relationship by demonstrating what happens to an outcome variable when another variable is manipulated. For example, according to Aristotle's theory of gravity, objects fall at a speed proportional to their masses, from which a hypothesis is derived that a sphere of a certain volume and a certain mass will fall faster than a sphere of the same volume but smaller mass.[7] Galileo Galilei, while developing his theory of acceleration, had another hypothesis, namely that two objects of the same volume but different mass would fall at the same speed. He set out to perform an experiment in which he dropped two spheres of the same volume but different mass from the Tower of Pisa.[8] He manipulated only the mass of the spheres, keeping other variables constant (including the volume of the spheres, air temperature, and distance, among many others), and measured how this single factor, mass, affected the outcome variable: the speed at which the spheres fall. The experiment proved his hypothesis correct, as both spheres fell at the same speed, thereby disproving Aristotle's theory of gravity.

In his experiment, Galileo could control for the effect of other variables except mass by replicating the conditions in which the speed of two falling spheres of different mass would be measured. The controlled variation of a single factor, while keeping all other factors that could affect the outcome variable constant, provides a crucial advantage for experiments to identify causal effects. There are strategies to identify causal relationships with observational data, involving collecting data from other variables that could be affecting the outcome and concomitantly controlling for their effects, or using other, more advanced econometric methods and strategies to identify the cause of a change.[9] As discussed below, they have many advantages over experiments, but the difficulty in proving causal relations, pervasive in this type of empirical research, is smaller in experiments. Experiments can thus serve as a powerful tool and method to establish causal relations, on their own or in combination with other forms of empirical research.

Experiments gained traction in the natural sciences primarily through the scientific method's advancement and emphasis on empirical validation. As scientists recognized the need for controlled testing to establish causal relationships and validate theories, experiments became fundamental tools across disciplines like physics, chemistry, biology, and more. The success and reproducibility of experimental findings further propelled their widespread adoption, solidifying experiments as essential methodologies for scientific inquiry

---

7 Simon Gindikin, *Tales of Physicists and Mathematicians* (1st edn, Birkhauser 1988) 29.

8 Thomas B. Settle, 'An Experiment in the History of Science' (1961) 133 *Science* 19.

9 For a review, see the chapter on empirical studies on contracts in this volume.

and discovery. Since the 19th century, experimental methods have been an integral part of most psychological research. However, the same did not occur in economics, political science, sociology, and other social sciences. The first experiments in economics were run after 1945, and it was only in the late 1960s, with experiments run by Vernon Smith studying the behavior of sellers and buyers in markets, auctions, and bargaining, that it managed to establish a presence.[10] It still took decades, perhaps until the 1990s, for a broader acceptance of the method in economics.[11]

The most important reason for this is related to the object of study. When designing an experiment, the researcher must think of how to manipulate the factor of interest. While some are straightforward—such as the price of a good or the monetary penalty for a certain action—others are much harder to modulate. In fact, up to the 1980s, one could read in one of the most famous economics textbooks that economists 'cannot perform the controlled experiments of chemists or biologists because they cannot easily control other important factors. Like astronomers or meteorologists, they generally must be content largely to observe'.[12] Samuelson and Nordhaus might have had macroeconomic phenomena in mind when making such an affirmation, and it is true that manipulating inflation or unemployment rates for a random group of citizens and not for another one is a daunting task.

Experiments can be implemented in the field, where individual behavior is directly observed in real-world settings, or in the laboratory, where such behavior is observed in more controlled environments designed by the researcher. Findings of field experiments have a higher external validity (the extent to which the results of the experiment can be generalized to other situations, people, and settings), as they are obtained in situations where people interact naturally. However, field experiments can be challenging to implement due to various uncontrollable factors present in natural environments that can potentially affect the experiment's reliability. On the other hand, lab experiments

---

[10] Vernon L. Smith, 'An Experimental Study of Competitive Market Behavior' (1962) 70 *Journal of Political Economy* 111. See also Vernon L. Smith, 'Effect of Market Organization on Competitive Equilibrium' (1964) 78 *The Quarterly Journal of Economics* 182; Vernon L. Smith, 'Experimental Auction Markets and the Walrasian Hypothesis' (1965) 73 *Journal of Political Economy* 387; Vernon L. Smith, 'Experimental Studies of Discrimination Versus Competition in Sealed-Bid Auction Markets' (1967) 40 *The Journal of Business* 56. Smith would later win the Nobel Memorial Prize in Economics for this work.

[11] Armin Falk and James J. Heckman, 'Lab Experiments Are a Major Source of Knowledge in the Social Sciences' (2009) 326 *Science* 535.

[12] See Paul A. Samuelson and William D. Nordhaus, *Economics* (12th edn, McGraw-Hill Companies 1985) 8.

provide controlled conditions, facilitating precise manipulation of variables; yet, they may lack the real-life context and might induce artificial behaviors not typical in natural settings, at times limiting the generalizability of results.

Field experiments manipulate factors in the real world and hence also implement the experimental ideal of controlled variation and random assignment in order to identify causal relationships.[13] Often conducted in cooperation with governmental agencies or non-governmental organizations, they have important ethical considerations to account for.[14] More often, social scientists can easily manipulate the factor they want to investigate in the lab and compare individual behavior of those randomly allocated to interact in the absence of this factor with those randomly allocated to interact with it in place. Consider the effect of including a stipulated damages clause in a service contract on the decision of the promisor of how much effort, care, and diligence to put into the service to be rendered to the promisee. Can we simply collect data from real-life contractual relations? This would be a difficult task. First, one would need to measure the effort made by promisors on the provision of the service, which, by itself, is extremely hard to measure. But say this is possible, and that one could collect data also from the type of contract that each promisor made, distinguishing between those with a stipulated damages clause and those without it. The researcher, when comparing effort levels under each type of contract, would be comparing apples with bananas because of self-selection into each type of contract. People with certain characteristics might systematically prefer one type of contract over the other, leading to a biased sample which may not be representative of the population that the study is trying to represent. Can we be sure that those who choose a contract with a stipulated damages clause are equally motivated as those who choose a contract without that clause? Are these promisors equally competent at the task in hand, or can it be that more competent promisors would tend to choose one type of contract over the other? In other words, we would not know if an observed difference in effort levels of promisors between contracts with and without that clause is caused by the clause or by competence, motivation, or any other factor that differs between people with the obligation to perform under different contracts.

In a laboratory experiment, the experimenter knows and controls the material gains that subjects can make, depending on how they behave, the order in which they act and react, the information they have, whether the game is repeated or not, and whether reciprocity or reputation is at stake, among other factors. These variables are rarely, if ever, controlled in the field, so

13 Esther Duflo and Abhijit Banerjee (eds), *Handbook of Field Experiments* (1st edn, Elsevier 2017).

14 Trisha Phillips, 'Ethics of Field Experiments' (2021) 24 *Annual Review of Political Science* 277.

lab experiments permit the testing of precise predictions from game-theoretical models. Moreover, most often, decisions are rewarded monetarily, and all interactions are anonymous, such that subjects do not know with whom they are interacting. Payment according to the way participants act and react ensures that they take their decisions seriously, and anonymity ensures that other factors, including concerns that conduct will have reputational repercussions outside the lab, are minimized by design.

There is, however, persistent criticism of the use of lab experiments in the social sciences. One key line of critique is that student samples—those usually used in these experiments—are not representative of the whole population and that the incentives normally provided to subjects, including monetary payments, consist of small sums.[15] While the influence of the size of the stakes has been found to be negligible in experiments involving simple games played between two participants,[16] this does not immediately extrapolate to other types of decisions and games. People in the 'real world' could behave differently because of demographics, higher monetary incentives involved in many decisions, or because the conditions in the experiment affect people's decision-making process in different ways than conditions in the outside world. Moreover, subjects self-select into the experiment, and even though they are never told about what the experiment will consist of before it starts, people willing to be recruited to take part might differ systematically from people who are not willing to register to be recruited.

These criticisms boil down to the issue of 'external validity'. Can we be sure that a causal effect identified in the lab also appears in the 'real world'? This is certainly a question one must have in mind when engaging in experimental research. Another question or common criticism is the lack of realism in lab

---

[15] Steven D. Levitt and John A. List, 'What Do Laboratory Experiments Measuring Social Preferences Reveal about the Real World?' (2007) 21 *Journal of Economic Perspectives* 153.

[16] Robert Slonim and Alvin E. Roth, 'Learning in High Stakes Ultimatum Games: An Experiment in the Slovak Republic' (1998) 66 *Econometrica* 569. See also Lisa Cameron, 'Raising the Stakes in the Ultimatum Game: Experimental Evidence from Indonesia' (1999) 37 *Economic Inquiry* 47; Robert Forsythe, Joel L. Horowitz, N.E. Savin and Martin Sefton, 'Fairness in Simple Bargaining Experiments' (1994) 6 *Games and Economic Behavior* 347; John A. List and Todd L. Cherry, 'Learning to Accept in Ultimatum Games: Evidence from an Experimental Design that Generates Low Offers' (2000) 3 *Experimental Economics* 11; Jeffrey Carpenter, Eric Verhoogen and Stephen Burks, 'The Effect of Stakes in Distribution Experiments' (2005) 86 *Economic Letters* 393. But see Steffen Andersen, Seda Ertaç, Uri Gneezy, Moshe Hoffman and John A. List, 'Stakes Matter in Ultimatum Games' (2011) 101 *The American Economic Review* 3427.

experiments. Reality is messy, so field data is messy, and conditions are less tightly controlled. An experiment, in isolating a single factor for study, creates an environment that might not be representative of 'real life' situations. However, if one is interested in testing predictions from theories, then the only real issue is determining the best way to isolate the effect one wants to test.[17]

3. THE EXPERIMENTAL METHOD IN LEGAL RESEARCH

Experiments allow the researcher to test hypotheses in decision environments that involve people, norms, sanctions, or other factors that are crucial to the law. Put simply, they allow the researcher to manipulate a variable, such as the presence of a specific legal norm, and to randomly assign some of the participants to a control group in which this norm is absent and other participants to a treatment group in which this norm is present. The conjunction of random assignment of participants to each group and the isolated variation of only one thing—in this case, the legal norm—that differs between the groups permits the identification of the causal effect of that specific legal norm on human behavior. If people randomly assigned to the treatment group in which this legal norm is present behave differently from people randomly assigned to the control group in which this norm is absent, and there is no other difference in the decision environments of both groups except for the presence of this legal norm, then the legal norm is seen to cause a change in the behavior of people.

A fundamental function of the law, albeit perhaps not the only one, is to influence and shape human actions and behavior. Liability rules induce people to take care and to invest in precautions to avoid liability from accidents. Damages for breach of contract induce promisees to make reliance investments since they are insured against loss of those investments caused by breach by the promisor; that is, knowing that, if the promisor breaches, then the promisee will be compensated for the loss of such reliance investments, the promisee has more incentives to invest. Damages also induce promisors to perform their contractual obligations to avoid the duty to pay damages in case they decide to breach.[18] The soundness of theoretical predictions such as these should be

---

17 Falk and Heckmann, 'Lab Experiments Are a Major Source of Knowledge in the Social Sciences' (n 11) 536.

18 Steven Shavell, 'Strict Liability Versus Negligence' (1980) 9 *The Journal of Legal Studies* 1. See also Steven Shavell, 'On Liability and Insurance' (1982) 13 *The Bell Journal of Economics* 120; Steven Shavell, 'A Model of the Optimal Use of Liability and Safety Regulation' (1984) 15 *Rand Journal of Economics* 271; Robert Cooter, 'Prices and Sanctions' (1984) 84 *Columbia Law Review* 1523;

verified empirically, as they provide normative foundations for why the law is as it is. Moreover, predictions from theory inform policy-makers on how the law should change to achieve higher levels of socially desirable reliance investment and contractual performance, and to provide insights for contract drafters on how best to design contracts to incentivize those actions.

Results from experimental investigations can and are used to improve theories or to develop new ones. Experimental findings on how high stipulated damages clauses for breaching a contract might erode the intrinsic motivation of promisors to perform, based on the value they place on keeping promises and contracts, led to a revision of the theoretical foundations underlying the use of liquidated damages clauses.[19] If promisors perceive the stipulated damages clause as a price for breach and feel less morally compelled to perform in the presence of such a clause, then the theoretical prediction that high liquidated damages clauses encourage the performance of contracts should be reviewed.

Experimental results, however, are not only useful for improving existing theories. They further inform policy-makers concerned with improving the law. If we can be more confident that a theory is correct, then we can use the theory to predict how people will change their behavior when the law changes. We can then have a higher degree of confidence that if we indeed change a legal norm, such as the norm limiting the amount of liquidated damages, or a certain policy, such as systematically including that clause in all contracts executed by a firm or a state, then resources will be well spent, and we can predictably achieve a desirable outcome.

Policy-makers need to know how to achieve their objectives, and theoretical predictions provide such answers. There are, however, classic examples of policy interventions that were backed by simple theoretical models but had an overall effect opposite to what theory would predict. For example, in theory, the introduction of a penalty that does not alter other factors should reduce the occurrence of the sanctioned behavior. Therefore, to deter late arrivals, we can impose a fine for being late. However, there is evidence that, at times, the opposite effect can be observed, perhaps because a fine crowds out guilt aversion or is interpreted as a price, reducing the moral disapproval of the act. For instance, the introduction of a penalty for being late increased the number of late arrivals in day-care centers in Israel.[20] Similarly, theories of human behavior predicted that the introduction of a premium or payment for a certain act should increase the occurrence of the rewarded behavior. To motivate

---

Richard Craswell, 'Contract Law, Default Rules, and the Philosophy of Promising' (1989) 88 *Michigan Law Review* 489.

[19] See section 4.3 below.

[20] Uri Gneezy and Aldo Rustichini, 'Pay Enough or Don't Pay at All' (2000) 115 *The Quarterly Journal of Economics* 791.

people to donate blood, we can add a payment for that action, inducing people to do it more often to earn the payment. However, at times, the opposite effect is observed, perhaps because of crowding out of intrinsic motivation or altruistic considerations. The introduction of payment for blood donation, in fact, reduced blood donations in several instances.[21]

Experimental research in law is often designed to address psychological or economic theories, and one can think about two types of paradigmatic experiments in each area.[22] Both types share the same core features, including random assignment of subjects to treatments and controlled variation of the variable or variables under study, both seeking to hold all other variables that could affect the outcome variable constant by design. There are some differences, though, which are described in the next paragraphs. These differences make one type of paradigmatic experiment more adequate to answer certain kinds of questions than the other, and knowledge of such differences can guide scholars to design their experiments and readers to better interpret the implications and generalizability of the findings. While the characteristics of economic experiments permit careful investigation of individual decisions and behavior, those of psychological experiments focus on individual perceptions and cognitive processes. Rather than being antagonists, these experiments often complement each other, delivering, when considered together, a broader picture of how people behave and think, depending on their perceptions and emotional mechanisms.

Economic experiments rely heavily on game theory, most often investigating how people behave when interacting with others (such as in a contract, where the action of one party will directly affect the other party). Participants are paid, in cash, according to the decisions they make in the experiment, and earn more or less depending on their choices and on the choices of other subjects, as fixed by the game-theoretical foundation of the interaction. Since such incentives vary with outcomes that result from subjects' choices, they provide motivation for subjects to undertake actions that maximize their preferences (i.e., to choose their most preferred action) in the experiment.[23] If there is a trade-off between acting in a way that maximizes one's profits and acting immorally (e.g., breaching a contract to earn extra profits and performing a

---

21 Richard M. Titmuss, *The Gift Relationship (Reissue)* (1st edn, Bristol University Press 2018). See also Carl Mellström and Magnus Johannesson, 'Crowding Out in Blood Donation: Was Titmuss Right?' (2008) 6 *Journal of the European Economic Association* 845.

22 Rachel Croson, 'Why and How to Experiment: Methodologies from Experimental Economics' (2002) (4) *University of Illinois Law Review* 921.

23 See Vernon L. Smith, 'Experimental Economics: Induced Value Theory' (1976) 66 *The American Economic Review* 247.

contract to respect the promisee's autonomy or the norm that promises should be kept), then subjects only face a real dilemma in economic experiments when their choices are rewarded monetarily. Economic experiments are especially adequate when studying individual decisions that have costs and benefits affecting the decision-maker, including those involved in negotiations, contracting, investing, and performing contracts.

Psychological experiments at times reward participants monetarily, but often do not, instead paying a fixed sum for participation. When the aim is to investigate individual perceptions of justice or the social appropriateness of an action, such experiments typically use vignette or scenario studies that differ in respect to the variable being manipulated. In a vignette or scenario study, subjects are provided with written descriptions of a legally relevant situation, and the key factor under investigation is manipulated while keeping all the remaining factors and details of the situation identical. Subjects are then asked to fill out a questionnaire where they report their perception, impression, opinion, or belief. For this, they might receive a fixed monetary payment, but this payment is not larger or smaller depending on the decisions and actions that subjects make.

In contrast to economic experiments, psychological experiments often deceive subjects. Psychological experiments that attempt to differentiate theories of how people reason require a comparison of how people reason when they believe one thing or another. Deceiving subjects about the existence of other subjects with whom they believe they are interacting, the payoffs others would be receiving, or other things is a valuable tool that is often used in psychological experiments.[24] Economic experiments do not generally use deception, and all the information that subjects receive must be true.

Validity and reliability are essential considerations in experimental research in law, as they influence the credibility and generalizability of findings. Validity concerns arise when experiments fail to accurately measure the intended concepts or adequately represent the complexities of legal relationships, potentially leading to erroneous conclusions about legal interventions or behavior. Similarly, reliability issues may emerge if experimental procedures lack standardization or exhibit substantial variability across experiments. Challenges to the validity and reliability of experimental results can occur through falsification, where errors in design, data collection, or data analysis undermine

---

24 One classic example of deception in psychological experiments is Stanley Milgram's obedience study. Participants were led to believe they were administering electric shocks to another person (who was actually an actor and not receiving any shocks), testing obedience to authority figures. The setup was designed to deceive participants into thinking they were causing harm, though, in reality, no harm was inflicted. Stanley Milgram, 'Behavioral Study of Obedience' (1963) 67 *The Journal of Abnormal and Social Psychology* 371.

the accuracy of the findings, casting doubt on the credibility of the outcomes. Replicability, crucial for confirming the robustness of results, is hindered in legal research due to contextual nuances and jurisdictional variations, among other reasons. Overcoming these challenges requires attention to experimental design and transparency in reporting methods and results, ultimately enhancing the reliability and applicability of experimental findings to inform legal policy-making and practice.

4. THE EXPERIMENTAL METHOD IN THE STUDY OF CONTRACT LAW

Experimental scholarship within contract law has emerged as an illuminating avenue, attempting to expand traditional legal analysis by integrating an empirical method. This dynamic field explores multifaceted dimensions of contractual relationships, delving into the intricacies of human behavior, perception, and cognition to understand how individuals engage in, perform, and enforce contracts. This approach contributes to the refinement of legal theory and practice, offering insights that bridge the gap between theoretical constructs and real-world contractual dealings.

The experimental literature in contract law includes economic and psychological experiments. The first category is especially informative in the study of individual behavior that has costs and benefits for the individual, and therefore predominates in the study of negotiations, contracting, and performing contracts. In the first subsection below, experiments focused on the decision to keep contractual promises and the causes of such decisions are presented. They reveal a rich debate on why people keep their promises, providing an example of how experiments can shed light on the factors that really drive promisors' decisions to perform.

Psychological experiments are especially useful for studying individual perceptions and cognition, and the second subsection presents recent examples of experiments studying people's perceptions of the moral value of breach, a factor that also affects the promisor's decision to perform and which interacts with the type of legal remedy for breach that the law adopts. The last two sections focus on studies of the effect of remedies for breach of contract that are agreed upon by the parties (stipulated damages clauses) or that are imposed by the law (legal damages for breach), focusing on two factors apt to induce promisors to perform their contracts, a decision with pervasive consequences in the economy. They reveal how stipulated damages have consequences not predicted by existing theories and how damages for breach have beneficial effects that go beyond inducing promisors to perform.

These are not, for sure, the only experiments in contract law, and the following subsections illustrate how the method can be and is applied, discussing methodological limitations and potential applications of experimental findings. The latter are, at times, more practical, offering guidance for contract drafters or negotiators. At times, experimental findings present challenges to existing predictions from theories on how people behave, paving the way for potential refinements in theory.

4.1 Non-Monetary Reasons to Keep Contractual Promises

Contracts, like promises more generally, commit individuals to a future course of action. A person who contracts has an obligation to take the promised action when the time comes to perform. Moreover, the promise creates expectations for the promisee that she or he will receive the promised performance. If the promisor breaks the promise, then the promisor disappoints the promisee and at the same time violates the norm that promises must be kept or that *pacta sunt servanda*. These two dimensions, i.e., fulfilling the expectations of the promisee and respecting the moral norms that promises ought to be kept, provide two different motives for promisors to keep contracts that are independent of material gains, i.e., that do not depend on sanctions, fines, or other material penalties.

The first motive for the promisor to perform even when performance is not profitable is to avoid feelings of guilt.[25] The theory of guilt aversion assumes that some people suffer a loss of utility when they believe they have let another person's expectations down. The promisee expects the promisor to perform, and the promisor knows that. If the promisor breaches, then he or she disappoints the promisee, and this will create feelings of guilt that bring disutility to the promisor. To avoid this loss of utility, the promisor might choose not to breach the contract even when doing so would bring monetary profits.

The theory was first tested in a laboratory experiment that implements a modified version of the trust game. In this game, subjects interact in pairs. The first person ('A') can choose *Out* or *In*. If A chooses *Out*, both A and the second person ('B') earn $5 each, and the game is over. If A chooses *In*, then the game continues and B can choose *Roll* or *Don't Roll*. If B chooses *Don't*

---

[25] As introduced in Gary Charness and Martin Dufwenberg, 'Promises and Partnership' (2006) 74 *Econometrica* 1579, formalized in Pierpaolo Battigalli and Martin Dufwenberg, 'Guilt in Games' (2007) 97 *The American Economic Review* 170, and Pierpaolo Battigalli and Martin Dufwenberg, 'Dynamic Psychological Games' (2009) 144 *Journal of Economic Theory* 1, and expanded in Topi Miettinen, 'Promises and Conventions – An Approach to Pre-Play Agreements' (2013) 80 *Games and Economic Behavior* 68, and later by Martin Kaae Jensen and Maria Kozlovskaya, 'A Representation Theorem for Guilt Aversion' (2016) 125 *Journal of Economic Behavior and Organization* 148.

Roll, B earns $14 and A earns 0. If B chooses *Roll*, then both parties earn $10.[26] Parties are better off if A chooses *In* and B subsequently chooses *Roll*, each earning $10. But player A has to trust that B will choose *Roll* if A chooses *In*, because after A chooses *In*, B can take the decision that maximizes his or her profits by choosing *Don't Roll* and earn $14 while A would then earn 0. The strict rational choice prediction for the game is for A to choose *Out* at the beginning, since A must anticipate that, if A chooses *In*, then B will choose *Don't Roll* to earn the most, and A would then earn nothing. It is hence better for A to choose *Out* and earn $5, and this is the equilibrium of the game.

To study the role of guilt aversion for promisors in keeping promises, the authors allowed B to send a message to A before they made any decision. Many Bs took this opportunity and sent messages with a promise or a similar statement of intent to induce A to trust them and to choose *In*. Although subjects were always free to repay trust or not, with the messages and promises being no more than 'cheap talk',[27] 79% of Bs who sent a promise to choose *Roll* indeed chose *Roll*, whereas only 33% who did not send a promise chose *Roll*. Promises, even in the absence of any enforcement mechanism, induced a substantial change in behavior and increased mutual gains considerably.

In order to study whether guilt aversion was a motive for this higher rate of choosing *Roll*, Charness and Dufwenberg asked As to guess the likelihood that Bs would choose *Roll*.[28] While As who received a promise believed that the likelihood *of Roll* was 64%, As who did not receive a promise had a significantly lower belief of 50%. Similarly, Bs who sent a promise reported higher guesses about As' guesses (63%) than those who did not send a promise (50%).

The authors concluded that the experiment provided support for the theory of guilt aversion. Legal sanctions are hence not the sole factor driving the decision to perform, as feelings of guilt induce some promisors to keep their promises. Guilt aversion will have an effect even in contractual relations in which parties know that the other one will not have the means or the interest in enforcing the contract in case of breach, perhaps because of high legal costs or time constraints. We therefore know that, even in those circumstances, or in jurisdictions where legal enforcement is lacking, contracts will still at times be kept, and parties might want to make clear to the other one what their

26 The original game had an additional slight detail that is omitted in this explanation since it does not substantially alter the trade-off and decisions that parties had to make. Please see the complete description in Charness and Dufwenberg, 'Promises and Partnership' (n 25).

27 See Joseph Farrell and Matthew Rabin, 'Cheap Talk' (1996) 10 *Journal of Economic Perspectives* 103, and Joseph Farrell, 'Talk is Cheap' (1995) 85 *The American Economic Review* 186.

28 Charness and Dufwenberg, 'Promises and Partnership' (n 25).

expectations are and how breach will affect them. In this manner, the role of guilt is enhanced, and we can expect a higher level of performance.

The second motive for a promisor to keep their promise, proposed by theory[29] and shown in experiments,[30] is related to preferences for complying with norms. There is a moral and social norm that people should keep promises.[31] Some individuals might derive disutility not from disappointing the promisee, as assumed by the theory of guilt aversion, but instead from disrespecting the moral norm, as assumed by the theory of moral costs.[32] Therefore, independent of whether the promisee expects the promisor to keep the promise or not, the promisor will derive disutility from violating a moral and social norm and has incentives to keep promises, even when doing so is unprofitable, to avoid the moral costs stemming from violating the norm of keeping promises, or of *pacta sunt servanda.*

Experiments that followed Charness and Dufwenberg provide evidence for the theory of moral costs. Vanberg attempted to prove that a desire to respect the moral norm of keeping promises leads promisors to keep their promises and designed an experiment to achieve independent variation in promises and in parties' beliefs.[33] He did so by building upon the experiment of Charness and Dufwenberg and randomly switching the promisor. In some cases, the promisee would be matched with the same promisor that made the promise, but in other cases, the promisee would face another person in place of the promisor who had made a promise to the promisee. The promisor knew, in the latter case, that the promisee had received a promise from another person and hence expected to receive performance, but the promisee did not know that they had been rematched with another promisor. Promisors who had sent a promise to repay another promisee did not repay the new, 'switched' promisee more often than in cases where there was no promise. This was observed independently of the fact that promisors knew that the switched promisee expected to receive performance. The experiment provides evidence that a preference for respecting moral norms can, by itself and independent of guilt aversion, induce promisors to keep their promises.

---

29 Tore Ellingsen and Magnus Johannesson, 'Promises, Threats and Fairness' (2004) 114 *The Economic Journal* 397.

30 Christoph Vanberg, 'Why Do People Keep Their Promises? An Experimental Test of Two Explanations' (2008) 76 *Econometrica* 1467.

31 See John Rawls, *A Theory of Justice* (Harvard University Press 1971) 344.

32 Ellingsen and Johannesson, 'Promises, Threats and Fairness' (n 29), and Navin Kartik, 'Strategic Communication with Lying Costs' (2009) 76 *Review of Economic Studies* 1359.

33 Vanberg, 'Why Do People Keep Their Promises?' (n 30).

In these experiments, subjects in fact received an amount of money that corresponded to their real choices. This is most adequate since using a hypothetical scenario and simply asking people what they would do in that situation would not present a dilemma for subjects, a dilemma that exists in real life. One cannot know if guilt or moral norms indeed lead people to keep their promises without this having real costs. If subjects received a fixed payment of x dollars or euros for their participation, then subjects could simply say they would keep the promise and earn x. In contrast, in the experiments above, if subjects decided to keep the promise, then they would earn $10 instead of $14, and avoiding guilt or respecting the moral norm has a real cost of $4.

In conclusion, there is, by now, causal evidence collected from different experiments for both motives, namely guilt aversion and a preference for compliance with moral norms, which may constrain parties to avoid breaching contracts even in the absence of legal sanctions for breach. More recent studies attempted to refine those theories. Kawagoe and Narita assumed that promisors feel guilt only if they disappoint another person's expectations that they themselves induced by their own actions, but do not find substantial evidence for such assumption.[34] Ederer and Stremitzer propose a lexicographic theory of guilt aversion in which a promisee's expectations matter only if there is a direct promissory link between the promisor and the promisee, and hence only if the promisor's own promise induced them, and find more robust evidence corroborating it.[35] There is mixed evidence, and both guilt aversion and moral norms can explain many but not all aspects of individual behavior observed in the lab.[36]

There are several applications of these findings to contract design. Since breaking a promise imposes costs on the promisor who decides to breach, either because of the violation of the moral norm or because of the guilt experienced, contracts should assign the responsibility for entrusting the promise to the party who might breach it. The study by Charness et al. indicates that, in a highly stylized setting, when workers take the lead in contract negotiations and specify their own effort commitments, both the effort they exert

---

34 Toshiji Kawagoe and Yusuke Narita, 'Guilt Aversion Revisited: An Experimental Test of a New Model' (2014) 102 *Journal of Economic Behavior & Organization* 1.

35 Florian Ederer and Alexander Stremitzer, 'Promises and Expectations' (2017) 106 *Games and Economic Behavior* 161.

36 Gary Charness and Martin Dufwenberg, 'Participation' (2011) 101 *The American Economic Review* 1211. See also Dorothee Mischkowski, Isabel Thielmann and Andreas Glöckner, 'Minimizing Inequality Versus Maximizing Joint Gains: On the Relation Between Personality Traits and Different Prosocial Motivations' (2019) 81 *Journal of Research in Personality* 153.

and their overall gains are greater compared to situations when the employer takes the initiative or sets the performance goal.[37] Stone and Stremitzer use guilt aversion theory to explore the investments made by those who receive promises.[38] In many real-world contracts, parties must invest in order to make profits, which might not come directly from performance of the contract. For instance, when hiring a singer to perform in a club, the person hiring the singer must buy beverages, food, and merchandise to make profits from such sales, and if the singer does not show up, then all those investments are wasted. The authors theorize that promisees may intentionally overinvest to increase the guilt that the promisor would suffer in case the promisor breaches. This is because the more promisees invest, the more they stand to lose in case of breach, and the higher the guilt that promisors would incur if they decided to breach. They find that the availability of legal recourse for broken promises mitigates this tendency to overinvest, which they describe as 'psychological lock-in'. Their experiment shows how the legal norm has advantages that are often overlooked.

4.2 Moral Value of Breach

Contract law is based on the principle that *pacta sunt servanda*, that people should keep their contractual promises. Understanding how people perceive, from a moral standpoint, their contractual obligations is crucial for understanding why they sometimes keep contracts and at other times breach them. If people believe that breaching a contract is morally wrong, then they are more likely to comply with the contract, even if they could breach it without legal penalty, or with a legal penalty that they consider affordable. A series of experiments has studied how people perceive the moral value or social appropriateness of breach of contract in different types of paradigmatic situations and under different legal norms. Consonant with the experimental idea, comparisons are made one at a time, as the researcher varies one factor and studies the effect of this single factor on people's perceptions. Given the object of study, experiments relying on psychological theories are of special interest, as people do not earn more or less, in reality, depending on how they perceive a certain act such as breach of contract.

Wilkinson-Ryan and Baron, using short scenarios in a psychological experiment, asked neutral individuals to levy damages on a promisor breaching a

---

[37] Gary Charness and others, 'Promises in Contract Design' (2013) 64 *European Economic Review* 194.

[38] See Rebecca Stone and Alexander Stremitzer, 'Promises, Reliance, and Psychological Lock-In' (2020) 49 *The Journal of Legal Studies* 33.

hypothetical contract.[39] There were no real subjects deciding to perform or breach, or bearing the monetary consequences of such acts, and this is why it is a scenario study and not an economic game. The authors first compared a situation in which the motive to breach was to earn higher profits with a situation in which the motive was to avoid economic losses. They found that people show a propensity to impose higher amounts of damages in the first case; that is, they appear to view breaching a contract to earn more profit as morally inferior to breaching a contract to avoid further losses. In addition, when comparing an intentional breach of contract that imposes a certain loss to the party with a negligent tort that imposes the same loss to someone who was not part of a contractual relationship, subjects were also more punitive toward the first party, which the authors interpret as showing that people treat willful breach as intentional harm-doing.[40] This appears to be because someone who behaves negligently, and thereby harms another person, does not have the intention to do so—unlike someone who intentionally breaches a contract, knowing that this act will harm the promisee. Wilkinson-Ryan and Hoffman studied these questions further and considered subjects' feelings of being betrayed and explored when victims of breach.[41] Similar to the results described above, subjects felt more highly betrayed, expressed higher levels of anger, and consequently imposed higher damages in case of breach of contract than in tort.

Mittlaender investigated people's perceptions of the moral value of breach by comparing breaches to profit with breaches to avoid an economic loss in conjunction with the efficiency of the breach.[42] Sometimes, a breach of contract is the action that maximizes social welfare (efficient breach), but at other times it is the performance of the contract that maximizes social welfare. When comparing situations in which the breach was efficient and inefficient, people's perceptions of the moral value of the breach did not change, but when comparing the motive to breach, people perceived breach to profit, independent of efficiency, as more inappropriate than breach to avoid losses. The fairness of the outcome is fundamental for the perception of the immorality of breach, as breaches to profit lead to a highly unequal outcome in which the promisor

---

39 Tess Wilkinson-Ryan and Jonathan Baron, 'Moral Judgment and Moral Heuristics in Breach of Contract' (2009) 6 *Journal of Empirical Legal Studies* 405.

40 Tess Wilkinson-Ryan, *Fool Proof: How Fear of Playing the Sucker Shapes Our Selves and the Social Order – And What We Can Do About It* (Harper Wave 2023) 104.

41 Tess Wilkinson-Ryan and David A. Hoffman, 'Breach is for Suckers' (2010) 63 *Vanderbilt Law Review* 1001.

42 Sergio Mittlaender, 'Morality, Compensation, and the Contractual Obligation' (2019) 16 *Journal of Empirical Legal Studies* 119.

increases his or her gains, something that does not occur in breaches to avoid losses, which lead to a more equal outcome. Second, the study investigated the effect of the payment of fully compensatory damages on people's perception of the moral value of breach. The payment of expectation damages reduced the perceived immorality of breach, and about half of the participants thought that an intentional breach of contract, when followed by the payment of expectation damages, was not immoral. These results contribute to the discussion on whether contract law, by adopting expectation damages as the default remedy for breach, as in common law jurisdictions, converges or diverges from commonsense morality.[43]

4.3 Behavioral Effects of Liquidated Damages Clauses

Liquidated damages clauses (also known as stipulated damages clauses) are widely used in contracts in common law jurisdictions. A liquidated damages clause is a provision in a contract that specifies the amount of money or other remedy that one party must pay to the other in case of breach of contract. The amount of liquidated damages, or a formula for calculating them, is typically agreed upon by the parties when the contract is signed. Liquidated damages clauses are designed to compensate the non-breaching party for the losses suffered and to deter the breaching party from breaching the contract. Economic theory predicts that imposing the duty to pay a predetermined amount in case of breach by the promisor should induce the promisor to perform, and that the higher the amount, the less breach we would observe. But by including such a clause in the contract, the party negotiating for it signals distrust in the promisor, and such a clause might well crowd out deontological reasons for the promisor to perform. The clause establishes what can be interpreted as a price to breach, and the sense of moral duty to keep the contract might be eroded. This is a testable hypothesis, which would imply more breach in the presence of such a clause, and which contrasts with the economic prediction that including such a clause would lead to less breach of contract. Evidence on the real effect of such clauses would provide useful knowledge for drafting contracts and for contract law's acceptance of such provisions.

Tess Wilkinson-Ryan investigated whether liquidated damages clauses can encourage, rather than discourage, breach of contract, a hypothesis derived

[43] Steven Shavell, 'Is Breach of Contract Immoral' (2006) 56 *Emory Law Journal* 439. See also Steven Shavell, 'Why Breach of Contract May Not Be Immoral Given the Incompleteness of Contracts' (2009) 107 *Michigan Law Review* 1569; Seana Shiffrin, 'The Divergence between Contract and Promise' (2007) 120 *Harvard Law Review* 708; Seana Shiffrin, 'Could Breach of Contract be Immoral?' (2009) 107 *Michigan Law Review* 1551.

from experiments which show that individuals may treat a fine as a price rather than a sanction.[44] She asked participants to indicate how much they would require to breach a hypothetical contract, comparing a situation in which the contract included a liquidated damages clause with another in which damages for breach were determined by general contract law. Except for this variation, the situations were identical. The hypothesis was that participants would require a lower amount to breach when the contract included a liquidated damages clause because such a clause makes the consequence of breach explicit, clarifying the expectations of the parties and thereby allowing breach without violation of the parties' mutual understanding. This is expected to make people's decision to breach more strategic and more self-interested, and to crowd out the promisor's intrinsic motivation to keep contractual promises for deontological reasons. Subjects, in fact, required less to breach the contract in the presence of a liquidated damages clause than in the case that damages were not explicit in the contract.

Depoorter, Freund, and Hoeppner investigated, in an economic experiment, whether proposing such a clause induces the other party to behave less cooperatively and trustworthily because of negative reciprocity.[45] In other words, proposing such a clause, when compared with a situation in which the consequence of uncooperative behavior is determined by the background legal regime or under no legal protection at all, induces negative reciprocal behavior by the promisor. That is, it signals a lack of trust in the promisor by the promisee who proposes it, and the promisor is apt to interpret the inclusion of such a clause as a negative act, to which the promisor would reciprocate negatively, i.e., by behaving in a less trustworthy manner. The authors find lower levels of trustworthy behavior under liquidated damages than under the background legal regime and under no legal protection.

Kornhauser, Lu, and Tontrup study the question further in another economic experiment, specifically testing whether stipulated damages clauses in contracts increase the likelihood of breach.[46] In contrast to the two experiments

---

44 Tess Wilkinson-Ryan, 'Do Liquidated Damages Encourage Breach – A Psychological Experiment' (2010) 108 *Michigan Law Review* 633. See also Uri Gneezy and Aldo Rustichini, 'A Fine Is a Price' (2000) 29 *The Journal of Legal Studies* 1.

45 Alvin W. Gouldner, 'The Norm of Reciprocity: A Preliminary Statement' (1960) 25 *American Sociological Review* 161. See also Sven Hoeppner, Lars Freund and Ben Depoorter, 'The Moral-Hazard Effect of Liquidated Damages: An Experiment on Contract Remedies' (2017) 173 *Journal of Institutional and Theoretical Economics* 84.

46 Lewis Kornhauser, Yijia Lu and Stephan Tontrup, 'Testing a Fine is a Price in the Lab' (2020) 63 *International Review of Law and Economics*.

described above, parties could not negotiate, offer, or request the inclusion of such a clause, and it hence resembles more a fine, not a liquidated damages clause. In an economic experiment, subjects had to perform the same real effort task under different contracts. In the first treatment, the contract specified no payment in case of breach; in the second, it stipulated a low fine to be paid to the promisee in case of breach; in the third, it stipulated a fine that was proportional to the burden created by the breach to the promisee; in the last treatment, the fine was not paid to the promisee but rather to the experimenter, which induces subjects to interpret the fine as a penalty. The authors do not find an overall effect of stipulated damages clauses to induce breach, but distinguishing between pro-social and selfish subjects, they find such an effect for the pro-social individuals, who breach more often under contracts with stipulated damages clauses.

These experiments do not prove that stipulated damages clauses are certain to induce, rather than discourage, breach of contract. Nor do they reveal that the economic prediction is wrong. They reveal only that a liquidated damages clause has a behavioral effect that might, in some cases, be larger than the economic effect. Liquidated damages clauses are often high enough to make the economic effect dominate the behavioral one, in which case we would observe that their inclusion discourages breach. The question of which effect will dominate cannot be answered via experiments that manipulate only one factor at a time, disregarding all other factors that might affect behavior in the case at hand. They reveal, however, that contract drafters should consider this behavioral effect, ponder the size of the stipulated damages, and the specific role that trust and distrust might have in the parties' relationship. These latter factors will depend on how well the parties know each other, whether their relationship might persist over time, and the social norms in that particular industry or community. Disregarding the behavioral effect might, however, lead to unexpected effects. Experiments are effective in proving that this effect exists, with their tight control of all other variables that could lead a party to breach, but they cannot provide a definite answer to whether such a clause should be included or not in contracts without considering the effect of other factors.

4.4 Behavioral Effects of Damages for Breach

Economic theory predicts that the promisee's right to receive damages in case of breach by the promisor encourages promisees to make investments that are valuable if the promisor performs, but that lose value if the promisor breaches.[47] This is because damages guarantee that, in case of breach, the promisee will be compensated for the loss of such investments, and the promisee will hence have greater incentives to invest than in the absence of damages, when the promisee expects to lose all their value in case of breach by the promisor. If the organizer of a show knows that if the hired singer does not perform, the losses from all investments made in catering and advertisement will be compensated, then the organizer has a greater incentive to make those investments.

More specifically, expectation damages completely insure the promisee, who is compensated for the whole value of the investments by the promisor in case the promisor breaches. Such damages are therefore predicted to lead to overinvestment in reliance.[48] That is, when fully insured, the promisee will disregard the probability that circumstances change and that performance of the contract might become impractical or impossible for the promisor. The promisee will invest too much, an amount that does not maximize the joint gains from the contract because it is excessive, a classical result from models of contractual behavior under different types of damages.[49] Sloof et al. performed an economic experiment in which subjects took the role of promisors or promisees, and promisees could decide how much to invest before the promisor decided to perform or breach.[50] All decisions were incentivized, and while the promisee could earn more by investing more as long as the promisor performed, he or she would lose more if the promisor breached. By comparing investment levels observed in the experiment with the theoretical level of investment that would be optimal, they find evidence for the theoretical prediction of overinvestment under expectation damages. Subjects behaved as predicted, with the expected consequences in terms of overinvestment in reliance. Their experiment reveals how contract law, by adopting the expectation measure for damages for breach, does have this negative effect on parties' incentives, leading to inefficient investment decisions.

In any contractual relationship, circumstances might change so that the performance of the contract becomes unprofitable for the promisor, who might then choose to breach in order to avoid losses. Economic models predict that expectation damages, when correctly measured and implemented with certainty, will induce promisors to perform when performance maximizes social

---

47 Shavell, 'On Liability and Insurance' (n 18) and Shavell, 'A Model of the Optimal Use of Liability and Safety Regulation' (n 18).

48 ibid.

49 ibid.

50 Randolph Sloof, Edwin Leuven, Hessel Oosterbeek and Joep Sonnemans, 'An Experimental Comparison of Reliance Levels Under Alternative Breach Remedies' (2003) 34 *Rand Journal of Economics* 205.

welfare and to breach when breach maximizes social welfare.[51] This is because such damages are high enough to make it more profitable for the promisor to perform rather than breach and pay damages in the first case, and to breach and pay damages in the second case.

Mittlaender and Buskens studied, in an economic experiment, whether expectation damages effectively induced promisors to perform when performance is efficient, and to breach when breach is efficient, as predicted by theory.[52] Subjects in the role of promisors had to decide whether to perform or breach under different circumstances. In some, performance was efficient, while in others, performance was inefficient, and subjects knew they would have to pay an amount equal to expectation damages to the promisee, who was a real person in the lab who would suffer monetary losses in case of breach by the promisor. Subjects had full information about the game they were playing, and their choices were incentivized, with their earnings in the experiment depending on the decisions they made. Promisors behaved as predicted and most often chose to perform when performance was efficient, and to breach and pay expectation damages when breach was efficient, in line with the predictions from economic theory. Second, the experiment investigated whether damages for breach would crowd out feelings of aggrievement and the associated tendency of promisees to retaliate against the promisor in breach. In different experimental treatments, promisees had the option to invest their own money to punish the promisor in breach, who would then lose an amount proportional to how much the promisee chose to invest in punishment. In the absence of the contractual duty to pay damages (or the right to receive compensation, from the promisee's perspective), promisees retaliated extensively against the promisor in breach. A comparison of rates of retaliation in the absence and presence of damages, with no other factor varying except for the payment of damages, revealed that damages had the additional effect of reducing this type of behavior, thereby crowding out retaliation by disappointed promisees. Overall, the experiment provided evidence supporting the theoretical prediction concerning incentives created by damages for promisors to perform, and further revealed that damages have another function beyond that one; a function that is intimately related to the role of legal redress to resolve

---

51 Robert L. Birmingham, 'Breach of Contract, Damage Measures, and Economic Efficiency' (1970) 24 *Rutgers Law Review* 273. See also Barton, 'The Economic Basis of Damages for Breach of Contract' (1972) 1 *The Journal of Legal Studies* 277; Steven Shavell, 'Damage Measures for Breach of Contract' (1980) 11 *The Bell Journal of Economics* 466; Steven Shavell, 'The Design of Contracts and Remedies for Breach' (1984) 99 *The Quarterly Journal of Economics* 121.

52 Sergio Mittlaender and Vincent Buskens, 'Retaliation, Remedies, and Contracts' (2019) 21 *American Law and Economics Review* 280.

the conflict without parties engaging in costly forms of retaliation and punishment against each other. The economic model is sound, as the experiment provided evidence for its predictions, but not necessarily complete, as damages have other functions, such as reducing conflict, that the model does not include.

5. CONCLUSION AND FUTURE RESEARCH AND USE OF EXPERIMENTS

The essence of experimental research lies in its empirical investigation seeking causal evidence in human behavior, cognition, and decision-making processes. Contrasted with observational empirical studies, experiments offer stronger control, facilitating precise identification of factors influencing behavior or cognition. In the context of contract law, experiments provide valuable insights into decisions like contract breaches, renegotiations, or reliance investments, impacting legal practice and policy-making beyond academic realms. Shedding light on instances where theoretical predictions diverge from real-world outcomes, experimental findings not only refine existing theories but also guide policy-makers in crafting effective legal interventions and contract drafters in improving contracts.

Since the idea behind the method is not complicated, and perhaps easy to understand for someone without a strong background in statistics and econometrics, practitioners and judges can read those studies and use the obtained results.[53] For this, they first need to assess whether the experiment indeed succeeded in varying only one factor at a time and then compare how subjects behaved differently in each situation. Practitioners and judges, moreover, have an advantage over experimenters with less knowledge of the legal system and legal practice to assess what other factors the experiment did not study, but that could be more important in terms of the study factor for individual behavior. That is, they must and should assess the external validity of the finding, and the importance of the factor under investigation, before advocating for a change in the law or in the manner that a certain contract is drafted. They can then use the knowledge gained from experimental studies to propose legal changes or contractual refinements that are more apt to achieve their objectives and to be effective.

---

53 Strahilevitz and Ben-Shahar, for instance, argue and show how surveys and experiments can and should be used in practice to shed light on important questions involving the interpretation of contracts that would otherwise remain under the scope of solely theoretical inquiries. See Omri Ben-Shahar and Lior Jacob Strahilevitz, 'Interpreting Contracts via Surveys and Experiments' (2017) 92 *New York University Law Review* 1753.

While the use of experiments has grown in the legal academy, there are many questions in need of empirical evidence that have not yet been explored. One such set of questions includes the combined effect of different legal norms on a certain decision, or the way in which the interaction between different legal norms that at times collide, and that at times are concomitantly applied, can affect parties' behavior. Many experiments, following the ideal of controlled variation of one single factor between control and treatment groups, study the effect of a single legal norm in isolation. But reality is messy, and multiple norms influence a single decision. Breach of contract leads to the duty to pay damages, but parties also have, at the same time, the duty to mitigate losses and face the risk that contractual clauses will be judged unconscionable. We do not know how promisors will decide when they face these different risks and duties. Such investigation is certainly not incompatible with the experimental method; it only involves more complicated and larger designs with several treatments and a focus on interaction effects. Lawyers and jurists are in the best position to identify which norms regulate certain decisions, and to suggest avenues for further experiments that account for the complexity of legal studies.

PART III

Challenging themes/perspectives

9. Research methods for contracts and sustainability

Kateřina Mitkidis

INTRODUCTION

The legal tool of private contract, stipulating the framework for a concrete transaction or business cooperation between two or more parties, seems at first ill-fitted to positively affect global sustainability aiming to benefit the global population as a whole.[1] Yet, it has become common for businesses to include sustainability requirements in their contracts.[2] Through these sustainability contractual clauses (SCCs), they require their suppliers and business partners to behave in an environmentally and socially sound manner—to, for example, reduce CO2 emissions, pay fair remuneration to employees, and avoid corruption. From the variety of business contracts, SCCs have especially proliferated in supply chain contracts, primarily due to the international community's attention to the sensitive topic of social and environmental conditions in global value chains (GVCs).[3]

---

[1] Gro Harlem Brundtland, *Report of the World Commission on Environment and Development: Our Common Future* (UN 1987), para. 27, <http://www.un-documents.net/our-common-future.pdf> accessed 26 May 2023.

[2] EcoVadis & Affectio Mutandi, *Sustainability Clauses in Commercial Contracts: The Key to Corporate Responsibility 2018 Study of CSR Contractual Practices Among Buyers and Suppliers* (2018), <https://www.eticanews.it/wp-content/uploads/2018/07/ecovadis_contrat_clauses_RSE__20.06.2018_eng_v5-1.pdf> accessed 26 May 2023.

[3] Yet, it is important to note that SCCs appear in a wide range of contracts, both private and public, and national and international ones, including public procurement contracts, international investment treaties, service agreements, and financial contracts. However, due to the length limitations of this chapter, private supply chain contracts were selected as the object of the study, as they epitomize the methodological challenges of the intersection between contracts and sustainability.

The production of goods is nowadays largely internationally outsourced through GVCs. While outsourcing may entail greater production efficiency, it is inseparable from a concurrent outsourcing of negative externalities, such as pollution. This is possible due to the governance gap, where international law regulating social and environmental issues is not directly applicable to private parties, while the application of national law is geographically and personally limited.[4] This allows for the occurrence of wrongful acts in GVCs without their 'adequate sanctioning or reparation'.[5]

SCCs aim to respond to this critique of GVCs and are an effort by businesses to accept their part of the responsibility within global sustainability efforts. In essence, SCCs are disconnected from the transactional elements and subject matter of an individual contract. Instead, through the inclusion of SCCs, supply chain contracts embrace a relational function,[6] they become a hybrid between a contract and organization,[7] and respond to legislative failures in the transnational sphere.[8] In other words, the traditional purpose of business contracts to facilitate transactions (transactional function) is in SCCs transformed into a regulatory function, where business contracts aim to influence the behaviour of contractual parties regarding aspects disconnected from the concrete transaction.

This shift in the contract's paradigm and purpose has not gone unnoticed by contract law scholars. Over the last two decades, a substantial amount of legal scholarship has emerged discussing the employment of commercial contracts for pursuing sustainability within GVCs both from theoretical and empirical perspectives, as well as through the lenses of contract law and regulatory doctrine. The methods employed by contract law scholars to study SCCs are as varied as the content of these clauses and the 'new' purposes contracts entail.

---

4 See Human Rights Council, 'Report of the Special Representative of the Secretary-General on the issue of human rights and transnational corporations and other business enterprises, John Ruggie. Protect, Respect and Remedy: A Framework for Business and Human Rights, Report of the Special Representative of the Secretary-General on the Issue of Human Rights and Transnational Corporations and Other Business Enterprises' (7 April 2008) A/HRC/8/5, para 3.

5 Ibid.

6 Ian R. Macneil, *The New Social Contract: An Inquiry into Modern Contractual Relations* (Yale University Press 1980).

7 George S. Geis, 'The Space Between Markets and Hierarchies' (2009) 95(1) *Virginia Law Review* 99.

8 Fabrizio Cafaggi and Paola Iamicelli, ''Private Regulation and Industrial Organization: Contractual Governance and the Network Approach' in Stefan Grundmann, Florian Möslein and Karl Riesenhuber (eds), *Contract Governance* (Oxford University Press 2015) 343.

Based on a literature review combining database searches with snowballing,[9] the present chapter documents and discusses the different streams in contract law scholarship on supply chain contracts and sustainability, and evaluates the contributions and challenges of the employed research methods.[10]

1. SUSTAINABILITY CLAUSES IN INTERNATIONAL SUPPLY CHAIN CONTRACTS

The primary goal of contracts is to formalize new relationships by recording the mutual rights and obligations of the contractual parties. The content of contracts is presumed legally enforceable, meaning that if a party breaches a contract, the other party may use the applicable contract law rules to seek a remedy. For businesses, contracting is essential, as it is through contracts that they enter into and maintain relationships with their stakeholders,[11] including suppliers, which are the focus of this chapter. It is through contracts that businesses make and lose money.

Traditionally, most business contracts were of a discrete character, related to one transaction, and thus centered around the contract's subject matter and the efficiency of the exchange. However, under the influence of intensifying globalization, business relations have increasingly become often long-term and/or transnational. This is especially true for supply chain contracts operating within the realities of present-day geographical separation of production and consumption. Supply chain contracts, connecting legally separate entities that constitute GVCs, are essential tools for GVCs' lead firms. They not only capture the mutual rights and obligations of the lead firm with its first-tier suppliers in respect to the subject matter of the specific contract but also stipulate the goals and values central to the business relationship and the whole GVC,

---

9 'Snowballing refers to using the reference list of a paper or the citations to the paper to identify additional papers'. Amanpreet Kohli, '"Snowballing" in Systematic Literature Review', Let's Talk, available at <https://www.linkedin.com/pulse/snowballing-systematic-literature-review-amanpreet-kohli/> accessed 21 February 2024.

10 It is acknowledged that extensive scholarship exists on the intersection between human rights, climate or other issues, and contracts that are not necessarily framed through the prism of contract and sustainability (see e.g. Olha O. Cherednychenko, 'Fundamental Rights, Contract Law and Transactional Justice' (2021) 17(2) ERCL 130). This article endeavours to engage with this exciting scholarship as far as it relates to GVCs.

11 Matthew J. Elsmore and Thomas Neumann, *International Business Law* (Gerbera Publishing 2014) 1.

establish rules for the GVC's organization, and regulate the impact of contracting within the GVC on external parties.

Turning from contracts to the other central concept of this chapter, achieving sustainability, as encompassed by the UN Sustainability Development Goals, is a global endeavour, which presumes realizing 17 goals covering widely diverse issues within the environmental, social, and economic areas.[12] However, while the 17 goals have been carefully formulated, specific targets defined, and indicators of progress developed, the implementation of the goals faces the lack of globally binding and applicable law. That is because 'the will and commitment to join any agreement as well as the interpretation and enforcement of any adopted rules are highly influenced by the economic and social development of a particular state'.[13] It is thus now recognized that states alone are unable to regulate effectively for global sustainability, but that private actors play a central role.[14] One way private actors may and are required to exert their (regulatory) influence is through their contracting. Both international soft law[15] and increasing amount of (supra)national hard law[16] expect businesses to employ their contractual relationships for the purpose of moving themselves and their business partners towards sustainability objectives. Therefore, it has become common for contractual parties to use the presumably enforceable form of a contract to influence the general, rather than the transaction-specific, behaviour of their business partners.

SCCs in supply chain contracts serve as a shining example of these developments in respect to GVCs and global sustainability endeavors. They may encompass diverse requirements for suppliers, ranging from those related to broad sustainability areas (e.g. respect for human rights) to those related to highly specialized ones (e.g. animal protection). Common to all SCCs is that they, rather than specifying the subject matter of the contract in question, aim

---

12 UNGA Res 70/1, 'Transforming Our World: The 2030 Agenda for Sustainable Development' (21 October 2015) A/RES/70/1.

13 Kateřina Peterková Mitkidis, *Sustainability Clauses in International Business Contracts* (Eleven International Publishing 2015) 9.

14 UNGA (n 12) para. 67.

15 See, e.g. OECD (2023), OECD Guidelines for Multinational Enterprises on Responsible Business Conduct, OECD Publishing, Paris, Commentary on Chapter II: General Policies, par. 23 ('Enterprises can use or increase leverage in a number of ways to influence entities with which they have business relationships, for example, … building expectations around responsible business conduct and due diligence specifically into commercial contracts …').

16 See, e.g., Directive (EU) 2024/1760 of the European Parliament and of the Council of 13 June 2024 on corporate sustainability due diligence [2024], OJ L1760, 5.7.2024, p.1, Arts. 10(2)b) and 11(3)c).

to influence the general behaviour of the business partners in an ethical and environmentally and socially responsible way. Thus, they are shifting the contract paradigm and methodologically challenging contract law scholars.

2. THEMES IN SUPPLY CHAIN CONTRACTS AND SUSTAINABILITY SCHOLARSHIP

The attention of legal scholars to the use of supply chain contracts for advancing global sustainability grew from the interdisciplinary discussions on corporate social responsibility and the role of the lead firms and their responsibility for environmental and social conditions in GVCs. Initiated by analyses of the regulatory landscape of GVCs and the contractual features of other tools, such as codes of conduct, contract law scholarship has gradually grown in volume and importance. It is largely varied as concerns the studied questions. However, it is possible to discern some major themes. Five of them are presented below by reviewing relevant literature. It should be noted that these five themes may be seen as overlapping to a certain extent. It is not uncommon that in one publication more than one of the themes are discussed. However, each of the themes is characterized by distinct aspects, theoretical underpinnings, and methodological approaches.

2.1 The Legal Nature of SCCs

The disconnection of SCCs from the contracts' subject-matter means that when the goods are delivered, it is not possible to discern from their physical appearance whether an SCC has been breached. For example, the Kraft Heinz Company binds their suppliers through the standard terms and conditions to comply with the Supplier Guiding Principles.[17] The text of the Supplier Guiding Principles states, among other things: 'Suppliers will not directly, or indirectly through its contractors or subcontractors, use child labor …'.[18] Yet, it is not possible to discern from, for example, delivered coffee beans whether a child worked to harvest the coffee. This ostensible incompatibility of supply chain contracts and sustainability objectives has stimulated academic discussion on what the legal nature of sustainability requirements included in supply

---

[17] The Kraft Heinz Terms & Conditions of Purchasing, para. 15.2, <https://www.kraftheinzcompany.com/terms_conditions_purchase/purchase_terms/EU_UK%20STANDARD%20TERMS%20AND%20CONDITIONS%2012%20August%202021.pdf> accessed 1 December 2023.

[18] Kraft Heinz, Supplier Guiding Principles, p. 8, < https://www.kraftheinzcompany.com/pdf/sgp/khc_supplierGuidingPrinciples_1.7.4_eng.pdf> accessed 5 February 2024.

chain contracts intends to be and factually is. Below, the perspective of the 'hardening' function of SCCs and its impact on the conceptualization of the role of business contracts in the spectrum of regulatory tools dealing with sustainability issues in GVCs, and the perspective on SCCs as trade usage, are discussed.

A mainstream understanding of using supply chain contracts as tools for global sustainability is that they render a binding nature to existing soft regulation. Due to the governance gap, most international regulation applicable to issues of social and environmental conditions in GVCs remains based on corporate voluntary action.[19] Besides, in navigating the regulatory environment, companies have largely availed themselves of the use of codes of conduct to respond to the requirements regarding the environmental and social governance of their supply chains while protecting their business interests. Both international soft law instruments and corporate suppliers' codes of conduct have faced criticism for not having a real impact and being more like corporate dress windows than truly affecting the conditions in GVCs. Using supply chain contracting has been seen as a possible way to react to this critique and 'harden' soft international regulation and voluntary codes of conduct.[20] By their inclusion in contracts by reference or their redrafting into contractual text, they take on the (seemingly) binding form of a contract. Using the above example of the Kraft Heinz Company, if their Supplier Guiding Principles were not incorporated into their contractual terms, they would remain a one-sided document without the possibility to use contract law to enforce them.[21]

The widespread incorporation of soft international regulation and codes of conduct into contracts has further impacts on legal development in the field, going beyond the borders of a specific contract. In this stream of literature, legal scholars have used and (further) developed the theoretical concepts of the

19 For example, United Nations Office of the High Commissioner for Human Rights (OHCHR), 'Guiding Principles on Business and Human Rights: Implementing the United Nations "Protect, Respect and Remedy" Framework', UN Doc. HR/PUB/11/04 (2011); United Nations Global Compact, 'The Ten Principles of the UN Global Compact', <https://www.unglobalcompact.org/what-is-gc/mission/principles> accessed 5 February 2024.

20 See, e.g., Fabrizio Cafaggi, 'New Foundations of Transnational Private Regulation' (2011) 38(1) *Journal of Law and Society* 20; Anna Beckers, *Enforcing Corporate Social Responsibility Codes* (Hart Publishing 2015) 48–49.

21 The doctrine of unilateral contract could present an exception; yet while it was tested in case law, it has not been successful in enforcing sustainability-related promises. See Mitkidis (n 13), 194–196.

'contractualization' of sustainability standards,[22] their 'spill over' effect[23] and their 'legalization' function.[24] Common to these theories is that they conceptualize the role of business contracts in the spectrum of regulatory tools dealing with sustainability issues in GVCs.

A separate stream of literature on the nature of SCCs investigates them as forming a new trade usage. Here, the argument is that by regular inclusion of SCCs in business contracts, they form a new trade usage and, thus, in the future—even if they are not expressly included in a contractual text—they can be understood as implied terms.[25] This presupposes that (the content of) SCCs are considered an international trade usage of which the parties knew or ought to have known (subjective element), and which is widely known to and regularly observed by the majority of traders involved in a particular field of trade (objective element).[26] Schwenzer and Leisinger conclude that, at least, minimum standards—including the prohibition of child labour and forced and compulsory labour—and a minimum of humane labour conditions may form a part of every international sales contract as implied terms.[27] Similarly, Poncibò argues that environmental protection and sustainability should be regarded as a trade usage by multinational corporations.[28] Some authors express a more critical attitude, questioning whether it is a trade usage that SCCs are included in supply chain contracts or whether it is trade usage that they are actually complied with and enforced.[29]

---

22 Fabrizio Cafaggi, 'The Regulatory Functions of Transnational Commercial Contracts: New Architectures' (2013) 36(6) *Fordham International Law Journal* 1557.

23 See, e.g., Attila Kun, 'From Transnational Soft Law to National Hard Law – Regulating Supply Chains' (2015) 8(1–2) *Pecsi Munkajogi Kozlemenyek* 53, 59–60.

24 Mitkidis (n 13), 237–263.

25 Ingeborg Schwenzer and Benjamin Leisinger, 'Ethical Values and International Sales Contracts' in Ross Cranston, Jan Ramberg and Jacob Ziegel (eds), *Commercial Law Challenges in the 21st Century: Jan Hellmer in Memoriam* (Juridiska Instituionem 2007) 249, 264–265.

26 Article 9(2) of the United Nations Convention on Contracts for the International Sale of Goods (CISG).

27 Schwenzer and Leisinger (n 25) 264–265.

28 Cristina Poncibò, 'The Contractualisation of Environmental Sustainability' (2016) 12(4) ERCL 335, 342–344.

29 Christina Ramberg, 'Emotional Non-Conformity in the International Sale of Goods, Particularly in Relation to CSR-Policies and Codes of Conduct', in Ingeborg Schwenzer and Lisa Spagnolo (eds), *Boundaries and Intersections: 5th Annual MAA Schlechtriem CISG Conference* (Eleven International Publishing 2015) 71.

2.2 Enforcement of SCCs in Supply Chain Contracts

Enforcement of contractual provisions can be understood in various ways. Traditionally, legal enforcement is understood as enforcement through courts securing remedies for a contractual party suffering damage from the breach of contract by the other contractual party. However, enforcement can also be understood as effectuating the contractual terms, which in the case of SCCs would mean factual change of behaviour of subjects in GVCs. While the first view on enforcement has mostly been studied using various types of doctrinal legal methods, the latter has been approached by theoretical and empirical research.

As outlined above, supply chain contracts are most often viewed as a vehicle for the 'hardening' of soft regulation on corporate sustainability. The underlying assumption is the possibility to employ contract law to enforce SCCs. Indeed, several scholars taking a regulatory doctrine perspective highlight the role of private law, in particular contract law, when it comes to the enforcement of private transnational regulation.[30] Some authors employed the expository legal approach to evaluate the applicability of contract law remedies to violations of SCCs.[31] For example, Schwenzer maintains that the CISG is flexible enough to deal with the enforcement of CSR standards.[32]

However, other authors point out challenges to using contract law to enforce SCCs, such as the complexity of the doctrinal system in question,[33] the need for a transformation of private international law related to choice of law[34] and the fact that formal enforcement is not the ultimate goal of these contractual

30 See, e.g., Jan M. Smits, 'Enforcing Corporate Social Responsibility Codes Under Private Law: On the Disciplining Power of Legal Doctrine' (2017) 24(1) *Indiana Journal of Global Legal Studies* 99; Anna Beckers and Mark T. Kawakami, 'Why Domestic Enforcement of Private Regulation Is (Not) the Answer: Making and Questioning the Case of Corporate Social Responsibility Codes' (2017) 24(1) *Indiana Journal of Global Legal Studies* 1; Cafaggi (n 22) 1565.

31 See, e.g., Ingeborg Schwenzer, 'Conformity of the Goods: Physical Features on the Wane?' in Ingeborg Schwenzer and Lisa Spagnolo (eds), *State of Play: The Third Annual MAA Schlechtriem CISG Conference* (Eleven International Publishing 2012) 103; Petra Butler, 'The CISG – A Secret Weapon in the Fight for a Fairer World?' (2017) 7(2) *Victoria University of Wellington Legal Research Papers*, Paper No. 10/2017.

32 Schwenzer (2012) (n 31) 112.

33 Smits (n 30).

34 Anna Beckers, 'Legalization Under the Premises of Globalization: Why and Where to Enforce Corporate Social Responsibility Codes' (2017) 24(1) *Indiana Journal of Global Legal Studies* 15, 30–35.

provisions.[35] For example, when an SCC forbids the release of chemical effluents from production into the environment, it is not helpful to the environment that the buyer can ask for damages, replacement of delivered goods, or termination of the contract when the SCC is breached. In this respect, Cafaggi maintains that the diverse logics of contract law on the one hand, and regulatory and certification regimes on the other hand, may give rise to tensions;[36] yet there could be an advantage in using both systems in combination.[37]

Others speak directly against focusing on formal sanctions, arguing that this may result in reducing corporate sustainability initiatives and in crowding out non-legal or social norms, as well as the intrinsic motivations of companies to be socially and environmentally responsible.[38]

Empirically, it has been observed that, rather than public enforcement through dispute resolution bodies, companies deploy private compliance mechanisms such as inspection, auditing, development of corrective action plans, and the use of certification schemes to monitor and enforce SCCs in their GVCs.[39] Nevertheless, private compliance mechanisms may prove inadequate in practice,[40] lacking the authority of public enforcement as well as oversight by public authorities.

2.3 The Role of Businesses as Regulators

As already noted, SCCs may have a regulatory rather than a transactional function. The regulatory power of corporations is not pertinent to the corporate

---

35 Mitkidis (n 13) 172–173 and 232–233.

36 Cafaggi (n 22) 1611–1616.

37 Fabrizio Cafaggi and Paola Iamiceli, 'Supply Chains, Contractual Governance and Certification Regimes' (2013) 37(1) *European Journal of Law and Economics* 131, 166–170.

38 Mark T. Kawakami, 'Pitfalls of Over-Legalization: When the Law Crowds Out and Spills Over' (2017) 24(1) *Indiana Journal of Global Legal Studies* 147, 161–174.

39 Anna Louise Vytopil, *Contractual Control in the Supply Chain: on Corporate Social Responsibility, Codes of Conduct, Contracts and (Avoiding) Liability* (Eleven International Publishing 2015) ch. 6; Mitkidis (n 13) 272–273; Paul Verbruggen, 'Private Regulatory Standards in Commercial Contracts: Questions of Compliance' in Roger Brownsword, Rob A.J. van Gestel and Hans-W. Micklitz (eds), *Contract and Regulation: A Handbook on New Methods of Law Making in Private Law* (Edward Elgar Publishing 2017) 284.

40 Marcia L. Narine, 'Disclosing Disclosure's Defects: Addressing Corporate Irresponsibility for Human Rights Impacts' (2015) 47(1) *Columbia Human Rights Law Review* 84.

sustainability area alone;[41] yet it is conspicuous there in the large absence of hard law. There are several reasons for businesses to engage in regulation through contracting, but two stand out. Firstly, companies are possibly in a better position than states to regulate this area not only given the governance gap but also due to their economic power, as large enterprises are often economically stronger than many sovereign states.[42] Secondly, by taking regulation into their own hands, companies manage risks, both economic and legal. The existing transnational regulation of corporate sustainability is of a soft nature or private character (or both) and as such suffers problems with respect to effectiveness and legitimacy.[43] This leaves companies in uncertainty as to the effects of such regulation as well as to whether and when hard national law will step in. The contractualization of sustainability standards represents a tool that 'hardens' soft corporate sustainability regulation and shields companies against accusations of acting irresponsibly as well as signals to national governments that more hard law is not necessary as the existing gap is adequately covered by corporate actions. In fact, most international soft regulation on corporate sustainability indirectly relies on the use of contracts as enforcement mechanisms.[44] A recent development is the EU's directive on Corporate Sustainability Due Diligence (CSDDD), which expressly requires companies to include SCCs in their supply chain contracts and use their contracting powers (including the contract suspension and termination possibility) to mitigate environmental and social risks in their value chains.[45]

However, so far, the regulation of corporate sustainability issues through supply chain contracts poses some fundamental challenges. Verbruggen raises the legitimacy deficit of businesses engaged with the regulation of their value chain owing to the lack of democratic processes or a delegation of powers by

---

41 On the regulatory function of contracts, see Hugh Collins, *Regulating Contracts* (OUP 1999).

42 In 2016, the 100 largest world economies comprised 31 states and 69 corporations. Global Justice Now, '10 Biggest Corporations Make More Money Than Most Countries in the World Combined' (*Globaljustice.org*, 12 September 2016, at <http://www.globaljustice.org.uk/news/2016/sep/12/10-biggest-corporations-make-more-money-most-countries-world-combined> accessed 5 February 2024).

43 Alice de Jonge, 'Transnational Corporations and International Law: Bringing TNCs out of the Accountability Vacuum' (2011) 7(1) *Critical Perspectives on International Business* 66, 72.

44 For a critical account of such reliance on contracts, see Martijn Scheltema, 'The Proliferation of Contractual Assurance in Environmental and Human Rights Due Diligence Supply Chains' (2022) 4 *Tijdschrift voor Compliance* 177.

45 See, n 16; see also Scheltema (n 44).

states.[46] This might partially be remedied by adoption of more laws similar to CSDDD. However, without waiting for public regulation to step in, legal scholars have been exploring various models of interactions between private and public actors, civil society, media, and consumer-investor community to overcome concerns regarding the concerns in respect to legitimacy of the regulation of international supply chains through contracts.[47] The leading idea is to create feedback loops among the actors, thus enhancing 'the visibility, identification, and internalization of the costs'[48] of environmental and social harms. However, as noted by Backer, a major limitation of such a system is that the source of norm-making is the behaviour (reactions) of companies' stakeholders rather than the supply chain contracts themselves.[49]

A distinct stream of scholarship approaching businesses as regulators in the sustainability arena adopts the comparative law perspectives of 'legal transplants'[50] and 'diffusion'.[51] It views the transmission of a new legal order to, particularly, developing countries by multinational corporations through codes of conduct in global supply chain contracts as constituting a form of legal transplantation.[52] The ability of supply chain contracts to extend sustainability requirements across jurisdictional borders has also been studied empirically.[53]

---

46 Paul Verbruggen, 'Regulatory Governance by Contract: The Rise of Regulatory Standards in Commercial Contracts' (2014) 35(3) *Recht der Werkelijkheid* 79, 91–92.

47 See, e.g., Stephen Kim Park and Gerlinde Berger-Walliser, 'A Firm-Driven Approach to Global Governance and Sustainability' (2015) 52(2) *American Business Law Journal* 255; Larry Cata Backer, 'Economic Globalization and the Rise of Efficient Systems of Global Private Lawmaking: Wal-Mart as Global Legislator' (2007) 39(4) *Connecticut Law Review* 1739; Fabrizio Cafaggi, 'Transnational Private Regulation and the Production of Global Public Goods and Private "Bads"' (2012) 23(3) EJIL 695.

48 Park and Berger-Walliser (n 47) 290–291.

49 Backer (n 47) 1777.

50 See, e.g., Tomaso Ferrando, 'Codes of Conduct as Private Legal Transplant: The Case of European Extractive MNEs' (2013) 19(6) ELJ 799.

51 See, e.g., Natasha Affolder, 'Looking for law in unusual places: cross-border diffusion of environmental norms' (2018) 7(3) TEL 425.

52 Li-Wen Lin, 'Legal Transplants Through Private Contracting: Codes of Vendor Conduct in Global Supply Chains as an Example' (2009) 57 *American Journal of Comparative Law* 711, 717–730.

53 Doreen McBarnet and Marina Kurkchiyan, 'Corporate Social Responsibility Through Contractual Control? Global Supply Chains and 'Other-Regulation' in Doreen McBarnet, Aurora Voiculescu and Tom Campbell (eds), *The New Corporate Accountability: Corporate Social Responsibility and the Law* (CUP 2007) 59.

Vandenbergh coined the term 'the new Wal-Mart effect', referring to 'the use of supply chain contracting to impose on suppliers requirements that are traditionally the subject of governmental regulation'.[54]

2.4 Effectiveness of SCCs in Supply Chain Contracts

The dual nature of SCCs in supply chain contracts—transactional and regulatory—has prompted a discussion on when an SCC can be considered effective. Thus, in assessing the effectiveness of SCCs, the first conundrum to be solved is against what we can measure their effectiveness. On the one hand, SCCs can be considered effective if they contribute to sustainability objectives. In this respect, for example, Poncibò argues that contract law should accommodate environmental sustainability objectives as a matter of social contractual justice.[55] Grounded in an extensive empirical investigation, Vandenbergh further argues that environmental standards in supply chain contracting have proved more effective in delivering on sustainability objectives compared to institutional alternatives, such as national and international regulation.[56] On the other hand, for example, Schlechtriem contests the appropriateness of employing contract law for imposing the moral values of one contracting party on another.[57] SCCs could thus be considered effective if they do not interfere with the transaction but instead preserve its efficiency. This is possibly done through strengthening the relationship (trust and cooperation) without necessarily delivering on the sustainability targets.

This clash between the regulatory and transactional character of sustainability requirements in supply chain contracts, evident from the discussions on SCCs' effectiveness, has further been investigated when analyzing the constraints that the doctrine of 'privity of contract' entails when it comes to the deployment of contracts for regulatory objectives.[58] Legal scholars have developed arguments and theories to overcome this limitation, mainly rooted in the concept of social justice.[59]

---

54 Michael P. Vandenbergh, 'The New Wal-Mart Effect: The Role of Private Contracting in Global Governance' (2007) 54(4) *UCLA Law Review* 913, fn 14.

55 Poncibò (n 28) 339–341.

56 Vandenbergh (n 54) 963–967.

57 Peter Schlechtriem, 'Non-Material Damages – Recovery Under the CISG?' (2007) 19(1) *Pace International Law Review* 89, 101–102.

58 See, e.g., Verbruggen (n 46) 83.

59 Leon E. Trakman, 'Public Responsibilities beyond Consent: Rethinking Contract Theory' (2016) 45(1) *Hofstra Law Review* 217; Jaakko Salminen, 'Contract-Boundary-Spanning Governance Mechanisms: Conceptualizing

The effectiveness of SCCs has also been challenged in respect to the achieved business parties' behavioural change, which arguably depends on the perceived enforceability of the contractual provisions.[60] For example, it has been argued that the inclusion of SCCs in business contracts may give rise to both psychological (e.g. internalization of values, expressive function of contract) and legal (e.g. standardization, development of a trade usage) effects.[61]

2.5 The Mutual Interaction between Private and Public Procurement

The use of SCCs in private supply chain agreements has also been studied in the context of its interaction with SCCs in public procurement. The use of public procurement to further sustainability constitutes a distinct branch of public procurement scholarship. It analyzes public procurement law, its possibilities, and limits in respect to the inclusion of environmental and social requirements for private bidders and contractors within all the public procurement stages.[62] Public procurement lies at the intersection of public and private law. This is because, within public procurement, the state essentially 'acts as a private actor seeking supply on the market'[63] and a public procurement process is completed by concluding a contract that is subjected to the rules and principles of contract law.[64] Private and public procurement contracts incorporating SCCs face similar challenges while operating against different moral and legal backgrounds. States remain the primary guarantors of social and human rights and protectors of the environment and are encouraged to use

Fragmented and Globalized Production as Collectively Governed Entities' (2016) 23(2) *Indiana Journal of Global Legal Studies* 709.

60 Verbruggen (n 46) 94.

61 Mitkidis (n 13) 242–253.

62 Marta Andrecka and Kateřina Peterková Mitkidis, 'Sustainability Requirements in EU Public and Private Procurement – a Right or an Obligation?' (2017) 1 *Nordic Journal of Commercial Law* 55, 69.

63 Anna Beckers, 'Using Contracts to Further Sustainability? A Contract Law Perspective on Sustainable Public Procurement' in Beate Sjåfjell and Anja Wiesbrock (eds), *Sustainable Public Procurement under EU Law* (CUP 2015) 206.

64 Doreen McBarnet, 'Corporate Social Responsibility Beyond Law, Through Law, for Law: The New Corporate Accountability', in Doreen McBarnet, Aurora Voiculescu and Tom Campbell (eds), *The New Corporate Accountability: Corporate Social Responsibility and the Law* (CUP 2007) 43.

their market power to deliver on this responsibility.[65] Yet, in their role as purchasers, they must also pursue the public interest in the rational use of public financial resources.[66]

The similarities and differences between SCCs in public and private contracts led contract law scholars to compare them and examine their mutual reinforcement, as well as tensions between them.[67] The main idea is that states can drive the adoption of sustainability requirements throughout the contracts within GVCs, lending them binding and regulatory power, while private procurement can contribute with experience, understanding of the power balances in the global value chains, and detailed market knowledge of a specific sector.[68]

A special attention has also been paid by contract law scholars to the questions of applicability of contract law on SCCs in public procurement contracts.[69] The reason is that while the award of public contracts is governed by rigid public procurement laws, the contract performance phase relies almost exclusively on national, often contract laws. Yet, the possibility to apply national contract law and the extent to which it is possible to do so depends on the jurisdiction in question and is also influenced by the distinct aims and functions of public procurement.

2.6 Semi-Conclusion on the Themes in the Supply Chain Contracts and Sustainability Scholarship

This section has identified five main streams in supply chain contracts and sustainability scholarship. They can be discerned based on the research questions the individual works aim to answer. The first stream, on *the legal nature of SCCs*, investigates the position of SCCs in the legal system and, more broadly,

65 Directive 2014/24/EU of the European Parliament and of the Council of 26 February 2014 on public procurement and repealing Directive 2004/18/EC [2014] OJ L94/65, preamble.

66 Ibid., art 67.

67 See, e.g., Andrecka and Mitkidis (n 62); BESTEK – Public Procurement Central, 'Purple Project' (*BestekProcurement.com*, N/A) <https://bestek-procurement.com/purple-project/> accessed 1 December 2023.

68 John Howe, 'The Regulatory Impact of Using Public Procurement to Promote Better Labour Standards in Corporate Supply Chains' in Kate MacDonald and Shelley Marshall (eds), *Fair Trade, Corporate Accountability and beyond: Experiments in Globalising Justice* (Ashgate 2013) 329; Kateřina Mitkidis, 'Sustainable Procurement of Pharmaceuticals: a Tool to Combat Global Antimicrobial Resistance' in Olivier Rubin, Erik Baekkeskov and Louise Munkholm (eds) *Steering Against Superbugs: The Global Governance of Antimicrobial Resistance* (OUP 2023) 260–261.

69 Beckers (n 63).

the regulatory environment. The second stream, on *enforcement of SCCs in supply chain contracts*, focuses on the research questions of whether contract law can be applied to formally enforce SCCs and whether it is, in fact, desirable that contract law renders remedies in the case of breach of an SCC. Empirical investigations then provide the knowledge on how SCCs are enforced in practice, both through formal legal processes and other means. Publications in the third stream, on *the role of businesses as regulators*, study the regulatory function of SCCs. The aim is not only to explain why and how businesses take on the regulators' role but also to identify any legal and theoretical problems with this phenomenon. The fourth stream, on *the effectiveness of SCCs in supply chain contracts*, aims to answer the question of whether SCCs are successful in delivering on their purpose. There is an evident clash between the scholars in this area about what the purpose of SCCs is: transactional efficiency or regulatory ability? Is it the efficiency of the exchange between the contractual parties or achieving a change in their behaviour regarding sustainability issues? Finally, the fifth stream, exploring *the mutual interaction between private and public procurement*, is the newest approach to SCCs. It identifies the similarities and differences in using SCCs in commercial and public contracts and investigates the applicability of contract law rules on SCCs in public contracts.

The summary above documents that only a fraction of supply chain contracts and sustainability scholarship deals with what could be understood as traditional contract law research questions. Most of the posed research questions need the researcher to step out of the methodological comfort zone and employ a combination of methods while carefully ensuring that the delivered research stays within the contract law field.

3. METHODS OF SUPPLY CHAIN CONTRACTS AND SUSTAINABILITY SCHOLARSHIP

In the past, legal scholarship was notorious for not addressing methodology at all or in a way that would facilitate intellectual exchange with other disciplines.[70] The main reason behind this silence regarding methodological choices was that legal scholarship stayed largely doctrinal[71] and that it was directed primarily to other legal scholars and practitioners. However, this has been challenged at least via three developments: a move from academic freedom to performance and quality monitoring, a move from mono-disciplinarity

---

[70] Paul Chynoweth, 'Chapter Three: Legal research', in Andrew Knight and Les Ruddock (eds), *Advanced Research Methods in the Built Environment* (John Wiley & Sons 2008) 28.

[71] *Ibid.*, 37 ('[...] no purpose would be served by including a methodology section within a doctrinal research publication and one is never likely to find one').

to multi-disciplinarity, and a move of focus from national to inter- and transnational contexts.[72]

All legal scholars face the challenges of the first move. Supply chain contracts and sustainability scholarship further directly face the challenges of the other two moves. As the sustainability topic is inherently interdisciplinary, contract law scholars working in this area need to engage in discussion with other disciplines (such as natural science, economics, and communication) and explain what the actual contribution of legal research is here. A careful description of research methods is a precondition for such an interdisciplinary exchange and for the perception of legal research as valid and reliable by other disciplines.[73] Moreover, GVCs are typically transnational, crossing various jurisdictions and interacting with multiple legal systems, both horizontally and vertically. This makes any implicit reliance on the understanding of legal doctrines of a particular legal system unusable. If one relies on legal doctrines of any particular legal system, this should be clearly expressed and the limits of such reliance in the context of GVCs research recognized and described.

Research methods applied in supply chain contracts and sustainability scholarship are as varied as the topics and themes they address. Scholars engaging in any of the five topics discussed in the previous section regularly employ multiple research methods, and simultaneously, the same research method is used to address several of the topics. This is natural, as when a scholar chooses methods to apply, she must consider the ability of the method to answer the posed research question as well as the existence and accessibility of the primary and secondary sources to use. Moreover, it is important that the scholar is clear about the objectives of the research, why the research question is posed, and what the purpose of answering it is. This is because such a heavily morally and politically loaded topic, as supply chain sustainability is, exposes related research to accusations of sustainability lobbying. Therefore, it is also important, especially in this field, to consider whether the formulated research question(s) is feasible, interesting, novel, ethical, and relevant.[74] Within the field of supply chain contracts and sustainability, the

---

72 Jan M. Smits, 'What is Legal Doctrine: On the Aims and Methods of Legal-Dogmatic Research' in Rob van Gestel, Hans-W. Micklitz and Edward L. Rubin (eds), *Rethinking Legal Scholarship: A Transatlantic Dialogue* (CUP 2017), Maastricht European Private Law Institute Working Paper No. 2015/06, 4.

73 Wendy Schrama, 'How to Carry out Interdisciplinary Legal Research: Some Experiences with an Interdisciplinary Research Method' (2011) 7(1) *Utrecht Law Review* 147, 148 ('Method is relevant and to ignore methodological standards may result in unreliable research').

74 Mike McConville and Wing Hong Chui, *Research Methods for Law* (Edinburgh University Press 2007) 53.

questions of feasibility and relevance are especially central when deciding on research questions, methods, and sources. The following sections explain why that is the case and discuss the methodological challenges and advances of various research methods in this field.

3.1 Doctrinal Legal Method

According to Smits, while no universal definition of the legal doctrinal method exists, there are three features of the method that are common in all of its understandings.[75] First, the doctrinal method adopts an internal perspective. The author places herself *inside* a legal system, and that legal system becomes the normative framework for the analysis. Secondly, the law is understood not only as a cumulation of rules applied in a specific society, but as a *system*. Finally, only *present* law is considered. Past, foreign, and future legal norms are left out. This description of the doctrinal legal method can also be called expository research, as it deals with the scholarly exposition, presentation, and explanation of legal doctrines in a given legal system.[76] When the doctrinal method moves away from its applied form, it is called legal theory or jurisprudence.[77]

The doctrinal method is sometimes understood as 'the' legal method. This is arguably because its expository version mimics the work of legal practitioners, mainly judges; expository scholarship is written primarily for them to be used in the application of law. Law students are trained mainly (and sometimes only) in the expository form of the doctrinal method, as most of them head for a career as legal practitioners. This naturally results in the expository form of the doctrinal method being present (to some extent) in most legal academic writings, including the supply chain contracts and sustainability scholarship where it has been applied both as the main and a supportive research method.

As stated above, it is the research question that leads the researcher in the selection of appropriate research methods. Looking at the streams of scholarship on supply chain contracts and sustainability in the previous section, the expository method plays a dominant role in works on the *enforcement of SCCs in supply chain contracts* through contract law. Authors have repeatedly examined SCCs against the doctrines of contract law, such as contract law remedies, unilateral contracts, and third-party beneficiaries. However, there

---

75 Smits (n 72) 5–7.

76 It must be noted that the term 'doctrinal legal method' is sometimes used interchangeably with 'dogmatic legal method' and 'expository research'. The understanding in this chapter is that 'doctrinal legal method' is a broader category including both 'expository research' and 'legal theory research'.

77 Chynoweth (n 70) 31.

is no universal answer to the question of whether SCCs are enforceable under the applicable contract law. The answer will necessarily depend not only on the specific legal system but also on the exact wording of the examined clause.

In general, though, investigating the availability of contract law remedies in cases of breaches of SCCs in supply chain contracts by the expository method, the researcher quickly faces the obstacle of the disconnection of SCCs from the subject matter of a contract. The 'disciplining power of legal doctrine'[78] works strongly here, raising doubts regarding the suitability of contract law remedies to SCCs, as the legal doctrine of non-conformity of delivered goods does not cater for sustainability aspects in supply chains. In other words, SCCs do not seem to fit within the well-established contract law doctrines, within the legal systems and, thus, presumably do not have legally binding power and cannot be enforced through contract law remedies.

In respect of the application of the third-party beneficiaries doctrine on SCCs, we face the obstacle of establishing the *intention* of the contractual parties to grant a *specific* right to one or an *identifiable* group of third parties.

We might presume that the relevant legal doctrines will accommodate sustainability claims in future in line with the increasing value given to sustainability concerns by the society.[79] However, for now, the results of expository legal analysis of the enforceability of SCCs do not provide tools to those experiencing harm from SCCs' breaches and, in fact, underline the mismatch between theory and practice. This is confirmed by the scarce (or largely non-existent) case law. The expository analyses could have a practical impact if they become the basis of more claims brought by contractual and third parties alike demanding the enforcement of SCCs. This might be ignited by experimenting with third-party beneficiary clauses by institutional buyers.[80] Further research combining different legal fields, such as combined contract and tort

---

78 Smits (n 30).

79 Kateřina Mitkidis, 'Enforcement of Sustainability contractual clauses in Supply Chains by Third Parties' in Vibe Ulfbeck, Alexandra Andhov and Kateřina Mitkidis (eds), *Law and Responsible Supply Chain Management: Contract and Tort Interplay and Overlap* (Routledge 2019) 3.2.

80 Charity Ryerson, Dean Pinkert and Avery Kelly, 'Seeking Justice: The State of Transnational Corporate Accountability' (2022) 132 *The Yale Law Journal Forum* 878, 810–811. (The authors describe an experiment run by Corporate Accountability Lab, where third-party beneficiary clauses naming the suppliers' employees as intended third parties are added into transnational supply-chain contracts concluded by public buyers.)

law perspectives,[81] can also boost the practical impacts of the expository method.

Next, considering enforceability of sustainability requirements in supply chain contracts, the expository form of the doctrinal method has also been applied to investigate *the legal nature of SCCs*. In the search for a legal doctrine that would legitimize sustainability requirements as being a part of international contract law[82] and the binding power of SCCs in supply chain contracts, several authors relied on the doctrine of trade usage.[83] Authors supporting this doctrinal underpinning of SCCs claim that the widespread use of SCCs constitutes proof of the inception of a trade usage. However, until empirical data confirm not only the widespread use but also the actual observance of sustainability requirements within international supply chains, the finding that the content of SCCs constitutes a trade usage and as such implied terms in international sales contracts seems to be more wishful thinking than a contractual reality.[84] Therefore, more empirical research into the compliance with SCCs is needed.

As mentioned above, the expository form of the doctrinal method is present to a certain extent in most scholarship on SCCs in international supply chain contracts. Often, though, rather than being the main method of analysis, its role is to 'set a stage' for an application of other research methods or a theory development.[85] This supportive role of the expository method stems from the research question(s), where the contractual features of SCCs are not the focus. Instead, the analysis is centered around their sustainability, regulatory, or management objectives. Many authors discuss contracts only as one of the tools for achieving these other objectives, usually as an enforcement

---

81 See, e.g., Vibe Ulfbeck, Alexandra Andhov and Kateřina Mitkidis (eds), *Law and Responsible Supply Chain Management: Contract and Tort Interplay and Overlap* (Routledge 2019).

82 Smits (n 30) 107.

83 Section on 'The Legal Nature of SCCs' above; see also Daniel Zatorski, 'Sustainable Development as a New Trade Usage in International Sale of Goods Contracts' in Piotr Szwedo, Richard Peltz-Steele and Dai Tamada (eds), *Law and Development Balancing Principles and Values* (Springer 2019) 227–241.

84 See also Butler (n 31).

85 See, e.g., Fabrizio Cafaggi, 'Regulation through Contracts: Supply-chain Contracting and Sustainability Standards' (2016) 12(3) ERCL 218; Cristina Poncibò, 'A Contract Law for Future Generations' (2020) 2(2) *Revija Kopaoničke škole prirodnog prava* 35, 52; Kawakami (n 38); Paul Verbruggen, 'Private Regulatory Standards in Commercial Contracts: Questions of Compliance' in Roger Brownsword, Rob A.J. van Gestel and Hans-W. Micklitz (eds), *Contract and Regulation: A Handbook on New Methods of Law Making in Private Law* (Edward Elgar Publishing 2017) 284–322.

tool.[86] This is then reflected in the methodology, which is usually based on a general legal discourse starting from a contract law doctrinal perspective and moving on to more regulatory and even interdisciplinary discourse. A problem is that the methodology is not always well explained. The scholarship, thus, may remain hanging between the contract law field and any other perspective taken, not clearly indicating the contribution to any of those.

3.2 Theoretical Research

Theoretical research is not a consolidated legal research method; rather it is an axis on which various types of theoretical research can be placed, ranging from theoretical 'research in law' to theoretical 'research about law'.[87] The theoretical 'research in law' can be seen as part of doctrinal legal research.[88] Yet, it is distinct from expository research, as it does not primarily rely on case law and black letter law, but rather on legal and regulatory theories and the normative understanding of the studied legal system. Given the already stated lack of case law on SCCs, as well as the difficulties in fitting them within the relevant contract law doctrines, theoretical research seems to be the prevalent methodological style in the supply chain contracts and sustainability scholarship. Theoretical research on supply chain contracts and sustainability has been used to answer research questions from all the five streams of scholarship discussed in the previous section; however, it is most pertinent to the questions regarding *the legal nature of SCCs*, *the role of businesses as regulators*, and *the effectiveness of SCCs in supply chain contracts*. There is a great variety of approaches to conducting theoretical research. In its pure form, theoretical research develops new theories about the examined legal phenomenon or presents theoretical advances.[89] Examples are many, such as Trakman's article, in which the author applies a theory of public responsibility to contract law to provide a rationale '[...] that transcends the artificial boundaries between private contracting and public responsibility for contracting'.[90] This research can still be categorized as 'research in law' and thus legal doctrinal research.[91]

---

86 Narine (n 40).
87 Chynoweth (n 70) figure 3.1 and accompanying text.
88 Ibid.
89 From the vast amount of literature, see e.g. Park and Berger-Walliser (n 47); Kun (n 23); Cafaggi (n 22); Mitkidis (n 13); Salminen (n 59); Backer (n 47); Trakman (n 59); Jaakko Salminen, 'Towards a Genealogy and Typology of Governance Through Contract Beyond Privity' (2020) 16(1) ERCL 25.
90 Trakman (n 59) 262.
91 Chynoweth (n 70).

However, much of the theoretical research in supply chain contracts and sustainability scholarship adopts some interdisciplinary aspects and thus moves more or less towards the 'research about law' category.[92] In order to keep the research 'legal', expository research is often used to build up the argument for stepping outside the legal system to use out-of-law justifications, methods, theories, and/or sources.[93] An example of such an approach to theoretical research is the application of an existing theory to a legal phenomenon where it has not been applied before. My previous work applying the legalization theory as discussed by Abbott et al.[94] to understanding SCCs in international business contracts as a type of regulation can serve as an example here.[95] Using a theory-based method where a theory from another discipline is used to study law, a legal concept, or a phenomenon of law in action can be seen as one of the lighter versions of interdisciplinarity. While it can bring new insights into law, to keep the research valid, the legal researcher using this method must provide persuasive argumentation about the appropriateness of the use of the specific non-legal theory to answer the legal research question(s).

Moving further away from doctrinal legal research towards 'research about law' and stronger interdisciplinarity, authors employ combinations of theoretical insights and methodological approaches from other, non-legal disciplines to build arguments about law. The final argument is not purely legal, but the object of study is legal norms or phenomena. For example, Scheltema assesses the effectiveness of various types of transnational private regulation, including contractual arrangements, in the corporate social responsibility arena. To do that, the author proposes an integrated methodology combining legal, economic, sociological, and psychological/behavioural approaches.[96]

The rich theoretical discourse on supply chain contracts and sustainability has advanced the theory of contract law. Yet, in the (virtual) absence of relevant case law, the academic debate remains largely disconnected from practice. This might be seen as problematic given the understanding of contracts as 'law in action' and might give rise to questions about the validity of this stream of research. For scholars pursuing theoretical research into this topic, regardless of where it lies on the 'research in law'/'research about law' axis, it is crucial to remember that the validity of theoretical research does not rest on

---

92 Ibid.

93 See e.g. Cafaggi (n 85); Kawakami (n 38); Poncibò (n 85).

94 Kenneth W. Abbott and others, 'The Concept of Legalization' (2000) 54(3) *Int'l Org.* 401.

95 Mitkidis (n 13) Chapter 8.

96 Martijn W. Scheltema, 'Assessing Effectiveness of International Private Regulation in the CSR Arena' (2014) 13(2) *Richmond Journal of Global Law and Business* 263.

an external reality, such as natural phenomena, but instead on the persuasiveness of the presented arguments, leading to the development of consensus in the epistemological community of legal scholars and practitioners.[97]

3.3 Empirical Methods

The review of the existing scholarship demonstrates a clear dominance of theoretical approaches to SCCs. This is not only because, as previously stated, legal doctrinal research is considered 'the' legal method, but also due to the methodological challenges inherent in empirical research distinctive to this area. The main challenges are that the texts of contracts are often confidential and supply chain relationships opaque or not easily detected. Moreover, the sample of companies participating in empirical research is limited, and the information obtained is often based on companies' claims rather than on the factual contractual texts. Affolder describes methodological strategies that scholars have developed and applied to avoid the practical problem of gaining access to the texts of commercial contracts, such as relying on contracts' proxies, for example, corporate mandatory reports, and studying contracts present in publicly accessible databases, for example, the United States Security and Exchange Commission filings.[98] Despite the methodological challenges, empirical research is essential to understand questions regarding the *enforcement of SCCs in supply chain contracts* and *the effectiveness of SCCs in supply chain contracts.*

Within the varied toolbox of empirical methods to study supply chain contracts and sustainability, three methods stand out. First, text analysis has been used since the inception of the field. In his pioneering work, Vandenbergh gathered and analyzed publicly available corporate policies and statements, giving insights into supply chain contracting, acquisition and credit agreements, and insurance agreements to examine the function of private contracting in global environmental governance.[99] Since then, the method of textual analysis has delivered essential information to companies and regulators about the existence and use of sustainability requirements in supply chain contracts. Yet, methodological challenges remain. Scholars adopting this method must be precise in describing the studied sample of companies and documents,[100] as well as the coding techniques and variables' descriptions[101] to allow the audience to judge the generalizability of the findings and allow for their

97 Chynoweth (n 70) 30.
98 Affolder (n 51) 5–6.
99 Vandenbergh (n 54).
100 See, e.g., Vytopil (n 39) 12–15.
101 See, e.g., Mitkidis (n 13) Annex 2.

replicability, which is a research standard often unfamiliar to legal scholars. Secondly, conducting interviews is another widespread method in this field. To my knowledge, it has never been used as the only method in any given work, but rather in combination with other empirical methods, such as a case study[102] or text analysis.[103] Conducting interviews is not a method commonly known to legal scholars. Therefore, an initial study of the method, and careful preparation before and disclosure after, is a precondition for this method to deliver valid legal research. The third empirical method to mention here is conducting a survey. This method has, however, been used primarily by professional associations rather than legal academics.[104] The practical barriers to conducting such research, as costs, gathering contacts of relevant people in the studied companies (and their limited time and concerns about confidentiality), and potentially the necessity of receiving IRB, discourage legal scholars from using this method more frequently.

Despite the challenges, empirical studies are highly valuable. Not only do they provide interesting data for theoretical debates, but they also establish a connection with business practice. The practical burdens of empirical research methods and their unfamiliarity to legal scholars can be at least partially overcome by connecting powers with researchers from other disciplines trained in these methods and the analysis of the gathered data.[105] Such a combinatory methodology is welcome, yet may face issues of siloization of academia and research outlets. Conducting empirical studies will foreseeably become more feasible and common as corporations' transparency commitments regarding their supply chain contracts become legislated.[106]

---

102 McBarnet and Kurkchiyan (n 53).

103 Affolder (n 51) 3.

104 Pace University School of Law and IACCM, 'The Triple Bottom Line: The Use of Sustainability and Stabilization Clauses in International Contracts' (2010); EcoVadis and Affectio Mutandi (n 2).

105 Kateřina Mitkidis, Sonja Perkovic and Panagiotis Mitkidis, 'Tendencies in Contractual Governance to Promote Human and Labour Rights in Transnational Supply Chains' (2019) 23(4) *Competition & Change* 397, pinpoint.

106 See, e.g., through CSDDD and the new Directive (EU) 2022/2464 of the European Parliament and of the Council of 14 December 2022 amending Regulation (EU) No 537/2014, Directive 2004/109/EC, Directive 2006/43/EC, and Directive 2013/34/EU, as regards corporate sustainability reporting [2022] OJ L322/15.

3.4 Comparative Method

The final method to be mentioned here is the legal comparative method or, more precisely, legal comparative methods. Despite the pervasive use of comparative methods across various legal disciplines, jurisdictions, and topics, there are no universal methodological standards for conducting legal comparative research;[107] in fact the character of comparative law being a method is frequently questioned,[108] and moreover, there is no one universal aim of legal comparison but a range of possible ones.[109] It has become common to compare not only two legal families or national systems but also both horizontally and vertically across legal systems. From the varieties of comparative law (sub) methods (that are determined by their particular objective), the legal transplants method has been deployed to study supply chain contracts and sustainability within the *role of businesses as regulators* stream of literature.[110] This scholarship stands very close to works of legal theoretical research.

Next to this use of comparison, comparative methods have become increasingly used to study the *mutual interaction between private and public procurement* in respect to sustainability issues. Scholars can, depending on their primary expertise, take the starting point in one of the fields and study its impact on the other,[111] or they can join the expertise from both disciplines by involving several authors.[112] Often, this work again connects expository research with theoretical research. The leading idea behind this research is that in sustainable procurement, the development of public-private regulatory synergies combining both the state's authority and legitimacy and companies' pragmatism would enhance the effectiveness of contracting as a sustainability regulatory tool.

---

107 Marie-Luce Paris, 'The Comparative Method in Legal Research: The Art of Justifying Choices' in Laura Cahillane and Jennifer Schweppe (eds), *Legal Research Methods: Principles and Practicalities* (Clarus Press 2016) 3.

108 Ibid, section A.1.

109 Mathias Siems, *Comparative Law* (Cambridge University Press 2022) 2.

110 Lin (n 52) 717–730; see n 53 above and the accompanying text; see also Chang-hsien Tsai and Yen-nung Wu, 'What Conflict Minerals Rules Tell Us about the Legal Transplantation of Corporate Social Responsibility Standards without the State: From the United Nations to the United States to Taiwan' (2018) 38(2) *Northwestern Journal of International Law & Business* 233; and Affolder (n 51).

111 Beckers (n 63); Maria Edith Lindholm Gausdal, 'Breaching the Interpretative Wall between Private and Public Commercial Contracts: Scandinavian Case Law on Fundamental Labor Standard Clauses in Public Contracts' (2020) 16(4) ERCL 511.

112 Andrecka and Mitkidis (n 62).

4. CONCLUSION

This chapter has mapped the main streams of supply chain contracts and sustainability scholarship and the methods used to study this topic. The review of relevant literature reveals the multifaceted character of this legal field, demonstrating a clear struggle of contract law doctrines and theories to accommodate and understand the use of SCCs in supply chain contracts and provide answers to the range of research questions that arise in this area of study. This struggle is reflected in the relatively little purely expository research that is confronted with a lack of case law and empirical evidence. Instead, most legal writings in this area initiate with expository research as a foundational point but subsequently utilize other research methods to complement and construct persuasive arguments. Consequently, much of the scholarship moves from black letter, applied research to more theoretical and empirical explorations and is positioned all around the axis between 'research in law' and 'research about law'. This move presents evident challenges to contract law and compels contract law scholars to broaden their methodological toolkit in response.

To maintain supply chain contracts and sustainability scholarship as an integral part of contract law scholarship, researchers must thoroughly elucidate their methodology. They should particularly emphasize the significance of the expository component and its relationship to any other employed methods. Moreover, researchers should be transparent about their starting point and the objectives of their research to prevent accusations of sustainability lobbying.

Finally, while much has already been written about supply chain contracts and sustainability, the topic has not been exhausted yet. Ongoing legal developments, such as the new CSDDD, emphasize the crucial role of contracts—and by extension, contract law—in the global sustainability endeavour. Contract law scholarship will thus continue to be methodologically challenged and will need to evolve accordingly to embrace the sustainability-related aspects while upholding its academic distinctiveness.

10. Research methods for contract law and technology

Pietro Ortolani

1. INTRODUCTION

The interaction between digital technologies and contract law is complex. Digitalization opens up unprecedented possibilities for contracting and has the potential to affect the entire lifecycle of contractual relations. At the same time, technological acceleration also has the potential to disrupt conventional contract law wisdom, forcing contract lawyers to reconsider some of the cornerstones of this field of law. What do these developments entail for contract law scholarship? What are the methodological implications of digitalization's impact on contracts for contract law scholars? This chapter will attempt to shed light on these questions, exploring the contours of "law and technology" methodologies and their application to contract law scholarship.

The chapter proceeds as follows. In order to set the scene, section 2 will provide an overview of the impact of digital technologies on contracts. On the one hand, this section will discuss the new possibilities that technology offers for contracting. Digital tools can function as veritable contractual facilitators, supporting the parties (and their counsel) during the negotiation and drafting of agreements, automating contract review and due diligence tasks, streamlining contract formation, enabling automatic performance, and opening up new possibilities for remedies. For each of these steps in the lifecycle of a contractual relationship, practical examples will be provided to illustrate the role of digital technology as a catalyst for innovation in the field of contracting and contract management. On the other hand, section 2 will also illustrate the new contract law challenges that arise in connection with digitalization, and the open questions that arise. Concrete examples will show how traditional contract law doctrines and concepts may need to be reconsidered and remodulated, or even radically altered, as a consequence of the widespread digitalization of many aspects of contractual relations.

Against this background, it will be possible to scrutinize the specific role of contract law scholarship, as well as the new methodological opportunities and challenges that arise in connection with the growing digitalization of contracting and contract law. To this end, the chapter will distinguish between "technology for contract law" and "contract law for technology", which are discussed in sections 3 and 4, respectively. The former refers to the application of technological tools to the lifecycle of a contract, including contract negotiation, drafting, review, formation, and performance, as well as remedies for non-performance. Section 3 will focus on "technology for contract law", discussing some technology-oriented research methods for contract law scholarship, and stressing the importance of a commitment to active interdisciplinary dialogue. Section 4 will consider "contract law for technology", i.e. the application of contract law to technological developments that do not specifically concern contracting, but that could nonetheless potentially upset some well-established contractual paradigms. The overarching focus, once again, will be on the position of contract law scholars and on the added value that a technology-focused methodological toolkit could bring to contract law as a field of study. Section 4 will also offer some practical examples of challenges that contract law scholars currently face and that interdisciplinary approaches could help tackle. Finally, section 5 will draw some general conclusions concerning the opportunities that technology-oriented research methodologies offer for contract law scholarship.

2. THE IMPACT OF DIGITAL TECHNOLOGIES ON CONTRACTS

Digital technologies bring about new possibilities and new challenges for contract law. This section will discuss both aspects, setting the scene for a reflection on contract law methodology and interdisciplinary dialogue.

2.1 New Possibilities

During the entire lifecycle of a contract, technology can help streamline contract-related workflows, support lawyers, and even automate some of their tasks. Indeed, digital tools can be used to draft, review, conclude, and perform contracts. By way of example, a number of frequently used contract software tools (or "contractware")[1] allow for automatic contract drafting. This type of

---

[1] See e.g. Avokka <https://avvoka.com/> accessed 25 April 2023, Lawlift <https://www.lawlift.com/> accessed 25 April 2023. On automated contract drafting in general see Kathryn D. Betts and Kyle R. Jaep, 'The Dawn of Fully

software is particularly useful for routine agreements that parties habitually enter into (such as a non-disclosure agreement that all people involved in a certain project or task are required to sign).[2] While firms typically rely on standard boilerplate models for this type of contract,[3] the task of adapting the contents of a document for each specific use case, as well as filling in the blanks, is time-consuming and potentially subject to human error.[4] By relying on contract-drafting software, firms can not only save costs and minimize the risk of mistakes, but also lower the threshold of legal expertise necessary to draft an agreement. For instance, it might be challenging for an employee with no legal expertise to decide whether a stipulated damages clause is appropriate, and (if yes) what amount of stipulated damages is both appropriate and legally enforceable. Contract drafting software, instead, can be instructed to automatically include or delete such a clause, as well as adjust its amount, based on a set of predetermined variables reflecting the firm's preferences.

Furthermore, contract software is already used frequently to review the content of existing agreements.[5] Conducting due diligence on a large number of contractual documents is intrinsically costly and, again, subject to human mistakes and inconsistencies. Many products currently existing on the market[6] allow users to review contracts automatically, summarize their contents, and flag aspects that require human review (for instance, whether a contract contains a stipulated damages clause or an arbitration clause). These tools can also help anonymize contracts where needed, thus allowing a firm to comply with

---

Automated Contract Drafting: Machine Learning Breathes New Life into a Decades-old Promise' (2016) 15 *Duke Law & Technology Review* 216.

2 Benjamin Werthmann, 'Legal Drafting and Automation' in André Janssen and others (eds), *The Cambridge Handbook of Lawyering in the Digital Age* (Cambridge University Press 2021); Claudio Elia, 'Automation of Non-disclosure Agreements: A Roadmap for a Legal Department to Gain Advantage Using AI (Artificial Intelligence)' (2019) 12 *International In-House Counsel Journal* 1.

3 See on the use of boilerplate clauses in international commercial contracts Giuditta Cordero-Moss, *Boilerplate Clauses, International Commercial Contracts and the Applicable Law* (Cambridge University Press 2011).

4 William E. Foster and Andrew L. Lawson, 'When to Praise the Machine: The Promise and Perils of Automated Transactional Drafting' (2017) 69 *South Carolina Law Review* 597.

5 Andrew Antos and Nischal Nadhamuni, 'Practical Guide to Artificial Intelligence and Contract Review' in Roland Vogl, Andrew Antos and Nischal Nadhamuni (eds), *Research Handbook on Big Data Law* (Edward Elgar Publishing 2021) 467.

6 See e.g. Kira <https://kirasystems.com/> accessed 25 April 2023; Lawgeex <https://www.lawgeex.com/> accessed 25 April 2023.

data minimization principles without the need to manually retrieve and delete personal data in a large set of documents.[7]

Contract formation is also affected by technology. In some sectors, such as finance, algorithmic trading has already been the norm for years, and agreements are routinely concluded without human intervention, based on the basis of pre-determined parameters.[8] For instance, a machine can be instructed to sell a certain quantity of a given security if and when the price drops below a certain level. Automatic contract formation, however, is not limited to financial markets: the rise of smart products and the interconnectedness of physical objects with the Internet (Internet of Things, or IoT), for instance, bring about a number of appliances that are able to automatically detect the need to restock household supplies (e.g. food or cleaning products), and place the relevant orders.[9] In the future, developments such as smart contracts may further extend the range of situations where agreements are concluded without direct human intervention or impulse.[10]

Along similar lines, digitalization has an impact on contract performance, ushering in an era of self-enforcing agreements. The aforementioned smart contracts enable users to automate the performance of contractual obligations, for instance, instructing a machine to perform a payment or transfer a digital asset when specific conditions are fulfilled. Thus, a car could be leased on a

---

7 Ira S. Rubinstein and Woodrow Hartzog, 'Anonymization and Risk' (2016) 91 *Washington Law Review* 703.

8 Lauren Henry Scholz, 'Algorithmic Contracts' (2017) 20 *Stanford Technology Law Review* 128; Maria José Schmidt-Kessen, Helen Eenmaa and Maya Mitre, 'Machines that Make and Keep Promises – Lessons for Contract Automation from Algorithmic Trading on Financial Markets' (2022) 46 *Computer Law & Security Review* 105717.

9 Silvia De Conca, 'From the Glass House to the Hive: The Private Sphere in the Era of Intelligent Home Assistant Robots' (Privacy and Identity Management: The Smart Revolution, International Summer School, Ispra, Italy, 4–8 September 2017); Silvia De Conca, 'Between a Rock and a Hard Place: Owners of Smart Speakers and Joint Control' (2020) 17 *SCRIPTed* 238; Silvia De Conca, 'Smart Home for Lawyers: IoT in the Home and Its Implications for the GDPR' (2021) *Tijdschrift voor Internetrecht* 231; Silvia De Conca, 'Bridging the Liability Gaps: Why AI Challenges the Existing Rules on Liability and how to Design Human-empowering Solutions' in Bart Custers and Eduard Fosch-Villaronga (eds), *Law and Artificial Intelligence: Regulating AI and Applying AI in Legal Practice* (Springer 2022).

10 Andre Janssen, 'Smart Contracting and the New Digital Directives: Some Initial Thoughts' (2021) 12 *Journal of Intellectual Property, Information Technology and Electronic Commerce Law* 196; John Linarelli, 'Artificial General Intelligence and Contract' (2019) 24 *Uniform Law Review* 330.

pay-as-you-drive basis, and a smart contract could be instructed to make periodic payments whose amounts are automatically adjusted depending on the vehicle's usage.[11]

One final instructive example concerns remedies for non-performance. In this context, the party suffering the consequences of non-performance may avail him/herself of technology-enabled self-help remedies.[12] For instance, cryptocurrencies and other digital assets are routinely stored in escrow, so as to guarantee the performance of contractual obligations.[13] As the IoT gains momentum, similar self-help devices may become available in relation to tangible assets as well: in the example of a pay-as-you-drive car lease, briefly sketched out above, the lessor may be able to remotely disable the car if the lessee fails to make a lease payment on time.[14]

Technology thus promises to enhance the efficiency of contractual relations, and of contract law as a whole.[15] This, in turn, raises fascinating challenges for contract law scholarship. Many doctrines and general notions of contract law are distinctively human-centric and do not necessarily fit with the reality of technology-driven contracts.[16] Hence, as contracts become increasingly permeated by technology, contract law scholars must re-think their conceptual toolbox, adapting it to this new reality. The next sub-section will expand on these aspects, describing some of the challenges that digitalization poses for contract law.

---

11 A.U. Janssen and Tom J. Vennmanns, 'Smart Dispute Resolution in the Digital Age: The Potential of Smart Contracts and Online Dispute Resolution for Dispute Prevention and Resolution in Consumer Law Cases' (2021) 9 *International Journal on Consumer Law and Practice* 52.

12 Larry A. Dimatteo and Cristina Poncibó, 'Quandary of Smart Contracts and Remedies: The Role of Contract Law and Self-Help Remedies' (2018) *European Review of Private Law* 805.

13 Pietro Ortolani, 'Self-Enforcing Online Dispute Resolution: Lessons from Bitcoin' (2015) 36 *Oxford Journal of Legal Studies* 595.

14 Janssen and Vennmanns (n 11).

15 Among the many factors, technology could potentially help reduce the risk of human error, share legal expertise, enhance consistency in contract-related decision-making, save time and resources, automate contractual performance, and/or discourage non-performance.

16 Mateja Djurovic and André Janssen, 'The Formation of Blockchain-based Smart Contracts in the Light of Contract Law' (2018) *European Review of Private Law* 753; Simon Gleeson, 'Legal Considerations Around Smart Contracts: Contracts Between Computer Programs' (2021) available at SSRN 3925127.

2.2 New Challenges

Digitalization generates not only opportunities but also challenges for contract law. Most national systems of contract law were developed in an era when the current degree of digitalization could not have been imagined. As a result, some aspects of contract law may be ill-equipped to deal with the current technological reality of contractual relations, and contract law reform may be necessary. This, in turn, raises important questions for contract law scholars and for the methodology of contract law research. To illustrate this point, it is useful to analyze the impact of technology at three stages of the lifecycle of a contract: formation, interpretation, and performance. For each of these stages, this section will provide a practical example, explaining how digitalization can disrupt received wisdom and stimulate us to re-think contract law.

Example 1: Algorithmic formation of contract

For a contract to validly come into existence, the law generally requires a meeting of the minds, with a plurality of parties undertaking obligations towards each other (according to the will theory)[17] or accepting liability for the counterparty's reliance on a party's future contractual performance (according to the reliance theory).[18] Thus, despite areas of disagreement, contract law scholars generally agree that, when entering into a contract, the parties make a decision. Accordingly, contract law typically sets forth certain objective requirements, in the presence of which a contract is deemed to have been validly formed. These assumptions (concerning the nature of the parties' consent to a contract, as well as the objective criteria evincing the valid formation of a contract) may be challenged by certain artificial intelligence (AI) applications, where a party deploys a complex algorithm to decide whether and under which conditions they will enter into a contract. As pointed out by Scholz, in these situations, the algorithm is more than a mere tool executing a party's pre-determined preferences.[19] A particularly important example is that of "black box" algorithms, i.e. algorithms whose output cannot be predicted by the party using it and, often, not even by the developer of the algorithm itself.[20]

---

[17] Charles Fried, *Contract as Promise: A Theory of Contractual Obligation* (Harvard University Press 1981).

[18] Peter Jaffey, 'A New Version of the Reliance Theory' (1998) 49 *Northern Ireland Legal Quarterly* 107.

[19] Lauren Henry Scholz, 'Algorithmic contracts' (2017) 20 *Stanford Technology Law Review* 128.

[20] Cynthia Rudin and Joanna Radin, 'Why Are We Using Black Box Models in AI When We Don't Need To? A Lesson from an Explainable AI Competition'

Thus, in cases where a party delegates the choice of whether and under which conditions to conclude a contract to such an algorithm, contract law scholars are faced with challenging questions concerning, inter alia, enforceability and agency.[21]

Example 2: Ex post gap-filling

Contract lawyers proceed on the assumption that agreements are inherently incomplete, both because they contain general standards that require case-by-case interpretation, and because they inevitably do not regulate all of the issues that may need to be adjudicated at a later point in time.[22] Contractual gaps are the result not only of factual uncertainty and unpredictability, but also of the parties' need to constrain bargaining costs and complexity during negotiations.[23] Digitalization may partially upset these well-established paradigms. Smart contracts, for instance, are based on the idea of encoding (portions of) the parties' agreement into software script that can be executed without human intervention. To the extent that such automation is possible, the role of general standards (such as good faith) may be marginalized in favor of a deterministic if/then logic that leaves no space for gaps. According to Casey and Niblett, AI could even enable the creation of fully "self-driving contracts", where the parties agree only on the general objectives of their agreement, and a machine drafts contractual terms that are so detailed as to fill all gaps, automate performance, and minimize the risk of breach.[24]

Example 3: Allocation of liability for breach of contract

Let us assume that a seller relies on a third-party carrier to have goods delivered to buyers. If the goods are not delivered on time, the seller will be liable towards the buyer as long as the applicable conditions for contractual liability are met. The carrier, in turn, may be liable vis-à-vis the seller for his/her failure to deliver the goods on time, under the same conditions. Contract law

(2019) 1(2) *Harvard Data Science Review*, <https://doi.org/10.1162/99608f92.5a8a3a3d> accessed 17 January 2024.

21 Lauren Henry Scholz, 'Algorithms and Contract Law' in Woodrow Barfield (ed.), *The Cambridge Handbook of the Law of Algorithms* (Cambridge Law Handbooks, Cambridge University Press 2020).

22 Ian Ayres and Robert Gertner, 'Filling Gaps in Incomplete Contracts: An Economic Theory of Default Rules' (1989) 99 *Yale Law Journal* 87; Omri Ben-Shahar, 'Agreeing to Disagree: Filling Gaps in Deliberately Incomplete Contracts Freedom from Contract Symposium' (2004) *Wisconsin Law Review* 389.

23 Ayres and Gertner (n 22) 93.

24 Anthony J. Casey and Anthony Niblett, 'Self-Driving Contracts' (2017) 43 *Journal of Corporation Law* 1.

thus allocates liability and determines who will ultimately suffer the negative economic consequences arising out of a (series of) failure(s) to perform. In many civil law systems, such allocation adheres to a fault-based approach.[25] Along similar lines, the systems that adhere to a strict liability approach often contain corrective devices based on the idea of fault.[26] Irrespective of whether fault constitutes the basis for contractual liability or a corrective to a strict-liability rule, these approaches all require the existence of a human agent that is expected to act with a certain degree of diligence. To a certain extent, thus, contract law presupposes the presence of a human, either directly performing the contractual obligations or otherwise ensuring their performance and assuming responsibility in his/her choice of diligent third-party intermediaries.

Let us now assume that, instead of relying on a traditional "analogue" carrier, the delivery of the goods is carried out entirely by an autonomous artificial agent, without any type of human intervention or control (e.g. a self-driving drone). In this scenario, the aforementioned liability allocation principles may not be entirely fit for purpose. The autonomous agent lacks legal personhood in most legal systems and thus cannot be held directly liable,[27] nor can it be deemed to be "at fault" in any traditional sense. The seller will typically be liable towards the buyer, but it is debatable whether, as a general policy choice, he/she should bear the ultimate negative consequences for the behavior of an autonomous agent, which he/she does not control or understand in any meaningful way. Alternatively, the manufacturer of the autonomous agent may, under certain conditions, be held liable. However, in order to establish manufacturer liability, the seller will often be required to prove a defect in the autonomous agent, as well as a causal link between that defect and the failure to deliver the goods in time. In practice, this might prove challenging for several reasons. Intellectual property constraints may limit the seller's

---

25 Karl Riesenhuber, 'Damages for Non-Performance and the Fault Principle' (2008) 4(2) *European Review of Contract Law* 119.

26 Melvin Aron Eisenberg, 'The Role of Fault in Contract Law: Unconscionability, Unexpected Circumstances, Interpretation, Mistake, and Nonperformance' (2008) 107 *Michigan Law Review* 1413; Eric A. Posner, 'Fault in Contract Law' (2009) 107 *Michigan Law Review* 1431; George M. Cohen, 'The Fault That Lies within Our Contract Law' (2009) 107 *Michigan Law Review* 1445.

27 However, some authors have called for the attribution of limited legal personhood to autonomous agents under some conditions: see, most prominently, Anna Beckers and Gunther Teubner, *Three Liability Regimes for Artificial Intelligence: Algorithmic Actants, Hybrids, Crowds* (Bloomsbury 2022). Beckers and Teubner argue that the law should attribute different degrees of legal personhood to autonomous agents and set forth different liability regimes depending on the type of interaction that takes place between the autonomous agent and its social surroundings.

ability to prove how the autonomous agent works in general and what caused its behavior in a specific case. Furthermore, it may be technically impossible to explain why the autonomous agent behaved as it did in a particular occurrence, due to the technical inscrutability of "black box" algorithms on which the autonomous agent relies.[28] In addition, in some cases, it may even be argued that the autonomous agent is, in fact, not defective at all, despite its failure to deliver the goods in a particular case. After all, AI hinges on statistics, and no statistical model (no matter how sophisticated) should typically be expected to perform with 100% accuracy in all circumstances. In this example, therefore, technology prompts contract law scholars to reconsider the very foundation of contractual liability and re-evaluate the fair allocation of liability in case of non-performance.[29]

Interim conclusion

The examples provided in this section, as well as the possibilities described in the previous section, illustrate how deep and multifaceted the impact of digitalization on contract law is. At the same time, these brief accounts also raise a delicate problem: it is often difficult to distinguish among (i) cases where new digital technologies are already being used in the practice of contracting; (ii) situations where technology is being developed but not yet ripe for use; and (iii) other scenarios where authors speculate about a technological future that (for the time being) belongs to the realm of science fiction. Going back to our examples: algorithmic "black boxes" undoubtedly exist, but how often do parties entrust this type of algorithm with the task of negotiating the terms of a contract? Automation is gaining traction, but to what extent and under which conditions can a contract be performed without any need for human

---

[28] Han-Wei Liu, Ching-Fu Lin and Yu-Jie Chen, in 'Beyond State v Loomis: artificial intelligence, government algorithmization and accountability' (2019) 27 *International Journal of Law and Information Technology* 122, distinguish between "legal" and "technical black boxes", illustrating the different reasons why the functioning of an algorithm may remain invisible to outside observers.

[29] To address these concerns, the European Commission recently proposed a reform of the Product Liability Directive (COM(2022) 495 – Proposal for a directive of the European Parliament and of the Council on liability for defective products), as well as the introduction of a new AI Liability Directive (COM/2022/496 final, Proposal for a Directive of the European Parliament and of the Council on adapting non-contractual civil liability rules to artificial intelligence). While different in many respects, both of these proposals aim at easing the burden of proof with respect to damages caused by AI. For a critical comment on these proposals, see Philipp Hacker, 'The European AI Liability Directives – critique of a half-hearted approach and lessons for the future' (2023) 51 *Computer Law & Security Review* 105871.

input? AI is advancing at an impressive speed, but is it already able to translate general contractual objectives into granular clause-drafting? Contract law scholars often lack the technical expertise necessary to answer these questions. In the absence of such knowledge, scholars may be tempted to apply their legal knowledge to factual premises that are ill-conceived or unrealistic. What type of methodological approach should contract law scholars adopt to avoid these pitfalls and tackle the diverse and rapidly evolving areas of intersection between contract law and technology? The following sections will propose an answer to this question, emphasizing the need for serious interdisciplinary commitment.

3. RESEARCH METHODS ON TECHNOLOGY FOR CONTRACT LAW

Some of the technologies mentioned in the previous section have been designed specifically for contracting and aim at assisting the parties (and their counsel) throughout the lifecycle of a contractual relationship, including drafting agreements, reviewing them, and automating their performance. In other words, there is a growing body of "technology for contract law", including contractware tools and other software developed with a specific view to contracting. These developments open up interesting opportunities for contract law scholars. Technology for contract law remains, to date, a relatively unexplored aspect of contracting, and scholars will find no shortage of unanswered research questions by observing how digital tools affect, for example, the negotiation of a contract, the drafting of clauses, and/or their performance.

This veritable treasure trove of research themes and questions cannot, however, be accessed without adopting interdisciplinary methodologies. To illustrate this point, it is useful to focus on four particularly important forms of interdisciplinary dialogue for contract law scholars: computer science, decision science, data sciences, and socio-technical studies. To be sure, these are not the only disciplines with which contract law scholars may fruitfully interact, and further channels of interdisciplinary dialogue can undoubtedly enrich contract law scholarship. However, these four examples are instructive and best lend themselves to practical illustrations of possible interdisciplinary research lines.

3.1 Interdisciplinary Dialogue with Computer Science

Current contract law scholarship often interrogates the impact of AI on contracting, contract interpretation, and adjudication of contract law disputes.[30] Such interest is certainly welcome and justified, considering the growing importance of AI in different societal spheres, and its potential impact on the legal professions as a whole. However, conducting this type of research requires a sound understanding of the underlying technology, at least in its basic features. In the absence of technical knowledge, any discussion of contract law and AI risks devolving into science fiction: "AI", in the worst-case scenario, becomes less a type of technology than a shorthand for technology-infused fantasies. This, in turn, entails a twofold risk. On the one hand, contract law scholars may write about the risks and potential of technologies that are not likely to arise or become market-viable in the near future. On the other hand, scholars may fail to grasp the practical relevance of actually existing technological developments.

To avoid the risks outlined above, some degree of interdisciplinary commitment is necessary. The gap between legal and technical expertise can be bridged in various ways. Certain strands of legal research and education are currently pushing towards an integration of expertise: according to this model, contract lawyers should become conversant in technology, so that the same person can, for example, both write smart contract code and understand the legal effects (if any) of that code.[31] At the same time, not all contract lawyers can or should be expected to become proficient computer scientists, and contract law scholarship can maintain its distinctiveness while gaining the

---

[30] Philipp Hacker and others, 'Explainable AI under Contract and Tort Law: Legal Incentives and Technical Challenges' (2020) 28 *Artificial Intelligence and Law* 415; Sean Semmler and Zeeve Rose, 'Artificial Intelligence: Application Today and Implications Tomorrow Technology' (2017) 16 *Duke Law & Technology Review* 85; Yonathan A. Arbel and Shmuel I. Becher, 'Contracts in the Age of Smart Readers' (2022) 90 *George Washington Law Review* 83; Noam Kolt, 'Predicting Consumer Contracts' (2022) 37(1) *Berkeley Technology Law Journal* 71; Noam Kolt, 'Algorithmic Black Swans' (2024) 101 *Washington University Law Review* 1177.

[31] Mark Fenwick, Wulf A. Kaal and Erik P.M. Vermeulen, 'Legal Education in a Digital Age' in Marcelo Corrales Compagnucci and others (eds), *Legal Tech and the New Sharing Economy* (Springer 2020); Ronald Leenes, 'Of Horses and Other Animals of Cyberspace: Editorial' (2019) *Technology and Regulation* 1.

necessary technical expertise through interdisciplinary dialogue with computer scientists.[32]

The aforementioned example of AI can help clarify the added value of interdisciplinarity in this context. The label "AI" is currently used to designate a very broad spectrum of technologies that differ from each other in many significant ways.[33] For instance, AI is routinely deemed to encompass expert systems, relatively rudimentary systems that have already for decades been able to display a pre-determined output, based on the input provided by the user.[34] However, the concept of artificial intelligence also encompasses neural networks, complex series of algorithms that attempt to replicate the functioning of a human brain and produce outputs that (unlike with expert systems) have not been pre-determined by a human expert.[35] Contract law scholars can benefit from understanding this distinction, and from contextualizing it in different contract-related settings. For instance, in the field of contract drafting, most of the currently available software products are expert systems: the user sets up the system on the basis of his/her preferences (e.g. inserting an ICC arbitration clause in a contract whenever the counterparty is established in a foreign jurisdiction). The system, in turn, automatically performs the desired drafting task on the basis of the input it receives (such as automatically inserting an ICC arbitration clause when the user specifies the counterparty's country). These systems are significantly different from neural networks, such as OpenAI's GPT-4.[36] When a party asks GPT-4 to draft a contract, he/she has no certainty as to the output that the system will generate, or whether and how that output will reflect his/her preferences. By familiarizing themselves with the

---

32 Mireille Hildebrandt, 'Law as Information in the Era of Data-Driven Agency' (2016) 79 *The Modern Law Review* 1; Peggy Valcke, Inge Graef and Damian Clifford, 'iFairness – Constructing fairness in IT (and other areas of) law through intra- and interdisciplinarity' (2018) 34 *Computer Law & Security Review* 707.

33 Pei Wang, 'On Defining Artificial Intelligence' (2019) 10 *Journal of Artificial General Intelligence* 1; Dagmar Monett and Colin W.P. Lewis, *Getting Clarity by Defining Artificial Intelligence—A survey* (Springer 2018).

34 Paul E. Johnson, 'What Kind of Expert Should a System Be?' (1983) 8 *The Journal of Medicine and Philosophy: A Forum for Bioethics and Philosophy of Medicine* 77; Randall Davis, 'Expert Systems: Where Are We? And Where Do We Go from Here?' (1982) 3 *AI Magazine* 3.

35 Anders Krogh, 'What Are Artificial Neural Networks?' (2008) 26 *Nature Biotechnology* 195; Arash Bahrammirzaee, 'A Comparative Survey of Artificial Intelligence Applicationsin Finance: Artificial Neural Networks, Expert System and Hybrid Intelligent Systems' (2010) 19 *Neural Computing and Applications* 1165.

36 <https://openai.com/research/gpt-4> accessed 27 April 2023.

basic features of different forms of AI (and engaging in direct dialogue with computer scientists, whenever possible), contract law scholars can understand AI-driven contract drafting in a more granular and realistic manner, unpacking the broad notion of AI and ensuring that their accounts of the technology comport with its current reality.

3.2 Interdisciplinary Dialogue with Decision Science

When applied to contract law, technology should never be observed in isolation. After all, contracts are interactions between parties, and the impact of digitalization on contract law can only be fully grasped when considering (among other aspects) the consequences of technology for the parties' decision-making processes. In other words, as digital technologies increasingly permeate different facets of contracting, they may increasingly affect the way parties behave. For instance, during the negotiation phase, parties often make pre-contractual representations and statements, which may have legal consequences depending on the facts of the case and the applicable law.[37] Are parties more or less likely to make such representations when technology is used during the negotiations? For instance, is a party inclined to think that pre-contractual representations are more or less appropriate when the counterparty is reacting to the negotiation proposals by using AI? This type of question is distinctly empirical in nature and cannot be conclusively answered without observing and measuring the behavior of contracting parties under different conditions. Once again, it would be unrealistic to expect every contract law scholar to master decision science and conduct their own behavioral experiments to test certain contract-related hypotheses. To the contrary, working in interdisciplinary research teams with decision scientists can be beneficial for all experts involved. Decision scientists can use the insights of contract law scholars to identify the relevant contract-related hypotheses to be tested and carry out the necessary experiments. Contract law scholars, in turn, can use the experimental outcomes to formulate normative arguments, such as whether and how the law applicable to pre-contractual representations and statements might be updated to take account of advances in AI.

---

[37] Paula Giliker, 'A Role for Tort in Pre-Contractual Negotiations? An Examination of English, French, and Canadian Law' (2003) 52 *International & Comparative Law Quarterly* 969; Rick Bigwood, 'Pre-Contractual Misrepresentation and the Limits of the Principle in With v. O'Flanagan' (2005) 64 *The Cambridge Law Journal* 94.

3.3 Interdisciplinary Dialogue with Data Science

Data science is gaining momentum in legal studies, and contract law scholars can benefit from its methodologies. While the label "data science" encompasses a broad range of methodological approaches and intersecting disciplines, a recurring feature is the idea of treating text (be it legislation, contracts, or any other type of document) as a corpus of data to be analyzed through computing techniques, rather than read by a human.[38] The applications of data science techniques to contract law are numerous. For instance, a group of researchers recently deployed machine learning methodologies to develop CLAUDETTE, an automated system aimed at detecting unfair contract terms pursuant to EU Directive 93/13 on Unfair Terms in Consumer Contracts.[39] Another group of researchers used machine learning to automate legal document review, so that documents (e.g. contracts) are classified by a computer based on their relevance, and human lawyers are aided in their subsequent manual work with the same documents.[40] These data science approaches do not negate the usefulness of doctrinal or qualitative empirical research on unfair contractual terms; to the contrary, they reinforce it, complementing it with a data-driven tool that allows for the processing of large datasets.

While contract law scholars should not shy away from data science approaches, they should remain mindful of their limitations. On the one hand, an emphasis on computing allows lawyers to process a higher volume of data than what would be possible through manual means and to take into account an entire corpus of text (e.g. all case-law issued in a given jurisdiction during a certain period of time) rather than selected portions of it (e.g. the judgments that a scholar deems to be the most instructive to understand a given contract

[38] Wolfgang Alschner, 'AI and Legal Analytics' in Florian Martin-Bariteau and Teresa Scassa (eds), *Artificial Intelligence and the Law in Canada* (LexisNexis 2021); Kevin D. Ashley, *Artificial Intelligence and Legal Analytics: New Tools for Law Practice in the Digital Age* (Cambridge University Press 2017); Daniel Martin Katz, Dirk Hartung, Lauritz Gerlach, Abhik Jana and Michael J. Bommarito II, 'Natural Language Processing in the Legal Domain' arXiv:2302.12039.

[39] Marco Lippi and others, 'CLAUDETTE: an automated detector of potentially unfair clauses in online terms of service' (2019) 27 *Artificial Intelligence and Law* 117.

[40] Maura R. Grossman and Gordon V. Cormack, 'Technology-assisted Review in E-discovery Can Be More Effective and More Efficient than Exhaustive Manual Review' (2011) 17 *Richmond Journal of Law & Technology* 11; Maura R. Grossman and Gordon V. Cormack, 'A Tour of Technology-assisted Review' in Jason R. Baron, Michael D. Berman and Ralph C. Losey (eds), *Perspectives on Predictive Coding and Other Advanced Search and Review Technologies for the Legal Practitioner* (ABA 2016) 63–95.

law doctrine). On the other hand, a focus on computing typically entails (at least for the time being) a loss of the type of qualitative nuance that only human reasoning can achieve. In light of this, contract law scholars should neither reject data sciences altogether, nor jump to the conclusion that data-driven approaches will make traditional doctrinal research obsolete. To the contrary, different methodologies are apt for different research questions, and scholars should strive to expand their toolkit so that they can make a conscious case-by-case choice as to whether a certain research question is better suited for data-driven analysis, human qualitative evaluation, or a blend of the two.

3.4 Interdisciplinary Dialogue with Socio-Technical Studies

Technology for contract law does not develop in a vacuum. Contractware, for instance, becomes part of the day-to-day operations of firms that use software tools to draft, analyze, and manage contracts. Hence, technology for contract law can be understood as a socio-technical system, i.e. a complex organization where human and technical resources interact in the performance of certain tasks.[41] This tendency is compounded by lawyers' inclination to see the law itself as a technical device, designed to achieve certain results;[42] technological advancements, in this context, are often seen as opportunities to improve the performance of the "machine of the law". Interdisciplinary exchanges with socio-technical studies, therefore, can help contract law scholars grasp the complexity of the relationship between technology and the professional practices of contracting. When contractware becomes integrated into the contract drafting practices of a given firm, it becomes part of its work organization, and it affects the way in which the people working in the firm conceive of contracting.

Qualitative methodologies (such as interviews or ethnographic studies) can help contract law scholars understand the real impact of technology on contract law in practice, rather than attempting to observe contractware as an isolated phenomenon. This engagement in qualitative empirical work can also help contract law scholars to overcome a recurring bottleneck of technology

41 Eric L. Trist, *The Evolution of Socio-technical Systems*, vol 2 (Ontario Quality of Working Life Centre Toronto 1981); Günter Ropohl, 'Philosophy of Socio-technical Systems' (1999) 4 *Society for Philosophy and Technology Quarterly Electronic Journal* 186; Fred Emery, 'Characteristics of Socio-technical Systems' in Eric Trist, Hugh Murray and Beulah Trist (eds), *The Social Engagement of Social Science, a Tavistock Anthology*, vol 2 (University of Pennsylvania Press 2016) 157.

42 Annelise Riles, 'A New Agenda for the Cultural Study of Law: Taking on the Technicalities' (2005) 53(3) *Buffalo Law Review* 973.

for contract law, i.e., the fact that most technological solutions are developed by and for the private sector and may not be readily accessible to academic lawyers. Thus, by observing the real-life operations of firms that use contractware on a daily basis, contract law scholars can gain first-hand experience of a given technology and the way it is used in practice. This type of exposure is, in many ways, preferable to demonstrations provided by software developers, where the products are presented in a simulated, not always realistic scenario, and descriptions of the technology are colored by commercial language more than real-life experience.

4. RESEARCH METHODS ON CONTRACT LAW FOR TECHNOLOGY

Conventional contract law wisdom can sometimes be upset by technological developments that appear at first glance to be irrelevant to contracting. As section 2 above illustrated, when technological developments gain sufficient momentum, their impact may extend to contract law. Thus, for instance, IoT devices (such as smart home appliances or smart cars) open up new possibilities for automatic contract formation and automatic contractual performance, as well as certain self-help remedies. Brain-computer interfaces have the potential to help parties demonstrate the development of their thinking processes, including, for instance, whether they relied on a given interpretation of a contract at the moment of formation. Importantly, these technologies (unlike those discussed in the previous section) were not developed with contracts in mind but nevertheless force us to re-evaluate well-established contractual paradigms and doctrines such as remedies or reliance, in an attempt to adapt contract law to new realities.

In this context, the task of legal scholars is to reflect on "contract law for technology". Two main questions will be relevant here. First, looking at the law as it exists today, the question is how to apply current contract law to new technologies (e.g. how to navigate the will versus reliance theoretical debate, in situations where the thinking processes of the contracting parties at the time of the formation of the contract can be scientifically demonstrated, rather than just speculated upon). Second, with an eye to the future, the question is whether and how contract law should be adapted or reformed (e.g. whether new regulations of self-help remedies in consumer contracts are necessary), to meet the challenge of disruptive technologies and match the new reality that those technologies bring about. An important task of contract law scholars is to reflect on both of those questions, identifying the relevant challenges and, where possible, anticipating the issues that will later emerge in case law and legislative reform processes.

From a methodological point of view, contract law scholars cannot meet the challenges of digitalization while relying exclusively on traditional doctrinal methodologies. To the contrary, the methodological toolkit of contract law scholars must be enlarged, embracing "law and technology" not only as a label to designate a set of research topics but also as a commitment to interdisciplinarity. In this respect, section 3 above has highlighted the importance of interdisciplinary dialogue with computer science, decision science, data science, and socio-technical studies, explaining how contract law scholars can benefit from observing the entire lifecycle of a contract through different disciplinary lenses, with reference to contract-specific technologies. Now, it is necessary to take a further step, reflecting on the added value of the same interdisciplinary dialogue, this time with reference to technologies that are not specific to contract law and contracting (e.g. IoT devices or brain-computer interfaces), but that nevertheless raise important contract-related issues. More specifically, when looking at "contract law for technology", the added value of an interdisciplinary commitment comes in at least three distinct forms: the ability to distinguish between resilience and rupture, the ability to spot the contract law effects of nascent technologies, and the possibility and urgency to reconsider some of the traditional tenets of contract law.

4.1 Distinguishing between Resilience and Rupture

Contract law scholars are presented with a diverse and ever-evolving technological landscape, with new products and services being launched daily. As a result, it is difficult for scholars not only to keep track of technological developments but also to understand what consequences those developments might entail for contract law in practice. In other words, some technologies can easily be accommodated within the current framework of contract law, as they do not raise difficult legal issues. Contract law, in these cases, shows its resilience in its ability to lead to predictable and fair results, despite the fact that a given technology did not exist at the time when the relevant contract law principles developed.[43]

A practical example may help clarify what is meant by the resilience of contract law: most national legal systems conceptualized party autonomy and consent at a time when the current level of digitalization could not have been anticipated. Thus, technology has brought about new ways in which parties can express their consent to a contract, for instance by clicking on boxes and

[43] Eliza Mik, 'The Resilience of Contract Law in Light of Technological Change' in Michael Furmston (ed), *The Future of the Law of Contract* (Routledge 2020) 112.

buttons on a website, or swiping on their smartphones[44]—or even texting an emoji.[45]

Despite the novelty of these technologies, no serious doubt has arisen as to the ability of contracting parties to validly express their consent through these new digital means.[46] In other cases, however, contract law has failed to show the same degree of resilience. Some technologies have a disruptive potential for contract law and require scholars to rethink fundamental doctrines and concepts. For instance, the wide availability of IoT devices may open up an unprecedented scope for self-help remedies, such as in the aforementioned example of a leased car that automatically stops working if the lessee misses a payment. This, in turn, raises delicate questions, such as concerning the protection of weaker parties (especially consumers and employees) and the avoidance of abusive behavior on the part of professional creditors.

Without a solid understanding of the underlying technology, it is impossible for contract law scholars to distinguish between resilience and rupture, evaluating whether a given technology calls for a reconsideration of contract law rules and concepts, or whether contract law in its current form is already well-equipped to deal with new technology. Often, commercial and marketing communications concerning technology contribute to obfuscation, promoting every new product or service as revolutionary or disruptive, even when it provides only marginal benefits in comparison with existing technology. In this context, interdisciplinarity is the best strategy for contract law scholars to tell real disruption from "hype".[47] Active dialogue with computer scientists, for instance, can help contract law scholars understand the basic features of IoT devices before they draw legal inferences. In other words, technology forces contract law scholars to seriously consider the real-life impact that different

---

44 Vincent Gautrais, 'The Colour of E-Consent' (2003) 1 *University of Ottawa Law & Technology Journal* 189.

45 *South West Terminal Ltd. v Achter Land*, 2023 SKKP 116.

46 Despite some initial attempts to conceptualize the internet as a self-contained space where State law would not apply (John Perry Barlow, 'A Declaration of the Independence of Cyberspace: The Past and Future of the Internet: A Symposium for John Perry Barlow' (2019) 18 *Duke Law & Technology Review* 5), in the wake of internet adoption, contract law quickly affirmed its applicability to internet-based contracts, and the validity of agreements concluded via the internet (see e.g. with reference to EU law Graham Pearce and Nicholas Platten, 'Promoting the Information Society: The EU Directive on Electronic Commerce' (2000) 6 *European Law Journal* 363; T.J. de Graaf, 'From Old to New: From Internet to Smart Contracts and from People to Smart Contracts' (2019) 35 *Computer Law & Security Review* 105322).

47 Kelvin F.K. Low and Eliza Mik, 'Pause the Blockchain Legal Revolution' (2020) 69 *International & Comparative Law Quarterly* 135.

technologies may have on the circumstances surrounding a contract, seriously engaging with other disciplines. In the absence of such an interdisciplinary dialogue, contract law scholars risk building unrealistic legal theories and reasonings that do not comport with the current practice of contractual relations, and are thus unable to guide the future development of this field of law. Interdisciplinarity can meaningfully help contract law scholars recognize moments of real rupture, identifying technological developments that call for new contract law research, and also eschew the siren song of technological hype in cases where a new technological development does not upset well-established contract law paradigms and doctrines.

4.2 "Spotting" Technologies and Legal Issues through Interdisciplinary Dialogue

Interdisciplinary approaches can help contract law scholars to "spot" technologies, i.e. to learn about new technological developments in their nascent stages, and detect the ways in which these technologies might impact contract law. For instance, interdisciplinary exchanges with computer scientists, socio-technical scholars, behavioral economists, and other specialists can help contract law scholars understand the growing ecosystem of the metaverse and identify new ways in which the metaverse enables and influences contracting practices.[48] In this way, contract law scholars can anticipate the legal relevance of technologies that are not yet ripe enough to have real-life impact. From this point of view, contract law scholars have an important task that is distinct from practitioners', as the former (unlike the latter) do not need to wait for a given technology to raise contract law questions in practice. Scholars can rely on multidisciplinary insights to hypothesize about the future of contract law, by learning about emerging technologies and reflecting on how they may influence contracting. Contract law scholarship, thus, can provide guidance to judges, arbitrators and policymakers of the future, developing frameworks that can be relied upon as soon as new issues materialize in the practice of contract law.

Importantly, however, contract law scholars are not the only ones who stand to gain from expanding their research horizons through interdisciplinary interactions. Other disciplines can similarly benefit from the insights that contract law scholars can provide. Often, computer scientists and technologists lack legal expertise, and they fail to foresee the contract law implications of the

---

48 Jon M. Garon, 'Legal Implications of a Ubiquitous Metaverse and a Web3 Future' (2022) 106 *Marquette Law Review* 163; Ben Chester Cheong, 'Avatars in the Metaverse: Potential Legal Issues and Remedies' (2022) 3 *International Cybersecurity Law Review* 467.

technologies they build. For instance, cryptocurrencies were originally developed as a decentralized payment system, but the potential of the underlying protocol has been exploited to enable expressions of private autonomy encoded in software script, thus opening up new possibilities for contracting. In this respect, it is telling that Ethereum founder Vitalik Buterin admits regretting the popularization[49] of the phrase "smart contracts". At the time when he chose to use this expression, Buterin did not consider the legal misunderstandings that it would raise, revolving around the question of whether software script deployed on a blockchain qualifies as a contract.[50] With the benefit of hindsight, we can see that Buterin would have benefited from the insights of a contract lawyer, as much as that contract lawyer would have learned from Buterin's ideas. Along similar lines, ascertaining the consent of two contracting parties is not likely to rank high on the agenda of developers of brain-computer interfaces, but contract law scholars can help those developers grasp the legal consequences of the technologies they are building.

4.3 Reconsidering the Tenets of Contract Law

Section 2.2 argued that technology challenges certain contract law tenets and invites us to rethink them. The three examples provided in that section (AI determining whether and under which conditions a party will enter into a contract; self-driving contracts leaving no space for gap-filling; autonomous agents causing a breach of contract) illustrate how digitalization can disrupt contract law and pose complex questions about whether the current legal framework is still fit for purpose. To answer those questions, interdisciplinary engagement is key: by taking technology seriously and learning from a wide range of technical experts, contract law scholars can look at old problems with new eyes. In other words, contract law scholars should engage in interdisciplinary dialogue not only to spot new legal questions but also to reconsider old ones and revisit traditional tenets and doctrines. An engagement with technology, in short, does not necessarily need to translate into a hunt for everything that is new and unexplored in contract law; the technological lens also allows contract lawyers to reconsider the very core of their discipline.

---

49 The phrase was originally coined by Nick Szabo in 'Smart Contracts: Building Blocks for Digital Markets' (1996) 18(16) *EXTROPY: The Journal of Transhumanist Thought* 28.

50 Tonya M. Evans, 'Role of International Rules in Blockchain-Based Cross-Border Commercial Disputes' (2019) 65 *Wayne Law Review* 1.

5. CONCLUSIONS

This chapter has argued for robust interdisciplinary dialogue and cooperation between contract law scholars and a wide range of other technology-related disciplines, including computer science, decision science, data science and socio-technical studies. To set the scene, the chapter has first illustrated the multifaceted impact of technology on contract law, distinguishing between "technology for contract law" and "contract law for technology". While the former refers to contract-specific technologies, such as automated contract-drafting software, the latter points toward the impact on contract law of technologies that were not developed with contracts in mind. This overview has shown how technology creates both new opportunities and new challenges for contract law, at times enhancing the efficiency in contractual relations, and at other times disrupting the very foundation of the discipline. To address both new possibilities and new challenges, an enlargement of the traditional methodological toolkit of contract law scholars is desirable and, in many cases, necessary. Importantly, such an enlargement does not need to entail a marginalization of traditional doctrinal methodologies, or of contract law's distinctiveness as an academic field. To the contrary, interdisciplinary dialogue reinforces the importance of contract law scholarship and enables scholars to tackle a wider range of contract-related questions in different ways. Such interdisciplinary exchange will benefit not only contract law scholars, but also the experts from the other disciplines engaging in the dialogue.

11. Research methods for 21st-century consumer contracts: new wines, old bottles?

Cătălin-Gabriel Stănescu and Liviu Damsa

1. THINKING ABOUT CONSUMER CONTRACTS IN THE DIGITAL AGE

Consider the following scenario. A retired person surfing the internet comes across an attractive cruise offer she had always dreamed of. However, she does not know that the websites she visited had collected her data and used algorithms to determine her preferences, lifestyle, and budget. The cruise offer was made possible due to these determinations. She has to click 'yes, I agree' to the terms to move forward and visit another site. But tucked away in the 'agreement' is a clause requiring arbitration in a distant forum.[1]

This clause, along with other mandatory clauses in this electronic document, removes most of the statutory responsibilities of the cruise company that would otherwise have applied. Payment and money transfers to the cruise companies are governed by opt-in 'contracts' signed with the bank transferring the funds or by electronic opt-in contracts that the retiree cannot or does not read. When the cruise company fails to deliver what it had promised, the retiree discovers she has no recourse except to pursue arbitration in a distant forum, following rules she does not know or understand, and only after paying high filing fees. The lawyers of the merchants or banks invoke the '*pacta sunt servanda*' rule to deprive the retiree of her money,[2] arguing that the agreement

[1] A similar situation and a dispute resolution clause can be found in *Carnival Cruise Lines Inc. v. Shute*, 499 U.S. 585, 111 S. Ct. 1522 (1991).

[2] In cases such as this, corporate lawyers might like to invoke this 'principle' to demand the execution of any obligation provided for in the contract for the consumer. Despite being a Latin catchphrase, *pacta sunt servanda* does not denominate a general principle derived from Roman law. There was no such principle in Roman law in the sense we attribute to it nowadays, and its elaboration is

she had signed should be enforced and the retiree should abide by her voluntary waiver of the statutory protections otherwise applicable by default.

1.1 Classical Contract Theory and its Limitations in Consumer Contracts

The lawyers representing the banks and the cruise companies rely on what is known as classical contract theory to win any dispute.[3] This theory assumes that agreements are concluded between parties with roughly equal bargaining power and perfect information, usually through exchanging proposals of contractual terms. It also takes it for granted that the parties' internal psychological aspects leading to decisions to enter an agreement are irrelevant, except for traditional means to render unfair contracts void, such as mistake, coercion, unconscionability, or fraud.[4]

Consumer contracts diverge from the classical paradigm of contract law in several ways. They are pre-drafted by the merchant and cannot be changed or negotiated by the consumer. They are executed between unfamiliar and unequal contracting parties. Consumers do not read or (fully) understand this information or the obligations they undertake by signing such contracts.[5]

---

from a later date. See in this regard, e.g., Dmitry Poldnikov, 'Origins of General Concept of Contract in Western European Legal Science (12th through 16th Centuries)' (2016) 7 *Journal on European History of Law* 53, 56–57; Anthony Jeremy, 'Pacta Sunt Servanda. The Influence of Canon Law upon the Development of Contractual Obligations' (2000) 144 *Law & Justice: The Christian Law Review* 4, 4–7; Malcolm P. Sharp, 'Pacta Sunt Servanda' (1941) 41 *Columbia Law Review* 783, 785–91; John W. Salmond, 'History of Contract' (1887) 3 *Law Quarterly Review* 166, 171–78; Christoph G. Paulus, 'The Erosion of a Fundamental Contract Law Principle: *Pacta Sunt Servanda* vs. Modern Insolvency Law' in UNIDROIT, *Eppur Si Muove: The Age of Uniform Law. Essays in Honour of Michael Joachim Bonell to Celebrate His 70th Birthday* (UNIDROIT 2016) 740–752; Kaius Tuori, '*Pacta Sunt Servanda*' (2023) 1 AASF (Finnish Academy of Science and Letters) 44, 48–50. However, the idea of the need to execute *in toto* a contractual obligation since it represents the free will of the party undertaking it would be recognisable for a lawyer from the classical period under the 'will theory'.

3 James Gordley, *The Philosophical Origins of Modern Contract Doctrine* (Clarendon Press 1991) 214–228.

4 For contemporary debates on these classical themes, see Gregory Klass, George Letsas and Prince Saprai (eds), *Philosophical Foundations of Contract Law* (Oxford University Press 2014), esp. Ch 1, 2, 3, 10, 15, 18.

5 See, e.g., Roseanna Sommers, 'What Do Customers Understand about Predispute Arbitration Agreements? An Empirical Investigation', (2024) 19(2)

Therefore, consumer contracts challenge classical contract law's fundamental assumptions and concepts, such as party autonomy, information symmetry, equilibrium, and fairness.[6]

1.2 The Poverty of Consumer Contracts? Outdated Assumptions and Prescriptions for New Predicaments of Contracting in the Digital Age

All these differences above call for reform of consumer contracts to re-establish substantive equality between consumers and sellers. However, as can be seen in relatively recent developments, such as the introduction of mandatory disclosures in consumer contracts,[7] industry and regulators remain bound within the limits and presumptions imposed by classical contract theory. In other words, what is being proposed as an 'alternative' capable of resolving doubts raised by consumer contracts regarding the assumptions of the classical theory ultimately appears to be no more than classical contract theory 2.0. This revamped version, like the original, is premised on equality between the parties and their presumed freedom of will. As a result, the new framework ignores the systemic inequality of the parties and the way new technologies amplify it.

What is more, the premises of the classical contract theory are further enhanced by these reforms when they assume that it is sufficient for the business to provide general information and mandatory disclosures. For example, the industry attempts to deflect critiques based on the psychological and technological aspects of consumer contracting[8] by offering a justification of

---

PLoS ONE e0296179, <https://doi.org/10.1371/journal.pone.0296179> accessed 20 May 2024.

[6] For an overview of these challenges, see, e.g., Shmuel I. Becher, 'A "Fair Contracts" Approval Mechanism: Reconciling Consumer Contracts and Conventional Contract Law' (2009) 42 *University of Michigan Journal of Law Reform* 749, 750–752; Aristides N. Hatzis, 'An Offer You Cannot Negotiate: Some Thoughts on the Economics of Standard Form Consumer Contracts' in Hugh Collins (ed), *Standard Contract Terms in Europe: A Basis for and a Challenge to European Contract Law* (Wolters Kluwer 2008) 43–44; Nora K. Duncan, 'Adhesion Contracts: A Twentieth Century Problem for a Nineteenth Century Code' (1974) 34 *Louisiana Law Review* 1081, 1082–1099.

[7] See Recitals 7 and 8 of Directive 2008/48/EC of the European Parliament and of the Council of 23 April 2008 on credit agreements for consumers and repealing Council Directive 87/102/EEC [2008] OJ L133/66. The Directive aims, among other things, to promote confidence in the use of consumer credit and secure contractual fairness.

[8] See for such criticism e.g., Jessica Silver-Greenberg and Michael Corkery, 'Efforts to Rein in Arbitration Come Under Well-Financed Attack', *New York*

adhesion contracts that borrows from the neoclassical economic theory at the heart of the Law & Economics movement.[9]

Industry representatives argue that efficiency is an intrinsic and desirable quality when assessing legal rules.[10] They argue that, when efficiency comes into conflict with other goals of legal rules, such as equality or fairness, contract law should promote efficient contracts even though they reduce consumers' ability to maximise utility via open market transactions.[11]

Moreover, new research has shown that traders design consumer contracts to exploit consumers' cognitive biases.[12] Mandatory disclosures in consumer contracts are a prime example of such exploitation. They can be drafted with

---

Times, 15 November 2015, <https://www.nytimes.com/2015/11/16/business/dealbook/efforts-to-rein-in-arbitration-come-under-well-financed-attack.html> accessed 30 June 2024; Myriam E. Gilles, 'A Force Created: The US Chamber of Commerce and the Politics of Corporate Immunity' (2022) 72 *DePaul Law Review* 139, 148–170; Peter Linzer, 'Contract as Evil' (2015) 66 *Hastings Law Journal* 971, 985–1008; Tess Wilkinson-Ryan, 'A Psychological Account to Consent to Fine Print' (2013–14) 99 *Iowa Law Review* 1745, 1758–1784; Nancy S. Kim, *Wrap Contracts: Foundations and Ramifications* (Oxford University Press 2013), 93–211; Stacy-Ann Elvy, 'Contracting in the Age of the Internet of Things: Article 2 of the UCC and Beyond' (2016) 44 *Hofstra Law Review* 839, 840–851.

9 For an overview of the main borrowings and links of Law & Economics movements with neoclassical economic thinking and some of the philosophical problems of neoclassical thinking, see, e.g., Richard Craswell, 'Contract Law: General Theories' in *Encyclopedia of Law and Economics* (2000) vol 3, 1–24; Eric A. Posner, 'Economic Analysis of Contract Law after Three Decades: Success or Failure?' (2002–2003) 112(4) *Yale Law Journal* 829; Richard A. Posner, 'The Law and Economics of Contract Interpretation' (2004) 83 *Texas Law Review* 1581; Steven Shavell, *Foundations of Economic Analysis of Law* (Harvard University Press 2004); Klaus Mathis, *Efficiency instead of Justice? Searching for the Philosophical Foundations of the Economic Analysis of Law* (Springer 2009); Robert Cooter and Thomas Ulen, *Law and Economics* (Addison-Wesley 2011); Elisabeth Popp-Berman, *Thinking Like an Economist. How Efficiency Replaced Equality in US Public Policy* (Princeton University Press 2022); Gary Gerstle, *The Rise and Fall of the Neoliberal Order. America and the World in the Free Market Era* (Oxford University Press 2022).

10 Eric A. Posner, 'Contract Theory' in Martin P. Goldin and William A. Edmunson (eds), *The Blackwell Guide to the Philosophy of Law and Legal Theory* (Blackwell Publishing 2005) 139; Andrea J. Boyack, 'The Shape of Consumer Contracts' (2023–2024) 1(101) *Denver Law Review* 1, 9–12.

11 Eric A. Posner, 'Contract Theory', 154.

12 Oren Bar-Gill, *Seduction by Contract*: *Law, Economics, and Psychology in Consumer Markets* (Oxford University Press 2012) 2–32.

consumers' biases in mind[13] or with complete disregard for people's cognitive abilities or literacy levels.[14] It has been repeatedly demonstrated that such disclosures 'are neither read, nor used, and beyond most people's interest or understanding'.[15] Therefore, many stakeholders – commentators, courts, civil society groups, and legislatures – agree that intervention is continually needed to protect consumers. Nevertheless, it is doubtful that such an intervention could advance consumer protection if outdated premises of the classical contract theory inspire it.

1.3 The Role of Mandatory Disclosures in Consumer Contracts

Disclosures have proven *ineffective* in overcoming asymmetric information or behavioural biases.[16] Even in online marketplaces, the EU's more protective system for consumers considers it sufficient to provide mandatory information

13 ibid 8–23.

14 Oren Bar-Gill and Omri Ben-Shahar, 'Regulatory Techniques in Consumer Protection: A Critique of European Consumer Contract Law' (2013) 50 *Common Market Law Review* 109, 118.

15 ibid 110, 116–119.

16 Becher (n 6), 749. Citing several empirical studies and academic works, the European Law Institute also notes the 'widespread understanding among consumer law scholars as well as in neuroscience, behavioural economics, and cognitive psychology that the information paradigm is not an effective way of protecting the interest of consumers' – European Law Institute, 'European Commission's Public Consultation on Digital Fairness – Fitness Check on EU Consumer Law. Response of the European Law Institute' (ELI 2023) 1–12, <https://www.europeanlawinstitute.eu/fileadmin/user_upload/p_eli/Publications/Response_of_the_ELI_to_the_European_Commission_s_Public_Consultation_on_Digital_Fairness_.pdf> accessed 12 December 2023. The limitations of 'disclosure, transparency, and consent as the only tools to effectively protect consumers' are also underlined by the European Consumer Organisation, in 'Towards European Digital Fairness. *European Consumer Organisation* (BEUC) framing response paper for the REFIT consultation' (2023), 5, 26 <https://www.beuc.eu/sites/default/files/publications/BEUC-X-2023-020_Consultation_paper_REFIT_consumer_law_digital_fairness.pdf> accessed 20 May 2024.

(known as 'pre-contractual information')[17] and a right of withdrawal,[18] albeit subject to several exceptions.[19]

Based on classical contract theory, the underlying assumption is that if consumers are provided with sufficient disclosure, they can protect themselves with minimal intervention by state authorities.[20] However, this emphasis on mandating information increases consumers' responsibility for protecting themselves, rather than providing protection.[21] The consumer is considered fully responsible for the obligations undertaken so long as accurate information is disclosed.[22] The responsibility to judge complex information is placed on consumers' shoulders.[23]

Ample research indicates that consumers have difficulties processing precisely the kinds of complex information and disclosures that merchants rely

---

17 Article 6a of Directive 2011/83/EU of the European Parliament and of the Council of 25 October 2011 on consumer rights, amending Council Directive 93/13/EEC and Directive 1999/44/EC of the European Parliament and the Council and repealing Council Directive 85/577/EEC and Directive 97/7/EC of the European Parliament and of the Council, [2011] OJ L304/64 (Consumer Rights Directive). Information requirements also appear in other EU legislation, such as the e-Commerce Directive, the Sale of Goods Directive, the Digital Content Directive, the Consumer Credit Directive, and the Consumer Mortgage Directive. For more details: Commission, 'Notice Guidance on the interpretation and application of Directive 2011/83/EU of the European Parliament and of the Council on consumer rights' [2021] OJ C525/1.

18 Articles 9–14 of the Consumer Rights Directive.

19 ibid Article 16.

20 Hans-Wolfgang Micklitz, Jules Stuyck and Evelyne Terryn (eds), *Cases, Materials and Text on Consumer Law* (Hart Publishing 2010) 372.

21 Cătălin-Gabriel Stănescu, 'The Responsible Consumer in the Digital Age' (2019) 24 *Tilburg Law Review* 49.

22 Micklitz, Stuyck and Terryn (n 20) 373. The increase in consumer responsibility, especially regarding financial products, was noticed, for instance, in the US and Australia. For the US, see John Y. Campbell and others, 'Consumer Financial Protection' (2011) 25 *The Journal of Economic Perspectives* 91, 94–109. For Australia, see Richard Sandlant, 'Consumer Financial Protection: Future Directions' (2011) 4 *JASSA: The Journal of the Securities Institute of Australia* 42, and Sandlant, 'Consumer financial protection: Future directions'. Australian Government. Treasury Economic Roundup, Issue 1 2012 <https://treasury.gov.au/publication/economic-roundup-issue-1-2012-2/economic-roundup-issue-1-2012/consumer-financial-protection-future-directions> [accessed 20 March 2024], (2–7).

23 Becher (n 6) 749.

upon and do not read essential legal documents.[24] A 2017 Deloitte survey found that 91% of people in the US consent to legal terms and service conditions without reading them, and the rate is even higher among young people aged 18–34 (97%).[25]

Another survey conducted in 2019 revealed that only 9% of Americans always read a company's privacy policy before agreeing to the terms and conditions, while an additional 13% do this often. Conversely, 36% of adults said they had never read a privacy policy.[26] Among the respondents who said they read policies, only a minority (22%) read them all the way through, while most (43%) merely glanced over them.[27] These results were reconfirmed in 2021.[28]

These studies show that it is challenging for consumers to process information even when it is provided, or to be willing to spend time and effort reading the fine print. Indeed, not reading the standard terms might be a rational decision if one considers their complexity or length, that they cannot be negotiated, and that if no problem arises, the fine print will not have any impact.

1.4 Further Challenges to Consumer Contracts in the Digital Age

In addition to cognitive biases and difficulties in processing information, technological advances further belie the assumptions of classical contract theory. Imagine that the hypothetical pensioner in the introduction searches and concludes that her cruise contract was 'aided' by non-visible AI assistants and all sorts of technological enhancements. She will face an exponential increase in cognitive and information processing difficulties caused by the rise in

---

24 Yannis Bakos, Florencia Marotta-Wurgler and David R. Trossen, 'Does Anyone Read the Fine Print? Consumer Attention to Standard Form Contracts' (2014) 43(1) *The Journal of Legal Studies* 1, 25, 35.

25 Caroline Cakebread, 'You're Not Alone, No One Reads Terms of Service Agreements', *Business Insider*, 15 November 2017, <https://www.businessinsider.com/deloitte-study-91-percent-agree-terms-of-service-without-reading-2017-11?r=US&IR=T> accessed 12 December 2023.

26 Brooke Auxier and others, 'Americans' Attitudes and Experiences with Privacy Policies and Laws', The Pew Research Center, 15 November 2019, <https://www.pewresearch.org/internet/2019/11/15/americans-attitudes-and-experiences-with-privacy-policies-and-laws/> accessed 12 December 2023.

27 ibid.

28 The Clearing House, 'Consumer Survey – Data Privacy and Financial App Usage' (December 2021) 5 <https://www.theclearinghouse.org/-/media/New/TCH/Documents/Data-Privacy/2021-TCH-ConsumerSurveyReport_Final.pdf?rev=eede5e57b1d94bbe93979e1c6aab9a4b&hash=AB7381B46AD085E1911CEDACD6A7C80E> accessed 12 December 2023.

automation and profiling in consumer contracts that come with these technological advancements.[29]

Automation refers to using technology to perform tasks where human input is minimised. Conversely, profiling uses personal data to evaluate, analyse, or predict aspects of a person's life, such as work performance, economic situation, health, personal preferences, interests, reliability, behaviour, location, or movements. Both automation and profiling could use algorithms,[30] which are processes or sets of rules to be followed in computer calculations or other computer problem-solving operations. With this increased use of algorithms, the scholarship even speaks of algorithmic contracts.[31]

---

[29] For a general overview and discussions of the exponential burden posed on customers' psychological capacity to process information or of the moral and legal dilemmas posed by this rise in automation and profiling, see, e.g., Veronica Barassi, *Child Data Citizen: How Tech Companies are Profiling Us from before Birth* (MIT Press 2020); Joseph Turow, *The Voice Catchers: How Marketers Listen in to Exploit Your Feelings, Your Privacy, and Your Wallet* (Yale University Press 2021); Shoshana Zuboff, 'You Are Now Remotely Controlled', *New York Times* (20 January 2020) <https://www.nytimes.com/2020/01/24/opinion/sunday/surveillance-capitalism.html> accessed 20 April 2024; Daniel Susser, Beate Roessler and Helen Nissenbaum, 'Online Manipulation: Hidden Influences in a Digital World' (2019) 4 *Georgetown Law Technology Review* 1; Moritz Büchi and others, 'The Chilling Effects of Algorithmic Profiling: Mapping the Issues' (2020) 36 *Computer Law & Security Review* 105; Axel Gautier, Ashwin Ittoo and Pieter Van Cleynenbreugel, 'AI Algorithms, Price Discrimination and Collusion: A Technological, Economic and Legal Perspective' (2020) 50(3) *European Journal of Law and Economics* 405; Jon Truby and Rafael Brown, 'Human Digital Thought Clones: The Holy Grail of Artificial Intelligence for Big Data' (2021) 30(2) *Information & Communications Technology Law* 140.

[30] An algorithm, according to the *Oxford Dictionary*, is a process or set of rules to be followed in calculation or other problem-solving operations, especially by a computer. Angus Stevenson, *Oxford Dictionary of English* (3rd edn, OUP 2010), 40. We should observe that not all automation is algorithmic (i.e., based on algorithms). Still, all algorithms automate, so the extension of algorithmic automation from purely mathematical computation to socio-technological infrastructures and aspects produces profound mutations in contemporary society. Similarly, while profiling involves more than the use of algorithms (Bernhard Anrig, Will Browne and Mark Gasson, 'The Role of Algorithms in Profiling' in Mireille Hildebrandt and Serge Gutwirth (eds), *Profiling the European Citizen: Cross-Disciplinary Perspectives* (Springer 2008) 65–86), it also uses algorithms to find correlations between separate datasets, and afterwards to make a wide range of (automated) decisions, e.g., to predict behaviour or to control access to products or services. So, at least a partial overlap exists between automation, profiling, and algorithms.

[31] Lauren Henry Scholz, 'Algorithmic Contracts' (2017) 20 *Stanford Technology Law Review* 128, 133–134. For Scholz, algorithmic contracts are

Yet, such utilisation of algorithms raises numerous problems in consumer contracts, which have been debated in a burgeoning literature.[32] Using algorithms could result in discrimination against consumers based on gender or race, violations of their fundamental rights, or denial of the benefits of similar contract terms or economic advantages from market transactions.[33] Such

---

agreements where an algorithm determines a party's obligations. In consumer contracts, sellers sometimes use algorithms as 'negotiators' before contract formation, e.g., for choosing which terms to offer or accept. Other times, algorithms could be used as gap fillers after the conclusion of the contract. The problem with this use of algorithms is that the contract law doctrine does not have a coherent approach to describing the creation and enforcement of such algorithmic contracts.

[32] Frank Pasquale, 'Restoring Transparency to Automated Authority' (2011) 9 *Journal on Telecommunications & High Technology Law* 235; Solon Barocas and Helen Nissenbaum, 'Big Data's End Run around Anonymity and Consent' in Julia Lane and others (eds), *Privacy, Big Data, and the Public Good Frameworks for Engagement* (Cambridge University Press 2014) 44–58; Frank Pasquale, *The Black Box Society: The Secret Algorithms That Control Money and Information* (Harvard University Press 2015); Solon Barocas and Andrew D. Selbst, 'Big Data's Disparate Impact' (2016) 104 *California Law Review* 671; Jenna Burrell, 'How the Machine 'Thinks': Understanding Opacity in Machine Learning Algorithms' (2016) *Big Data & Society* 1; Madalina Busuioc, 'Accountable Artificial Intelligence: Holding Algorithms to Account' (2020) 81(5) *Public Administration Review* 825.

[33] Jon Kleinberg and others, 'Discrimination in the Age of Algorithms' (2018) 10 *Journal of Legal Analysis* 113; James Zou and Londa Schiebinger, 'AI Can Be Sexist and Racist – It's Time to Make It Fair' (2018) *Nature*, <https://www.nature.com/articles/d41586-018-05707-8> accessed 4 June 2024; European Union Agency for Fundamental Rights, 'Bias in Algorithms – Artificial Intelligence and Discrimination' (EU AFR 2022); Michal S. Gal and Niva Elkin-Koren, 'Algorithmic Consumers' (2016) 30 *Harvard Journal of Law and Technology* 309, 332–341; Laura Drechsler, 'The Price Is (Not) Right: Data Protection and Discrimination in the Age of Pricing Algorithms' (2018) 9(3) *European Journal of Law and Technology* <https://ejlt.org/index.php/ejlt/article/view/631/853> accessed 14 July 2024; Sandra G. Mayson, 'Bias in, Bias out' (2019) 128 *Yale Law Journal* 2218; Robert Bartlett and others, 'Consumer-Lending Discrimination in the FinTech Era' (2022) 143(1) *Journal of Financial Economics* 30; Salil K. Mehra, 'Price Discrimination-Driven Algorithmic Collusion: Platforms for Durable Cartels' (2021) 26(1) *Stanford Journal of Law, Business and Finance* 171; Jon Kleinberg and others, 'Discrimination in the Age of Algorithms' (2019) 10 *Journal of Legal Analysis* 113; Gerhard Wagner and Horst Eidenmüller, 'Down by Algorithms? Siphoning Rents, Exploiting Biases, and Shaping Preferences: Regulating the Dark Side of Personalized Transactions' (2019) 86 *The University of Chicago Law Review* 581; Kate Crawford, 'The Hidden Biases in Big Data', *Harvard Business Review*, 1 April 2013, <https://hbr.org/2013/04/the-hidden-biases-in-big-data> accessed 4 June 2024; Alexandra Reeve Givens, 'How Algorithmic Bias Hurts People with Disabilities', *Slate Magazine*, 6 February

discrimination is often due to biases inherent in the construction of algorithms, where 'algorithmic biases' are defined as systematic and repeatable errors in a computer system that create unfair outcomes in ways that are different from the intended function of the algorithm.[34]

To prevent such biases, the public should be able to scrutinise the algorithms and the data utilised to train them. However, such scrutiny is difficult since the algorithms employed in automation and profiling are often considered proprietary information by the industry and are not disclosed to the public. Similarly, the data used to train the algorithms is considered proprietary and not disclosed. This makes detecting any discrimination the algorithms produce because of inherent biases difficult, if not impossible.[35] Even if a legal norm would forbid it, consumers would have a hard time proving that discrimination occurred in violation of the law.[36]

Furthermore, in the case of profiling, which relies on massive data sets of personal information, consumers find it challenging to understand, let alone control, the 'free' circulation of their data among third parties on which the profiling business model is based. At the same time, consumers sign adhesion contract clauses for products or services, which often provide collectors with legal rights to monetise such data. The result is that consumers unknowingly collaborate in the development of algorithms that discriminate against them.

Moreover, these are only some of the challenges that technological advancements pose for classical contract theory. Another common practice is that many consumer contracts expressly reserve for merchants the right to make amendments without seeking separate consent. This undermines the classical theory ideas of 'personal autonomy' and 'meeting of the minds'.[37] Additionally, there are triangular transactions used by digital platforms, which leave consumers

---

2020, <https://slate.com/technology/2020/02/algorithmic-bias-people-with-disabilities.html> accessed 4 June 2024.

34 Maya C. Jackson, 'Artificial Intelligence & Algorithmic Bias: The Issues with Technology Reflecting History & Humans' (2021) 16 *Journal of Business and Technology Law* 299, 300.

35 Sandra Wachter, Brent Mittelstadt and Luciano Floridi, 'Why a Right to Explanation of Automated Decision-Making Does Not Exist in the General Data Protection Regulation' (2017) 7(2) *International Data Privacy Law* 76, 94.

36 Marco Giraudo, 'On Legal Bubbles: Some Thoughts on Legal Shockwaves at the Core of the Digital Economy' (2022) 18(4) *Journal of Institutional Economics* 587, 589–93; Monique Mann and Tobias Matzner, 'Challenging Algorithmic Profiling: The Limits of Data Protection and Anti-discrimination in Responding to Emergent Discrimination' (2019) 6(2) *Big Data & Society* 1, 2–3.

37 Shmuel I. Becher and Uri Benoliel, 'Sneak in Contracts' (2021) 55(2) *Georgia Law Review* 657, 660.

with inadequate protection.[38] Online platforms also have the power to unilaterally alter consumer contract fees, dispute resolution mechanisms, and privacy policies.[39] This gives them maximum flexibility with minimal transparency requirements.[40]

1.5 Regulatory Adaptation to the Digital Age

Thus far, the consequences of digitalisation have not been fully addressed in regulation. However, EU legislation has already started to respond to the need to adapt contract law to the realities of the digital age.[41] Uniform laws have been implemented for geo-blocking,[42] portability,[43] and, more recently, by the private law parts of the Platform-to-Business Regulation,[44] the Digital

---

38 Christoph Busch and others, 'The Rise of the Platform Economy: A New Challenge for EU Consumer Law?' (2016) 5(1) *Journal of European Consumer and Market Law* 3, 4.

39 Becher and Benoliel (n 37) 660–661.

40 ibid 668.

41 While the EU apparently has more consumer protection doctrines and consequently extensive regulatory initiatives for protecting customers, similar trends exist around the globe. For an overview of e-commerce regulation, including business-to-consumer commerce in the US, see, for instance Victor J. Castelucci, 'Digital Business Laws and Regulations USA 2023-2024', ICLG, 2 June 2023, <https://iclg.com/practice-areas/digital-business-laws-and-regulations/usa> accessed 20 May 2024. Alberto De Franceschi and Reiner Schulze, 'Harmonizing Digital Contract Law – An Introduction' in Alberto De Franceschi and Reiner Schulze (eds), *Harmonizing Digital Contract Law: The Impact of EU Directives 2019/770 and 2019/771 and the Regulation of Online Platforms. A Handbook* (Bloomsbury Publishing 2023) 2.

42 Regulation (EU) 2018/302 of the European Parliament and of the Council of 28 February 2018 on addressing unjustified geo-blocking and other forms of discrimination based on consumers' nationality, place of residence or place of establishment within the internal market and amending Regulations (EC) No 2006/2004 and (EU) 2017/2394 and Directive 2009/22/EC, [2018] OJ L60I/1. For an overview of consumers' struggle against geo-blocking around the globe, see Sabrina Earle, 'The Battle Against Geo-Blocking: The Consumer Strikes Back' (2016) 15 *Richmond Journal of Global Law and Business* 1, <http://scholarship.richmond.edu/global/vol15/iss1/2> accessed 20 May 2024.

43 Regulation (EU) 2017/1128 of the European Parliament and of the Council of 14 June 2017 on cross-border portability of online content services in the internal market, [2017] OJ L168/1.

44 Regulation (EU) 2019/1150 of the European Parliament and of the Council of 20 June 2019 on promoting fairness and transparency for business users of online intermediation services, PE/56/2019/REV/1, [2019] OJ L186/57.

Markets Act,[45] and the Digital Services Act.[46] Concurrently, the Omnibus Directive,[47] the Digital Content and Digital Services Directive,[48] and the Sale of Goods Directive[49] have continued the harmonisation of the laws of the Member States.

The last two directives have harmonised some of the most important parts of contract law in the digital age: the supply of digital content and services and the sale of goods, including goods with digital elements, covering millions of consumer contracts.[50] Moreover, they make several innovative contributions to adapting contract law to the challenges of digitalisation. One prominent example is the recognition of the importance of data as the subject of performance and counter-performance in modern contracting.[51]

The EU consumer protection directives are also oriented towards standardised objective criteria for conformity with the contract.[52] Such objective criteria further limit the traditional view, according to which the parties' mutual intentions determine the contract, to enhance consumer protection.[53] This marks a legislative recognition that the traditional conception of individually-negotiated contracts no longer reflects the reality of mass production and mass

---

45 Regulation (EU) 2022/1925 of the European Parliament and of the Council of 14 September 2022 on contestable and fair markets in the digital sector and amending Directives (EU) 2019/1937 and (EU) 2020/1828 (Digital Markets Act), PE/17/2022/REV/1, [2022] OJ L265/1.

46 Regulation (EU) 2022/2065 of the European Parliament and of the Council of 19 October 2022 on a Single Market for Digital Services and amending Directive 2000/31/EC (Digital Services Act), PE/30/2022/REV/1, [2022] OJ L277/1.

47 Directive (EU) 2019/2161 of the European Parliament and of the Council of 27 November 2019 amending Council Directive 93/13/EEC and Directives 98/6/EC, 2005/29/EC and 2011/83/EU of the European Parliament and of the Council as regards the better enforcement and modernisation of Union consumer protection rules, PE/83/2019/REV/1, [2019] OJ L328/7.

48 Directive (EU) 2019/770 of the European Parliament and of the Council of 20 May 2019 on certain aspects concerning contracts for the supply of digital content and digital services, PE/26/2019/REV/1, [2019] OJ L136/1.

49 Directive (EU) 2019/771 of the European Parliament and of the Council of 20 May 2019 on certain aspects concerning contracts for the sale of goods, amending Regulation (EU) 2017/2394 and Directive 2009/22/EC, and repealing Directive 1999/44/EC, PE/27/2019/REV/1, [2019] OJ L136/28.

50 De Franceschi and Schulze (n 41) 3.

51 ibid 4.

52 ibid 5–6.

53 ibid.

contracting in the 21st century. There is also an increased impetus to compensate for structural asymmetries in bargaining power.[54]

1.6 Roadmap

Technological developments have revolutionised how consumer contracts are formed, executed, and personalised.[55] In light of these transformative changes, researchers must use several research methodologies and keep up with the latest developments.

This chapter aims to provide an overview of the challenges posed by digitalisation to some of the fundamental concepts of contract law and outline the research methods that will enable researchers to study consumer contracts in the digital age.

The remainder of the chapter comprises several sections, each organised around an essential aspect of the digital economy and the problems it poses for consumer contracts. Following the Introduction, section 2 provides an overview of the development of theoretical frameworks for contracts since the end of the 19th century and contemporary ideas about consumer contracts. Section 3 explains several essential aspects of modern trade that are impacted by technological change: digitalisation, automation, and personalization. The main argument is that, collectively, these phenomena render the classical conceptions of contracts inapplicable or obsolete as they apply to consumer contracts. Section 4 concludes by proposing that sociological and interdisciplinary approaches are essential to respond to contemporary challenges and generate practical solutions to aid consumers in the digital age.

2. CONTRACTS: WHAT'S IN A NAME? THE HISTORY OF THE DISTINCTIVE SET OF IDEAS IN CLASSICAL CONTRACT THEORY AND CONTEMPORARY CONSUMER CONTRACTS

Margaret Jane Radin, an influential American legal and political philosopher, explores the limits of classical contract theory in her book, *Boilerplate*, which examines the normative and theoretical problems posed by the adhesion

---

[54] ibid.

[55] Cristoph Busch and Alberto De Franceschi (eds), *Algorithmic Regulation and Personalized Law: A Handbook* (Beck/Hart Publishing 2021) 130–135; Omri Ben-Shahar and Ariel Porat, *Personalized Law: Different Rules for Different People* (Oxford University Press 2021) 1–13.

clauses that plague contemporary consumer contracts.[56] She focuses on the consequences for consumers when they enter into adhesion contracts, a topic generally ignored by classical theory based on the presumption that parties to a contract have voluntarily agreed to all of its terms. Radin argues that by repeatedly agreeing to these 'agreements', the retiree in our opening example gave up the legal rights granted to her by the political order, the constitution, and other sources of law.[57]

When consumers agree to adhesion contracts, they are offered only a limited selection of legal rights allowed by the firms that supply the electronic equivalent of bureaucratic paperwork. This raises an obvious question: what justifies a contractual outcome whereby a party is denied her legal rights just because she clicked a box next to a link to the full text of a pre-drafted instrument? The brief answer, detailed in the following subsection, is that ideas about contracts – developed primarily during the long 19th century, in the Gilded Age or the high point of classical liberalism,[58] but still widely utilised – are to blame for such outcomes. This answer would not be satisfactory to consumer contracts theory that primarily asks what happens to consumers' legal rights when they enter into adhesion contracts.

To comprehend why certain questions are raised in consumer contracts research and why they sometimes differ from those formulated in classical contract theory, it is essential to understand the variations in ideas and legal philosophies that inspire these two related but distinct fields.

2.1 Contracts and the Development of Legal Consciousness

One way to examine these two often contrasting perspectives on contracts is by considering the history of ideas and their impact on legal teaching and research. This requires tracing the transition of 'law' from a purely practical and unsystematic endeavour in the early 1800s to a recognisable academic discipline by the final decades of the 19th century.

The architects of this remarkable transformation believed that, for the law to hold a crucial place in academia or to be accepted as an academic discipline,

---

56 Margaret Jane Radin, *Boilerplate: The Fine Print, Vanishing Rights, and the Rule of Law* (Princeton University Press 2013).

57 Margaret Jane Radin, *Boilerplate* (n 56) xiv.

58 For additional explanations related to the main ideas of this period, see, e.g., Jason Brennan and John Tomasi, *Classical Liberalism* (Oxford University Press 2012); M. Todd Henderson (ed.), *The Cambridge Handbook of Classical Liberal Thought* (Cambridge University Press 2018), 20–371.

it should become 'scientific'.[59] Thus, the discipline of law underwent a significant shift in the 19th century from a medieval institution to a modern enterprise.[60] This period in the second half of the 19th century corresponds to what Duncan Kennedy described as the first era of legal globalisation, with the law professor occupying centre stage.[61] Kennedy argues that what was globalised during this period was a mode of legal consciousness that viewed law as a 'system' with internal structural coherence.[62]

These intellectual threads were brought together in the 'will theory', whereby private law rules are understood as a set of rational deductions from the principle that governments should protect the rights of legal persons. When the will theory was first developed, the concept of 'consumer' did not yet exist because there was no mass production or mass sales concluded at a distance.[63]

Classical legal thought was increasingly challenged in the period from 1900 until World War II. This period, which Kennedy calls the 'second globalisation', saw the rise of the 'social' as the primary determinant of legal

---

59 David S. Clark, 'Tracing the Roots of American Legal Education – A Nineteenth-Century German Connection' (1987) 51(3) *Rabels Zeitschrift für ausländisches und internationales Privatrecht / The Rabel Journal of Comparative and International Private Law* 313, 327; Bruce A. Kimball, 'Langdell on Contracts and Legal Reasoning: Correcting the Holmesian Caricature' (2007) 25(2*) Law and History Review* 345; Bruce A. Kimball, *The Inception of Modern Professional Education: CC Langdell, 1826–1906* (University of North Carolina Press 2009) 206; Andrew Charles Forsyth, *Common Law and Natural Law: A Case Study: The Changing Shape of American Legal Education from the Puritans to the Legal Realists* (Yale University Press 2017) 20.

60 Laura I. Appleman, 'The Rise of the Modern American Law School: How Professionalization, German Scholarship, and Legal Reform Shaped Our System of Legal Education' (2004–2005) 39 *New England Law Review* 251, 252, 298.

61 Duncan Kennedy, 'Three Globalizations of Law and Legal Thought' in David Trubek and Alvaro Santos (eds) *The New Law, and Economic Development: A Critical Appraisal* (Cambridge University Press 2006) 19. For criticism, Karlson Preuß, 'Legal Formalism and Western Legal Thought' (2023) 14(1) *Jurisprudence* 22, 50–51.

62 Kennedy (n 61) 22–26; Duncan Kennedy, 'Towards a Historical Understanding of Legal Consciousness: The Case of Classical Legal Thought' (1980) 3 *Research in Law and Sociology* 3. For an extensive discussion of philosophical ideas inspiring the elaboration of 'classical' theory of contract in the 19th century, inspired by Kennedy's paradigm, see Gonçalo de Almeida Ribeiro, *The Decline of Private Law, A Philosophical History of Liberal Legalism* (Hart 2019).

63 Kerry Higgins, *Collision Course: Endless Growth on a Finite Planet* (MIT Press 2014), 65–79.

consciousness.[64] This development was influenced by the work of preeminent jurists such as Jhering, Gierke, or Ehrlich in Germany and Saleilles, Geny, Duguit, Lambert, Josserand, or Gounod in France.[65] In the United States, the development was most visible in the work of jurists writing in what was later known as the legal realism tradition.[66] Legal science became a distinct category, and the 'study' of law focused on supporting regulatory regimes in service of the 'public interest' rather than on partisan political grounds.[67]

The social critique raised during this period aimed at classical legal thought's pretensions to maintain an appearance of objectivity. This critique led to a successful reform program, from labour legislation to the regulation of landlord-tenant relations, from the regulation of financial markets to developing new ways of thinking and new institutions, including in the area that would later be known as consumer contracts. Concerning its fundamental assumptions about law and its functions in society, the social period could be seen as an antithesis of the classical period.[68]

However, after 1968, with the advent of neoliberalism, the 'social' began to lose its influence. This period, called by Kennedy the third globalisation of legal consciousness, was not a synthesis of the first two periods.[69] Instead, it was an unsynthesised or instrumentalist opportunistic coexistence of transformed elements of classical and social legal theories. There was no discernible integrating concept that could mediate between normative projects and subsystems of positive law. In this third era of globalisation, judges have become the

---

64 Kennedy (n 61) 37.

65 For an overview of such developments in France, see, e.g., Marie Claire Belleau, 'The "Juristes Inquiets": Legal Classicism and Criticism in Early Twentieth-Century France' (1997) 2 *The Utah Law Review* 379; Marie-Claire Belleau, 'Les juristes inquiets: classicisme juridique et critique du droit au début du XXe siècle en France' (1999) 40(3) *Les Cahiers de droit* 507.

66 Kennedy (n 61) 22–26. In the United States, preeminent representatives of this legal thought were the jurists writing in what was called the legal realism tradition. See Laura Kalman, *Legal Realism at Yale, 1927 1960* (The University of North Carolina Press 1986); John Henry Schlegel, 'American Legal Realism and Empirical Social Science: From the Yale Experience' (1978) 28 *The Buffalo Law Review* 459; Michael Steven Green, 'Legal Realism as Theory of Law' (2004) 46 *The William and Mary Law Review* 1915; John Henry Schlegel, 'American Legal Realism and Empirical Social Science: From the Yale Experience' (1978) 28 *The Buffalo Law Review* 459.

67 The interdisciplinary insistence of contemporary legal research has its origins in this period.

68 Kennedy (n 61) 40.

69 ibid.

heroic figures who resolve disputes and make law.[70] Judges use policy analysis or formalism to adjudicate these disputes, sometimes with the implications and outcomes described by Radin.[71]

'Human rights' are now as significant in contemporary legal consciousness as 'private rights' were in classical legal theory and 'social rights' in the 'social' period. The role of the 'individual' in classical legal theory and of classes and national minorities in the social period has been replaced by 'identity'. Pluralism is recognised as an instrumental device to identify and manage 'difference.' Moreover, rights claimants are organised based on their plural, cross-cutting identities. Nevertheless, as each of us has many identities, we arrive at paradoxical situations when some of our identities are protected and others are not.

To add to the confusion, employers, creditors, and sellers of tangible and intangible goods have made a sustained effort to reconfigure property and contract rights as parallels to minority/identity rights, which is symbolic of contemporary legal consciousness.[72] However, there has not been any dominant reconstruction project, like that based on the individual's 'will' in the late 19th century, which could mediate between normative projects and the subsystems of positive law.[73] This is also reflected in the methodological realm, where many methodologies are designed to understand the relationship of law to other domains, yet no single dominant method has emerged.

Nevertheless, the success of the third globalisation should not be construed as absolute. Of particular relevance, the concept of 'consumer', the contemporary consumer movement, and even the positive law on consumer contracts have all developed after the onset of the 'third globalisation'.[74]

---

70 ibid.

71 Radin (n 56), 3–33. Kennedy also notes that policy analysis done by judges is now based on 'conflicting considerations' (also called balancing or proportionality), which tends to produce rules that are 'ad hoc compromises, rather than social rules dictated by single social purposes in coherently adaptive new legal regimes' – Kennedy (n 61) 40.

72 For a good description of the political alliance between neoliberals and human rights activists, which enabled after the fall of the Soviet Union the advent of courts in the adjudication process of the global neoliberal order, see, e.g., David M. Trubek, 'The "Rule of Law" in Development Assistance: Past, Present, and Future' in David Santos and Alvaro Trubek (eds), *The New Law, and Economic Development: A Critical Appraisal* (Cambridge University Press 2006) 74–94. For the pedigree of a long tradition in law that supports stronger parties, see Katharina Pistor, *The Code of Capital* (Princeton University Press 2019), x–xi, 1–24.

73 Kennedy (n 61) 65.

74 Luisa Antoniolli, 'Consumer Law as an Instance of the Law of Diversity' (2005) 30 *Vermont Law Review* 855, 856–862.

The revival of classical contract theory had a limited window of opportunity between the fall of the Iron Curtain and the onset of the 2009 financial crisis.[75] This revival is supported by the initial success of big digital companies, such as Google, Facebook, and Apple, in defining property rights over (personal) data via contracts, thus creating a multi-billion dollar industry in the first 15 years of the new millennium. However, scandals such as the Snowden or Cambridge Analytica affairs have shattered the trust in this model, leading to a pushback against such business practices in the courts and among regulators.[76]

Moreover, with the failure of privatised Keynesianism,[77] the global financial crisis of 2009 (and the related exhaustion of neoliberalism's promissory legitimacy in Europe, North America, and elsewhere),[78] and the poly-crisis post-Covid-19,[79] there has been a renewed call for ideas from the 'social period' to be employed to temper the excess and inequality unleashed by neoliberalism, including in the field of contracts.[80]

---

75 Fukuyama describes this historical period as the 'end of history'. See Francis Fukuyama, *The End of History and the Last Man* (Free Press 1992), 27–29. Even the internet, the byword for technological advance at the dawn of the millennium, came to be governed by widespread utilisation of contracts. See, e.g., Lee A. Bygrave, *Internet Governance by Contract* (Oxford University Press 2015), 28–84.

76 Giraudo (n 36).

77 Colin Crouch, 'Privatised Keynesianism: An Unacknowledged Policy Regime' (2009) 11(3) *The British Journal of Politics and International Relations* 382. Crouch argues that following the state's retreat from the economy from the late 1970s onwards and in the face of a decline in wages, states encouraged private banks to assume the role previously held previously by the state by allowing access to easy credit, which would compensate for the wage losses, at least until the 2008 global crisis. In other words, states still countered the effects of business depression cycles by creating money as they did during the heights of Keynesianism, but banks as private institutions administered access to this money and its distribution instead of the state via welfare and general distribution.

78 Jens Beckert, 'The Exhausted Futures of Neoliberalism: From Promissory Legitimacy to Social Anomy' (2020) 13(3) *Journal of Cultural Economy* 318.

79 Adam Tooze, 'Welcome to the World of the Polycrisis', *Financial Times*, 28 October 2022, <https://www.ft.com/content/498398e7-11b1-494b-9cd3-6d669dc3de33> accessed 4 June 2024; David Henig and Daniel M. Knight, 'Polycrisis: Prompts for an Emerging Worldview' (2023) 39(2) *Anthropology Today* 3; Attila Ágh, 'The EU Polycrisis and Hard Populism in East-Central Europe: From the Copenhagen Dilemma to the Juncker Paradox' (2017) 13(2–3) *Politics in Central Europe* 7.

80 Jeddediah Britton-Purdy and others, 'Building a Law-and-Political-Economy Framework: Beyond the Twentieth-Century Synthesis' (2019) 129 *The Yale Law Journal* 1784.

The technological, political, and economic transformations discussed here render 'classical' contract law theory ill-suited to deal with the issues posed by these transformations and, at worst, reactionary and endorsing legal rules that favour antisocial behaviour. The realisation that 'general social theory is the indispensable setting for any credible legal theory'[81] is bound to impact legal methodology, including for consumer contracts.

2.2 Consumer Contracts and The New Private Law Theory

As researchers explore consumer contracts, it is useful to consider the insights of the 'new private law theory' developed by European scholars like Grundmann, Micklitz, and Renner.[82] Although they do not offer any methodological innovations, their insights can help develop research ideas related to consumer contracts, particularly when the researcher is looking at the contract in conceptual terms and attempts to describe the power and information imbalances and the impact of new technologies on the consumers' side. The new private law theory can assist in overcoming the situation in which the researcher is caught between the hammer of the 'will' in the classical theory and the anvil of lack of coherence (synthesis) characteristic of the third globalisation of legal consciousness.

According to Grundmann, Micklitz, and Renner, private law should be pluralistic, comparative, and application-oriented. As used by them, the term 'pluralistic' means not only a variety of cultural or national perspectives but also a variety of interdisciplinary perspectives. Private law, they write, 'must take into account the findings of different disciplines to develop an adequate description of society'.[83] 'Comparative' means that the new theory must consider different legal systems and theoretical traditions since pure functionalist knowledge is no longer sufficient.[84] Finally, private law theory should be 'application-oriented', since only by addressing the concrete problems of private law and applying theoretical insights to these problems can one 'fruitfully combine the findings of different disciplines and traditions'.[85] Theory is tested by practice and must be grounded in it.

The new private law theory addresses transactions and risk, placing private law in a market context where the contract is central. Grundman's

[81] Samuel Moyn, 'Reconstructing Critical Legal Studies' <https://papers.ssrn.com/sol3/papers.cfm?abstract_id=4531492> accessed 1 July 2023.

[82] Stefan Grundmann, Hans-Wolfgang Micklitz and Moritz Renner, *New Private Law Theory. A Pluralist Approach* (Cambridge University Press 2021).

[83] ibid 1.

[84] ibid 2.

[85] ibid 3, 10.

discussion of the functions of contracts is particularly relevant to consumer contracts because it considers the justifications for freedom of contract and its limitations in a consumer contract setting, where private autonomy, the need to protect systematically weaker parties, and the public good are related.[86] Grundmann shows that contract and consensus grounded in autonomy may be one of the (if not *the*) leading paradigms in private law.[87] However, the limits to freedom of contract are not drawn from considerations of distributive justice but of commutative or corrective justice'.[88] Thus, freedom of contract has two justificatory functions: fostering parties' interests and fostering social goods (including the protection of weaker parties).

Grundmann continues his theoretical exposé by comparing two opposing views. The first argues that providing sufficient protection to weaker parties, such as consumers, risks favouring those already better off in the protected group.[89] The second view argues that the law intervenes to protect weaker parties who meet the standard assumptions according to which consumers are active and purely rational market actors.[90]

This discussion leads Grundmann to question biases and disclosures in consumer contract law. He suggests that disclosure rules combined with limits on contract length could help consumers recognise the most relevant terms before entering a contract.[91] His proposal highlights some challenges related to general contract law theory and consumer contract theory that are still relevant in the digital age, as will become apparent in the following sections.

2.3 The Emergence of Dedicated Consumer Law Methodologies

It seems paradoxical that voluntary contract obligations could arise when one party – a consumer – is unaware that their legal rights are implicated. Yet such an outcome is made possible by the 19th-century conceptions of contract that are still widely circulated today. They are promoted by employers, creditors, and sellers of tangible and intangible commodities, who profit the most from their application. These ideas were thoroughly contested, and their assumptions and theoretical biases demolished, during the first four decades

86 Stefan Grundmann, 'Negotiation, the Function of Contract and the 'Justice of Consensus' in Grundmann, Micklitz and Renner (n 82) 207–208.

87 ibid 210.

88 ibid 216.

89 ibid 218. This could be seen as an application of Kennedy's (n 61) discussion of dilemmas posed by the legal conscience of third globalisation, where the law protects some interests but not others, and so on.

90 Grundmann (n 86) 224–225.

91 ibid 227.

of the 20th century. Nevertheless, they retain currency partly because they are advantageous to commercial parties who contract frequently and partly because, today, there is no single dominant conception of contract to replace them.

As we argued, following Duncan Kennedy, the mainstream developments of legal consciousness at the end of the 20th century did not provide a coherent theoretical framework of contracts that researchers could use without much ado on consumer contracts, but rather a multitude of methods and practices. In this context, insights on the 'new private law' developed by Grundmann, Micklitz, and Renner and their analysis of customers' behaviour could be helpful as a starting point for consumer contracts researchers. Seminal works of Micklitz, Sibony, and Esposito have also emphasised the importance of behavioural approaches in consumer law research.[92] These authors argue that empirical approaches are necessary due to the often unrealistic nature of consumer concepts developed by courts.[93] Ishwara Bhat also sees consumer law as an appropriate area for empirical legal research combining multiple methods.[94]

As the theoretical framework of contracts developed during the classical period diverges significantly from contemporary frameworks, research in the field of consumer contracts cannot remain agnostic. Furthermore, insights developed in the new private law theory highlight its pluralistic, comparative, and application-oriented character. Finally, the emergence of what we refer to as dedicated consumer law methodologies emphasises the need for empirical and behavioural insigthts into consumer contracts. The following sections will provide examples of research methodologies and their possible use for studying major topics in digital consumer contracts.

3. THREE MAJOR THEMES OF CONSUMER CONTRACTS IN THE DIGITAL AGE

In the Introduction, we argued that regulators' and industries' responses to research on consumer contracts have paradoxically reinforced classical contract theory. Despite doubts about its suitability to address contemporary consumer agreements, these responses have primarily adopted the assumptions of classical theory. They proposed a classical contract framework 2.0

---

92 Hans-Wolfgang Micklitz, Anne-Lise Sibony and Fabrizio Esposito, 'The Bright and Adventurous Future of Consumer Law Research' in Hans-Wofgang Micklitz, Anne-Lise Sibony and Fabrizio Esposito (eds), *Research Methods in Consumer Law: A Handbook* (Edward Elgar 2018) 12–13.

93 Micklitz, Sibony and Esposito (n 92) 34.

94 P. Ishwara Bhat, *Idea and Methods of Legal Research* (Oxford University Press 2020) 489.

as a 'solution' to the problems posed to consumer contracts by technological advances and the consolidation of power in today's neoliberal society.

The hypothetical scenario that opened this chapter demonstrates that three major trends in modern consumer contracting – digitalisation, automation, and profiling – strengthen businesses' ability to create their own (self-serving) legal universes when entering consumer agreements. As a result, consumers are limited to an increasingly constricted set of legal rights that the businesses select, instead of the full spectrum of rights granted by law.[95] This is primarily the case in the US, where the law permits consumers to contract out of a wide swath of legal rights,[96] but less so in Europe, where consumers can only do so in a limited number of cases and only after a dispute has arisen.[97]

Nevertheless, studies influenced by the classical theory of 'will' from the late 19th century,[98] which strongly supports legal interpretative formalism and the protection of the rights of legal persons,[99] would have little to say about such a restriction of consumers' rights. Researchers adopting this framework would instead tend to provide normative justifications for such restrictions.[100] However, since the realist and socio-legal attacks on the classical will

---

95 Radin (n 56).

96 Christopher R. Drahozal and Raymond Friel, 'Consumer Arbitration in the European Union and the United States' (2003) 28(2) *North Carolina Journal of International Law and Commercial Regulation* 357, 374–377.

97 Annex, point 1 (q) of the Council Directive 93/13/EEC of 5 April 1993 on unfair terms in consumer contracts, [1993] OJ L95/29.

98 Kennedy (n 61) 22–26.

99 ibid. Also, Kennedy (n 61) 3–24.

100 An extended discussion of the links between general theoretical frameworks and ideas about society and discrete legal institutions such as contracts is beyond the scope of this chapter. In this context, however, it is essential to remember that the overall ideas about society or law one adopts influence what one considers vital as a research subject and the methods one uses. So, nowadays, with the existing plurality of methods described by Kennedy, the problem for one adopting the classical view is not necessarily related to the possible lack of sophistication of research methods but rather to what the classical framework obscures or renders invisible in the functioning of society and law. In this regard, the classical theory views the 'market' as external, self-regulating, metaphysical 'living,' which the state should leave alone, even if we know nowadays that the state creates markets (Karl Polanyi, *The Great Transformation: The Political and Economic Origins of Our Time* (Beacon Press 2001)). Similarly, it sees law as external, technocratic, and autonomous, even if we know that law plays a significant role in the market's creation – Pistor (n 72) 4, 20, Britton-Purdy (n 80) 1820. With the market-state-law relations eliminated from the onset as subjects of inquiry, what is left is to take an arrangement in society at a given moment, which is historically contingent,

theory,[101] it has become clear that theorization within the framework provided by the classical theory was based on a premise (or conceptualisation) of free, informed, and equal contracting parties that no longer applies to modern consumer contracting. Scholars and policymakers must employ more rigorous research approaches to identify gaps, shortcomings, and necessary adaptations to ensure the effectiveness and relevance of the classical framework in the digital age.

3.1 Digitalisation

Classical contract theory cannot fully explain the consequences of consumers' reduced bargaining power in digital transactions.[102] The classical view of parties in an agreement as perfectly rational and fully informed actors who appreciate what obligations they assume cannot account for important aspects of contractual reality in the digital economy. These include power imbalances, lack of transparency, uncertainty about the legal implications of torts or contracts, the widespread use of digital surveillance or data collection for profiling 'consumers', non-transparent use of algorithms to determine contract terms, non-transparent ranking and listing of products, or 'free' digital services in exchange for personal data.[103] While the classical theory of contracts does not

---

economic and political, and to 'naturalise' this arrangement, attributing it characteristics of 'nature' and then to look for justifications of such an arrangement outside of historical, economic, political, or social factors that it has produced. For this reason, there is a tendency of this literature to produce, with little exception, just normative justifications of present legal, political, and economic arrangements based on abstract analyses, which could be further recycled by the legal profession when arguing in the courts for the preservation of the status quo.

[101] Kennedy (n 61).

[102] Ajar Rab, 'Smart Contracts & Blockchain: The Panacea to the Unequal Bargaining Power of Consumers?' (2020) 8 *International Journal on Consumer Law and Practice* 41, 54–57; Joshua Fairfield, 'Smart Contracts, Bitcoin, Bots and Consumer Protection' (2014) 71(2) *Washington and Lee Law Review Online* 35, 37–39 <https://scholarlycommons.law.wlu.edu/cgi/viewcontent.cgi?article=1003&context=wlulr-online> accessed 20 May 2023.

[103] For good descriptions of these and a litany of problems that besiege traditional understanding of contracts when analysing consumer contracts in the digital age, see, e.g., Vanessa Mak, 'Challenges of Digitalisation for Consumer Contracts' (2020) 11 *Annuario Di Diritto Comparato E Di Studi Legislativi* 63; Reiner Schulze and Dirk Staudenmayer (eds), *Digital Revolution. Challenges for Contract Law in Practice* (Bloomsbury Publishing 2015); Pasquale, *The Black Box Society* (n 32); Shoshana Zuboff, *The Age of Surveillance Capitalism: The Fight for a Human Future at the New Frontier of Power* (Profile Books 2019).

address these concerns, researchers can use empirical studies, surveys, and data analysis to determine how much digital consumers can exercise freedom of contract, as conceived by the classical theory. For example, researchers can explore the impact of standardised contracts – such as clickwrap agreements – on consumer autonomy, and make policy recommendations to address power imbalances and promote fair contracting practices.[104]

An important social and economic phenomenon accompanying digitalisation is the rise of digital platforms.[105] Digital platforms have dramatically changed how consumers engage with businesses by providing convenient and accessible purchasing channels.[106] For instance, e-commerce websites like Amazon allow consumers to browse, select, and buy products online with just a few clicks. However, various challenges have emerged with these opportunities, and a burgeoning literature explores platforms' economic, societal, and philosophical drawbacks. These challenges include regulatory and legal difficulties faced by consumers when contracting through digital platforms, fake reviews, dissemination of illegal content, unfair business conditions for business users, abuse of dominant position, weak competition in digital markets

---

104 For an example of good discussions on overall concerns and problems faced by consumer law in digital content and smart contracts, and areas where policy could be improved, see Natali Helberger and others, 'Digital Content Contracts for Consumers' (2013) 36 *Journal of Consumer Policy* 37; Alberto R. Salazar V, 'Unconscionability, Smart Contracts, and Blockchain Technology: Are Consumers Really Protected against Abuses in the Digital Economy?' (2021) 9 *International Journal on Consumer Law and Practice* 74.

105 For more information on the rise of platforms see Nick Srnicek, *Platform Capitalism* (Polity Press 2017); Frank A. Pasquale, 'Two Narratives of Platform Capitalism' (2016–2017) 35 *The Yale Law and Policy Review* 309; Vanessa Mak, 'Regulating Online Platforms – The Case of Airbnb' in Stefan Grundmann (ed), *European Contract Law in the Digital Age* (Cambridge University Press 2018) 87; Matthieu Montalban, Vincent Frigant and Bernard Jullien, 'Platform Economy as a New Form of Capitalism: A Régulationist Research Programme' (2019) 43(4) *Cambridge Journal of Economics* 805; K. Sabeel Rahman and Kathleen Thelen, 'The Rise of the Platform Business Model and the Transformation of Twenty-First-Century Capitalism' (2019) 47(2) *Politics & Society* 1; Vili Lehdonvirta, *Cloud Empires: How Digital Platforms are Overtaking the State and How We Can Regain Control* (MIT Press 2022).

106 Mohammad Anisur Rahman and others, 'Consumer Buying Behaviour towards Online Shopping: An Empirical Study on Dhaka City, Bangladesh' (2018) 5(1) *Cogent Business & Management* 1.

due to gatekeepers' control over the platform ecosystem, unfair commercial practices towards consumers, and ineffective supervision of services.[107]

Without suggesting a hierarchy of possible topics inspired by the literature discussing digital platforms, researchers can, for example, use website and transaction data analysis methods to study consumer interactions with these platforms. This can help determine whether platforms function as marketplaces only or exert control over operations, which is a relevant factor in establishing a platform's liability to consumers for defective products or other contract breaches by third-party suppliers who sell through the platform.[108]

Researchers can also examine factors influencing contract formation, such as user interface design, product recommendations, and bogus social validation of inferior products via social networks. Additionally, they can explore the role of user reviews and ratings in shaping consumer trust and purchase decisions on digital platforms, including how these systems can be 'gamed',[109] the problems posed by 'personalisation' via algorithms and AI, and discrimination arising from algorithmic decision-making.[110]

Digitalisation has streamlined contract execution processes, enabling consumers to fulfil their contractual obligations quickly and efficiently. For instance, digital payment systems like PayPal, Apple Pay, and mobile wallets

---

107 Srnicek (n 105); Pasquale 'Two Narratives of Platform Capitalism' (n 105); Busch (n 38) 3–10; Vanessa Mak, 'Challenges of Digitalisation for Consumer Contracts' (2020) *Annuario Di Diritto Comparato E Di Studi Legislativi* 63, <https://hdl.handle.net/1887/3277831>, accessed 30 April 2024; European Commission, 'How Do Online Platforms Shape Our Lives and Businesses?' (EU 2019) <https://digital-strategy.ec.europa.eu/en/library/how-do-online-platforms-shape-our-lives-and-businesses-brochure> accessed 12 December 2023.

108 UNCTAD, 'Strengthening Consumer Protection and Competition in the Digital Economy' (29 July 2020) UN Doc TD/RBP/CONF.9/4, 5.

109 Tao Chen and others, 'The Impact of Online Reviews on Consumers' Purchasing Decisions: Evidence from an Eye-Tracking Study' (2022) 13 *Frontiers in Psychology* 865702; George Lăzăroiu and others, 'Consumers' Decision-Making Process on Social Commerce Platforms: Online Trust, Perceived Risk, and Purchase Intentions' (2020) 11 *Frontiers in Psychology* 890; Semila Fernandes and others, 'Measuring the Impact of Online Reviews on Consumer Purchase Decisions – A Scale Development Study' (2022) 68 *Journal of Retailing and Consumer Services* 103066; M. Narciso, 'The Unreliability of Online Review Mechanisms' (2022) 45(3) *Journal of Consumer Policy* 349.

110 Joanne Atkinson, 'Inside the Black Box: The Impact of Machine Learning on the Creditworthiness Assessment' in Cătălin-Gabriel Stănescu and Asress Adimi Gikay (eds), *Discrimination, Vulnerable Consumers and Financial Inclusion* (Routledge 2021) 141; Pasquale, *The Black Box Society* (n 32) 23, 27.

have simplified payment transactions.[111] Researchers can employ data analysis techniques to study transaction patterns, identify trends, and understand the factors influencing payment preferences in digital consumer contracts. By doing so, they can gain insights into consumer behaviours, preferences, and perceptions of contract execution processes.[112] They can then contrast these insights with the industry allegations on these matters. Research is not limited to empirical methods; as our understanding of the landscape of consumer contracts continuously evolves, there is ample room for doctrinal and theoretical research. Researchers favouring the latter approaches could re-examine the premises of contract theory and furnish better explanations and integration of this theory with the insights supplied by interdisciplinary empirical research.

Further, the dynamic nature of digital platforms presents a significant challenge for researchers investigating platforms and consumer contracts as they continually adapt to meet consumer demands. To accurately capture the implications of digitalisation, researchers must remain current with platform features, algorithms, and policies. The vast amount of data generated by digital platforms requires effective data management and analysis techniques. Researchers must understand the various issues caused by the mass collection of data, such as privacy concerns.[113]

Finally, researchers have a range of methods available for investigating how digital platforms impact consumer contracts. One approach is to use surveys and online questionnaires to gather quantitative and qualitative data on consumer experiences, satisfaction levels, and preferences related to digital contracts. For instance, researchers can conduct surveys on large samples of consumers to quantify their satisfaction with contract terms or to evaluate their mindset during contract formation (e.g., whether the meeting of minds or the idea of private autonomy still matters in the consumer's decision to enter a contract), as well as their comprehension and acceptance of contractual obligations (e.g., whether the contract is still perceived as a two-way bargain or a one-sided agreement in favour of the platform). The data collected can then be analysed using statistical techniques to identify correlations between platform

---

111 FISERV, 'Mobile and Digital Payments Continue Upswing' (2021) <https://www.fiserv.com/en/about-fiserv/resource-center/consumer-research/2021-expectations---experiences--consumer-payments.html> accessed 5 May 2023.

112 Shasha Teng and Kok Wei Khong, 'Examining Actual Consumer Usage of E-Wallet: Case Study of Big Data Analytics' (2021) 121 *Computers in Human Behaviour* 106778 <https://doi.org/10.1016/j.chb.2021.106778> accessed 20 May 2024.

113 For a good overview of these concerns and of the limits of traditional paradigms and approaches, see, e.g., Ignacio Cofone, *The Privacy Fallacy: Harm and Power in the Information Economy* (Cambridge University Press 2023).

features and consumer behaviours. Similarly, website and app analytics can provide valuable insights into user interactions, navigation patterns, and conversion rates, which can help researchers better understand contract formation and user experience.

Another way to study digital consumer contracts is through case studies. Researchers can select representative cases and analyse contract terms, user feedback, and dispute resolution processes to assess the strengths and weaknesses of digital consumer contracts based on consumers' perspectives. For example, researchers could select a group of retirees who were offered 'the trips of their lives', analyse their contract terms, and obtain feedback from these retirees. This approach provides researchers with contextualised insights into the challenges and benefits of digital platforms.

Ethnographic methods like participant observation and interviews can help researchers understand how consumers interact with digital contracts daily. Researchers can document their experiences, perceptions, and challenges by observing and interacting with consumers navigating digital platforms. In-depth consumer interviews can provide valuable insights into their decision-making processes, trust-building mechanisms, and interactions with digital contracts.

Qualitative research methods complement quantitative data by capturing subjective aspects of consumer behaviour and attitudes that may not be apparent from quantitative analyses alone. By combining research methods, researchers could gain comprehensive insights into the impact of digital platforms on consumer behaviour, trust, and satisfaction.[114] These insights could contribute to developing consumer-centric contract practices and evidence-based policies that align with the evolving digital landscape. Ultimately, these empirical observations may substantiate the increasing inadequacy of classical contract theory concepts for consumer agreements.

3.2 Automation

Automated processes have become a prominent feature of the consumer contracts landscape, revolutionising every stage of the contract life cycle. With automated chatbots, intelligent contracts, algorithmic pricing, and personalised offers, automation has streamlined processes and transformed how consumers (and businesses) interact with contracts.[115]

---

114 Chen and others (n 109); Lăzăroiu and others (n 109).

115 Carlos Severino and Enrique Manso, 'How Intelligent Automation Is Transforming Customer Service Experience', Ernst & Young Global, 2020, <https://www.ey.com/en_gl/strategy/how-intelligent-automation-is-transforming-customer-service-experience> accessed 5 September 2023.

If we think about how automation intervenes in all steps of the 'agreement' in the case of the retiree surfing the internet for cruise offers, we can see, for example, that automated profiling of the consumers' preferences occurs not only far before the actual search but even independent of any search for a cruise. Search engines automatically collect a wealth of data related to consumers' preferences, characteristics, and priorities. These data are aggregated automatically and sold to sellers using computerised processes to construct sophisticated consumer profiles. Via automated personalised advertising, an offer for a cruise could pop up on the consumer's screen even without the consumer having actually searched for cruise offers. If the consumer takes the 'bait', further automated processes determine a 'personalised price' for the cruise based on the data indicating the consumer's lifestyle, financial means, appetite for risk, and other characteristics. Finally, automation intervenes in adhesion contracts delivered for signature, with boilerplate clauses inserted automatically in a process not supervised by humans.

The process described could not be further from the classical contract theory of will, which posits that parties determine what they need and enter into contracts to secure those needs through exchanging offers until an offer is accepted. Therefore, it is crucial for researchers studying consumers in the digital age to comprehend the different types of automation and their implications for the assumptions held by classical contract theory.[116]

Researchers can investigate the effects of automation on consumer contracts by comparing traditional contract processes with their automated counterparts. They can conduct comparative studies to analyse automated chatbots' efficiency, accuracy, and user experience versus human consumer service representatives in contract-related interactions. Additionally, they can examine the impact of algorithmic pricing on consumer perceptions of fairness and trust compared to fixed pricing models. By identifying the advantages and limitations of automation, researchers can provide valuable insights to consumers, businesses, and policymakers.

Researchers can also employ various research methodologies to study how automation affects consumer decision-making in contract settings. Experimental research designs provide controlled environments to investigate consumer behaviours and preferences. For instance, researchers can

---

116 Martin Adam, Michael Wessel and Alexander Benlian, 'AI-based Chatbots in Customer Service and Their Effects on User Compliance' (2021) 31 *Electron Markets* 427 <https://doi.org/10.1007/s12525-020-00414-7> accessed 20 May 2023; Katharina Klein and Luis F. Martinez, 'The Impact of Anthropomorphism on Customer Satisfaction in Chatbot Commerce: An Experimental Study in the Food Sector' (2023) 23 *Electronic Commerce Research* 2789, 2798–2800 <https://doi.org/10.1007/s10660-022-09562-8> accessed 20 May 2023.

create scenarios where consumers engage under controlled conditions with automated or human-mediated processes and observe their decision-making patterns. They can design experiments to compare consumer trust levels in mechanical contract negotiation systems versus human negotiation processes. They can also examine the effectiveness of different disclosures in influencing consumer decision-making in online contracts.[117]

Behavioural analysis techniques, such as eye-tracking studies or MRI scans of blood flow to different parts of the brain, can provide deeper insights into consumers' cognitive and emotional responses when interacting with automated contract processes. By monitoring neurological or physiological responses or analysing eye movements, researchers can understand how automation influences attention, arousal, and emotional engagement in contract-related interactions.

'Big data' approaches are also beneficial for studying the impact of automation on consumer contracts. Researchers can analyse large datasets from automated contract systems, such as transaction records, contract terms, and user feedback. By employing data analytics techniques, they can identify patterns, trends, and correlations that reveal the effects of automation on consumer behaviours, contract outcomes, and satisfaction levels.

Researchers can conduct quantitative surveys of consumers to evaluate their attitudes towards automated contract renewal processes. By analysing the survey responses, researchers can determine how much consumers prefer manual or automatic renewal and identify factors influencing their decision-making.

In addition, qualitative research methods such as in-depth interviews and focus groups allow researchers to gain more detailed insights into consumer experiences and perceptions of automated contract processes. These methods can uncover nuanced aspects, such as consumer trust, concerns, and challenges related to automation in consumer contracts. Researchers can explore consumer narratives, probing their understanding of automated processes and eliciting feedback on the benefits and drawbacks of automation. For instance, researchers can interview consumers to explore their experience with personalised contract terms offered by digital platforms. This will help uncover consumers' perceptions of the benefits and challenges of personalised contracts and gain insights into the factors that influence their acceptance or rejection of such terms.[118]

117 Sibony, in Micklitz, Sibony and Esposito (n 92) 210.
118 ibid 168.

3.3 Profiling

Consumer profiling involves using advanced data analytics and algorithms to collect and analyse consumer data. Profiling aims to segment, target, and personalise contract offerings. Although merchants claim that profiling benefits consumers by providing tailored experiences and improving efficiency,[119] it raises ethical concerns regarding privacy, fairness, and informed consent. We address these concerns with examples of financial products offered to consumers by the financial industry based on profiling.

Profiling plays a significant role in consumer credit agreements, where lenders leverage consumer data to determine creditworthiness, interest rates, and customised loan offers.[120] They create consumer profiles by leveraging demographic data, financial histories, and online behaviour to evaluate risk more accurately and offer customised credit products to consumers. However, reliance on profiling algorithms raises concerns about fairness and discrimination.[121] Profiling algorithms rely on various data points and factors to assess creditworthiness. Such factors inevitably involve generalisations; if they are associated with protected attributes such as race, gender, or religion, there is a risk of illegal discrimination.[122] Extensive data collection and analysis can also intrude on individuals' privacy rights. Profiling often involves collecting sensitive personal information, such as financial data and behavioural patterns, which must be protected to ensure individuals' privacy and data security.

Researchers can assess the effect of profiling algorithms on consumer interest rates by comparing rates provided to individuals with similar credit profiles but differing demographic characteristics. This can help them identify potential biases and discriminatory practices.[123] Such analyses contribute to discussions on fair lending practices and possible policy interventions.

---

119 ibid 209.

120 Profiling is used not only in consumer credit agreements but in all interactions with consumers, from the beginning of a simple search of products and services, through the results offered for these searches, to terms of contracts for the sales, through credit offered. We chose to discuss the example of credit because, in the debtor society of privatised Keynesianism, credit becomes somehow as important as the sale of the products, if not even more important, but what we say under this rubric applies to all other aspects aforementioned.

121 Cătălin-Gabriel Stănescu and Asress Adimi Gikay, 'Introduction: Discrimination, Vulnerable Consumers and Financial Inclusion' in Stănescu and Gikay (eds) (n 110) 1.

122 ibid.

123 Matthias Stefan and others, 'Ethnical Discrimination in Europe: Field Evidence from the Finance Industry' (2018) 13(1) *PLoS ONE* e0191959 <https://

Profiling algorithms often use alternative data sources, such as social media information, to assess creditworthiness, especially for individuals with limited credit histories. Researchers can investigate the impact of incorporating alternative data, such as utility payment history or rental records, into profiling algorithms. They can examine whether including such data helps reduce disparities and provides more accurate credit assessments for individuals who may not have traditional credit histories.[124] Such research could contribute to understanding the benefits and pitfalls of using alternative data in credit profiling.

Finally, researchers can analyse consumers' perceptions of profiling to test merchants' arguments. Qualitative research methods like interviews or focus groups allow researchers to gather in-depth insights into individuals' understanding, concerns, and attitudes towards profiling in consumer credit agreements. Researchers can explore how consumers perceive the use of their data, their awareness of the profiling process, and their opinions on the fairness and transparency of credit decisions based on profiling algorithms. Such qualitative approaches can provide a nuanced understanding of the psychological and emotional impacts of profiling, empowering researchers to advocate for consumer-centric credit practices.

4. CONCLUSIONS

This chapter argued that classical contract theory, advocated by industry and still dominantly employed in the legal profession and courtrooms, has severe limitations when applied to consumer contracts. Sociological and interdisciplinary approaches are better suited to respond to contemporary challenges and generate practical solutions. These approaches can reveal flawed assumptions and help develop more appropriate frameworks for consumer contracts. More specifically, they can unpack the implications of the three major trends of digitalisation, automation, and profiling for contract theory and practice. They can also highlight the gap between classical contract theory and digital contracts, and support policy development. The insights gained from these approaches could be utilised as building blocks in developing a better doctrinal understanding of consumer contracts.

---

doi.org/10.1371/journal.pone.0191959> accessed 20 May 2023.

[124] Consumer Protection Financial Bureau, 'CFPB Explores Impact of Alternative Data on Credit Access for Consumers Who Are Credit Invisible', *CFPB*, 16 February 2017, <https://www.consumerfinance.gov/about-us/newsroom/cfpb-explores-impact-alternative-data-credit-access-consumers-who-are-credit-invisible/> accessed 5 September 2023.

Recent advancements in neuropsychology and the understanding of cognition challenge many of the assumptions underpinning classical 19th-century contract theory, which serves as the foundation for party autonomy. According to this theory, if one party reads and agrees to clauses drafted by the other party, they are bound by them. However, these assumptions must be reconsidered in light of the latest scientific and philosophical findings. Advancements in political economy, nuanced explanations provided by sociology and anthropology, and intellectual developments in ethics and political philosophy provide a new understanding of individuals and the challenges faced by society that were inconceivable two centuries ago. Over time, these insights could lead to the development of an entirely different doctrine for digital consumer contracts or, at the very least, shape the methodological framework for analysing and researching consumer contracts.

12. Research methods for contracts in Indigenous legal orders

Alan Hanna

INTRODUCTION

The law of contract as we understand it today has European origins. The fundamental conception of these origins on contracts is unnecessary, as contract scholars are aware of these foundations.[1] However, the meaning of a contract is contingent upon the cultural context in which those conceptions arose. Keeping this foundational Eurocentric origin in the background, where then is there space for conversations about the laws of non-Western societies with disparate societal origins, values, beliefs, mores, and trajectories over time? Responses to this overarching question, as explored in this chapter, provide the insight to developing research methods for contract law in Indigenous legal orders, the results of which may provide a critical lens for assessing contemporary contract law in Western and non-Western societies.

The chapter begins with a discussion on the distinction between Western and Indigenous concepts of contract. The discussion involves identifying the existence and relevance of Indigenous perspectives about law, relationality, and voluntary obligations within a few Indigenous nations in Canada. Next, I offer a view of appropriate methodological approaches to researching contract-based relationships within Indigenous legal orders. The chapter concludes with some suggestions for researching contract law in Indigenous legal orders.

[1] Theodore Plucknett, *A Concise History of the Common Law* (Liberty Fund 2010) 628. James Gordley, 'Contract in Pre-commercial Societies and in Western History' in Arthur Von Mehren et al. (eds), *International Encyclopedia of Comparative Law Volume VII* (Tübingen and Nijhoff 1997) 12.

1. WESTERN AND INDIGENOUS APPROACHES TO CONTRACT LAW

There is a distinction between Western constructions of contract law and the manner in which voluntary obligations attract legal weight in an Indigenous legal order. On the one hand, state law in Canada, consisting of common and civil law traditions, is imposed on Indigenous peoples under what legal scholars and practitioners refer to as Aboriginal law.[2] On the other hand, Indigenous peoples have always managed relationships and obligations arising in those relationships under their own organic legal traditions, commonly referred to as Indigenous legal orders. Indigenous legal orders emerged in Indigenous societies before the arrival of Europeans and the introduction of the Western legal systems Europeans brought with them to Indigenous lands. Similar to European legal systems, Indigenous legal orders change over time according to the changing needs of the particular society. More importantly, Indigenous laws co-exist to varying degrees of recognition and comprehension of the outside world with Aboriginal law.[3] Aboriginal law is relatively uniform, as Canadian state law gets applied to all Indigenous groups in what is now Canada; whereas, Indigenous laws vary according to the specific Indigenous group to which one legal tradition is connected. For example, Secwepemc peoples (a large nation in the central interior of what is now British Columbia) have a legal order, which varies according to each individual Secwepemc community comprising the larger Nation. Secwepemc laws are different from other Indigenous legal orders, such as Blackfoot, Cree, Mi'kmaq, Inuit, or Métis. Understanding the discrete, distinct existence of these legal orders and state law provides a helpful framework for the following section.

1.1 Aboriginal Law

Present day contract law gained much of its profile from a particular European context over a specific historical path, a temporal trajectory, and worldview.[4] When we think about contracts, we think about contracts under state law. In

---

2 For a straightforward articulation of the difference, see Federal Court of Canada, *Practice Guidelines for Aboriginal Law Proceedings* (4th edn, September 2021) 3 <https://www.fct-cf.gc.ca/Content/assets/pdf/base/Aboriginal%20Law%20Practice%20Guidelines%20Sept-2021%20(ENG)%20FINAL.pdf> accessed 29 November 2023.

3 Indigenous laws may provide evidence in Canadian common law courts to prove an aboriginal rights claim.

4 I use the term worldview loosely to mean the epistemological, ontological, cosmological ways of understanding the self and collective in their world.

Canada, contract law resides within the common law and civil law traditions. Without delving too deeply into European – particularly Anglo – foundations of contract law, the development of maritime and mercantile law helps render the structure for the contemporary law of contracts and the relationships they embody in Canadian law.[5] Advances in technology, manufacturing, and commercial ventures over the last 200+ years have solidified the formalistic tenets of offer, acceptance, and consideration in contract law as it is practiced in the 21st century. The European origins of contract law were imported into Canada with the influx of French and British settlers, which forms the foundations of contract law as it exists today. The imposition of this Eurocentric legal system on Indigenous peoples became commonly known as Aboriginal law.[6]

Aboriginal law is an area of legal practice within Canadian state law. When Indigenous nations[7] enter into agreements with third parties and colonial governments in Canada,[8] the rules of common or civil law, and equity in contract apply.[9] In other words, Indigenous nations contract with others on a regular basis as part of their daily governance and administrative operations, such as employment contracts with band administration staff, contracts for the purchase and supply of various goods and services, from office equipment to the construction of housing, and contracts for revenue-sharing in resource development. These contemporary contracts are governed under Canadian contract law in the area of Aboriginal law.[10] Aboriginal law is different

---

5 See for example, Theodore Frank Thomas Plucknett, *A Concise History of the Common Law* (5th edn, Little, Brown & Company 1956, reprinted 2010) 657.

6 Jim Reynolds, *Aboriginal Peoples and the Law: A Critical Introduction* (Purich 2018) 3, 174–175. Also, Federal Court of Canada, cf (n 2) 3.

7 Indigenous nations include First Nations, Métis, and Inuit. See Constitution Act, 1982, Schedule B to the Canada Act 1982 (UK), 1982, c 11, section 35.

8 Colonial governments refer to Canadian governments, federal and provincial, which derive their authority and model after British Parliament, and territorial and municipal governments, which receive their jurisdiction under federal and provincial statutes.

9 The jurisprudence in Canada is rife with contracts litigation involving Indigenous parties. See for example, Alan Hanna, 'An Introduction to Indigenous and Aboriginal Laws in Contracts' in Stephanie Ben-Ishai and David Percy (eds), *Contract: Cases and Commentaries* (11th edn, Thomson Reuters 2022) 17. See also, V.N. Brock Folkersen, 'Capacity of First Nations to Contract: A Review of Recent Canadian Case Law with Special Reference to Saskatchewan', 1995 Contract Drafting: New Perspectives on Familiar Territory (Law Society of Saskatchewan, Continuing Professional Development 1995) <https://canlii.ca/t/tbbj> accessed 24 July 2023.

10 The distinction is articulated in several documents. See for example, the Federal Court's *Practice Guidelines for Aboriginal Law Proceedings* (4th edn,

from Indigenous law, which refer to the laws of Indigenous people arising in Indigenous societies.

1.2 Indigenous Law

This section offers a cursory introduction to Indigenous law for the purpose of providing some foothold for reference, as Indigenous laws are not recorded in legal texts, but rather they are carried in the fabric of human beings. In contrast to Aboriginal law, Indigenous law refers to the laws, norms, rules, and practices of Indigenous peoples rooted in a pre-colonial social past, which continue to the present.[11] To be clear, I do not generalize about Indigenous law or the legal orders from which they emerge. By Indigenous legal order, I mean the decentralized system of law produced and practiced by every member of an Indigenous community, in contrast to a centralized legal system of courts, lawyers, and legislatures.[12] There are common principles which may weave through various Indigenous legal orders, but each Indigenous society and their legal order will have distinct variations, applications, and understandings of common principles.[13] In short, Indigenous legal orders are nuanced by the shared language, history, beliefs, and values of each particular Indigenous nation. As an Indigenous person of mixed ancestry trained in the common law, and invested in a lifelong process of learning Indigenous laws, I believe we cannot rely on Western understanding of what law is and Western depictions of society in an effort to an understand Indigenous law. In other words, we need to depart from restraints of Western paradigms and attempt to understand the totality of the operation of Indigenous societies and what can be framed as contracts in those societies. To do otherwise would skew the meaning and content of Indigenous laws and make them appear Western. To better explain, I will emphasize some contrasts between Indigenous law and Western law.

One notable distinction between Western law and Indigenous law is the specialization training and professional practice of the former, and the

---

September 2021) 3 <https://www.fct-cf.gc.ca/Content/assets/pdf/base/Aboriginal%20Law%20Practice%20Guidelines%20Sept-2021%20(ENG)%20FINAL.pdf> accessed 29 November 2023. The word Aboriginal, which was applied to Indigenous peoples without consultation in Canada's colonial past, is drawn from the federal language of aboriginal peoples in the Constitution Act, 1982, cf (n 7).

11 For a concise introduction, see Val Napoleon, 'Thinking about Indigenous Legal Orders' in René Provost and Colleen Sheppard (eds), *Dialogues on Human Rights and Legal Pluralism* (Springer 2013) 231–232.

12 I align with Val Napoleon's definition of a legal order, ibid at 231.

13 Darcy Lindberg, 'Drawing upon the Wealth of Indigenous Laws in the Yukon' (2020) 50 *The Northern Review* 179, 181.

experientially lived practice of the latter. Indigenous laws are taught to children through their upbringing in an Indigenous community. Parents, grandparents, elders and other knowledge holders pass teachings along to children and adults alike in Indigenous communities through a process of being in relationship with one another and with the world around. This practice is more intuitive than it is prescribed. Laws are embedded in most aspects of life, as in most societies, from language to stories, and artistic expression to landmarks. The people from whom I have learned, primarily Dene, Tŝilhqot'in, and Secwepemc, often do not talk about these teachings as law (although this word is commonly used today).[14] Rather they talk about the teachings as *ways of being*. A people's way of being contains the rules and practices about how a person should conduct themselves in order to have a healthy, sustainable life, where they can provide for their families and maintain respectful relationships with others as they understand those aspects.[15]

In addition to the professional and sociocultural difference of how law is learned and practiced, another notable distinction between Western and Indigenous perspectives on law is the decentralization of institutions.[16] Unlike, yet distinctly similar to, institutions such as legislatures, courts, and police departments, where law-making, adjudication, and enforcement are centrally located, Indigenous law is made through the distinct processes of each nation. Law-making, adjudication, and enforcement may be carried out by families, groups of people with specific knowledge or skills, and even by the natural and sacred worlds. In decentralized societies, people know to whom they should turn first when attempting to address a problem, which may be the head of a family, a responsible sibling or other family member, a grandparent or elder, or a respected leader. These authorities are in contrast to Weber's theory of charismatic authority, as the people who are recognized as authorities in certain matters (e.g. elders and hunters may address matters with the land, medicine people address illnesses and hunting matters, parents tend to address inter- and intra-family cohesion) are recognized for the skills and knowledge they

---

14 These are large Indigenous national collectives, each of which are comprised of smaller local communities, referred to as First Nations. For example, The Tŝilhqot'in Nation is comprised of six First Nations (or bands according to the *Indian Act*) ?Esdilagh, Tl'etinqox, Xeni Gwet'in, Yunesit'in, Tŝideldel, and Tl'esqox.

15 There are many definitions of what constitutes *healthy*, *sustainable*, and *respectful* across different Indigenous perspectives. John Borrows offers a few examples of different Indigenous legal orders in *Canada's Indigenous Constitution* (Toronto University Press 2010) 59–104.

16 See cf. Napoleon (n 11) 5–6.

acquired over a lifetime of learning.[17] Rather than the routinization of charisma to a bureaucratic model of authority, Indigenous decision-makers are specialized knowledge-holders who apply reasoned responses to legal issues. Although these groups do not resemble the centralized institutions of Western society with a courthouse or legislature, they perform similar functions such as adjudicating legal matters and deciding on appropriate rules of conduct in changing circumstances, which explains my comment that they are unlike, yet distinctly similar.

One more distinction to identify is that notions of liberal autonomy and economic benefit also differ from those underpinning Western foundations of law. This is not to say that Indigenous societies are devoid of individual autonomy or interest in economic gain. To make a claim such as this would be false. Understanding how these function in Indigenous societies is helpful to understand how laws, such as the law of contracts, operates under unique legal reasoning. Anthropologist Robert Lane, who worked with Tŝilhqot'in people in British Columbia in 1950s, wrote that

> [f]ormal social controls were minimal. Individuals had a high degree of autonomy. In theory, beyond the confines of the family, no one could force anyone else to do anything. People were guided to internalized morality and recognition of the need to maintain good relations with others in anticipation of the need for future aid and support.[18]

At first blush, the statement implies full autonomy of individuals, able to act without regard for or interference from others, which reflects a general notion of liberalism.[19] Under this view of liberalism, an individual's autonomy aligns with the party autonomy for entering a contract espoused by the common law. However, a closer look at Tŝilhqot'in life and law shows that individuals possess a duality of autonomous belonging that appear to be at odds. The first piece is stated above, a "high degree of autonomy". The second piece is understood from within the Tŝilhqot'in worldview, part of which is also captured in the statement, "the need to maintain good relations with others in anticipation

---

17 Max Weber, *Theory of Social and Economic Organization* (A.R. Anderson and Talcott Parsons trs, Oxford University Press 1947). For one example of how leaders are chosen in the Haudenosaunee Confederacy, see Haudenosaunee Confederacy, 'Chiefs' <https://www.haudenosauneeconfederacy.com/government/> accessed 29 November 2023.

18 Robert Lane, 'Chilcotin' in June Helm (ed), *Handbook of North American Indians, vol 6: Subarctic* (Smithsonian Institution 1981) 408.

19 Liberalism is a loaded term. For a discussion on liberalism and Indigenous peoples, see Isabel Altamirano-Jiménez, *Indigenous Encounters with Neoliberalism: Place, Women, and the Environment in Canada and Mexico* (UBC Press 2013).

of the need for future aid and support". Another section of Lane's paper states: "sharing was the ideal. If someone had something to spare it would be given on request and a return would be made later. [...] A wealthy man was one who produced for distribution".[20] The Tŝilhqot'in worldview embraces the autonomy of individuals, while simultaneously accepting that people are bound by obligation to others. In other words, although at liberty to act according to one's own interests and aspirations, a person is always responsible for others in their community. They are effectively both autonomous and bound by obligation.

This broader, entangled view of an individual's autonomy complicates whether a party is sufficiently autonomous to enter a contract within the liberal underpinnings of what it means to be an autonomous party. How can a party be autonomous if they are simultaneously always under obligations to others, which, arguably may influence a party's decision to enter a contract? For example, is an individual entering a contract for their own benefit and of their own volition or are they entering it because their obligations to others compel them to seek a benefit that they are required to share with others, making them feel as they don't have a choice? This oversimplification of a complex relational world where everyone is both at once individual and collective sets the framework for understanding how contract functions in the Indigenous legal orders I have studied.

2. CONTRACTS IN INDIGENOUS LAW

Some people may not agree that there is such a thing as a contract in Indigenous legal orders outside of Aboriginal law, where a First Nation enters into a contract for goods or services in the global economy. At the heart of this disagreement is a working definition of contract. If we adhere rigidly to the common law's construction of a contract with offer, acceptance, consideration, capacity, intention, and certainty as its construction, then identifying a contract from within an Indigenous legal order requires interpretation and translation of events, concepts, and parties to assess whether that definition of a contract is satisfied. However, if we look to a definition shaped from within an Indigenous legal perspective using principles of sharing, reciprocity, and respect, we may find that contracts arise in the form of voluntary obligations, which carry more flexibility than the common law may bear.

Principles of sharing, reciprocity, and respect form the basis for many Indigenous laws. In contract, these principles inform the relationship between parties, which are generally meant to endure beyond any single contractual

20 Ibid at 404.

commitment. Respect, sharing, and reciprocity as concepts are common across Indigenous legal orders; however, the meaning and limits of each are nuanced by each disparate legal order. For example, for Tŝilhqot'in people, respect may mean that people should remain wary of uncertain or dangerous situations. In another legal order it may mean that uncertain situations should be avoided altogether. Respect for a person with whom a party is in relationship may mean that a person should be prepared to provide mutual aid if requested or obviously required. When relationships are guided by principles of respect, sharing, and reciprocity the groundwork for enduring commitment is laid, which establishes an internalized enforcement mechanism to ensure voluntary obligations are fulfilled. When these principles inform a relationship, people are more likely to fulfil an obligation than if they are not present, as all three balance party needs to ensure nobody suffers unnecessarily in times of scarcity or need. Internal enforcement is a more practical and effective means of ensuring parties remain committed to fulfilling obligations to others than, for example, the threat of having to pay damages, because the relationships are often interdependent for the purpose of access to resources and ultimately a person's or group's ongoing survival.

An Indigenous relationship framed in terms of a contract allows flexibility as fulfilling obligations may be carried out over time and parties may include more than just those involved in the immediate contract relationship. A member of one of the party's family may fulfill obligations, or the whole community may fulfil an obligation. When this manner of flexibility is introduced into a common law contract without it being captured within the four corners of the contract, its validity comes into question for ambiguity or privity. If a person has an obligation to share, and they share what they have, perhaps a certain species of fish, rather than what the other party wanted, such as some moose meat, the validity of a common law contract may be scrutinized for certainty; whereas the Indigenous agreement permits for substitutions with whatever may be available at the time of performance according to rules around subsistence gathering under their legal order. In addition to foundational principles, the construction of who constitutes a competent party also varies from the common law.

A significant difference in common law and Indigenous contracts is that in the latter, non-human relations may constitute legitimate parties to a relationship bound in voluntary obligations. I have written elsewhere how animals are parties to contracts based in Indigenous legal orders.[21] For the purpose

---

[21] Alan Hanna and Emmaline English, 'Can a Moose Be a Party to a Contract? Nuanced Spaces for Indigenous Perspectives in Canadian Contract Law' (2023) 109 *Supreme Court Law Review* 129.

of elucidating this concept, I offer the following construction. Consider for example this excerpt from a larger story.[22] In the story, a blind man had been abandoned in the forest.

> The man, being left alone, was helpless and was very sad. After a while he heard a Loon a long way off, and started to work slowly toward the sound of the Loon's call, and marked his path by fur which he pulled from his blanket of ground-hog skin. At last he reached the lake where the Loon was, and he called to him and said, "Loon, if you will give me back my sight, I will give you a necklace of shells". And the Loon answered, "Come into the water, and I will try". The man waded out, and the Loon told him to dip himself under the surface. He obeyed; and when he came up and opened his eyes, he could see dimly, but not well. And the Loon asked him, "Are your eyes all right now?" When he replied, "Not yet, I can only see dimly", the Loon told him to go under again, which he did. When he emerged this time, his eyes were as good as ever. Then the man took his shell necklace and threw it over the neck of the Loon, and said, "Wear this always". And that is how the Loon got his white collar.[23]

There are multiple dimensions to oral stories. In this one, we are focusing on the voluntary obligations created and fulfilled between the blind man and the loon – a necklace in exchange for the return of sight. In common law terms, there is an offer – if you heal me, then I will give you something in exchange; acceptance – "I will try"; consideration – the necklace. Based on this rendering alone, this looks to be the formation of a valid common law contract. However, there are problems. Primarily, how can a loon be a party to a contract? Regarding the loon as a party, we must be capable of accepting that Western categories of animals as property, devoid of human qualities, is only one way of understanding the world. In any Indigenous worldview from which I have learned, animals are beings capable of agency, and are often considered kin to the people with whom they are in relation.[24] Of course an animal can be

---

22 Oral traditions are a form of precedents for Indigenous groups, who were preliterate societies before the arrival of Europeans. Oral traditions recorded rules, norms, principles, and beliefs, which were capable of being passed down from generation to generation. See John Borrows, *Recovering Canada: The Resurgence of Indigenous Law* (University of Toronto Press 2002) 16–20. Also, Hadley Friedland and Val Napoleon 'Gathering the Threads: Developing a Methodology for Researching and Rebuilding Indigenous Legal Traditions' (2015–2016) 1(1) *Lakehead Law Journal* 1, 22.

23 'The Blind Man Who was Cured by the Loon" in Livingston Farrand, 'Traditions of the Chilcotin Indians' (1900) 4(1) *Memoirs of the American Museum of Natural History (New York)* 35 <http://digitallibrary.amnh.org/handle/2246/39> accessed 29 November 2023.

24 Robin Wall Kimmerer, *Braiding Sweetgrass: Indigenous Wisdom, Scientific Knowledge, and the Teachings of Plants* (Milkweed Editions 2013) 183; Paul

a party to an agreement under Indigenous law, as they are capable of fulfilling their obligations to humans.[25]

Another problem trying to attribute the events of this encounter to fit the rules of formation in the common law involves the epistemology of the interaction. What if the meaning of the exchange does not meet our common law construction of the contract, with the requirements of offer, acceptance, and consideration? Activities that may appear to be elements of contract formation, often reveal different origins and meaning within Indigenous worldviews. This story of the blind man and the loon is from the Tŝilhqot'in oral tradition. The appearance of an offer and acceptance is relatively straightforward. However, the necklace is not consideration (i.e. something of value in the eyes of the law) upon which the obligations crystalize to form a legally binding contract.[26] Rather, the necklace is a gift performing several functions, namely to honour the loon's willingness to help the man, to show respect for the loon's healing powers, and to create an enduring relationship based in reciprocity that is written into the white markings around a loon's neck. This interpretation of the purpose of the necklace follows extensive research with Tŝilhqot'in people.[27] The interpretation begs the question: does the necklace as a gift mean the exchange does not amount to a binding contract? The answer is not a simple *yes* or *no*. For example, Canadian law does not consistently require consideration as an element of contract formation.[28] Under the Quebec Civil Code, a contract is formed when there is an object and a cause.[29] The obligations under this regime may be moral, civil, or natural.[30] The main difference between the first two obligations is that the civil obligation is legally binding at law, whereas the moral obligation is not binding beyond a person's conscience.[31] An obligation in an Indigenous legal order is similar to a moral obligation, as the enforcement to ensure its fulfilment is largely left to the internal commitment of the promisor. Although moral obligations are not legally binding in civil law, arguably, they are legally binding in many Indigenous legal orders. What makes them binding in Indigenous law is the expectation that the obligation

---

Nadasdy, 'The Gift in the Animal: The Ontology of Hunting and Human–Animal Sociality' (2007) 34(1) *American Ethnologist* 25, 25.

25 For a deeper discussion on this matter, see Nadasdy, ibid; and cf. Hanna and English (n 21), 134.

26 *Thomas v Thomas* (1842) 2 QB 851; 114 ER 330.

27 I have worked with the Tŝilhqot'in Nation on different legal research projects since 2012.

28 Code Civil Du Québec CCQ 1991.

29 Ibid para 1371.

30 *Bruker v Marcovitz*, 2007 SCC 54 (CanLII); [2007] 3 SCR 607 para 49.

31 Ibid para 50.

will be fulfilled or the relationship between parties will be jeopardized. If the relationship fails, the potential loss of a resource-sharing partner follows, and ultimately, the loss of access to the resource itself potentially leading to starvation. In other words, the breach of an obligation may lead to death.

Under the common law, gifts are repugnant to the law as a binding agent (consideration), as once given, the giver relinquishes any right to the gift, nor can they be forced to give their gift once promised. The giver of a gift is considered a volunteer, who can not be bound by obligation.[32] Although the legal landscape of gifts varies across societies,[33] many Indigenous legal orders view a gift as the mechanism that binds ongoing relationships between the giver and receiver.[34] In the example above, the gift of the necklace to the loon (the act of giving of the gift rather than the physical object itself) is the substance that creates the obligation.[35] The blind man and loon story was published by ethnographer Livingston Farrand in 1900 as part of a collection of stories Tŝilhqot'in informants shared with him, suggesting the stories have pre-contact (with European settler) origins. The obligations stemming from this exchange endure in present day Tŝilhqot'in society.

Today, Tŝilhqot'in people continue to receive sight from loons. For example, loons fishing in certain parts of a lake show people where they are likely to catch fish. They also show people which lakes and ecosystems are healthy by their presence in them, in contrast to their absence in a watercourse which may be struggling with the impacts of human disturbance (e.g. logging, mining, agriculture). Today, the loon continues to wear the necklace around its neck as a means of recording the laws of reciprocity, respect, and helping others in the Tŝilhqot'in legal order.

---

32 Although the law has shifted in more recent times through legislation that may require a charitable donor to fulfil their promise to donate. Compare the decision in *The Governors of Dalhousie College at Halifax v The Estate of Arthur Boutilier* (1934) SCR 642 with the Province of Nova Scotia's Public Subscriptions Act, RSNS 1989, c 378.

33 For example, in some societies, such as many European societies, the giver of a gift relinquishes all rights to the gift as property, while in other societies, gifts may come attached with obligations, such as an obligation to reciprocate at some later date, as symbolic of a relationship created.

34 Marcel Mauss, *The Gift: Forms and Functions of Exchange in Archaic Societies* (first published 1925, Ian Cunnison tr, WW Norton & Company 1967) 10.

35 Ibid 9. For comparison, where one party's performance of an obligation agreed upon binds the other party, see F.P. van R. Whelpton, 'The Indigenous Contract as Legal Phenomenon' (2006) 29 (3–4) *Anthropology Southern Africa* 144.

Source: Photo by Michael Davidson.

Figure 12.1 *A loon bird*

Beyond the original gift of the necklace, Tŝilhqot'in people are bound by the original exchange, as they continue to receive sight, and they are required to honor and respect the loon by honoring and respecting its habitat. The logic behind Tŝilhqot'in reasoning is straightforward, as without a healthy habitat, loons will no longer exist on the Tŝilhqot'in landscape, and the relationship necessarily collapses. No more loons means they can no longer help people to see. If loons cannot survive in the Tŝilhqot'in landscape because of an unhealthy environment, the ability of Tŝilhqot'in people to continue to exist in a healthy manner on their lands will likely also be in jeopardy. As such, the obligations in this relationship are reciprocal and enduring, with people and loons inextricably bound in a relationship rooted in the past and dependent on a healthy environment into the future. I argue this arrangement is an example of a contract under one Indigenous legal tradition, although I use the term *contract* with some discomfort to make a loosely analogous connection to common law.

As discussed elsewhere, I understand the term contract to be defined by the common law construction established under its criteria of formation (offer, acceptance, consideration). This is not to suggest Indigenous people do not contract under that definition (purchase of property or services). However, this articulation of contract does not represent my understanding of a legally binding voluntary obligation in an Indigenous legal order. Nor does a moral obligation align with my understanding. I am not convinced morality underpins the impetus to fulfill one's obligation in an Indigenous legal obligation as much as necessity does. When considering Mauss' work, refusing to participate in the giving or receiving of a gift may be tantamount to a declaration of war.[36] A person would be compelled to participate for the benefit they gain from the relationship with their counterpart in the exchange while potentially avoiding violent conflict.

In some respects, I believe the relationship created, replete with legal obligations, in an Indigenous legal order is more akin to a treaty. The defining acts which complicate the relationship as being one of treaty is that there is an exchange, similar to a contract, an expectation of some benefit, as in a contract, and these may involve individuals, as in a contract. Yet the resulting enduring relationship is more treaty-like. Perhaps the legal obligations between parties exist somewhere between a treaty and a contract.[37] The impetus for fulfilling obligations flows from the necessity of being in relationship with others, both humans and non-humans, for the mere continued existence of the parties. Breaching an obligation is not followed by a threat of consequence, but some negative impact is ingrained in the person who may choose not to fulfill their obligation, internally recognizing that they may not be able to feed their family. Obligations bearing this manner of weight are outside the world of common law and civil law contracts, not driven by threat of damages or moral imperative; they are driven by the necessities of life and the protection of future generations. This is what I mean by an Indigenous contract. It is a relationship bound by obligations that do not have common law or civil law remedies but rather they impact the lives of the parties, their families, and communities. Accepting that there is something akin to a contract in Indigenous legal orders, the next step is to consider approaches to researching those voluntary obligations.

---

[36] cf. Mauss (n 34).

[37] For a discussion comparing treaty with social contract, see Aaron Mills, 'What is a Treaty: On Contract and Mutual Aid' in John Borrows and Michael Coyle (eds), *The Right Relationship: Reimagining the Implementation of Historical Treaties* (University of Toronto Press 2017) 208.

3. INTRODUCTION TO INDIGENOUS LEGAL RESEARCH

Research methodologies applied by university scholars (rather than land-based learners) are inherently Western in form and practice. Indigenous scholars continue to push back against the forms and formalities of Western research (e.g. scientific method, testable hypotheses, observable results, objectivity), developing instead Indigenous research methodologies.[38] For some Indigenous scholars, the requirements of funding, writing, and presenting, regardless of whether the researcher and their subject matter are Indigenous, force Indigenous scholarship into foreign institutional boxes, such as applying for a research grant, publishing a peer-reviewed article, defending a thesis or dissertation using a European language. As Anishinaabe writer and artist Leanne Betasamosake Simpson argues, Indigenous scholarship is rooted in the sacred passing of knowledge to humans through the land, rather than through Western academic institutions,

> For countless generations, Nishnaabeg children grew up within the milieu of Nishnaabewin [all things Nishnaabe], not within the institutionalized schooling system. [...] You can't graduate from Nishnaabewin; it is a gift to be practiced and reproduced. And while each individual must have the skills and knowledge to ensure their own safety, survival and prosperity in both the physical and spiritual realm, their existence is ultimately dependent upon intimate relationships of reciprocity, humility, honesty and respect with all elements of creation, including plants and animals.

Indeed, the selection and refinement of an appropriate research methodology for contracts in Indigenous law require careful consideration, humility (to know one's own limits and rely on the generosity of knowledge holders),

---

[38] Indigenous research methodologies are developed by Indigenous scholars to create a more organic space for Indigenous researchers. Recognizing the validity of these Indigenous research methodologies is central to the reality that western academic institutions are not the monolith of valid research and knowledge production. One example arises in recruitment of professors, where a PhD is viewed as the standard for most appointments, which fails to recognize knowledge gained from a life lived on the land. See Linda Tuhiwai Smith, *Decolonizing Methodologies: Research and Indigenous Peoples* (Zed Books 1999); Margaret Kovach, *Indigenous Methodologies: Characteristics, Conversations, and Contexts* (University of Toronto Press 2009); Shawn Wilson, *Research is Ceremony: Indigenous Research Methods* (Fern-wood 2008); Alan Hanna, 'Going Circular: Indigenous Legal Research Methodology as a Legal Practice' (2020) 65(4) *McGill Law Journal* 671.

and specificity to prepare to work within the legal and research traditions arising from an Indigenous nation's worldview.[39] The interplay between life and legal principles such as those Simpson identifies above provides the foundation upon which analysis and comprehension are structured. The more embedded a researcher is in an Indigenous worldview, the more depth of analysis they will be able to provide. However, at some point, the deeper the embedded meaning within an Indigenous worldview, the more difficult it becomes for a researcher to translate that meaning into a Western worldview using Western concepts.

I have listened to elders tell me they don't have law because the definition of law is foreign to them, translating conceptually to courts, governments, written documents, and police. Yet, when engaged in dialogue, the same elder will sit for hours explaining the proper way to take an animal in a hunt. Even the word *hunt* has different meanings. In a Western worldview, it roughly means to stalk and kill an animal.[40] From a generalized Indigenous perspective, it means to be in relationship with an honoured relative and rely on that relationship to provide sustenance. It also means to engage in a complicated relationship of reciprocity that, while removing one animal from their population, also requires ensuring the sustainability of the population, largely requiring important decision-making processes around land use and protection of habitat. To hunt involves maintaining a good relationship with the animal's spirit and one's own ancestors in the other world to ensure good physical and spiritual health here on earth. The deeper a researcher works, the more complicated the research results. From having no law to having a complex system of law that simply is not bound by the same definitions of law with which legal scholars or practitioners are familiar. To access and learn the nuances and meanings when researching contracts in Indigenous legal orders requires relationships with and within an Indigenous community.

3.1 History of Indigenous Laws Research

Learning, unpacking, interpreting, and articulating Indigenous law is not a new academic pursuit. Anthropologists of the early 20th century visited and studied with Indigenous groups around the world. Despite the problematic Western language of those times, the interest behind much of the anthropological

39 For an additional discussion see Gordon Christie, 'Indigenous Legal Theory: Some Initial Considerations' in Benjamin Richardson, Shin Imai and Kent McNeil (eds), *Indigenous Peoples and the Law: Comparative and Critical Perspectives* (Hart 2009) 195.

40 'Hunt': In the *Marriam-Webster.com Dictionary*, first definition for 'hunt' is 'to pursue for food or in sport' <https://www.merriam-webster.com/dictionary/hunt> accessed 7 November 2023.

research was a sincere understanding of how these non-Western societies functioned.[41] Of the anthropological work from this era, two are particularly relevant for this discussion on research methods in contract law. The first, written by Llewellyn and Hoebel, is relevant as it is one of a few early Indigenous legal research projects in North America. The second (previously mentioned) Marcell Mauss, relates directly to the concept of contract.

The first notable early 20th century work on Indigenous law is by anthropologist E. Adamson Hoebell and jurist Karl Llewellen, whose work of understanding Cheyenne law was ahead of its time. Their work identified the legal principles, or as they called them, "law-ways", underpinning resolutions to internal conflict within Cheyenne society. Relevant for our discussion is their wise caution about using a Western framework for investigating Indigenous law, as Western tools "may dictate what one sees and makes use of, and may dictate also a general frame into which the data may be squeezed", to make it cognizable to Western jurists.[42] In other words, they were aware of the potential for distortions that may occur when using a common law lens for analysis, primarily because Indigenous law "sets its own premises and becomes impenetrable on any premises except its own".[43] Their research was focused on "trouble-cases", stories about conflict between people.[44] They included some discussion on whether some of the exchanges had the appearance of contracts in the Western definition.[45] However, my reference to Llewellen and Hoebel here is not to unpack their work on contracts in Indigenous law, but because they were mindful of the potential for distortions when using methods from the American legal system as methods for understanding Indigenous law.

As discussed briefly elsewhere, to avoid distorting what a researcher may believe they are identifying across legal orders, that researcher should immerse themselves as much as possible into the society under study. Immersion allows various meanings to become clearer, when initially, according to the

---

41 Some of the anthropological works include, Alfred Reginald Radcliffe-Brown, *Structure and Function in Primitive Society* (first published in 1952, Lowe and Brydone 1986); Isaac Schapera, *A Handbook of Tsawana Law and Custom* (first published in 1938, Frank Cass and Company 1970); Robert S. Rattray, *Ashanti Law and Constitution* (first published in 1929, Oxford University Press 1956); Bronislaw Malinowski, *Crime & Custom in Savage Society* (first published in 1926, Routledge and Kegan Paul 1970).

42 Karl Nickerson Llewellyn and E. Adamson Hoebel, *The Cheyenne Way: Conflict and Case Law in Primitive Jurisprudence* (University of Oklahoma Press 1941) 39.

43 Ibid at 49.

44 Ibid at 29.

45 Ibid at 45, 228.

researcher's worldview and legal order, the observable practice of a people, such as what may appear to be the construction of a contract, may actually be an entirely different social activity (such as the fulfilment of a reciprocal obligation under a gift exchange). The discipline of comparative law has its strengths and weaknesses when applied to Indigenous legal orders. Using comparative law techniques when researching Indigenous law allows a researcher from another legal order to see analogous concepts. For example, in many legal orders, killing another person is prohibited (I avoid the use of the word murder, which has specific meaning in Canada's *Criminal Code*). Studying across from one order to another, the comparativist may identify rules and processes for dealing with someone who kills another. However, the fine details about the substantive and procedural aspects of an offence such as killing likely will not be available to the researcher.

To discover the nuances around killing, a researcher almost always requires some depth of immersion with the people and their ontological and epistemological perspectives to learn about the nuances surrounding killing. For example, in Tŝilhqot'in society the word killing can take on many meanings.[46] A person who does not return from a hunt will be viewed as being killed, despite possible alternatives, such as simply moving to another part of the territory or joining another group. Likewise, a person's status may be killed if they commit another offense, such as disturbing a salmon spawning bed. Likewise, human relationships, such as a marriage, may be killed. Regarding nuance, one of the concerns I have with comparative law is the potential to privilege the legal order of the comparatist researcher. The potential to assess the merits of another's legal order exists with comparative techniques, as the baseline of knowledge is the researcher's own knowledge. Comparative techniques seem better suited to researching across similar legal orders (European to European, or Indigenous to Indigenous) when both are from a similar ontological perspective. Not having an inside perspective gained from immersion will create barriers by way of potential misunderstandings or misinterpretations.[47] However, this does not mean that working across legal orders without immersion is futile. Often, a comparative approach is helpful for gaining an initial understanding of the legal order being studied. It likely also reveals

---

46 Robert Lane, *Cultural Relations of the Chilcotin Indians of West Central British Columbia* (DPhil thesis, University of Washington, Department of Anthropology 1953) 166.

47 Aaron Mills argues that understanding an Indigenous legal order from a Western legal perspective doesn't make sense, as the systems of logic and reasoning differ too significantly. *Miinigowiziwin: All That Has Been Given for Living Well Together. One Vision of Anishinaabe Constitutionalism* (DPhil thesis, University of Victoria, Faculty of Law 2019) 28.

problems associated with what a researcher doesn't know, but needs to know before proceeding with their work, including problems of language barriers and the importance of access to communities.

One scholar who appears to be an exception to the necessary commitment of direct engagement with a community or nation was French anthropologist Marcel Mauss. Mauss never actually set foot in any of the communities about which he wrote, working extensively from his home in Paris.[48] Specifically, as it relates to the topic of this chapter, Mauss wrote on how perpetual agreements arise within various Indigenous societies in his publication, *The Gift: Forms and Functions of Exchange in Archaic Societies*.[49] Mauss explores what he calls "permanent contracts" between the peoples of a given society and their outside relations.[50] According to anthropologist Michael Asch, Mauss identified "a set of practices associated with the establishment and fulfillment of agreements between certain societies that have neither a state form of organization nor a common culture".[51] These agreements, or contracts, were self-regulating and did not require state authority enforcement, as in a court awarding a judgment against a party for their breach of a contractual obligation. A breach in a party's obligation, such as "to refuse to give, or to fail to invite, is – like refusing to accept [a gift to form the contract] – the equivalent of a declaration of war; it is a refusal of friendship and intercourse".[52] Through his analysis, Mauss interpreted the gift exchange in Polynesian society as a system of contract, which could be brought into conversation with the European model of financial lending (contracts for borrowing and repaying money).

The reason for discussing Mauss in the context of this chapter is to recognize that anthropologists of the time were interpreting language, concepts, and practices of Indigenous law. Through his European lens, Mauss was able – as best he could given his lack of immersion in a community – to understand the Indigenous practice of gift exchange and its legal effects in the communities whom he studied. Mauss's reach was limited, by necessity, to the work others had performed while in community. Many of his contemporaries were lost to the battlefields of World War I. He wanted to honour them by continuing the research they had conducted with Indigenous peoples. Mauss' ability to provide his analysis in many respects is attributable to the in-community engagement his colleagues had conducted, providing him appropriate and relevant data

48 Wendy James and Nicholas Justin Allen, *Marcell Mauss: A Centenary Tribute* (Berghahn Books 1998) 11.

49 cf. Mauss (n 34). Also cf Gordley (n 1) 5–6.

50 Ibid at 6.

51 Michael Asch, *On Being Here to Stay: Treaties and Aboriginal Rights in Canada* (University of Toronto Press 2014) 167.

52 cf. Mauss (n 34) 11, also cited in Asch, ibid.

upon which he relied. A fascinating question is how different might Mauss' analyses and conclusions be had he attended the communities of the people about whom he wrote.[53] Much contemporary scholarship on Indigenous laws and legal orders can draw connections to these early anthropological methods of research and analysis, through what is now commonly referred to as doctrinal legal research.

4. DOCTRINAL LEGAL RESEARCH

Doctrinal research is an appropriate method for the study of Indigenous law. There is no uniform definition of doctrinal research. Perhaps most simply put, a doctrine in law is "a principle of law established through past decisions".[54] Yet, this is only one, perhaps limiting, definition. An expanded definition is warranted when contemplating how Indigenous peoples preserve knowledge, decisions, and resolutions that either change or maintain ongoing relationships with others. These details are central to authoritative internal reasoning in that they characterize how a legal issue may be explored, understood and approached. Doctrinal legal research is inextricably linked to social realities, which are best studied through an interdisciplinary approach to access internal knowledge.[55] Similar to scholars applying doctrinal legal research in the traditional sense, a scholar researching an Indigenous legal order must have full understanding of what constitutes the internal logic, as it is this logic that constitutes the authority for the reasoning within the respective legal order.[56] Understanding a legal order in its totality, which is a lifelong commitment, provides access to the authoritative internal logic underpinning Indigenous law.

The simple definition of researching legal precedents may be suitable for Aboriginal law within the jurisprudence. However, under the more expansive definition, doctrinal research moves beyond the study of legal precedents to include "disparate legal strands" and "general principles" through an interdisciplinary approach, hence my use of anthropology and history in addition to Indigenous research methods. A significant challenge in accessing Indigenous legal doctrine is possessing the ability to recognize where it is recorded and

53 Marshall Sahlins critique's Mauss work in *The Gift*, calling into question the accuracy of his analyses on the *hau* (spirit) of the gift, and in the context of the social contract. Marshall Sahlins, *Stone Age Economics* (Routledge 1972) 149.

54 'Doctrine': *Merriam-Webster.com Dictionary* <https://www.merriam-webster.com/dictionary/doctrine> accessed 29 November 2023.

55 P. Ishwara Bhat, *Idea and Methods of Legal Research* (Oxford University Press 2020) 147.

56 For a detailed discussion on internal logic systems, see cf. Mills (n 47) 28.

being able to interpret the information once located.[57] Knowing the local oral traditions and the landscape or landmarks to which they may adhere is only accessible when a researcher is engaging directly with a community in their geographic locale. The knowledge of how law is embedded in the land, art, ceremonies, songs, and stories (to name a few) varies between nations, and is not something a person can pick up in a book. They need to be present and on the land with knowledge holders, otherwise mountains look like mountains, rivers look like rivers, baskets hold physical things rather than repositories of legal knowledge. Not having inside insight is probably the biggest challenge to locating law's archive in an Indigenous community.

Most Indigenous societies did not have systems of writing as commonly understood today (i.e. words on paper). Rather, Indigenous people recorded their laws in a variety of other forms, such as through artistic expression (totems, crests, clothing), oral stories, and cultural practices.[58] The guswenta, or two row wampum, is an example of Indigenous law, specifically an agreement, recorded in an object. The guswenta, or two-row wampum, contains two parallel rows of white wampum shells amid a bed of purple wampum shells. The two rows of white shells

> symbolize two paths or two vessels, travelling down the same river together. One, a birch bark canoe, will be for the Indian people, their laws, their customs and their ways. The other, a ship, will be for the white people and their laws, their customs, and their ways. We shall each travel the river together, side by side, but in our own boat. Neither of us will try to steer the other's vessel.[59]

The Western version of this agreement is captured in the *Royal Proclamation, 1763*. The relevant and related statement being "the several Nations or Tribes of Indians with whom We are connected, and who live under our Protection, should not be molested or disturbed in the Possession of such Parts of Our Dominions and Territories as, not having been ceded to or purchased by Us, are reserved to them".[60] Although one contains words, and the other contains

---

57 Borrows writes of the challenges of accessibility and intelligibility in cf. Borrows (n 15) 138 and 142.

58 cf. Borrows (n 15) 139.

59 John Borrows, 'Wampum at Niagara: The Royal Proclamation, Canadian Legal History, and Self-Government' in Michael Asch (ed), *Aboriginal and Treaty Rights in Canada: Essays on Law, Equality, and Respect for Difference* (UBC Press 2002) 164, citing Robert A. Williams, Jr., 'The Algebra of Federal Indian Law: The Hard Trail of Decolonizing and Americanizing the White Man's Indian Jurisprudence' (1986) *The Wisconsin Law Review* 219, 291.

60 UBC Indigenous Foundations, *Royal Proclamation, 1763* <https://indigenousfoundations.arts.ubc.ca/royal_proclamation_1763/> accessed 29 November

symbolic representation, they both stand to memorialize the meeting and agreement of Indigenous leaders and the Crown at the time the agreement was made in 1763.[61] A researcher may review the historical activities expressed in various forms when open to the concept that the documentation of these events exist in places other than only written publications, such as the guswenta. Although a researcher may identify some object that holds a record of past events (or laws), engaging directly with people in their communities is necessary to unlock relevant embedded meanings.

Another form of legal doctrine containing Indigenous law is the land itself. In many Indigenous societies, the law is embedded in stories, which are connected to some aspect of the land, either a particular place or landform.[62] For example, the Tŝilhqot'in oral tradition contains stories about Tŝ'il?os and ?Eniyud.[63] These individuals were married with six children. At some point, Tŝ'il?os and ?Eniyud grew tired of one another, as there was trouble between them, and they decided to separate. Tŝ'il?os moved to one location with three of the children and ?Eniyud stayed in her location with the other three children. The individuals, Tŝ'il?os and ?Eniyud, were once human, but are now mountains on the Tŝilhqot'in traditional territory. They are geographically located far enough apart that they cannot see one another over the natural curvature of the earth. This story, which is more involved than my cursory recounting here, is about resolving marital conflict, and addresses responsibilities to the children. This is another example of how law is written into landforms as a means of providing a record for future generations. Again, relationships with Indigenous people living in their communities is the entry point for learning and understanding meaning. Although a legal researcher may gain access to this esoteric knowledge, they still have to interpret that information to have meaning with regard to law (Indigenous and Western). This paragraph reaffirms a point made earlier, which is that understanding and interpreting knowledge written onto the land requires access to the authoritative internal logic and reasoning of the relevant Indigenous group. Otherwise, what outsiders see are mountains, rock formations, trees, and rivers devoid of internal meaning. Stories anchored to the local landscape serve as an important repository of Indigenous knowledge.

2023.

[61] cf. Borrows (n 59) 156.

[62] Marianne Ignace and Ronald Ignace, *Secwepemc People, Land, and Laws: Yeri7 re Stsqeys-kucw* (McGill-Queen's University Press 2017) 490.

[63] Story shared with me by several Tŝilhqot'in elders.

4.1 Ethnographic Research

Because Indigenous laws are embedded in human beings and exercised through lived experience, empirical research with human beings is necessary. Given the abundance of scholarly work on ethnographic methods, I will limit my comments here to the basics pertaining to ethics, relationships, and interviews.[64] If an expansive definition of doctrinal research applies, as suggested, then other disciplines, particularly in social science (anthropology, sociology, psychology, linguistics) are relevant, providing research with a variety of tools for accessing knowledge.

4.1.1 Ethics

Nobody should do research with human collaborators without ethics approval from their affiliated institution, funders, and relevant governing bodies, including that of the research collaborator.[65] Ethics provides oversight in an effort to ensure a researcher does not harm their research collaborators in the process of acquiring knowledge. Harm may include, but is not limited to, publishing information that may be harmful to individual participants, their families or communities, publishing information that should not be made public, exploiting people for their knowledge where only the researcher (and their institution) benefits from the work. There are many reasons for acquiring ethics approval. Simply engaging in the process of applying for an ethics certificate forces researchers to carefully consider the potential ramifications of their work on their collaborators. Before getting to the ethics stage, a researcher should have a collaborator who wants to engage in some manner of research with them.

4.1.2 Relationships

As I mentioned elsewhere in this chapter, research into Indigenous contracts, or any matter in Indigenous law, cannot occur without developing or maintaining existing relationships.[66] The reason for this approach is that it follows a principle of respect and with the principles of ownership, control, access and possession (OPEC) protecting against the exploitation of Indigenous peoples

---

64 See for example, Madhulika Sahoo, S. Jeyavelu and Anjali Kurane (eds), *Ethnographic Research in the Social Sciences* (Routledge 2023); and Leah Shagrir, *Journey to Ethnographic Research* (Springer International Publishing 2017).

65 See for example, Canada, *Tri-Council Policy Statement: Ethical Conduct for Research Involving Humans* <https://ethics.gc.ca/eng/policy-politique_tcps2-eptc2_2018.html> accessed 29 November 2023.

66 Alan Hanna, 'Reconciliation through Relationality in Indigenous Legal Orders' (2019) 56(3) *Alta Law Review* 817, 828.

and knowledge.[67] I teach a field course and conduct research with and for a small, remote Dene community in the Northwest Territories. In addition to ethics, I adhere to Dene legal principles to guide the relationship. A few key principles include reciprocity (both parties offer gifts to exchange and maintain balance in the relationship), respect (for all parties, time, knowledge, contribution), humility (knowing that I am and always will be a learner, that my best intentions may not produce beneficial results, that I do not expect anything when engaging in research in community). There is a great deal of knowledge, skill, and experience that informs this part of the discussion, which goes beyond the scope of this chapter.[68] The benefits of entering and maintaining a relationship with an Indigenous group are many, from providing access to esoteric knowledge to having new acquaintances. Without these relationships, the perspectives of the researcher will prevail, despite their not being grounded in Indigenous knowledge through relationships with people whose lived experiences generate and transmit knowledge through generations.

4.1.3 Interview

For many, myself included, the interview is the most challenging and rewarding part of the research process. As with the relationship, interviews come with their own unique characteristics.[69] There is no single approach to interviewing people. One interview may occur smoothly, as a researcher might expect. The very next interview, on the same day with the same people, can go entirely sideways for any number of reasons (anxiety, heat, fatigue, interpersonal tension, distractions). I have had the most cordial conversations with people with whom I would soon be sitting down to interview, and when the interview begins, the same person lashes out to vent their frustration for years of harm caused by colonialism. This is perfectly acceptable, provided the hostility is not threatening or potentially dangerous. Hostility from frustration is to be expected from people who have been subject to a variety of harms from any number of sources. With patience, empathy, and respect, these interviews most often result in the most meaningful conversations. Occasionally an interview may begin with tension, as people try to determine whether the interviewer is trustworthy, honest, and will take the participant's knowledge seriously. In

---

67 First Nations Information Governance Centre, *The First Nations Principles of OCAP* <https://fnigc.ca/ocap-training/> accessed 29 November 2023.

68 I have written on these matters elsewhere. See cf. Alan Hanna (n 38); Alan Hanna, 'Reconciliation Through Relationality in Indigenous Legal Orders' (2019) 56(3) *Alberta Law Review* 817.

69 See the complexity of interviewing people in, Alan Hanna, 'Art of the Interview: Research in Indigenous Communities' in Laura Forsythe and Jennifer Markides (eds), *Walking Together in Indigenous Research* (DIO Press 2020) 79.

other words, the participant is testing to see if the interviewer understands how to be respectful.

Ethics, relationships, and interviews are only part of a complex world of ethnographic research with Indigenous peoples. There are many other facets to consider, particularly once a research collaborator relationship has been established, as the particular nuances of the individual's community and nation require attention and care. There is much a researcher can do before they ever step foot into a community with whom they will be working, which is related to respect and humility, called preparation.

4.2 Approach and Application of Methods

Equipped with some of the basic empirical research tools discussed above, a researcher is relatively prepared to engage in their work with and within community. The approach is important to how the relationship develops, or not, and will shape the content of what is exchanged in the relationship. Often the exchange involves the researcher's ability to compile data, while the community provides access to the data and helps inform the research question(s).

A legal researcher should never walk into an unfamiliar community, invited or not, without having conducted some preliminary research. Entering a meeting with collaborators, leadership, or liaisons empty-handed, without having some sense of the community, is insulting and disrespectful. Printed materials, electronic resources, media archives are available to researchers to provide some foundational knowledge which, once informed, allows a researcher to show their respect by not expecting their potential collaborator to provide the context that is already available. Once the researcher has a general grasp of their collaborator (history, struggles, society, economy, language, legal and political perspectives), the face-to-face time is more efficiently spent working on the important details of the collaboration, such as the parameters of the proposed work, research outputs, and partnership (collaborator) agreements. Indigenous scholars have written on Indigenous research methodologies to inform approaches to working with and for Indigenous communities.[70]

Once prepared and in a good working relationship with a collaborator community or nation, the research may commence. As this book pertains to research in contracts methods, and I am writing about Indigenous legal research generally and Indigenous contracts specifically, I will discuss a couple of matters that require particular attention – interpretation and translation.

Interpretation and translation are two of the more complicated aspects of Indigenous laws research, if the researcher is to understand knowledge and

70 See cf. Smith, Wilson and Kovach (n 38).

perspective reasonably accurately. This is particularly relevant for a researcher who is not from a community with whom they are working and have little to no knowledge of the language. The researcher is, and always will be in many respects, a beginner in each new community with whom they collaborate, trying to absorb and understand the unspoken nuances of community life without having had the childhood upbringing from within that community. Additionally, a lack of knowledge of the language adds another layer of complication.[71]

Meaning is directly linked to language. Working in the researcher's mother language offers a means to initial access.[72] Learning an Indigenous language to a level of fluency is not always achievable or practical. Many Indigenous peoples do not know their language, which often makes using the researcher's language necessary to work with an Indigenous legal order.[73] Not knowing the language of the collaborative Indigenous group, or not having been raised in a particular community, does not render research efforts futile. A person raised in a community will also struggle through their own challenges, such as internal politics, disparate viewpoints on the law, different teachings, some of which may come from people whose authority in a particular community is questionable according to other community members (lineage often plays a role in this latter challenge). Accuracy, therefore, is often a fluctuating concept.

A researcher's efforts to achieve accuracy in interpretation and translation of Indigenous laws is strengthened by the application of multiple research methods such as those discussed elsewhere in this chapter. Knowing how to interpret what is being received is a challenge only overcome by time and thought from within an Indigenous legal perspective. When teaching Indigenous law, I provide direction toward the oral traditions of a First Nation, instructing students to read the stories, speak the stories aloud to friends or family allowing them to breathe life into them, and live with the stories for a while. Only time living with Indigenous stories will begin to open access to their meaning. Then, a researcher may begin to identify linkages that connect stories to the lived realities underpinning an Indigenous legal perspective. Learning this knowledge and applying what is learned to Western legal concepts is fraught with challenges, such as misinterpreting the meaning behind certain actions.

---

71 On challenges with language, see Lorraine Weir, 'Oral Tradition' as Legal Fiction: The Challenge of Dechen Ts'edilhtan in *Tsilhqot'in Nation v. British Columbia*' (2016) 29 *International Journal for the Semiotics of Law* 159.

72 James (Sákéj) Youngblood Henderson, *First Nations Jurisprudence and Aboriginal Rights: Defining the Just Society* (Native Law Centre 2006) 163.

73 John Borrows, 'Heroes, Tricksters, Monsters, and Caretakers: Indigenous Law and Legal Education' (2016) 61(4) *McGill Law Journal* 795, 810.

4.3 Contracts Specific Research

When I was first invited to teach Indigenous laws relating to contracts, I was concerned. I had never heard of the idea of contract arising in conversations with elders and community members. However, I was keenly aware of obligations which arise among and between people and others. The challenge I faced was identifying the logic mechanism that connected the two disparate concepts of contract to allow a conversation across these understandings. I often rely on the following excerpt from a larger Secwepemc story to show the challenge and pitfalls of recklessly accepting superficial connections without the advantage of deeper knowledge of a community's worldview.

In this story about two warring groups, the birds and the animals, Chief Swan asks if someone from his community would carry an invitation to the chief of their enemy to attend a feast. It was the middle of winter, and the snow was deep.

> Whoever would undertake the journey was to receive a large present of dentalia [small white shells used to make jewellery and adorn clothing].
>
> Coyote volunteered to go, and prepared for the journey by putting on his finest clothes, embroidered moccasins, and all his dentalia and necklaces. At dusk he left the house, but, not caring to face the deep snow, he ran around the underground house all night, admiring himself, and was still running in the morning, when the people awoke. The Swan asked him why he had not gone; and Coyote answered, "I was just playing and running around for practice. I will start to-night". When evening came, the people saw him leave, and watched him until he was out of sight. Coyote soon found the snow too deep, returned after dark, and lay down underneath the top of the ladder, where he fell asleep. When the people awoke in the morning, they found him fast asleep, and Swan asked him why he had not gone. Coyote answered, "Oh! I was playing, became tired, and lay down to sleep. I will start to-night".
>
> Then Swan asked the people which one of them was best able to undertake the journey, and they all agreed that Porcupine was the fittest person, for she was accustomed to walking in the high mountains where there was much deep snow. Porcupine was thus selected … [*Porcupine succeeds in the task, which results in peace between the bird people and the animal people.*] Porcupine got [her] rich present of dentalia, and was much envied by Coyote.[74]

To most common law lawyers, the formation of a simple contract is obvious, with an *offer* to carry a message in exchange for dentalia as *consideration*, and Coyote's *acceptance*. Is this a common law contract being formed within an Indigenous legal order? The answer is quite simply *no*. Although the story was translated into English and written down by a non-Indigenous ethnographer

---

74 James Teit, *The Shuswap, Vol II The Jesup North Pacific Expedition: Memoir of the American Museum of Natural History* (GE Stechert & Co 1909) 658.

(James Teit), we can look to the translated words Teit used combined with some understanding of the Secwepemc worldview to show a different analysis. The word *present* associated with the dentalia, suggests this is not consideration, but a gift, which, as discussed earlier in the chapter with the Tŝilhqot'in story about the blind man and loon, carries obligations. The word *volunteered* associated with Coyote's acceptance strips obligation when viewed from a common law perspective, as volunteers cannot be bound by legal obligation. These two words, *present* and *volunteer* suggest something other than a legally binding contract.

In the Secwepemc worldview, an offer of a *present*, or gift, is likely associated with acknowledging an individual's sacrifice and commitment to protect their community, sometimes at great cost to the individual's personal safety, such as walking into the enemy's camp carrying a message. The word *volunteer* suggests that Coyote, or anybody else for that matter, could choose whether to accept the Chief's request, as it is not an enforceable obligation in the contractual sense, and no sanction was imposed on Coyote for his 'breach' of the obligation. However, every member of the community carries an obligation to protect their community. When Coyote failed to perform the task for which he volunteered, his status likely diminished in the community, and the community decided who was best suited to perform the task, Porcupine.[75]

Once the community deliberated and rendered their decision, the obligation would have weighed heavily on Porcupine, who was chosen as being the most appropriately skilled individual to fulfill the task. Yet, selected, and thus bound by obligation at the result of a community decision, Porcupine consented to her performance of it, binding her in obligation to the community, otherwise, like Coyote, she could have avoided performance. That said, whether Porcupine actually had independent choice over her obligation to community protection once selected by the community is a matter for deeper research. Obligations of protection are strong and deeply engrained responsibilities in Indigenous communities. The remedy, or consequence, for Coyote's failure to perform his accepted task was not administered by an authority from within the community, as he was not legally bound (he volunteered). Rather, his consequence was internally driven by his own jealousy when Porcupine accepted and successfully performed the task. His own jealousy would be a fitting consequence for a trickster character such as Coyote, as it would not give him much peace for a while.

---

[75] Coyote is a trickster in the Secwepemc world, meaning people likely weren't surprised that he would not perform his obligation, but still wanted the gift of dentalia. Coyote is an anomalous figure who simultaneously has sacred status and no status. The insight and knowledge of this important and often polarizing figure goes beyond the scope of this chapter.

In this brief analysis, we see obligations to community, rather than individual parties, as carrying the binding force of law coming from collective decision-making and an individual's willingness to perform. There is also a gift to honour the courage and commitment of the individual who puts the community's safety ahead of their own, and fulfilled their obligation, which contributes to their longevity through the protection of future generations. Clearly, there is much more to be understood and said here than can be accommodated in this chapter, but hopefully this offers some helpful insight.

5. CONCLUSION

One of the questions I propose to students is whether there is such a thing as a contract within an Indigenous legal order. Certainly, Western conceptions of contracts are created and performed regularly in Aboriginal law when Indigenous groups and governments regularly contract for services or the acquisition of property (real and otherwise). However, Indigenous laws are founded on worldviews that are different from and which long pre-date European worldviews rooted in liberalism and capitalism, meaning that obligations flow from sources unrelated to offer, acceptance, consideration. The difference in worldview begs a multi-juridical approach to studying and recognizing contracts from various legal perspectives. Legal pluralism is one approach that offers some helpful insights to working across distinct legal orders.[76] Accepting the multiple sources of Indigenous law, including oral traditions, lived experience, and recording law on the land, transdisciplinary and interdisciplinary approaches offer sensitive and effective methods for accessing esoteric information through the establishment and maintenance of ongoing relationships with Indigenous nations and their communities. As an Indigenous legal scholar and practicing lawyer with undergraduate and graduate degrees in anthropology, I appreciate and draw upon an interdisciplinary approach to research, often in conversation with scholars in other disciplines (e.g. history, political science, sociology, psychology). Unsurprisingly, considering this background, when tasked with identifying contracts outside of common or civil law constructions, the answer to whether Indigenous laws have contracts is challenging. My answer is: it depends.

---

[76] Discussions on legal pluralism and Indigenous legal orders come with critiques that go beyond the scope of this chapter. See for example, Nicole Roughan, *Authorities: Conflicts, Cooperation, and Transnational Legal Theory* (Oxford University Press 2013); Perry Shawana, 'Legal Processes, Pluralism in Canadian Jurisprudence, and the Governance of Carrier Medicine Knowledge' in Law Commission of Canada (eds), *Indigenous Legal Traditions* (UBC Press 2007) 114.

Whether we identify contracts in an Indigenous legal order depends on a range of factors, such as how are we defining a contract, who constitutes a party, what does competence require, how do these concepts translate from an Indigenous language, worldview, and legal perspective? Under an Indigenous definition of contract, which may be rendered loosely as an obligation voluntarily entered into that binds a party or parties to performance under no threat of judgement for breach beyond the individual's internalized sense of obligation to their community, then yes, there are contracts in Indigenous law. If we limit the definition to that of the common law, then the answer is no, resulting in no need to learn new approaches to research contracts from these disparate and longstanding legal orders.

Regardless of how we answer this question, new research methods for studying whether contracts, or legally binding agreements, exist in Indigenous legal orders may provide a critical lens for assessing contemporary contract law in both Western and non-Western societies. Ultimately, research will generate new knowledge highlighting differences in disparate legal orders, affording scholars and lawyers the ability to discern how the legal orders operate based on their relevant worldviews. Recognizing and respecting difference through critical analysis requires an ethical commitment by researchers, particularly where different legal orders co-exist on Indigenous lands shared by colonizing and colonized peoples, as the imbalance of power remains a tangible aspect of the relationships between disparate nations. Scholars should be mindful that their work embraces difference in a manner facilitating and encouraging coexistence in the contemporary milieu of legal systems around the world.

13. Research methods for transnational contract law

Joshua Karton

1. INTRODUCTION: TRANSNATIONAL LAW AS A CHALLENGE TO TRADITIONAL CONTRACT LAW CONCEPTS

Like the other 'challenging topics' presented in Part III of this book, transnational law is not an area of law. Rather, it is a conceptual category, a label we use to help define and understand observed phenomena. What distinguishes transnational law from both national and international law is its polymorphous character. Aside from the capacity to have an effect across jurisdictional borders (which is implied by the name), there is no single characteristic or criterion shared by all transnational laws. The leading definition—an old one, but still regularly cited—is both broad and vague. It comes from Phillip Jessup's 1956 book, *Transnational Law.* There, Jessup defined transnational law 'to include all law which regulates actions or events that transcend national frontiers. Both public and private international law are included, as are other rules which do not wholly fit into such standard categories'.[1]

As this oft-quoted passage shows, from the very first articulations of transnational law as an object of scholarship, it has been characterized by a conceptual uneasiness, a lack of fit with established categories.[2] Transnational

1 Phillip C. Jessup, *Transnational Law* (Yale University Press 1956). More an extended essay than a book, *Transnational Law* compiles a series of three lectures given by Jessup as part of the 1956 Storrs Lectures on Jurisprudence at Yale Law School. It is not clear whether Jessup coined the term 'transnational law', but his book was the biggest factor in popularizing it.

2 In a review of Jessup's book published in 1957, Katzenbach describes Jessup as arguing for 'an approach which is quite different—and much more sensible—than that of more traditional scholarship', and 'employing a broad-gauged view [that] seeks to open up to the domain of legal scholarship a large and important area of rules and practices now too often arbitrarily excluded by *a priori* classification'.

law is not national law, but neither is it international law, a 'law of nations'. Transnational contract law reaches around and across state boundaries, often ignoring them altogether as it governs cross-border contractual relationships wherever they arise. This chapter focuses on the transnational law governing contractual relationships between commercial entities.[3] This is not the only kind of transnational contract law; in particular, modern consumer regulation often has a transnational dimension. However, the law of commercial contracts was the earliest area of law to develop transnationally, and it remains the most extensively transnationalized of any area of private law.

Unlike the other 'challenging topics' discussed in Part III, transnational contract law does not pose a challenge *to society*, a challenge that can be answered partly with contract law doctrines. Rather, transnational law challenges *contract law itself.* The emergence of transnational contract law as a legal and economic phenomenon challenges once-established notions of what contract law is, where it comes from, and what forms it takes. Transnational contract law forces researchers to confront a range of meta-questions that traditional contract law scholarship is not forced to confront (and which are usually the province of general jurisprudence): Where does law come from? What constitutes law? How do different legal sources relate to each other? If law is simply a matter of choice, is it still law?

At the same time, transnational contract law also challenges traditional research methodologies. While doctrinal methods continue to have relevance and to play a unique role—as they do in conceptualizing and describing any area of law—transnational law upends the notion of what constitutes legal doctrine. To be specific, transnational law forces contract scholars to confront assumptions that many would not even realize were assumptions: that law comes from states (and, correspondingly, that a private agreement among parties may be rendered binding upon them by operation of law, but is not law in itself); that contract law is associated with a particular territory, within which it applies; and that law constrains contracting practice, such that parties may order their own affairs but do so within a framework imposed upon them by state law. Indeed, transnational contract law presents particular challenges because it is not a single category, but rather a multifaceted phenomenon. It encompasses a variety of state laws (applying both within the state's territory and extraterritorially), treaties, model laws, codes of conduct, standard form contracts, and uncodified trade usages—which have in common only that they

---

Nicholas de B. Katzenbach, Review of *Transnational Law* (1957) 24(2) *University of Chicago Law Review* 413, 413–414. See also Craig Scott, '"Transnational Law" as Proto-Concept: Three Conceptions' (2009) 10(7) *German Law Journal* 859.

[3] See the extensive definition of 'commercial' in Giuditta Cordero-Moss, *International Commercial Contracts* (Cambridge University Press 2023) 2.

apply to some category of contractual relationships and that they are treated as binding by parties to those contracts.

Transnational contract law is distinguished by the marginal role of state power. It is not so much law *beyond* the state, as some have described it,[4] but rather law *regardless of* the state. Many of the rules of transnational contract law are embodied only in standard form contracts, are 'codified' in the limited sense that they are written out in a code of conduct or privately-published set of standards, arise entirely from commercial custom, or were drafted as an international model law that states may or may not adopt, but which can apply to contracts even though they have not been formally adopted into applicable national laws.

This is not to say that states have been rendered superfluous or irrelevant by the growth of transnational contract law. State rulemaking and—especially—state enforcement powers are vital to the perpetuation and flourishing of transnational law. However, states play a marginal role as generators of transnational contract law (and indeed of any area of transnational law). Instead, states are largely sanctifiers of rules and structures developed elsewhere: in industry associations and other private sector bodies, nongovernmental and intergovernmental organizations, and through the everyday contracting practices of private firms.[5] That is, while states' adoption or acceptance of transnational rules remains necessary to make them practically effective and to confer legal validity (in the positivist sense) upon them, transnational law develops at the speed of business, frontrunning and setting the agenda for state lawmaking processes.[6]

---

[4] Ralf Michaels, 'The True Lex Mercatoria: Law Beyond the State' (2007) 14 *Indiana Journal of Global Legal Studies* 447; Larry Catá Backer, 'Private Actors and Public Governance Beyond the State: The Multinational Corporation, the Financial Stability Board, and the Global Governance Order' (2011) 18 *Indiana Journal of Global Legal Studies* 751.

[5] See, e.g., Jürgen Basedow, 'The State's Private Law and the Economy: Commercial Law as an Amalgam of Public and Private Rule-Making' (2008) 56 *American Journal of Comparative Law* 703; Michaels (n 4). Berger describes the gradual process by which privately generated norms become instantiated in state laws as 'creeping codification'. Klaus Peter Berger, *The Creeping Codification of the Lex Mercatoria* (2nd edn, Kluwer 2010).

[6] Joshua Karton, 'Sectoral Fragmentation in Transnational Contract Law' (2018) 21 *University of Pennsylvania Journal of Business Law* 142, 145 (arguing that, 'in a reverse of the traditional conception, formal contract law is being remade in the shadow of private contracts'). On the interplay between public and private governance, see, e.g., Tehila Sagy, 'What's so Private About Private Ordering?' (2011) 45 *Law and Society Review* 923.

In a pioneering study that continues to influence transnational law scholarship, Ellickson documented how commercial communities come to create their own legal orders.[7] But despite this insight, even Ellickson did not take the step necessary to understand transnational contract law. He named his seminal 1994 book *Order without Law*, thus showing that even he worked under the influence of the traditional assumption that what states decree is 'law', while what parties privately agree to is something else—'order' perhaps, but not law. With the benefit of thirty more years of experience with transnational law, we can now understand that only two requirements are needed for the legality of a contract law rule: widespread and willing acceptance within a defined commercial community, and willingness by state courts to enforce the implications of that rule by granting legal remedies. Everything else is contingent. This concept is summed up with the label 'autopoiesis', a term borrowed from biology that, in the transnational law context, refers to the spontaneous generation of legal rules without formal lawmaking processes.[8]

Whether or not one subscribes to the notion of autopoietic law, it is evident that transnational contract law is, at heart, a spontaneous, bottom-up phenomenon. Transnational law arises as an organic response to the 'universality of human problems', as Jessup titled the opening chapter of *Transnational Law*.[9] While it often includes formal rulemaking at the global, regional, and national levels, transnational law is ultimately a legal response to economic and social globalization.[10] Just as, say, transnational family law, such as the Hague Convention on the Civil Aspects of International Child Abduction, is a legal response to people increasingly forming romantic relationships across borders, so transnational contract law is the legal expression of, and an organic response to, the globalization of commerce.

Commercial practices may not track national borders, and traders in a particular industry tend to have more in common with foreign firms in the same

---

7 Robert Ellickson, *Order without Law: How Neighbors Settle Disputes* (Harvard University Press 1994).

8 The theory of autopoietic law is most associated with two German scholars, Luhmann (a sociologist) and Teubner (a socio-legal theorist). See Niklas Luhmann, *Social Systems* (J. Bednarz and D. Baeker, tr, 2nd edn, Stanford University Press); Niklas Luhmann, *Law as a Social System* (Klaus Ziegert tr, 2nd edn, Oxford University Press 2003); Gunther Teubner, *Law as an Autopoietic System* (A. Bankowska and R. Adler tr, Blackwell 1993). See also Gralf-Peter Calliess and Peer Zumbansen, *Rough Consensus and Running Code: A Theory of Transnational Private Law* (Hart 2010).

9 Jessup (n 1).

10 C.B. Soyapi, 'A Case for Transnational Law in Contemporary Times' (2020) 23 PER/PELJ 1.

line of business than with their neighbors plying different trades. Yet, if they do business across borders, counterparties may operate on the basis of different implicit norms, which means that parties must either invest more resources in specifying contractual terms in greater detail, or else accept a greater risk that the adjudicator of an eventual dispute may adopt an adverse interpretation of the contract. Moreover, parties in cross-border commerce run the risk that a foreign law will apply, putting them in unfamiliar territory, confronted with risks that they did not contemplate and having to hire foreign lawyers who are unfamiliar with their business.[11] As Lord Justice Kennedy (of the English Court of Appeal) put it in a 1909 address, at roughly the apogee of the first age of economic globalization:

> Conceive the security and the peace of mind of the shipowner, the banker, or the merchant who knows that in regard to his transactions in a foreign country the law of contract, of movable property, and of civil wrongs is practically identical with that of his own country. Or, to put the same thing in the concrete, that the Courts of the foreign country would deal with questions arising out of collisions at sea, questions of salvage, limitation of liability, freight, mortgages, liens, insurance, agency, sale of goods, stoppage in transition, and bills of exchange ... as they would be dealt with in his own country's Courts.[12]

As globalization increasingly takes hold, there is 'an urgent need for a corresponding legislative policy' that is globally consistent and independent of national legal systems.[13] Indeed, the higher transaction costs associated with conflicting national laws can deter commercial parties from entering the cross-border market altogether.[14]

For this reason, from its beginnings in the first great age of globalization around the beginning of the 20th century, transnational contract law has been associated with harmonization or unification of law at the global level. At the beginning, attempts at legal harmonization were almost laughably small-bore, such as the 1891 Madrid Agreement for the Repression of False or Deceptive Indications of Source on Goods. But from these small acorns a vast forest of

---

11 Larry E. Ribstein, 'Choosing Law by Contract' (1993) 18 *Journal of Corporate Law* 245.

12 Lord Justice Kennedy, 'The Unification of Law' (1909) 10 *Journal of the Society of Comparative Legislation* 212, 212.

13 Franco Ferrari, 'The International Sphere of Application of the 1988 Ottawa Convention on International Factoring' (1999) 8 *International Business Law Journal* 895, 895.

14 J.J. Callaghan, 'UN Convention on Contracts for the International Sale of Goods: Examining the Gap-Filling Role of CISG in Two French Decisions' (1995) 14 *Journal of Law and Commerce* 183, 185.

transnational oaks has grown, with a dizzying array of treaties, model laws, standard-form contracts, codes of conduct, and uncodified but highly globalized trade usages.

Transnational law has also emerged in response to technological change, especially in communications technology and digitalization, since these are the technologies that most directly reduce the impact of distance and borders. Technological change has, without reverse,[15] fostered the globalization of commerce and, with it, the demand for a globalized commercial law. The transnationalization of commerce through technology reaches its apogee (at least so far) in the fully online world of digital commerce, in which digital products and services are created, delivered, and paid for in an entirely online global ecosystem, one that ignores national borders altogether except to the extent that national governments intrude to require observance of their laws—to levy sales taxes, to fight money laundering, to protect consumers, to ban child pornography, and so on.

The close ties between transnational contract law and technological development did not begin with the digital age, but instead have existed for as long as transnational law has existed. In his 1909 address hailing the international unification of law, Lord Justice Kennedy observed that the first age of globalization was made possible by new technologies: 'electricity and the printing press have, as it were, drawn together the ends of the earth. Swift intercommunication, the facility of frequent personal intercourse, and the ceaseless interweaving of the devious and tenacious threads of commercial enterprise'.[16] A half-century later, Hynning observed that 'The prime motivating forces for the international unification of law are technological and economic. The great discoveries of science and their application by technology have radically altered the nature of man's world, what he produces, how he travels, and the manner in which he communicates'.[17]

The transnational contract law movement has long been associated with libertarian capitalist ideals—perhaps unsurprising, since commercial communities have always been its most active driving forces. Still today, although less than in the past, the literature on transnational law is inspired by a kind of technocratic utopianism. Eliminating the legal impact of national borders—which, from the perspective of business, are entirely arbitrary—makes possible a new era of globally-harmonized, economically efficient contract law

---

[15] Slowdowns and reverses in globalization have, thus far in human history, been traceable to wars, economic recessions, or pandemics—that is, to social and natural phenomena rather than technological ones.

[16] Kennedy (n 12) 214.

[17] Clifford J. Hynning, 'International Law: Unification of Private Property Laws' (1956) 42 *American Bar Association Journal* 1135, 1136.

that evolves in sync with business practices.[18] Zumbansen captures the tone of this strain of capitalist idealism well: 'One view insists on emphasizing and lamenting the alleged weakness of (the state's) regulatory law that finds its most persuasive illustration in the triumphant proliferation of private norm-setting and suggests that law cannot escape death by suffocation in the oxygen-free atmosphere of globalization'.[19]

Implicit in this account is the assumption that legal globalization means legal unification.[20] However, as transnational law has continued to evolve, it has confounded this assumption. Despite the unification of certain areas of substantive contract law, transnational contract law is increasingly pluralistic, rather than increasingly unified, and may simply represent a reconfiguration of boundaries rather than their erasure. There are several reasons for this. First, parties in different industries or based in different regions might well prefer one substantive law over another to govern their contract, or prefer one forum over another in which to resolve disputes.[21] Second, the piecemeal way in which transnational contract law has been codified has left a multitude of gaps, with many areas continuing to be governed only by national laws.[22] Third, even where a single codified uniform text exists, courts and arbitral tribunals in different jurisdictions—none of which are hierarchically superior to the others or are bound by *stare decisis*—inevitably interpret those texts in diverse ways, the so-called 'homeward trend'.[23] Fourth, states continue to exert power unilaterally by implementing regulations with extraterritorial effect, regulations that may conflict with each other, increasing the complexity (and cost) of

---

18 Reza Dibadj, 'Panglossian Transnationalism' (2008) 44 *Stanford Journal of International Law* 253; Ralf Michaels, 'Dreaming law without a state: scholarship on autonomous international arbitration as utopian literature' (2013) 1 *London Review of International Law* 35.

19 Peer Zumbansen, 'Transnational Private Regulatory Governance: Ambiguities of Public Authority and Private Power' (2013) 76 *Law and Contemporary Problems* 117, 122.

20 See, e.g. Ingeborg Schwenzer, 'Global unification of contract law' (2016) 21 *Uniform Law Review* 60.

21 See generally Franco Ferrari, *Forum Shopping Despite Unification of Law* (Recueil des cours of the Hague Academy of International Law, vol. 413, 2021).

22 Sylvia Ferreri, 'General Report: Complexity of Transnational Sources' (2012) 1 *European Review of Private Law* 3, 14.

23 An extensive literature exists investigating the 'homeward trend' and how it may be combatted so as to preserve the harmonizing promise of uniform law instruments. See generally Mads Andenas and Camilla Baasch Andersen (eds), *Theory and Practice of Harmonisation* (Edward Elgar 2012).

compliance.[24] Fifth, the same demand-side forces that drive legal globalization may lead to a division of the law across industry sectors, as specialized commercial entities exert pressure to have their legal affairs treated by specialized experts. I have labeled this phenomenon 'sectoral fragmentation'—the tendency of transnational law to split along industry sector lines, even as it transcends national boundaries.[25] Similarly, van Krieken posits a 'refeudalization' of the global order[26] and Riles argues that a transnationalized world is simply one where regulatory arbitrage and forum-shopping run rampant.[27] The upshot is that transnationalization does not always equal harmonization and can yield further complexification.

While transnational law challenges traditional state-centric theories of contract law, it is not necessarily inconsistent with more general jurisprudential theories, even positivist ones like H.L.A. Hart's concept of legality, the dominant conceptual model in the common law world. Hart, the arch-positivist, wrote *The Concept of Law* at a time when the only law that crossed borders was that which governs state-to-state relations, i.e. public international law. Famously, he dismissed international law as not constituting a legal system. But Hart saw the rule of recognition—the criterion by which laws may be identified within a given legal system—as a kind of social fact, with popular legitimacy as the ultimate source of legality.[28] The emergence of transnational law requires us only to widen our frame of who can constitute the 'people' conferring that popular legitimacy. As Halliday and Shaffer observe, 'transnational

---

24 On the persistence of state-centred spheres of influence, see, e.g. Pascal McDougall, 'Global Value Chains, Labor Rights, and the Nature of Transnational Law' (2024) 72 *American Journal of Comparative Law* 33; Matthew S. Erie, 'The New Legal Hubs: The Emergent Landscape of International Commercial Dispute Resolution (2020) 60 *Virginia Journal of International Law*; Poul F. Kjaer, 'Transnational Normative Orders: the Constitutionalism of Intra- and Trans-Normative law' (2013) 20 *Indiana Journal of Global Legal Studies* 777.

25 Karton (n 6).

26 Robert van Krieken, 'Refeudalization and Law: From the Rules of Law to Ties of Allegiance' (2023) 19 *Annual Review of Law and Social Science* 337.

27 Annelise Riles, 'Managing Regulatory Arbitrage: A Conflict of Laws Approach' (2014) 47 *Cornell International Law Journal* 32. See also Larry Catá Backer, 'Private Actors and Public Governance Beyond the State: The Multinational Corporation, the Financial Stability Board, and the Global Governance Order' (2011) 18 *Indiana Journal of Global Legal Studies* 751, 762–772.

28 See, e.g., Stephen Perry, 'Hart on Social Rules and the Foundations of Law: Liberating the Internal Point of View' (2006) 75 *Fordham Law Review* 1171.

legality' can be just as durable and powerful a source of legitimacy as the populace of a Westphalian nation-state.[29]

While Jessup's pioneering 1956 study of transnational law reads in many ways as if it had been published just last year, he fell short in that he continued to apply traditional doctrinal methods to this new phenomenon. Even by the 1950s, it was already clear that transnational law can only be fully understood if legal scholars incorporate 'insights into the legal and political processes which other social scientists can offer to this task'.[30] Due to the enormous variety of sources and processes that yield transnational law rules, transnational legal scholarship forces contract researchers to confront, case by case, the relationship between law and its social context.

For that reason, transnational law is intimately connected with socio-legal methods and perspectives, including techniques from sociology, anthropology, and psychology.[31] Indeed, at the level of theory, the existence of transnational law as a legal category depends on a recognition that 'law' should not be defined according to formalistic criteria; instead, any rules that act upon parties with the effective force of law should be treated as legal rules.[32] Understanding transnational law on its own terms means discarding legal formalism and embracing a conception of law that, to paraphrase Forrest Gump, law *is* aslaw *does*.[33] Thus, transnational law includes not only rules produced through the recognized processes for rule-making in various jurisdictions—legislation, regulations, case law, etc.—but also rules that bind parties in other ways—contractual terms (especially where these become standardized across industries and across borders), codified codes of conduct, recognized technical and documentation standards, and commercial customs widely observed in a given economic sector.

29 See generally Terence C. Halliday and Gregory Shaffer, *Transnational Legal Orders* (Cambridge University Press 2015).

30 Katzenbach (n 2) (1957) 24(2) *University of Chicago Law Review* 413, 416.

31 See generally Terence C. Halliday and Pavel Osinky, 'Globalization of Law' (2006) 32 *Annual Review of Sociology* 447; Sally Engle Merry, 'Anthropology, Law, and Transnational Processes' (1992) 21 *Ann Rev Anthropology* 357; Lawrence M. Friedman, 'Borders: On the Emerging Sociology of Transnational Law' (1996) 32 *Stanford J Int'l L* 65.

32 Peer Zumbansen, 'Transnational Law as Socio-Legal Theory and Critique: Prospects for "Law and Society" in a Divided World' (2019) 67 *Buffalo Law Review* 909.

33 *Forrest Gump* (Robert Zemeckis, dir., 1994).

2. THE NATURE AND CHARACTERISTICS OF TRANSNATIONAL CONTRACT LAW

The bulk of the literature on transnational contract law consists of explorations of the ways in which it is distinct from state laws, often in the form of case studies of the transnationalization of a particular aspect of contract law, or the practice of transnational contracting in a particular region or industry sector. This section, therefore, expands on the characteristics of transnational contract law that distinguish it from 'traditional' (i.e. national) contract law, and which also constitute the ways that transnational contract law challenges traditional theoretical conceptions of contract law and practice.

For ease of exposition, I have gathered these characteristics under three headings: the sources of contract law rules, the form of governance they provide (public vs. mixed public and private), and the mechanisms by which rules are promulgated and diffused. Note, however, that all of these relate to the most fundamental characteristic of transnational contract law, which is its pluralism. State contract law constitutes a closed set of approved doctrines, which can be added to only in defined ways and by defined actors within the legal system (legislatures, regulators, judges). Transnational contract law comes in a variety of 'hard' and 'soft' law forms, which derive from a variety of sources, apply to a variety of overlapping categories of contractual relationships, and are promulgated through a variety of means.

Forms and Sources of Transnational Contract Law

Within any given jurisdiction, the sources of legal rules are well known and clearly delineated: constitutions, codes, statutes, and regulations, as well as court judgments or academic writings (depending on the jurisdiction). These categories of legal sources remain stable over time, even as the content of the laws evolves. In transnational law, by contrast, legal rules come from a variety of sources and accordingly take on a variety of forms. For ease of categorization, I have divided the rules that come from public or private sources. However, as will be discussed in the following section, the boundaries between public and private governance have become significantly blurred.

Public sources of transnational contract law rules include the following:

- A prime source of transnational contract law rules is treaties; that is, agreements among sovereign states.[34] While the traditional purpose of treaties

[34] In this way, transnational law is part of international law, and *vice versa*. See Cordero-Moss (n 3) 5–7. Indeed, in recent years transnational law has come

is to govern relations between states, these treaties are instead intended to harmonize the treatment of some category of private relationships.[35] That is, by signing and then ratifying the treaty, states pledge to each other that they will apply the same sets of rules to some areas of private law. (Such treaties need not deal with contracts or commercial law, although the bulk of them do.) Prominent examples include the United Nations Convention on Contracts for the International Sale of Goods (CISG), the United Nations Convention on Independent Guarantees and Standby Letters of Credit, and the Cape Town Convention on International Interests in Mobile Equipment.

- Treaties can be hard to conclude because they require states to agree on a single text. Model Laws can therefore constitute a more feasible alternative; typically, they are drafted by committees of experts convened by an international organization such as the UN Commission on International Trade Law (UNCITRAL), the Hague Conference on Private International Law, or the International Institute for the Unification of Private Law (UNIDROIT). Like treaties, model laws are 'born transnational' in the sense that they do not originate in any national legal system, but rather become incorporated into national legal systems through the adoption of laws based on the model law. Prominent examples include the UNCITRAL Model Laws on International Commercial Arbitration, on Cross-Border Insolvency, and on Electronic Commerce. To the extent that a given model law becomes widely adopted by states and sub-national jurisdictions around the world, it becomes not merely transnational but global.
- Modern regulatory states, especially in developed countries, often deliberately extend the scope of their regulations extra-territorially. (I use 'regulation' here in a broad sense, not specifically to refer to the kinds of rulemaking technically labeled as 'regulation'.) The growth of such extraterritorial regulations has created a transnational body of rules that apply to commercial dealings—and in many cases specifically to contracts. This body of rules is not 'international' or 'global' in that there is little or no attempt to coordinate or harmonize regulations, although extraterritorial

---

to 'encroach' into core areas of public international law. See, e.g. Josh Martin, 'A Transnational Law of the Sea' (2021) 21 *Chicago Journal of International Law* 419; Weimin Shen, 'The Role of Transnational Legal Process in Enforcing WTO Law and Competition Policy' (2021) 30 *Journal of Transnational Law and Policy* 59.

35 For this reason, Lo calls these 'treaties for private matters'. Chang-Fa Lo, 'Should Domestic Court's and Commercial Arbitral Tribunal's Interpretation of "Treaties for Private Matters" be Based on the VICLT or Other Rules?' (2016) 9 *Contemporary Asia Arbitration Journal* 1.

regulations may be intended to deal with transboundary problems, such as the bribery of government officials by foreign investors[36] or transboundary environmental harm.[37] But equally, extraterritorial regulation may represent an attempt by states to impose their values or put their 'stamp' on cross-border commerce.[38]

- In particular industries, a single national law can become so pervasively applied by parties in the choice of law provisions of their contracts that it becomes the *de facto* transnational or even global law of that industry. This development is a consequence of the near-universal enforcement of contractual choice of law clauses in modern private international law.[39] The clearest example, one with a long history, is the adoption of English law for charter parties and other international shipping contracts.[40] This history is preserved in the standard form contracts most frequently used for shipping contracts, those issued by the Baltic and International Maritime Council (BIMCO), all of which provide for the application of English

---

[36] Addressed by a mix of national laws with extraterritorial application (such as the US's *Foreign Corrupt Practices Act*) and international laws (such as the OECD's Anti-Bribery Convention, officially the Convention on Combating Bribery of Foreign Public Officials in International Business Transactions).

[37] See, e.g., Ioanna Hadjiyianni, 'The extraterritorial reach of environmental law: legitimacy concerns and the role of domestic courts in controlling transnational regulatory power' in Austen Parrish and Cedric Ryngaert (eds), *Research Handbook on Extraterritoriality in International Law* (Edward Elgar 2023); Markus Vordermayer, 'The Extraterritorial Application of Multilateral Environmental Agreements' (2018) 59(1) *Harvard International Law Journal* 59.

[38] The US and EU are the foremost practitioners of this form of extraterritorial regulation. See generally Nico Krisch, 'Jurisdiction Unbound: (Extra)territorial Regulation as Global Governance' (2022) 33 *European Journal of International Law* 481.

[39] See Peter Nygh, *Autonomy in International Contracts* (Oxford University Press 1999) 13; Symeon C. Symeonides, *Codifying Choice of Law Around the World: An International Comparative Analysis* (Oxford University Press 2014) chapter 13 (both describing the 'triumph' of party autonomy with respect to choice of law). The autonomy of the parties to choose to be governed by any rules of law extends to the direct choice of transnational laws, even those that may not have been codified into any national legal system. See, e.g., Jane Willems, 'Party Autonomy and the Selection of Non-State Norms in International Commercial Contracts' (2018) 48 *Hong Kong Law Journal* 953.

[40] As noted by Lord Wright in *Vita Food Products v Unus Shipping Company* [1939] AC 277, 290.

law.[41] Preferred national laws can shift over time as a result of regulatory competition among states.[42] For example, if a given state enacts a pro-insurer regulatory regime, insurance companies will rush to include a choice of that state's law in their standard forms.[43]

Private sources of transnational contract law rules include the following:

- Comprehensive standard form contracts are widely adopted by firms in a globalized industry sector, regardless of their nationality. To the extent that a standard form contract sets out the bulk of the obligations of parties to it and is used across an industry sector, it comes to constitute the law *of* that sector.[44] A good example is the set of construction contract forms developed by FIDIC (the International Federation of Consulting Engineers).[45] In disputes where the contracting parties adopt one of the FIDIC forms, the contract is frequently so comprehensive that the dispute can be resolved

41 Available at https://www.bimco.org/contractual-affairs/bimco-contracts (accessed 22 June 2025).

42 It is uncontroversial that regulatory competition exists with respect to contract law, but its extent may be overstated. See Gilles Cuniberti, 'The International Market for Contracts: The Most Attractive Contract Laws' (2014) 23 *Northwestern Journal of International Law and Business* 455; Stefan Vogenauer, 'Regulatory Competition Through Choice of Contract Law and Choice of Forum in Europe: Theory and Evidence' in Horst Eidenmüller (ed), *Regulatory Competition in Contract Law and Dispute Resolution* (Bloomsbury 2013); Horst Eidenmüller, 'The Transnational Law Market, Regulatory Competition, and Transnational Corporations' (2011) 18 *Indiana Journal of Global Legal Studies* 707.

43 For example, in the US, most consumer credit contracts are subject to the laws of South Dakota or Delaware, states that have enacted laws favorable to creditors. Erin A. O'Hara and Larry E. Ribstein, *The Law Market* (Oxford University Press 2009) 145–148.

44 For a discussion of standard contracts as a form of global governance, see chapters by Axel Metzger, Hugh Collins, Thomas Ackermann, Giesela Rühl, and Andreas Engert, in Horst Eidenmüller (ed), *Regulatory Competition in Contract Law and Dispute Resolution* (Oxford University Press 2013).

45 The various FIDIC forms are summarized at http://fidic.org/bookshop/about-bookshop/which-fidic-contract-should-i-use [https://perma.cc/FK74-PJ2V] (accessed 10 October 2024).

without resorting to any exogenous rules of law[46] (except, of course, the rules that govern the enforceability and interpretation of contracts).[47]

- Many commercial contracts make use of sets of alternative standardized contract terms from which parties can choose, which were developed for use in cross-border commerce. The most familiar example is the 'commercial terms' used in sale of goods contracts—the three-letter acronyms such as FOB or FAS that each encode suites of obligations of buyer and seller (and, indirectly, carrier) related to the transportation of the goods. The commercial terms were developed largely through the practices of English shipping clerks and the case law of the English courts. However, they are today best known in the codified form of the INCOTERMS promulgated by the International Chamber of Commerce (ICC). The INCOTERMS' widespread use and their absolute stability of meaning regardless of which contract they are incorporated into give them the character of transnational law. In international sale of goods disputes, tribunals have held that the use of one of the three-letter acronyms constitutes incorporation of the INCOTERM meaning of that acronym (as opposed, for example, to the English common law meaning); in this way, the INCOTERMS have moved from the purely private realm into positive law.
- Self-contained sets of rules, drafted in the style of statutes, are a common feature of transnational contract law. They are not binding in themselves, but can inspire national legislation, can be applied by international arbitral tribunals as governing 'rules of law', and can be expressly adopted as the governing law in cross-border contracts. These are often promulgated under the auspices of an international organization in the public or private sector, but can also be academic initiatives; examples of these pertaining to general contract law include the UNIDROIT Principles of International Commercial Contracts (UPICC) and the Principles of European Contract Law (PECL).

---

46 As one experienced construction arbitrator put it, 'Very often you don't need the applicable law that has been chosen by the parties. It is not that relevant. What is relevant is what is written in the contract.' Interviewed in Joshua Karton, *The Culture of International Arbitration and the Evolution of Contract Law* (Oxford University Press 2013) 92. Cordero-Moss provides a helpful label for attempts by the parties to contract regarding matters that are usually resolved by the governing law, so that reliance upon that law becomes unnecessary: 'self-sufficient contract drafting'. Cordero-Moss (n 3) 22 et seq.

47 Despite the extraordinary growth of transnational contract law, there remains no comprehensive alternative to state law for providing rules of interpretation and validity. Ibid at 43.

While the UPICC and (to a lesser extent) PECL have been influential, private sector initiatives have had more impact in practice. A frequently cited example is the Uniform Customs and Practices for Documentary Credits (UCP), also promulgated by the ICC. References to the UCP (whether in contracts, regulations, or judgments) often use the language of choice of law, such as a term in a letter of credit providing that the instrument is 'governed by UCP'; however, they are better understood as an extensive set of contractual terms incorporated into individual contracts by reference. Properly speaking, they have no legal force except to the extent that they are incorporated into private contracts, and then are binding only on the parties to those contracts. However, the UCP are so commonly incorporated into letters of credit that they are indistinguishable in practice from default rules imposed by statute.

In some cases, these kinds of rules are incorporated by states into their national regulations or legislation or are adopted as default rules in case law. For example, the 1968 'Hague-Visby Rules' relating to the carriage of goods by sea (formally the International Convention for the Unification of Certain Rules of Law relating to Bills of Lading) were codified in some states as schedules to pre-existing legislation.[48] In England, the House of Lords formally recognized the Hague-Visby Rules as applicable by default to international bills of lading.[49] Revisions promulgated under the auspices of UNCITRAL in Hamburg (1978) and Rotterdam (2009) represent modern industry practice but have not yet been widely adopted by states.[50]

- 'Common law' principles arise from the decisions of national courts and international arbitral tribunals on cross-border commercial disputes. These principles go under various names (*lex mercatoria*, general principles of international commercial law, etc.), and their vitality and legitimacy

---

48 For example, in some countries, the Hague-Visby Rules relating to the carriage of goods by sea have been codified as schedules to pre-existing domestic legislation. See, e.g. Carriage of Goods by Sea Act, 1991 (Cth), sch 1 (Austl.) (codifying the Hague-Visby Rules in the Australian Carriage of Goods by Sea Act through a schedule); see also Marine Liability Act, S.C. 2001, c 6, Part 5 and Schedule 3 (Can.) (incorporating the Hague-Visby Rules into the Marine Liability Act by virtue of a schedule).

49 *JI MacWilliam Co. Inc. v Mediterranean Shipping Co., SA* [2005] UKHL 11; [2005] 2 AC 423.

50 G.A. Res. 63/122, annex, United Nations Convention on Contracts for the International Carriage of Goods Wholly or Partly by Sea (Dec. 11, 2008) ('The Rotterdam Rules').

are debated.[51] Typically, they are recognized through a comparative law process of identifying principles common to a range of legal systems.[52] Despite their continued uncertainty, it is undeniable that there exist at least a few substantive principles of law developed through the accretion of case law that are regularly followed in international adjudication.[53] Of these, the most successful exist with respect to specific types of transactions or specific industry sectors, such as the *lex petrolea*[54] and *lex sportiva*.[55] More loosely, commentators agree that a *de facto* system of precedent (technically non-binding but normally followed) now exists in some areas of international contract law, especially with respect to sports.[56]

---

51 See, e.g. Nikitas E. Hatzimihail, 'The Many Lives—and Faces—of Lex Mercatoria: History as Genealogy in International Business Law' (2008) 71 *Law and Contemporary Problems* 169; Michaels (n 4); Michael Mustill, 'The New Lex Mercatoria: The First Twenty-Five Years' (1988) 4(2) *Arbitration International* 86; Berthold Goldman, *La lex mercatoria dans les contrats et l'arbitrage internationaux* (Clunet 1979); Ugo Draetta et al., *Breach and Adaption in International Contracts: An Introduction to Lex Mercatoria* (Butterworths 1992); Georges R. Delaume, 'Comparative Analysis as a Basis of Law in State Contracts: The Myth of Lex Mercatoria (1989) 63 *Tulane Law Review* 575.

52 Cordero-Moss (n 3) 79. This notion of *lex mercatoria* or general principles of transnational commercial law constituting the product of comparative law analysis is most associated with Gaillard. See, e.g., Emmanuel Gaillard, 'Transnational Law: A Legal System or a Method of Decision Making?' (2001) 17(1) *Arbitration International* 59.

53 See generally Gilbert Guillaume, 'The Use of Precedent by International Judges and Arbitrators' (2011) 2(1) *Journal of International Dispute Settlement* 5; Gabrielle Kaufmann-Kohler, 'Arbitral Precedent: Dream, Necessity or Excuse?' (2007) 23(3) *Arbitration International* 357.

54 The seminal publication on the topic describes published arbitral awards as 'the source material from which customary law may be drawn'. R. Doak Bishop, 'International Arbitration of Petroleum Disputes: The Development of a "Lex Petrolea"' (Centre for Petroleum & Mineral Law & Policy, Discussion Paper No. DP 12, 1, 1997), reprinted in (1998) 23 *Yearbook of Commercial Arbitration* 1131. See also Thomas C.C. Childs, 'Update on Lex Petrolea: The Continuing Development of Customary Law Relating to International Oil and Gas Exploration and Production' (2011) 4 *Journal of World Energy Law and Business* 214, 214–15.

55 See generally Robert C.R. Siekmann and Janwillem Soek (eds), *Lex Sportiva: What is Sports Law?* (Springer 2012).

56 See, e.g., Chui Ling Goh and Jack Anderson, 'The Credibility of the Court of Arbitration for Sport' (2022) 13 *Harvard Journal of Sports and Entertainment Law* 233; Lorenzo Casini, 'The Making of *Lex Sportiva* by the Court of Arbitration for Sport' (2019) 12(5) *German Law Journal* 1317; Annie Bersagel, 'Is There a Stare

- Codes of best practices and product standards are enacted to help harmonize business operations. These may be incorporated directly into contracts by dominant parties (in individual contracts or throughout a supply chain) or may be drafted by industry groups or by committees of legal experts and are not intended to assume a coercive character.[57] Either way, they are often binding on market participants in practice.[58]
- Finally, uncodified trade usages are an important source of binding obligations for parties engaged in cross-border commerce, both as direct sources of obligations and as sources of content for codified transnational law instruments.[59] Indeed, many of the instruments mentioned above are themselves codifications of pre-existing trade usages. Under the classic view of *lex mercatoria*, this putative autonomous transnational commercial law consists of the collective usages observed in cross-border trade.[60] When disagreements over the obligations created by trade usages arise, it is important to remember that usages are not self-validating and their content is often disputed; they may require recognition in decisions of national and international courts and arbitral tribunals to be considered binding.[61]

Decisis Doctrine in the Court of Arbitration for Sport?' (2012) 12 *Pepperdine Dispute Resolution Journal* 189.

57 Such as the voluntary *Code of Conduct for Litigation Funders* adopted by the Association of Litigation Funders of England and Wales, available at https://associationoflitigationfunders.com/code-of-conduct/ (accessed 10 October 2024).

58 See, e.g., Axel Marx et al. (eds), *Private Standards and Global Governance* (Edward Elgar 2012); Harm Schepel, *The Constitution of Private Governance: Product Standards in the Regulation of Integrating Markets* (Bloomsbury 2005); Julia Zenker, 'Made in Misery: Mandating Supply Chain Labor Compliance' (2018) 51 *Vanderbilt Journal of Transnational Law* 297. However, there are limits to the governance powers of industry associations. See, e.g., Sarah Dadush, 'The Internal Challenges of Associational Governance' (2017) 111 *American Journal of International Law Unbound* 125.

59 Clayton P. Gillette, 'Harmony and Stasis in Trade Usages for International Sales' (1999) 39 *Virginia Journal of International Law* 707, 707–709; Charles J. Goetz and Robert E. Scott, 'The Limits of Expanded Choice: An Analysis of the Interactions between Express and Implied Contract Terms' (1985) 73 *California Law Review* 261.

60 Roy Goode, Herbert Kronke and Ewan McKendrick, *Transnational Commercial Law: Texts, Cases and Materials* (2nd edn, Oxford University Press 2015), paras 1.63 et seq.

61 Cordero-Moss (n 3) 48. For example, the place of good faith within transnational contract law remains fraught and contested. Ibid 83–87.

Transnational Law as a Mix of Public and Private Governance

As the previous section indicates, transnational laws come from a wide range of sources, both public and private. In the commercial sphere, the most significant aspect of this broader phenomenon is the rise of private contractual governance in transnational rulemaking. The concept of contractual governance embodies the socio-legal insight that contracts often regulate a wide range of behavior in ways that are distinct from their legally binding character,[62] and that therefore contracts themselves take on the character of governance, especially where common sets of standard terms are shared across members of a commercial network.[63]

Definitionally, formal state laws involve public governance. That is, to the extent that contracts are governed by state law, private contracting is conducted within frameworks established by state organs (legislatures, regulators, courts) and enforced by them. Transnational contract law, true to the pluralistic character of transnational law more generally, involves a mix of public and private governance, including varying degrees of hybridity among the two.[64] In transnational contract law, moreover, both public and private governance can be exerted at the local, national, regional, and global levels, sometimes simultaneously.

Even leaving aside the hybrid character of governance in transnational contracting, the distance between public and private transnational governance is not as large as one might think. Even public governance displays a voluntary character absent from national legal regimes (not counting situations of regulatory capture). Given the widespread enforcement of choice of law agreements and respect for separate corporate personality,[65] private parties in transnational commerce can choose which legal regime they want to be governed by, employing a combination of choice of law clauses and incorporation of special purpose entities in friendly jurisdictions. Thus, while it would be going too far to suggest that transnational commerce is self-governed or un-governed, governance structures are sufficiently complex, fluid, and voluntary that parties

62 The ur-text of this field of contracts scholarship is Stewart Macaulay, 'Non-Contractual Relations and Business: A Preliminary Study' (1963) 28 *American Sociological Review* 55. See generally Hugh Collins, *Regulating Contracts* (Oxford University Press 1999).

63 See Peter Vincent-Jones, 'Contractual Governance: Institutional and Organizational Analysis' (2000) 20 *Oxford Journal of Legal Studies* 317.

64 Zumbansen (n 19).

65 Nygh (n 39); Symeonides (n 39).

to cross-border commercial relationships can generally ensure that they are governed by their preferred regulatory regime.[66]

Another byproduct of the multilevel governance that prevails in transnational contracting is the overall incoherence of the legal regime. The traditional picture of private law at the national level (especially in civil law jurisdictions) is of a coherent, all-encompassing system.[67] Systematicity and coherence have historically been hailed as the great strengths of the civil codes, and the same ideals have manifested in the transnational law sphere, leading to the harmonization/unification efforts described above. But despite those efforts, different aspects of contract law continue to be 'dealt with by different "lawgivers" without an overall responsibility for coherence and unity in the hands of one overarching institution. This has led to diverging substantive norms, all with an equal claim to validity.'[68] In the political science literature, multilevel governance is associated with the breakdown of traditional state-centric conceptions of the international order.[69]

Indeed, the rise of private governance is partly due to stagnation in formal international rulemaking.[70] Until roughly the beginning of the 21st century, rules generated through private governance processes served largely to fill gaps in public governance, but now private governance has moved beyond gap-filling and is dominating more broadly.[71] Industry associations have been particularly active in transnational rulemaking, both in promulgating rules

---

66 As a result, law itself becomes a market good, and jurisdictions compete against each other in a global market. See generally O'Hara and Ribstein (n 43).

67 Jan Smits, 'Dutch Report: Coherence and Fragmentation of Private Law' (2012) 1 *European Review of Private Law* 153, 155. This conception has always been less widely shared by common law scholars than among civilians.

68 Ibid at 66.

69 Gary Marks et al., 'Competencies, Cracks and Conflicts: Regional Mobilisation in the European Union' (1996) 29 *Comparative Political Studies* 164, 167.

70 Joost Pauwelyn et al., 'When Structures Become Shackles: Stagnation and Dynamics in International Lawmaking' (2014) 25(3) *European Journal of International Law* 733, 734–38. Pauwelyn et al. identify three reasons for this slowdown: 'saturation' such that treaties already exist in many areas, 'backlash' to treaty-making after the wave of new treaties in the 1990s, and the financial crisis, which has made American and European leadership more preoccupied with domestic problems and cautious about entering into new international obligations and structures. Ibid at 738–744. See also Halliday and Shaffer (n 29) 9; Ilias Bantekas, 'Signature of Multilateral Treaties: Still Meaningful in the Era of Transnational Law?' (2022) 21 *Santa Clara Journal of International Law* 24.

71 Tim Büthe and Walter Mattli, *The New Global Rulers: The Privatization of Regulation in the World Economy* (Princeton University Press 2011); Annelise

themselves and in shaping the development of treaties and other instruments drafted under the auspices of international organizations such as UNCITRAL and the Hague Conference on Private International Law.[72] In line with the libertarian (or at least neoliberal) ethos that pervades much of the transnational contract law literature,[73] Druzin argues that market forces, while imperfect as an enforcement mechanism, are 'sufficient to sustain legal order where central enforcement mechanisms are lacking, which is largely the case in the international context'.[74] The upshot is that '[a] space has been created, outside the normative reach of municipal authorities and international agencies established by treaties or conventions, for new agencies to elaborate the emerging *ratio* of transnational law'.[75]

The Spread and Scope of Transnational Contract Law Rules

In addition to state and sub-state governments, there are now at least four types of actors promulgating legal rules governing commercial relationships: supranational governmental entities like the European Union, technocratic non-governmental and intergovernmental bodies like the United Nations Commission on International Trade Law (UNCITRAL) and the International Institute for the Unification of Private Law (UNIDROIT), adjudicative bodies, both permanent like the WTO Appellate Body and ad hoc like international arbitral tribunals, and private groups like NGOs and trade associations.[76]

Riles, 'The Anti-Network: Private Global Governance, Legal Knowledge, and the Legitimacy of the State' (2008) 56 *American Journal of Comparative Law* 605.

72 See, e.g., Susan Block-Lieb, 'Soft and Hard Strategies: The Role of Business in the Crafting of International Commercial Law' (2019) 40 *Michigan Journal of International Law* 433; Melissa J. Durkee, 'The Business of Treaties' (2016) 63 *UCLA Law Review* 264; Sarah Dadush, 'The Internal Challenges of Associational Governance' (2017) 111 *American Journal of International Law Unbound* 125; Kishanthi Parella, 'Outsourcing Corporate Accountability' (2014) 89 *Washington Law Review* 747, 753–756; Gregory C. Shaffer, 'How Business Shapes Law: A Socio-Legal Framework' (2009) 42 *Connecticut Law Review* 147; Mark J. Sundahl, 'The "Cape Town Approach": A New Method of_Making International Law' (2006) 44 *Columbia Journal of Transnational Law* 339, 341–344.

73 See above, nn. 17–18 and accompanying text.

74 Bryan H. Druzin, 'Anarchy, Order, and Trade: A Structuralist Account of Why a Global Commercial Order is Emerging' (2014) 47 *Vanderbilt Journal of Transnational Law* 1049, 1058.

75 Roger Cotterrell, 'What is Transnational Law?' (2012) 37 *Law and Social Inquiry* 500, 517.

76 Ibid at 518; Gunther Teubner, 'Breaking Frames: The Global Interplay of Legal and Social Systems' (1997) 45 *American Journal of Comparative Law* 149,

The promulgation of rules in some kind of codified form is only one way in which transnational contract law rules are enacted and spread. To explain these phenomena, transnational law scholars have reached for concepts from political science. The 'diffusion' of transnational contract law rules cannot be explained by 'any single causal mechanism but in the succession and reinforcement of multiple mechanisms'.[77] These mechanisms overlap with those applicable to legal transplantation across national legal systems.

- First, groups or states may *emulate* rules adopted in other jurisdictions or by other private sector organizations; emulation is a function of the natural human instinct, when confronted with a question or problem, to take lessons from the experience of others.[78]
- Second, transnational law rules may spread through *coercion*, which involves the direct imposition of legal rules, such as by a colonial power, or indirectly through the threat of negative consequences if a rule is not adopted.[79]
- Third, rules may spread through *contractualization*, whereby parties (whether states or individual firms) promulgate their preferred rules through the exploitation of their stronger bargaining power in concluding treaties or contracts.
- Fourth, *regulatory competition* can lead to the spread of rules to counteract the adoption of more attractive rules by early adopters. Lawmakers may adopt foreign rules, regardless of whether they serve domestic political goals, in order to better position their jurisdiction in a competitive marketplace to attract international transactions and dispute resolution proceedings.[80] Regulatory competition can result in a 'race to the bottom' toward less regulation of cross-border contracting.[81] Equally, though, regulatory

157.

77 Jean-Frédéric Morin and Edward Richard Gold, 'An Integrated Model of Legal Transplantation: The Diffusion of Intellectual Property Law in Developing Countries' (2014) 58 *International Studies Quarterly* 781, 781.

78 Daniel Berkowitz, Katharina Pistor and Jean-Francois Richard, 'The Transplant Effect' (2003) 51 *American Journal of Comparative Law* 163; Richard Rose, 'What Is Lesson-Drawing?' (1991) 11(1) *Journal of Public Policy* 3.

79 David P. Dolowitz and David Marsh, 'Learning From Abroad: The Role of Policy Transfer in Contemporary Policy-Making' (2000) 13(1) *Governance* 5, 9.

80 Claudio M. Radaelli, 'The Puzzle of Regulatory Competition' (2004) 24(1) *Journal of Public Policy* 1; Pamela Bookman, 'The Adjudication Business' (2020) 45 *Yale Journal of International Law* 227.

81 Daniel W. Drezner, 'Globalization and Policy Convergence' (2001) 3(1) *International Studies Review* 53, 57.

competition can yield a 'race to the top', whereby states or private sector organizations seek to burnish their reputations for reliability, responsiveness, or general competence. States, in particular, may actively transnationalize their laws in order to generate legitimacy and attract businesses to their jurisdiction.[82]

- Fifth, transnational contract law rules can spread by *socialization*, meaning a process by which legal actors internalize the principles, beliefs, and norms of a foreign community or the international community.[83] Legal professionals play a key role in the socialization process as 'vectors' of transnational contract law rules. Transactional lawyers draft contracts that contain choices of foreign laws or transnational laws, advise their clients to adhere to transnational standards, and lobby governments to adopt transnational rules into national law.[84] Disputes lawyers can advise on choice of law or choice of forum agreements, and more commonly advocate for arbitration under the auspices of major international arbitral institutions, whose rules tend to converge toward global standards.[85]

As discussed above, while transnational law is associated with the harmonization or unification of law, it does not necessarily yield global rules. Rather, transnational contract law is produced by a network of cross-cutting mutual influences between local business cultures, industry practices, and globalization. The structure of any individual rule or set of rules takes the shape of the transnational networks that give rise to them and that are bound by them.[86] Accordingly, the scope of application of different transnational contract laws can vary enormously. Specific rules or codified sets of rules may apply globally, may apply to a specific industry sector regardless of where the parties to

---

[82] David Vogel, *Trading Up: Consumer and Environmental Regulation in a Global Economy* (Harvard University Press 1995).

[83] Frank Schimmelfennig, 'International Socialization in the New Europe: Rational Action in an Institutional Environment' (2000) 6(1) *European Journal of International Relations* 109, 112; Jeffrey T. Checkel, 'International Institutions and Socialization in Europe: Introduction and Framework' (2005) 59(4) *International Organization* 801, 804.

[84] See, e.g., Jeremy J. Kingsley, 'Drafting Inter-Asian Legalities: Jakarta's Transnational Corporate Lawyers' (2021) 41 *Adelaide Law Review* 197.

[85] Kun Fan, '"Glocalization" of International Arbitration—Rethinking Tradition: Modernity and East-West Binaries Through Examples of China and Japan' (2016) 11 *University of Pennsylvania Asian Law Review* 243; Karton (n 46) 64–67.

[86] On the nature and structure of the legal orders generated by transnational communities, see generally Halliday and Shaffer (n 29).

any given transaction are located, may apply within a particular region, or may apply to transactions that interact with a given state legal regime regardless of the parties' location (whether because that state's law governs the contract, one party is domiciled there, or the contract is performed there).

Transnational contract law therefore has a highly particularistic character when compared with national contract law systems. Most transnational law instruments, whether treaties, model laws, codes of conduct, or codified trade usages, constitute specialized law for specialized circumstances. The prevailing approach in transnational law scholarship sees this particularism as a reflection of the growing particularism of global society; different social groups and different industry sectors operate relatively autonomously from each other, and therefore exhibit distinct senses of what kinds of conduct are acceptable. In legal scholarship, this view is most associated with Teubner, who writes that '[i]nternal differentiation of law can be seen as a response to the fragmentation of society into various systems and discourses'.[87] Similarly, Cotterrell describes 'networks of community' as the loci of transnational rule-making.[88] Such networks are defined objectively by 'stable sustained interactions' between members of the community and subjectively by a 'sense of attachment' among community members.[89] These develop into webs of common understanding that can, over time, gain the force of law.[90] Whichever vocabulary one adopts, it is clear that the structure of transnational law is pluralistic and polycentric, corresponding to the structure of the overlapping national, subnational, and transnational communities that contribute to it and that choose—actively or passively—to be bound by it.[91]

---

87 Gunther Teubner, 'De collisione discursuum: Communicative Rationalities in Law, Morality and Politics' (1996) 17 *Cardozo Law Review* 901, 916. See also Gunther Teubner, *Constitutional Fragments: Societal Constitutionalism and Globalization* (Gareth Norbury tr, Oxford University Press 2012) 162–166; Gunther Teubner and Peter Korth, 'Two Kinds of Legal Pluralism: Collision of Transnational Regimes in the Double Fragmentation of World Society' in Margaret A. Young (ed), *Regime Interaction in International Law: Facing Fragmentation* (Cambridge University Press 2012) 23–25.

88 See Roger Cotterrell, 'Transnational Networks of Community and International Economic Law' in Amanda Perry-Kessaris (ed), *Socio-Legal Approaches to International Economic Law: Text, Context, Subtext* (Routledge 2013) 133; Roger Cotterrell, *Law Culture and Society: Legal Ideas in the Mirror of Social Theory* (Routledge 2006) 68–73.

89 Ibid at 70.

90 Ibid at 73.

91 Legal pluralists have long recognized that 'people belong to (or feel affiliated with) multiple groups and understand themselves to be bound by the norms of these multiple groups'. Paul Schiff Berman, 'Global Legal Pluralism' (2007)

3. TOPICS AND METHODS FOR TRANSNATIONAL CONTRACT LAW SCHOLARSHIP

While transnational law is not an area of law in itself (an internally coherent category of legal rules pertaining to an identifiable set of relationships or exercises of rights or powers), it can be studied as if it were an area of law. By this, I mean that the research methods employed by legal scholars for any aspect of law can be appropriate for studies of transnational law in general, and transnational contract law in particular.

'Transnational contract law' as a whole is too wide a category to be researched except at the broadest level of theory-generation.[92] Most studies narrow their focus to one of the following topics (which can overlap with each other in individual studies):

- The evolution, content, and structure of transnational contract law rules that apply to particular industry sectors.[93]
- The adoption and/or implementation of transnational law in specific jurisdictions or regions, including studies of the interactions between local

---

80 *Southern California Law Review* 1155, 1169. See also Larry Catá Backer, 'The Emerging Normative Structures of Transnational Law: Non-State Enterprises in Polycentric Asymmetric Global Orders' (2016) 31 *Brigham Young University Journal of Public Law* 1; Peer Zumbansen, 'Defining the Space of Transnational Law: Legal Theory, Global Governance, and Legal Pluralism' (2012) 21 *Transnational Law and Contemporary Problems* 305, 325; Harlan Grant Cohen, 'Finding International Law, Part II: Our Fragmenting Legal Community' (2012) 44 *International Law and Politics* 1049, 1064.

[92] Such as William Twining, *General Jurisprudence: Understanding Law from a Global Perspective* (CUP 2009); Halliday and Shaffer (n 29); Calliess and Zumbansen (n 8); Andrew Halpin and Volker Roeben (eds), *Theorising the Global Legal Order* (Hart 2009).

[93] Riles (n 71); Mark Hsiao, 'From the Global ISDA Master Agreement to the Chinese Version of NAFMII: A Standard Form Contract as the Source of Legal Transplant, Irritation, and Integration' (2023) 15 *George Mason Law Journal* 1; J.H. Dalhuisen, 'Globalization and the Transnationalization of Commercial and Financial Law' (2015) 67 *Rutgers University Law Review* 19; Dionysia Katelouzou and Peer Zumbansen, 'The New Geographies of Corporate Governance' (2020) 42 *University of Pennsylvania Journal of International Law* 51.

specificities and global generalities[94] and of the 'downloading' of international norms into national law.[95]

- Legal harmonization or unification through the transnationalization of specific sub-fields or doctrines of contract law.[96]
- Individual codified transnational law instruments (treaties, model laws, etc.), including their implementation and interpretation by courts and arbitral tribunals.[97]
- The interrelationships between transnational and national contract law, including the extent to which transnational law influences, displaces, or supplements national laws[98] and the uses of transnational law to interpret national law (and *vice versa*).[99]
- The role of states in promulgating transnational laws, including as a means of extending states' soft power.[100]

---

[94] Fan (n 85); Christopher A. Whytock, 'Domestic Courts and Global Governance' (2009) 84 *Tulane Law Review* 67.

[95] Ngoc Son Bùi, 'Vertical Law and Development' (2021) 54 *Cornell International Law Journal* 1.

[96] Fabien Gélinas, 'Toward a Transnational Law of Trade Usages' (2015) 7 *Yearbook on Arbitration and Mediation* 49; Sandeep Gopalan, 'Transnational Commercial Law: The Way Forward' (2003) 18 *American University International Law Review* 803.

[97] There are too many examples to mention, even if one limits oneself to commentaries on codified contract law instruments. Commentaries abound on, for example, the CISG, the UPICC, the PECL, the Cape Town Convention, and other uniform law instruments.

[98] See, e.g., Johanna Hoekstra, 'The Normative Influence of the UNIDROIT Principles of International Commercial Contracts on Courts' (2019) 23 *Vindobona Journal of International Commercial Law and Arbitration* 54; Cassie D. Roberts, 'The Gap-Filling Role of Private Environmental Governance: A Case Study of Semiconductor Supply Chain Contracting' (2018) 51 *Vanderbilt Journal of Transnational Law* 591; Christine M. Whited, 'The UNIDROIT Principles of International Commercial Contracts: An Overview of their Utility and the Role they have Played in Reforming Domestic Contract Law Around the World' (2011) 18 *ILSA Journal of International and Comparative Law* 167.

[99] Ryan C. Black et al., 'Upending a Global Debate: An Empirical Analysis of the US Supreme Court's use of Transnational Law to Interpret Domestic Doctrine' (2014) 103 *Georgetown Law Journal* 1; Luke Nottage, 'Practical and Theoretical Implications of the Lex Mercatoria for Japan: CENTRAL's Empirical Study on the Use of Transnational Law' (2000) 4 *Vindobona Journal of International Commercial Law & Arbitration* 132. See generally Klaus Peter Berger (ed.), *The Practice of Transnational Law* (Kluwer 2002).

[100] Krisch (n 38); Matthew S. Erie, 'The Soft Power of Chinese Law' (2023) 61 *Columbia Journal of Transnational Law* 1; Farshad Ghodoosi, 'The Trump

- The mechanisms by which transnational law rules emerge and are diffused,[101] including studies of private vs. public governance[102] and of the institutions that promulgate and disseminate transnational rules.[103]
- The role of lawyers in developing, implementing, and diffusing transnational laws.[104]

As can be seen with other research methods and challenging topics described in this book, different research methods are best suited to answering different kinds of research questions. Many studies of transnational contract law employ traditional doctrinal methods that examine the rules of transnational law on their own terms from an 'internal' perspective. There is now such a profusion of norms of varying sources and forms that much material exists for the doctrinalist to study. Indeed, transnational law rules are susceptible to the same techniques employed by doctrinal scholars in various legal traditions; all that needs to change is for the doctrinalist to adopt a flexible sense of what constitutes a legal rule and a corresponding agnosticism about the sources of rules. Once one accepts that standard terms, industry codes of best practices, and the like are *legal*, one can perform the familiar moves of doctrinal scholarship to study them.

Indeed, what might be called methodologically traditional studies of transnational laws are becoming more common in the academic literature. This

---

Effect: Assertive Foreign Policy Through Extraterritorial Application of Laws' (2019) 51 *George Washington International Law Review* 661.

[101] Ralf Michaels, 'Private Law Theory and the "Global Legal Community"' (2022) 23 *German Law Journal* 851; Ilias Bantekas, 'Signature of Multilateral Treaties: Still Meaningful in the Era of Transnational Law?' (2022) 21 *Santa Clara Journal of International Law* 24.

[102] Roy Goode, 'Private Commercial Law Conventions and Public and Private International Law: the Radical Approach of the Cape Town Convention 2001 and its Protocols' (2016) 65 *International and Comparative Law Quarterly* 523; Riles (n 71); Hsiao (n 93).

[103] Erie (n 24).

[104] John Flood, 'Lawyers as Sanctifiers: The Role of Elite Law Firms in International Business Transactions' (2007) 14 *Indiana Journal of Global Legal Studies* 35; John Flood, 'Institutional Bridging: Engage in Globalization' (2013) 54 *Boston College Law Review* 1087; John Flood and Fabian P. Sosa, 'Lawyers, Law Firms and the Stabilization of Transnational Business' (2008) 28 *Northwestern Journal of International Law and Business* 489; Kingsley (n 84); Galit Sarfaty, 'Corporate Actors as Translators in Transnational Lawmaking' (2021) 115 *American Journal of International Law Unbound* 278; Arm Tungnirun, 'Practising on the Moon: Globalization and Legal Consciousness of Foreign Corporate Lawyers in Myanmar' (2018) 5 *Asian Journal of Law and Society* 49.

is partly due to a resurgence of doctrinal scholarship in the legal academy generally,[105] but also to the growth and maturation of transnational contract law itself. Even twenty or thirty years ago, the total volume of transnational contract law rules was drastically smaller and more restricted to definable categories of transactions or specific industry sectors. Today, transnational law rules have blossomed to encompass a significant range of cross-border relationships—still primarily commercial relationships, but now others as well. There is sufficient material for doctrinal scholarship to discern underlying principles, categorize rules, elucidate their logical relationships to each other, explore their interpretation by courts and arbitral tribunals, and so on—the traditional tasks of doctrinal research.

Most doctrinal research on transnational law is comparative in its orientation. Some of these are what one might call traditionally comparative studies, in that they compare two or more jurisdictions with each other, such as comparing different states' implementation of a harmonized uniform law instrument. However, they may also engage in comparison along a wide number of axes other than across jurisdictions.[106] Many such studies compare national and transnational law rules in a given sub-field of contract law, such as the sale of goods or secured transactions, identifying congruences and divergences between the national and transnational, uncovering transnational law rules' origins in specific national laws or legal families, or charting the progress of harmonization or unification of transnational law. Comparative law techniques are also valuable for exploring the transnationalization of rules in different areas of law, or the impact of transnational law on domestic law.

Despite this growth in doctrinal scholarship, transnational law research is most associated with social science methods, and theoreticians with a socio-legal orientation have been the most active in transnational law theory.[107] Different social science methods, in particular, are well-suited to provide

---

105 In the United States, at least, where interdisciplinary scholarship became dominant in the academy in the later decades of the 20th century, this school of thought has been called 'the new doctrinalism'. Although it is now is applied to a range of legal fields, the term was coined in the constitutional law context. Brandon P. Denning, 'The New Doctrinalism in Constitutional Scholarship and *Heller v. District of Columbia*' (2008) 75 *Tennessee Law Review* 789.

106 Mathias Reimann, 'Beyond National Systems: A Comparative Law for the International Age' (2001) 75 *Tulane Law Review* 1103; William Twining, 'Globalisation and Comparative Law' (1999) 6 *Maastricht Journal of European and Comparative Law* 217; David Kennedy, 'New Approaches to Comparative Law: Comparativism and International Governance' [1997] *Utah Law Review* 545.

107 Prime examples are Roger Cotterrell and Gunther Teubner. See, e.g., Cotterrell (n 75); Teubner (n 76).

empirical answers to questions about *how* and *why* given legal rules are adopted, spread, or evolve, which are the questions that continue to predominate in transnational contract law scholarship.

The social sciences have not been equally represented; thus far, sociological and anthropological approaches have dominated the interdisciplinary literature on transnational contract law. For example, there has been extensive ethnographic scholarship involving surveys, interviews, and observations by researchers embedded in a given industry sector,[108] or rapidly-globalizing emerging economy,[109] or with lawyers working in cross-border practices.[110] There are also empirical studies of rule diffusion, many of them mixed-method studies that identify a transnational legal phenomenon by using quantitative data then seek to explain why and how that phenomenon arises by using qualitative data gathered from surveys and interviews.

On the other hand, despite frequent claims that transnational contract law rules are more efficient, little rigorous economic research has been conducted to test these claims or to model the economic effects of transnational law rules.[111] In-depth economic studies of transnational contract law are likely to provide useful insights, whether they involve economic modeling of transnational contracting behavior or empirical investigations of the incentives created by transnational contract laws or practices.

---

108 Ellickson (n 7); Riles (n 71); Hsiao (n 93). For an overview of this literature, see Matthew C. Canfield, 'The Anthropology of Legal Form: Ethnographic Contributions to the Study of Transnational Law' (2023) 48 *Law and Social Inquiry* 31.

109 David B. Wilkins, David M. Trubek and Bryon Fong, 'Globalization, Lawyers, and Emerging Economies: The Rise, Transformation, and Significance of the New Corporate Legal Ecosystem in India, Brazil, and China' (2020) 61 *Harvard International Law Journal* 281.

110 Flood (n 104), Kingsley (n 84); Sarfaty (n 104); Tungnirun (n 104); Karton (n 46).

111 Some exceptions include Shen Wei, *Rethinking the New York Convention: A Law and Economics Approach* (Intersentia 2013); Sabine Frerichs, 'Transnational Law and Economic Sociology' in Peer Zumbansen (ed), *The Oxford Handbook of Transnational Law* (Oxford University Press 2021); Bo Yuan, 'A Law and Economics Approach to Norms in Transnational Commercial Transactions: Incorporation and Internalisation' (2016) 1 *Erasmus Law Review* 5; Horst Eidenmüller, 'The Transnational Law Market, Regulatory Competition, and Transnational Corporations' (2011) 18 *Indiana Journal of Global Legal Studies* 707.

While there now exists a growing body of transnational legal theory,[112] legal philosophers have not extensively explored transnational contract law. H.L.A. Hart—infamously among international law scholars—did not regard international law as a legal system.[113] Many of the analytic philosophers who followed in Hart's footsteps have similarly neglected international law.[114] The most sustained (and to my mind, convincing) attempt to update general jurisprudential theories to encompass transnational law is Twining's *General Jurisprudence: Understanding Law from a Global Perspective*.[115] There, Twining's primary concern is to update what he sees as the two core propositions of legal positivism (that there is no necessary connection between law as it is and law as it should be—morally or otherwise—and that the existence of law is ultimately a matter of social fact) for the age of globalization. In particular, Twining attacks 'Western academic legal culture' as 'state-oriented, secular, positivist, "top-down", North-centric, unempirical, and universalist in respect of morals'.[116] He argues that legal theory must evolve to embrace legal pluralism, socio-legal information about how legal rules are actually experienced, and 'post-colonial, subaltern perspectives'.[117] Such philosophical approaches are appropriate for theorizing the nature of transnational law, especially in comparison with law enacted at the state level.[118]

However, most of the transnational legal theory literature is descriptive, exploring what makes transnational law *legal*, what its sources are, what the nature of transnational law rules is, and so on. There is substantially less literature applying ethical and other normative theories to transnational law, and philosophically minded scholars working in the tradition of theorists like Twining could profitably explore these areas. Similarly, transnational contract law, due to its association with multinational businesses and its potential to be

112 Indeed, an entire journal is dedicated to publishing such scholarship: *Transnational Legal Theory*, now in its 15th volume.

113 H.L.A. Hart, *The Concept of Law* (3rd edn, Clarendon 2012); see Mehrdad Payandeh, 'The Concept of International Law in the Jurisprudence of H.L.A. Hart' (2011) 21 *European Journal of International Law* 967.

114 There are, of course, exceptions, in particular William Twining, Jeremy Waldron, and Brian Tamanaha.

115 Twining (n 92).

116 Ibid at 6.

117 Ibid at 7.

118 See, e.g. John Linarelli, 'Analytical Jurisprudence and the Concept of Commercial Law' (2009) 113 *Penn State Law Review* 119; Sidney Richards, 'Globalization as a Factor in General Jurisprudence' (2012) 41(2) *Netherlands Journal of Legal Philosophy* 129.

used to insulate such businesses from national regulations, is particularly suitable for assessment from a critical theory perspective.[119]

None of the above is intended to suggest that socio-legal approaches have outlived their usefulness for conducting research on transnational contract law. For example, numerous studies have been conducted on transnationalization of private law in specific regions. Europe can be fairly characterized as the center of gravity of transnational law research; it began to transnationalize its private law earlier than other regions and has taken the greatest formal steps toward the transnationalization of law through the European Union and related institutions. In some other regions, such as East Asia, academics have spearheaded transnational law projects, most notably in Singapore and Hong Kong, two jurisdictions whose economic success depends on their ability to serve as hubs for cross-border commercial activity. More recently, the Association of Southeast Asian Nations (ASEAN)[120] and China's Belt and Road Initiative have acted as loci for the harmonization and exportation, respectively, of private law norms.[121] However, the literature is sparser with respect to legal transnationalization in Africa, the Americas, and Oceania. These areas are promising regions in which to conduct ethnographic studies of transnationalized legal professionals, of legal transplants and their interaction with postcolonial dynamics, and of the role of international institutions such as the Organization for the Harmonization of Business Law in Africa (OHADA) and the Southern Common Market (Mercosur).

Similarly, little-to-no academic research has been conducted on transnationalization of Indigenous law; scholars could, for example, explore legal relations and harmonization between Indigenous communities, especially across the Americas and Oceania, or could explore the transnationalization of non-Indigenous laws from an Indigenous perspective.

---

119 For a rare example of a critical theory approach to transnational law, see Mohsen al Attar, 'Reframing the "Universality" of International Law in a Globalizing World' (2013) 59 *McGill Law Journal* 95. By contrast, critical treatments of international economic law abound.

120 Paul J. Davidson, 'The ASEAN Way and the Role of Law in ASEAN Economic Cooperation' (2004) 8 *Singapore Yearbook of International Law* 165; Chad Patrick Osorio, 'Enhancing the ASEAN Way: Integrating international law into local initiatives in the ASEAN' in Heru Susetyo et al. (eds), *Advancing Rule of Law in a Global Context* (CRC Press 2017); Basil C. Bitas, 'Legal Convergence, Transnational Rule-Making and Regional Integration in ASEAN – from "Open Regionalism" to "Open Legal Architecture"' [2014] *Lawasia Journal* 1.

121 Bùi (n 95); Matthew Erie, 'Chinese Law and Development' (2021) 62 *Harvard International Law Journal* 51.

Researchers might also consider how the same mechanisms by which transnational contract law rules are created and diffuse might operate in public law. Public law (including not just administrative and constitutional law but also criminal law, taxation, and other areas directly tied to public policy preferences and the exercise of state power) has always been more varied than private law across jurisdictions, as it is tied more closely to cultural values, governmental structures, and traditions that are particular to each polity. For the same reasons, states are less likely to be willing to 'compromise' their policies in public law areas by adopting transnational rules or delegating rulemaking or adjudicative authority to transnational institutions.

However, the same demand-side phenomena that drive a desire for uniformity in the regulation of cross-border contracts also affect commerce-oriented areas of public law, such as competition, bankruptcy, customs and excise, and banking and investment regulation. International investment law, for example, has been described as 'global administrative law'[122] or 'global public law', showing that globalization impacts public law and private law alike.[123] While this characterization of investment law is controversial, international investment law shares many of the characteristics of transnational contract law, so the same strategies for developing and effectively implementing transnational rules may be employed in both.[124] Researchers could focus on the transnationalization of public law, applying theories and methodological practices developed for transnational contract law.

Procedural law, too, can be analyzed using the techniques of transnational private law, since transnational norm diffusion occurs in very similar ways in procedural rulemaking.[125] Areas in which procedural styles and norms from different legal systems are brought into confrontation with each other, such as

---

122 See, e.g., Gus Van Harten and Martin Loughlin, 'Investment Treaty Arbitration as a Species of Global Administrative Law' (2006) 17 *European Journal of International Law* 1; Benedict Kingsbury and Megan Donaldson, 'Global Administrative Law' in Anne Peters (ed), *Max Planck Encyclopedia of Public International Law* (Oxford University Press 2012).

123 See, e.g., Stephan W. Schill, 'International Investment Law and Comparative Public Law – An Introduction' in Stephan W. Schill (ed), *International Investment Law and Comparative Public Law* (Oxford University Press 2010).

124 Joshua Karton, 'Reform of Investor-State Dispute Settlement: Lessons from International Uniform Law' in Jean E. Kalicki and Anna Joubin-Bret (eds), *Reform of Investor-State Dispute Settlement: In Search of a Roadmap* (Brill | Nijhoff 2015).

125 Alyssa King, 'Global Civil Procedure' (2021) 62 *Harvard International Law Journal* 223; Anthony J. Colangelo, 'Procedural *Jus Cogens*' (2022) 60 *Columbia Journal of Transnational Law* 377.

international commercial arbitration, display many of the same processes of hybridization, demand-led rule generation, and codification of standard practices, as well as a central role for soft law instruments. These developments are apt for analysis from a transnational law perspective.

Finally, it is worth considering the role of the contract law scholar as educator and the implications of transnational contract law for the ways that we teach contracts to law students. With an increasing number of lawyers working for multinational firms and an increased ability for lawyers to become licensed in multiple countries, the practice of law itself increasingly crosses borders, and legal education must adapt accordingly.[126] As far back as 1994, Abel argued that legal education had failed to adapt to the demands of transnational legal practice.[127] Since then, scholars have begun to explore how best to train lawyers—in particular, business lawyers—for the realities of transnational

[126] H. Patrick Glenn, 'Comparative Law and Legal Practice: On Removing the Borders' (2001) 75 *Tulane Law Review* 977. See also Lawrence M. Friedman, 'Erewhon: The Coming Global Legal Order' (2001) 37 *Stanford Journal of International Law* 347.

[127] Richard L. Abel, 'Transnational Law Practice' (1994) 44 *Case Western Reserve Law Review* 737.

legal practice.[128] However, with a few notable exceptions,[129] university law programs have proven hesitant to change their mandatory curricula or degree structures, and legal education at the undergraduate level remains stubbornly territorial. Further research on transnational law pedagogy would help address the increasingly anachronistic way lawyers are trained.

128 See, e.g., César Arjona et al., 'What law for transnational legal education? A cooperative view of an introductory course to transnational law and governance' (2015) 6(2) *Transnational Legal Theory* 253; Eve Darian-Smith, 'Transnational Legal Education' in Peer Zumbansen (ed), *The Oxford Handbook of Transnational Law* (Oxford University Press 2021); Simon Chesterman, 'The Evolution of Legal Education: Internationalization, Transnationalization, Globalization' (2009) 10(7) *German Law Journal* 877; Sébastien Lebel-Grenier, 'What is a Transnational Legal Education?' (2006) 56(2) *Journal of Legal Education* 190; Carole Silver, 'Internationalizing US Legal Education: A Report on the Education of Transnational Lawyers' (2006) 14 *Cardozo Journal of International and Comparative Law* 143; Raymond J. Friel, 'Special Methods for Educating the Transnational Lawyer' (2005) 55(4) *Journal of Legal Education* 507; William Twining, 'A Cosmopolitan Discipline? Some Implications of "Globalisation" for Legal Education' (2001) 8(1) *International Journal of the Legal Profession* 23; Alberto Bernabe Riefkohl, 'Tomorrow's Law Schools: Globalization and Legal Education' (1995) 32 *San Diego Law Review* 137.

129 Such as the Center for Transnational Legal Studies, a London-based consortium of several partner institutions led by Georgetown University, the 'trans-systemic' program offered by McGill University's Faculty of Law, and the Peking University School of Transnational Law.

Index